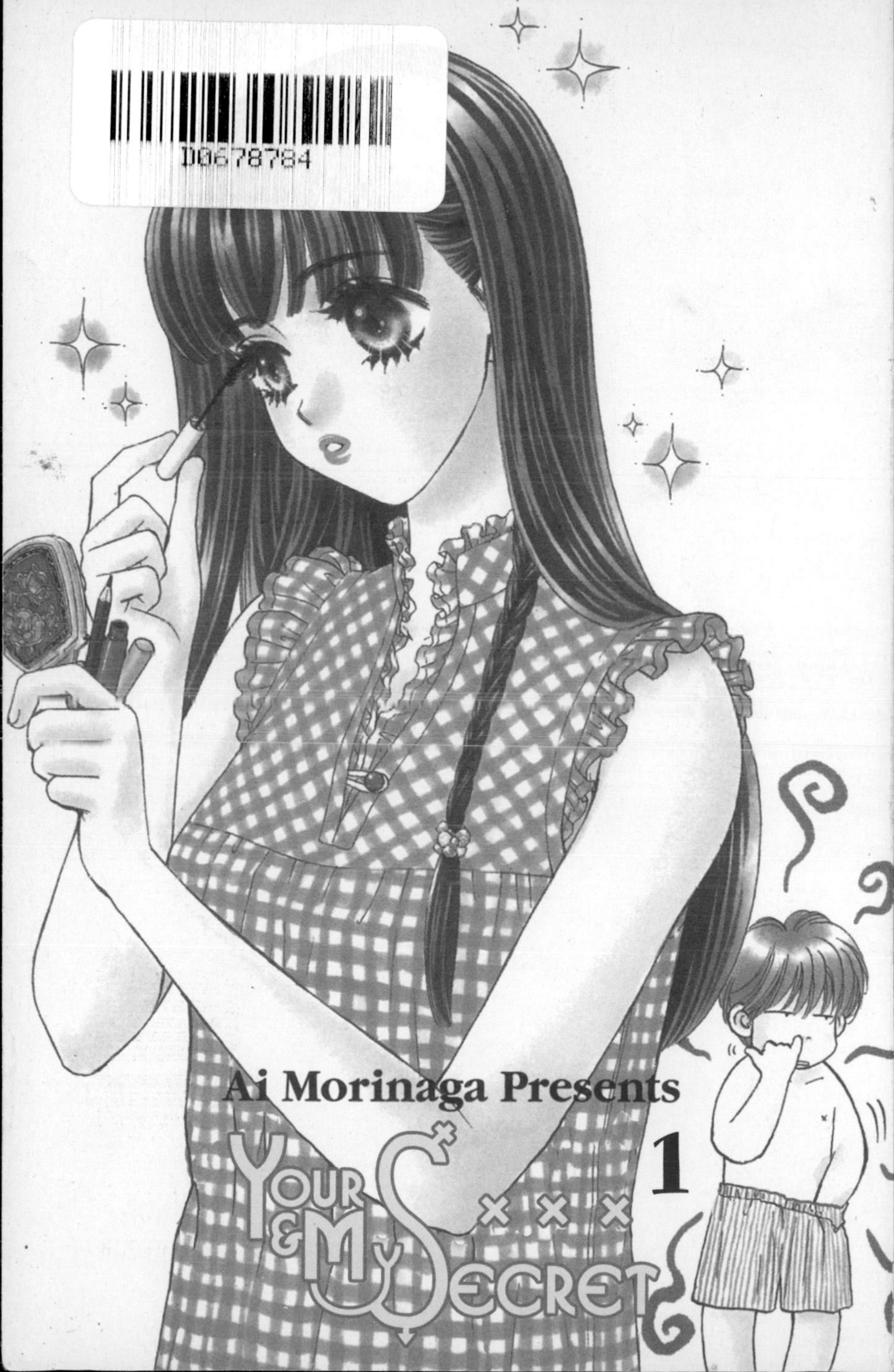
Ai Morinaga Presents
Your & My Secret
1

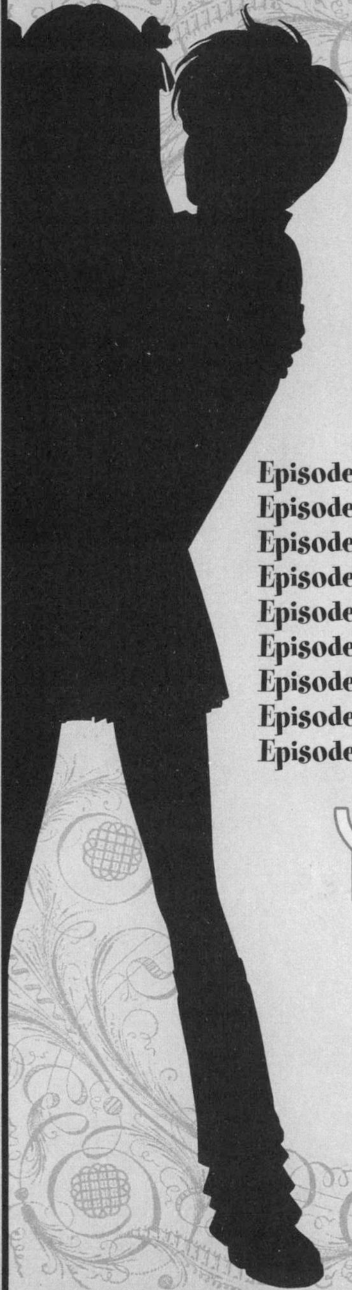

Contents

Your & My Secret ×××

1

Your & My Secret

Volume 1
by
Ai Morinaga

HAMBURG // LONDON // LOS ANGELES // TOKYO

Your & My Secret Volume 1
Created by Ai Morinaga

Translation - Yuya Otake
English Adaptaion - Jay Antani
Associate Editor - Jessica Chavez
Copy Editor - Shannon Watters
Retouch and Lettering - Star Print Brokers
Production Artist - Michael Paolilli
Graphic Designers - Jose Macasocol, Jr. & Niyaz Mahmud

Editor - Paul Morrissey
Digital Imaging Manager - Chris Buford
Pre-Production Supervisor - Erika Terriquez
Production Manager - Elisabeth Brizzi
Managing Editor - Vy Nguyen
Creative Director - Anne Marie Horne
Editor-in-Chief - Rob Tokar
Publisher - Mike Kiley
President and C.O.O. - John Parker
C.E.O. and Chief Creative Officer - Stuart Levy

A  Manga

TOKYOPOP and  are trademarks or registered trademarks of TOKYOPOP Inc.

TOKYOPOP Inc.
5900 Wilshire Blvd. Suite 2000
Los Angeles, CA 90036

E-mail: info@TOKYOPOP.com
Come visit us online at www.TOKYOPOP.com

ISBN: 978-1-4278-0522-5
First TOKYOPOP printing: March 2008
10 9 8 7 6 5 4 3 2
Printed in the USA

Episode 1
Destined Soul Mate

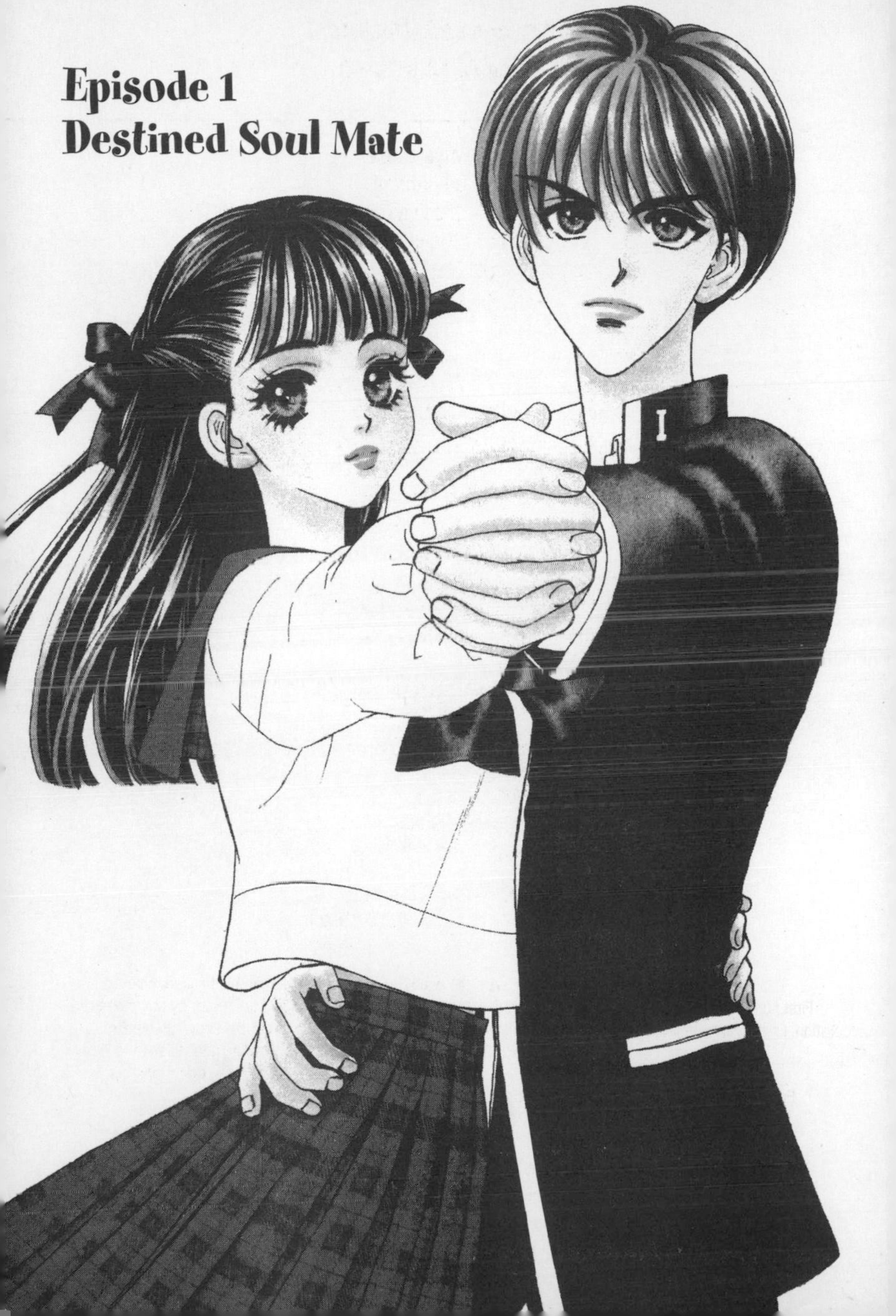

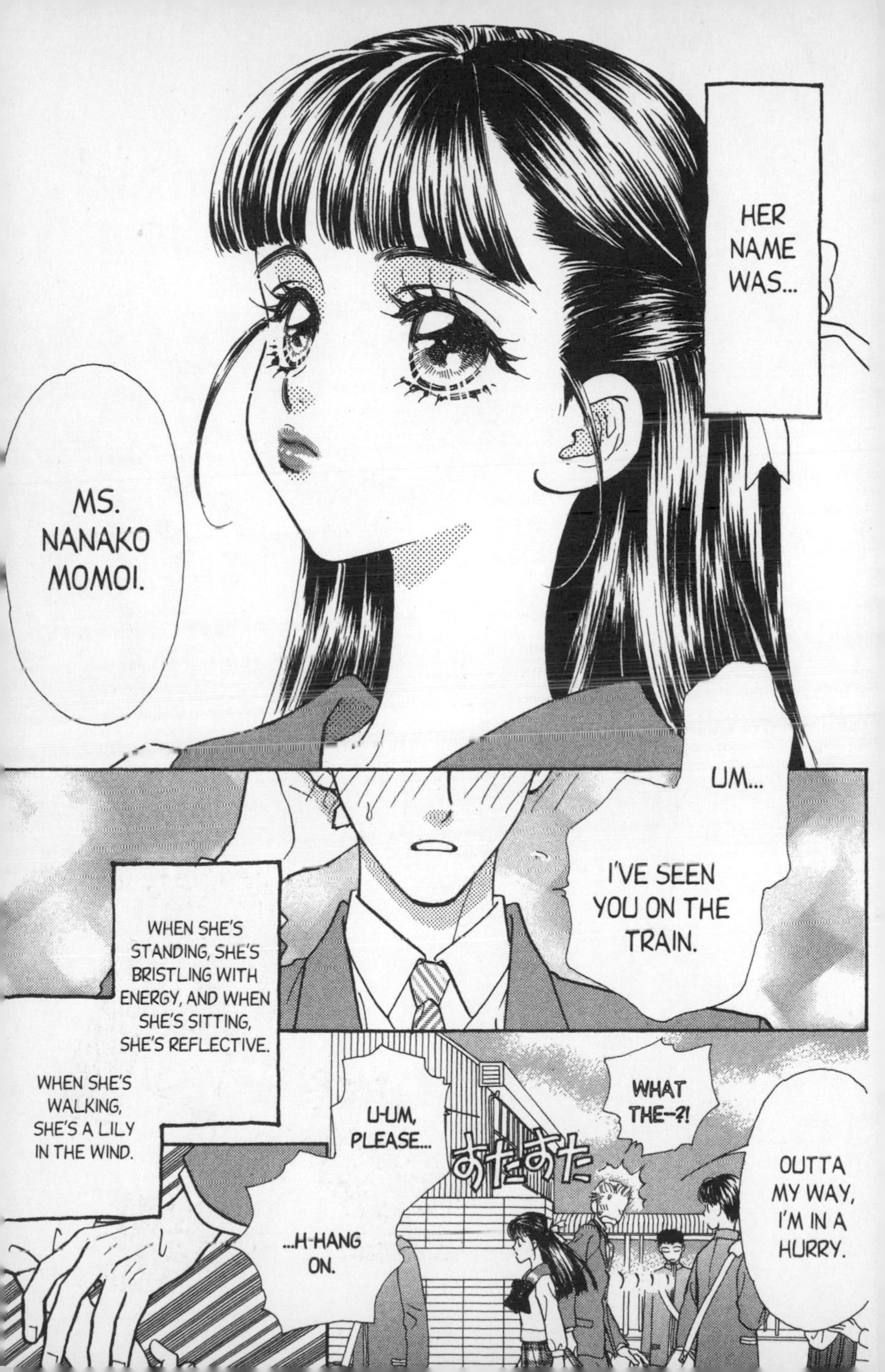
HER NAME WAS...
MS. NANAKO MOMOI.
UM...
I'VE SEEN YOU ON THE TRAIN.
WHEN SHE'S STANDING, SHE'S BRISTLING WITH ENERGY, AND WHEN SHE'S SITTING, SHE'S REFLECTIVE.
OUTTA MY WAY, I'M IN A HURRY.
WHAT THE--?!
U-UM, PLEASE...
あたあた
...H-HANG ON.
WHEN SHE'S WALKING, SHE'S A LILY IN THE WIND.

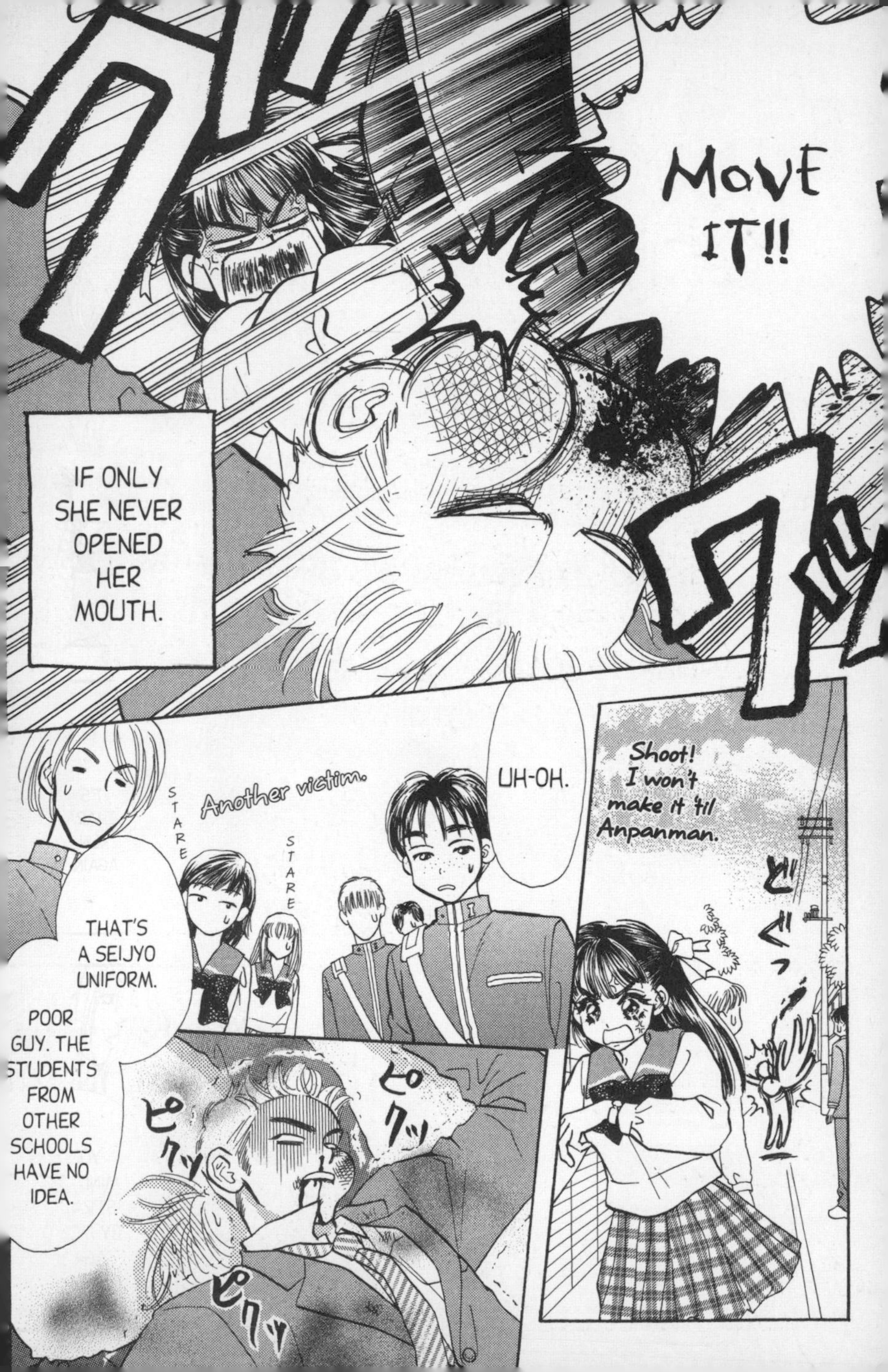
MOVE IT!!
IF ONLY SHE NEVER OPENED HER MOUTH.
Shoot! I won't make it 'til Anpanman.
どぐっ
UH-OH.
Another victim.
STARE
STARE
THAT'S A SEIJYO UNIFORM.
POOR GUY. THE STUDENTS FROM OTHER SCHOOLS HAVE NO IDEA.
ピクッ
ピクッ
ピクッ

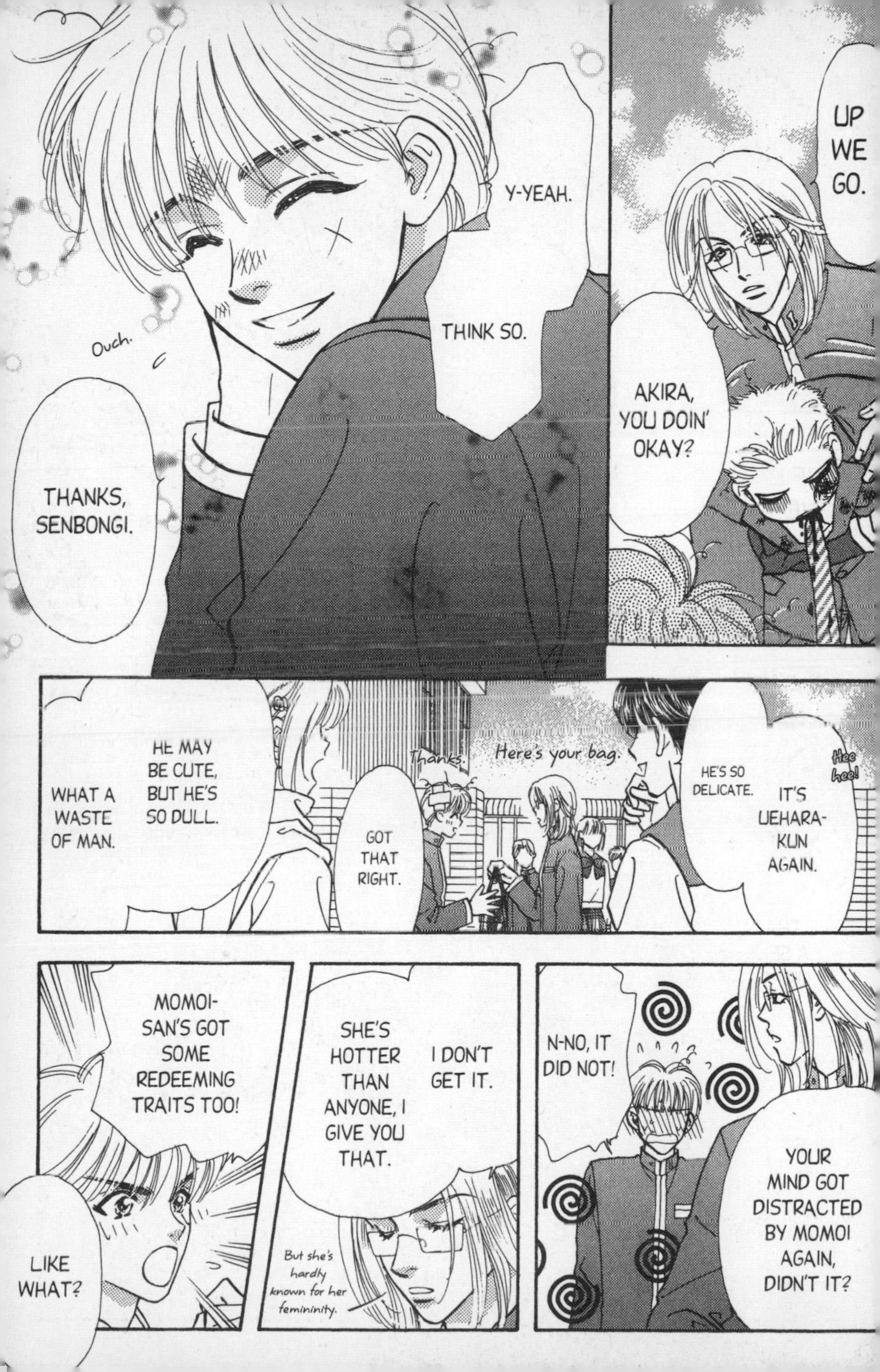
UP WE GO.
AKIRA, YOU DOIN' OKAY?
Y-YEAH. THINK SO.
Ouch.
THANKS, SENBONGI.
Hee hee!
IT'S UEHARA-KUN AGAIN.
HE'S SO DELICATE.
Here's your bag.
Thanks.
GOT THAT RIGHT.
HE MAY BE CUTE, BUT HE'S SO DULL.
WHAT A WASTE OF MAN.
YOUR MIND GOT DISTRACTED BY MOMOI AGAIN, DIDN'T IT?
N-NO, IT DID NOT!
I DON'T GET IT.
SHE'S HOTTER THAN ANYONE, I GIVE YOU THAT.
But she's hardly known for her femininity.
MOMOI-SAN'S GOT SOME REDEEMING TRAITS TOO!
LIKE WHAT?

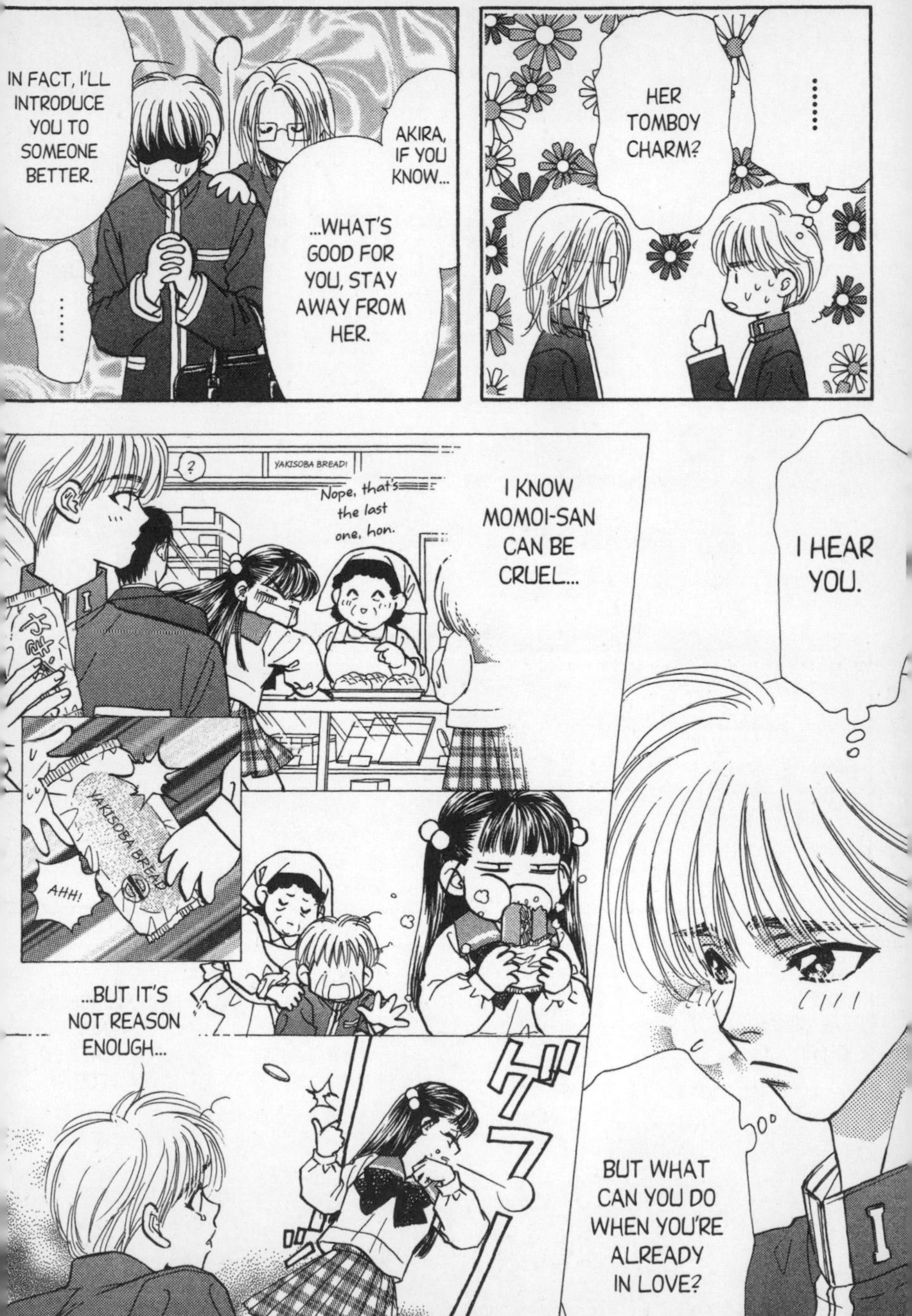
......
HER TOMBOY CHARM?
AKIRA, IF YOU KNOW...
...WHAT'S GOOD FOR YOU, STAY AWAY FROM HER.
IN FACT, I'LL INTRODUCE YOU TO SOMEONE BETTER.
......
I HEAR YOU.
BUT WHAT CAN YOU DO WHEN YOU'RE ALREADY IN LOVE?
I KNOW MOMOI-SAN CAN BE CRUEL...
YAKISOBA BREAD!
Nope, that's the last one, hon.
?
YAKISOBA BREAD
AHH!
...BUT IT'S NOT REASON ENOUGH...

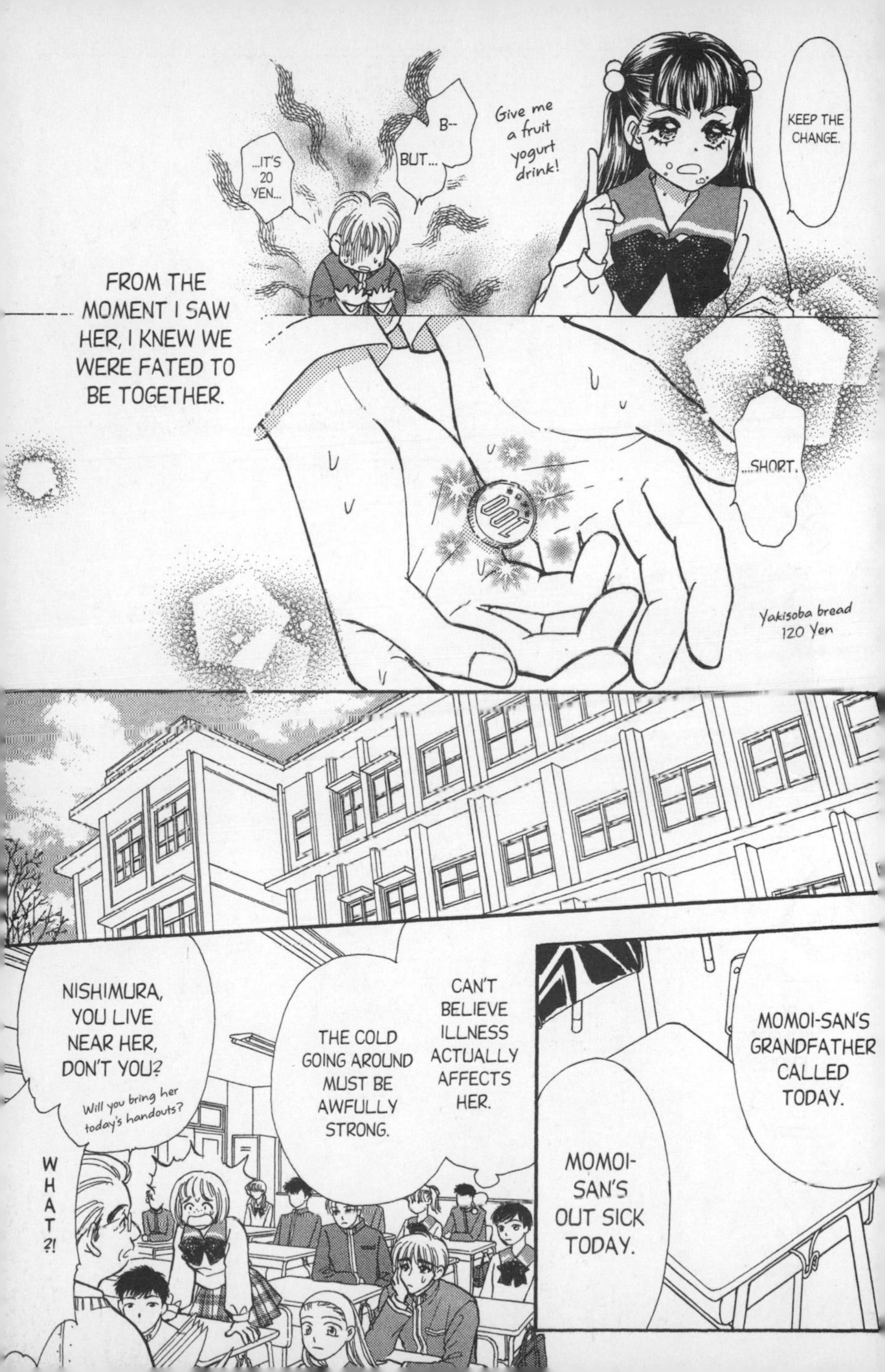
KEEP THE CHANGE.
Give me a fruit yogurt drink!
B-- BUT...
...IT'S 20 YEN...
FROM THE MOMENT I SAW HER, I KNEW WE WERE FATED TO BE TOGETHER.
...SHORT.
Yakisoba bread 120 Yen
MOMOI-SAN'S GRANDFATHER CALLED TODAY.
MOMOI-SAN'S OUT SICK TODAY.
CAN'T BELIEVE ILLNESS ACTUALLY AFFECTS HER.
THE COLD GOING AROUND MUST BE AWFULLY STRONG.
NISHIMURA, YOU LIVE NEAR HER, DON'T YOU?
Will you bring her today's handouts?
WHAT?!

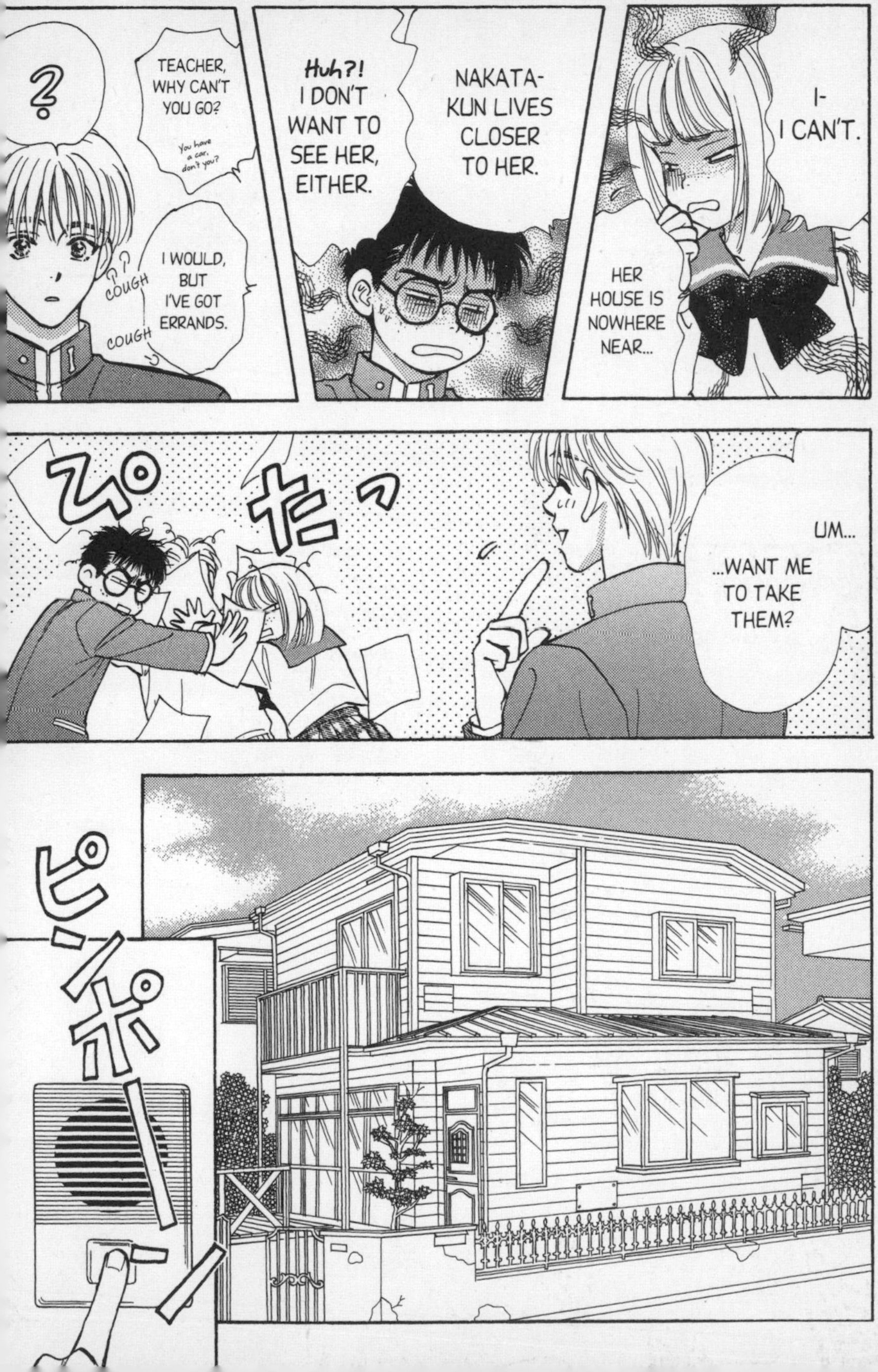
I-
I CAN'T.
HER HOUSE IS NOWHERE NEAR...
NAKATA-KUN LIVES CLOSER TO HER.
Huh?! I DON'T WANT TO SEE HER, EITHER.
?
TEACHER, WHY CAN'T YOU GO?
You have a car, don't you?
I WOULD, BUT I'VE GOT ERRANDS.
COUGH
COUGH
UM...
...WANT ME TO TAKE THEM?
ぴたっ
ピンポーン

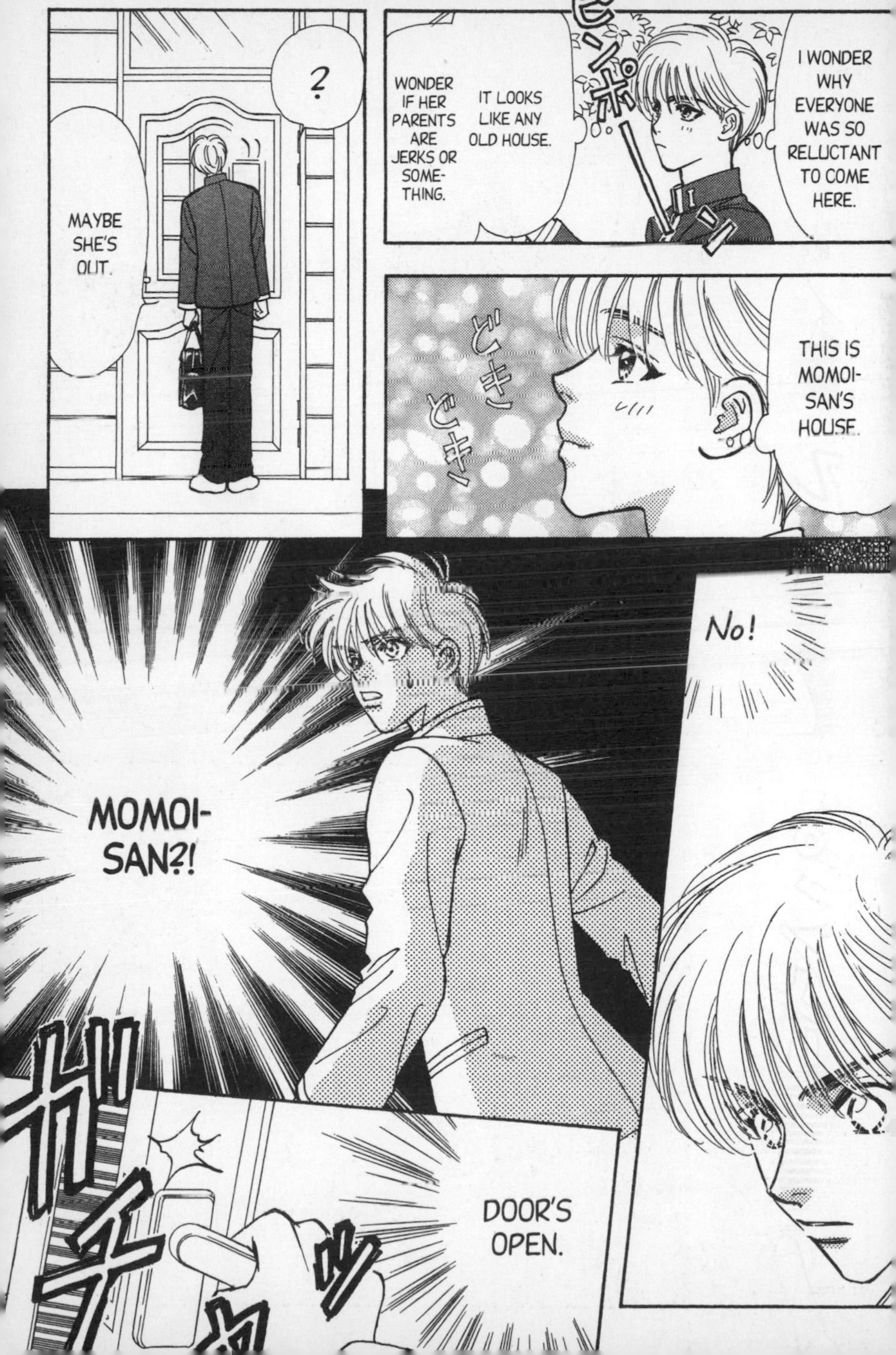
ピンポーン
I WONDER WHY EVERYONE WAS SO RELUCTANT TO COME HERE.
IT LOOKS LIKE ANY OLD HOUSE.
WONDER IF HER PARENTS ARE JERKS OR SOME-THING.
どきどき
THIS IS MOMOI-SAN'S HOUSE.
?
MAYBE SHE'S OUT.
No!
MOMOI-SAN?!
ガチャッ
DOOR'S OPEN.

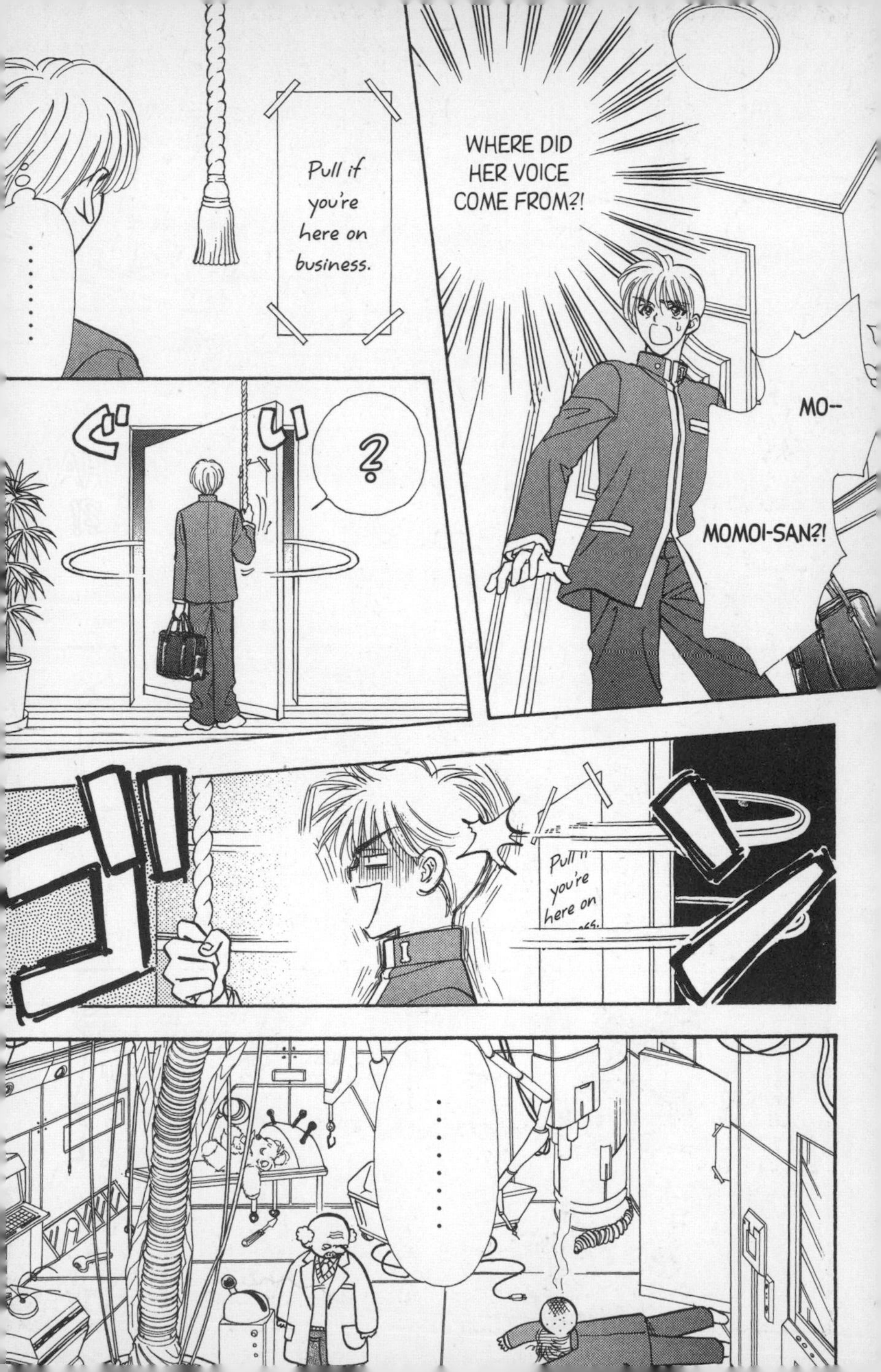
WHERE DID HER VOICE COME FROM?!
MO--
MOMOI-SAN?!
......
Pull if you're here on business.
ぐい
?
you're here on
......

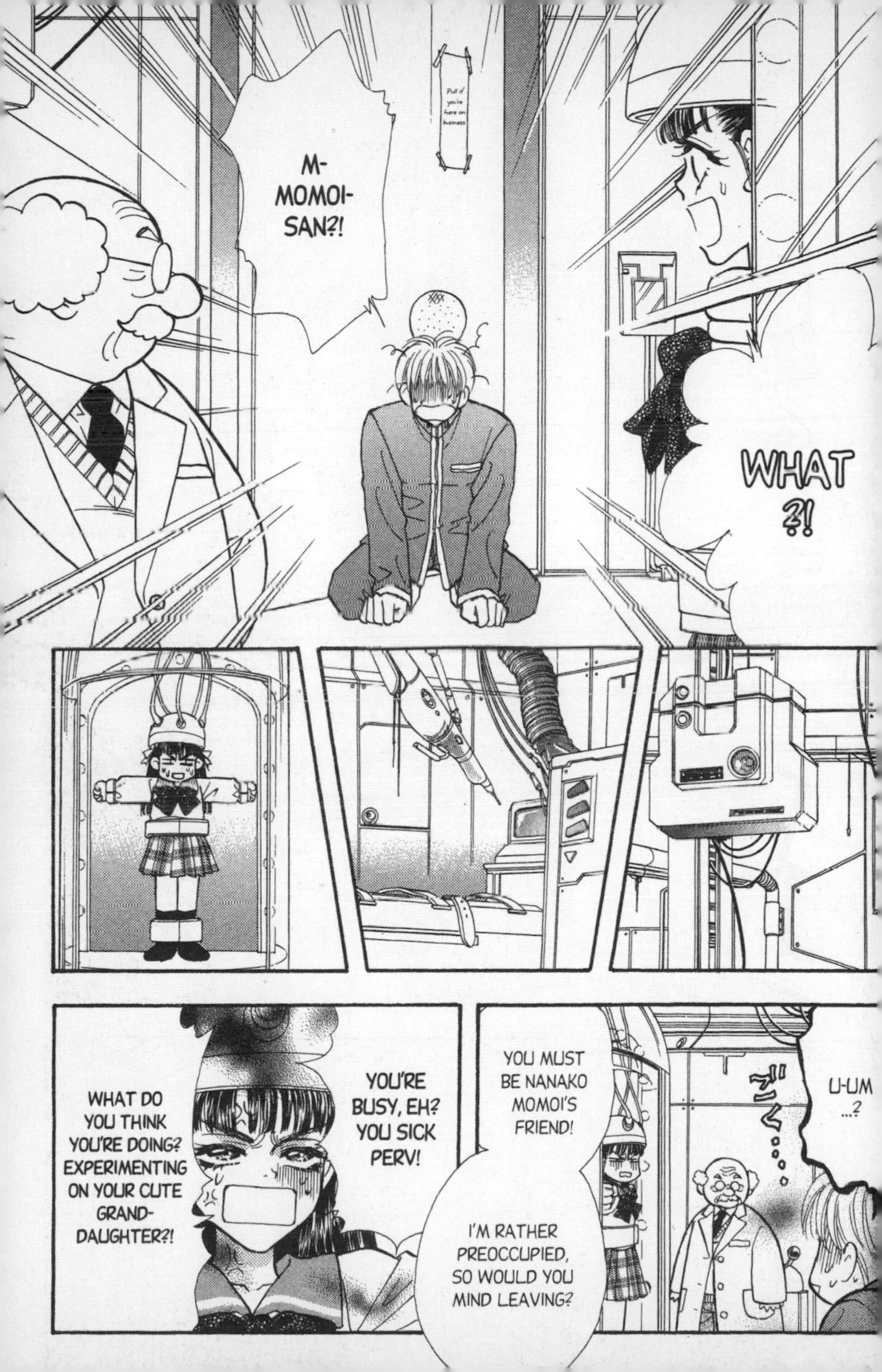
Pull if you're here on business.
WHAT ?!
M-MOMOI-SAN?!
U-UM ...?
YOU MUST BE NANAKO MOMOI'S FRIEND!
I'M RATHER PREOCCUPIED, SO WOULD YOU MIND LEAVING?
YOU'RE BUSY, EH? YOU SICK PERV!
WHAT DO YOU THINK YOU'RE DOING? EXPERIMENTING ON YOUR CUTE GRAND-DAUGHTER?!

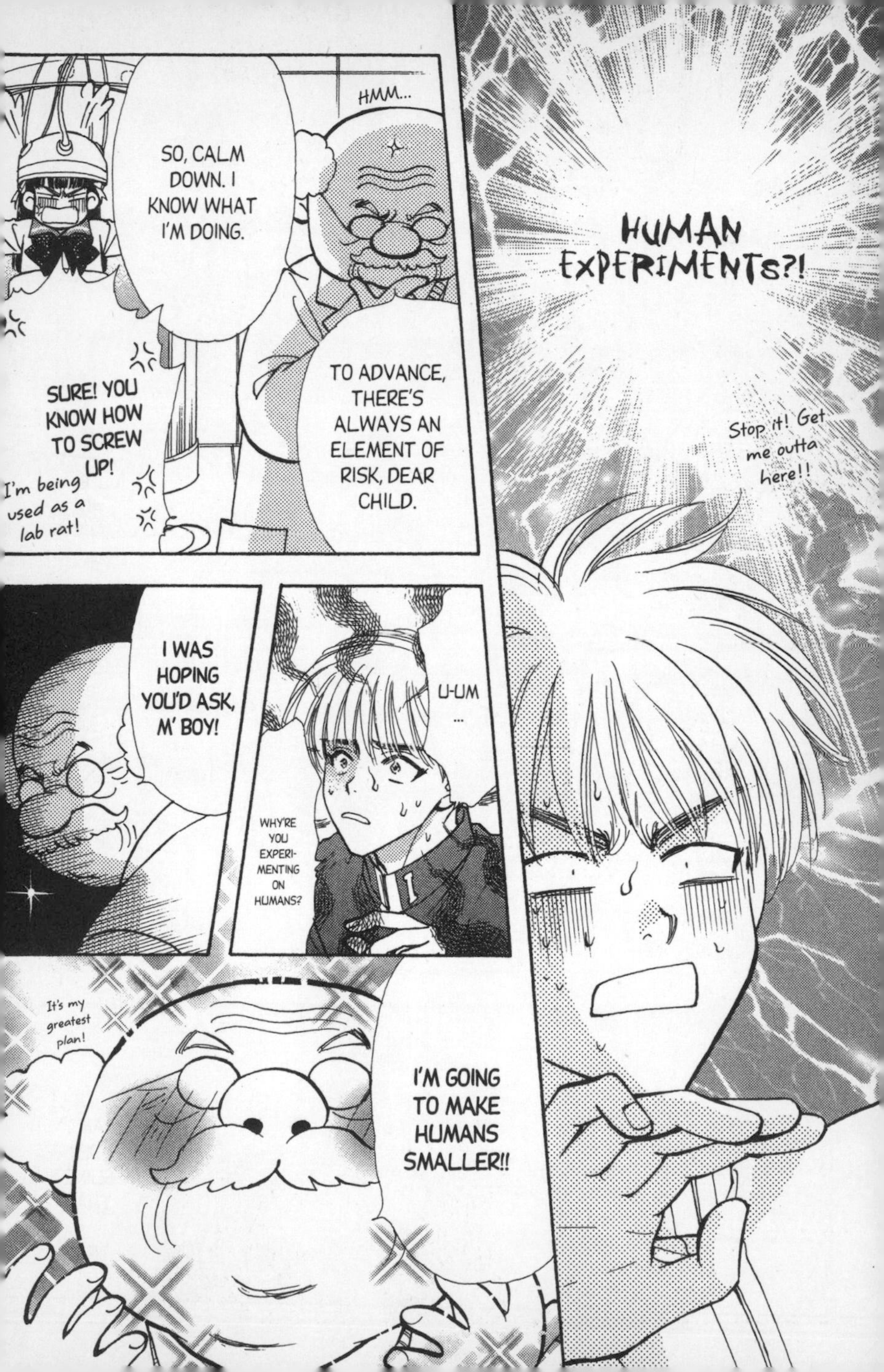
HUMAN EXPERIMENTS?!
Stop it! Get me outta here!!
HMM...
SO, CALM DOWN. I KNOW WHAT I'M DOING.
TO ADVANCE, THERE'S ALWAYS AN ELEMENT OF RISK, DEAR CHILD.
SURE! YOU KNOW HOW TO SCREW UP!
I'm being used as a lab rat!
U-UM ...
WHY'RE YOU EXPERIMENTING ON HUMANS?
I WAS HOPING YOU'D ASK, M' BOY!
I'M GOING TO MAKE HUMANS SMALLER!!
It's my greatest plan!

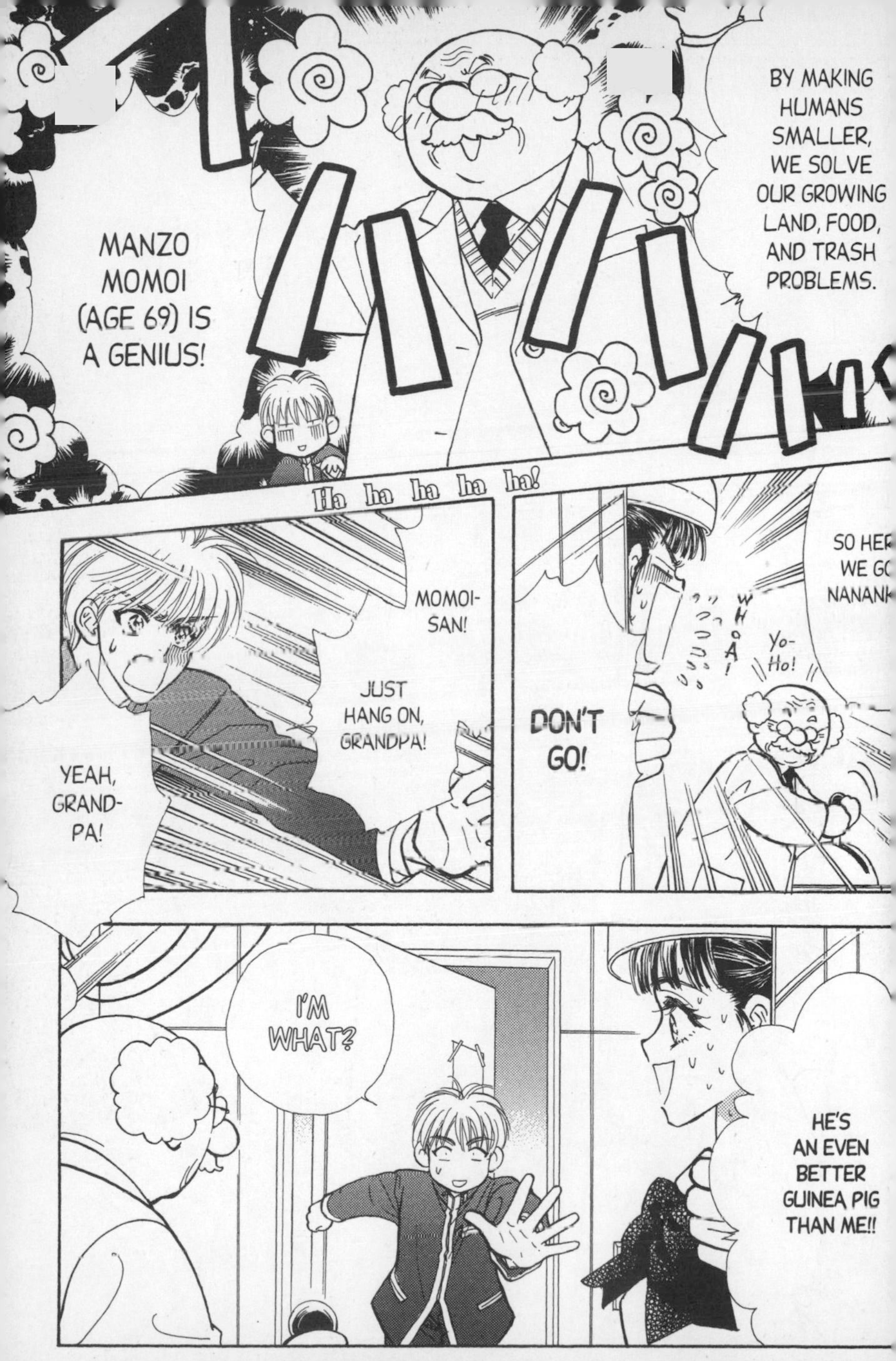
BY MAKING HUMANS SMALLER, WE SOLVE OUR GROWING LAND, FOOD, AND TRASH PROBLEMS.
MANZO MOMOI (AGE 69) IS A GENIUS!
Ha ha ha ha ha!
SO HER
WE GO
NANANK
Yo-Ho!
WHOA!
DON'T GO!
MOMOI-SAN!
JUST HANG ON, GRANDPA!
YEAH, GRANDPA!
HE'S AN EVEN BETTER GUINEA PIG THAN ME!!
I'M WHAT?

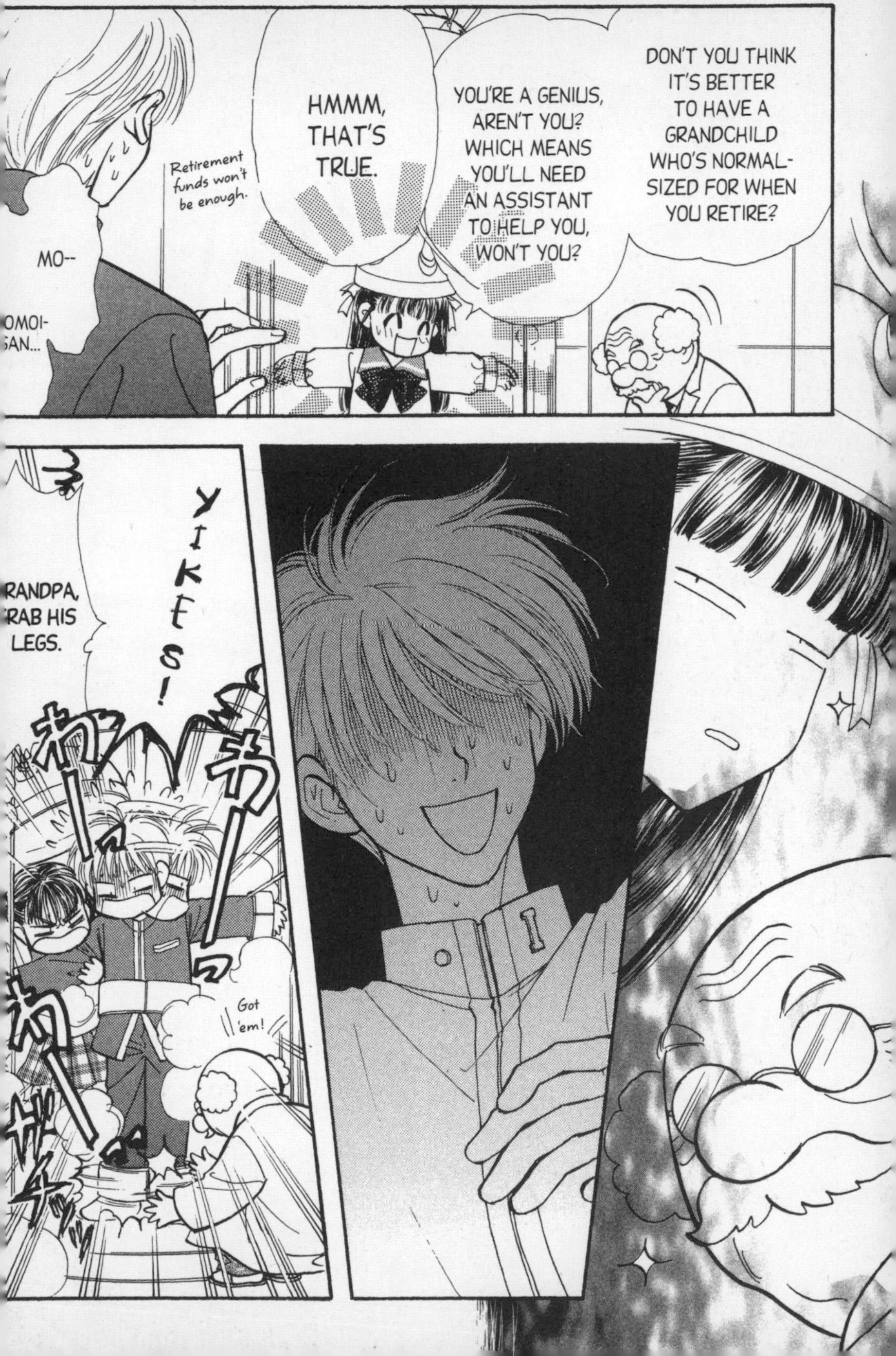

DON'T YOU THINK IT'S BETTER TO HAVE A GRANDCHILD WHO'S NORMAL-SIZED FOR WHEN YOU RETIRE?
YOU'RE A GENIUS, AREN'T YOU? WHICH MEANS YOU'LL NEED AN ASSISTANT TO HELP YOU, WON'T YOU?
HMMM, THAT'S TRUE.
Retirement funds won't be enough.
MO--
OMOI-SAN...
YIKES!
RANDPA, RAB HIS LEGS.
Got 'em!

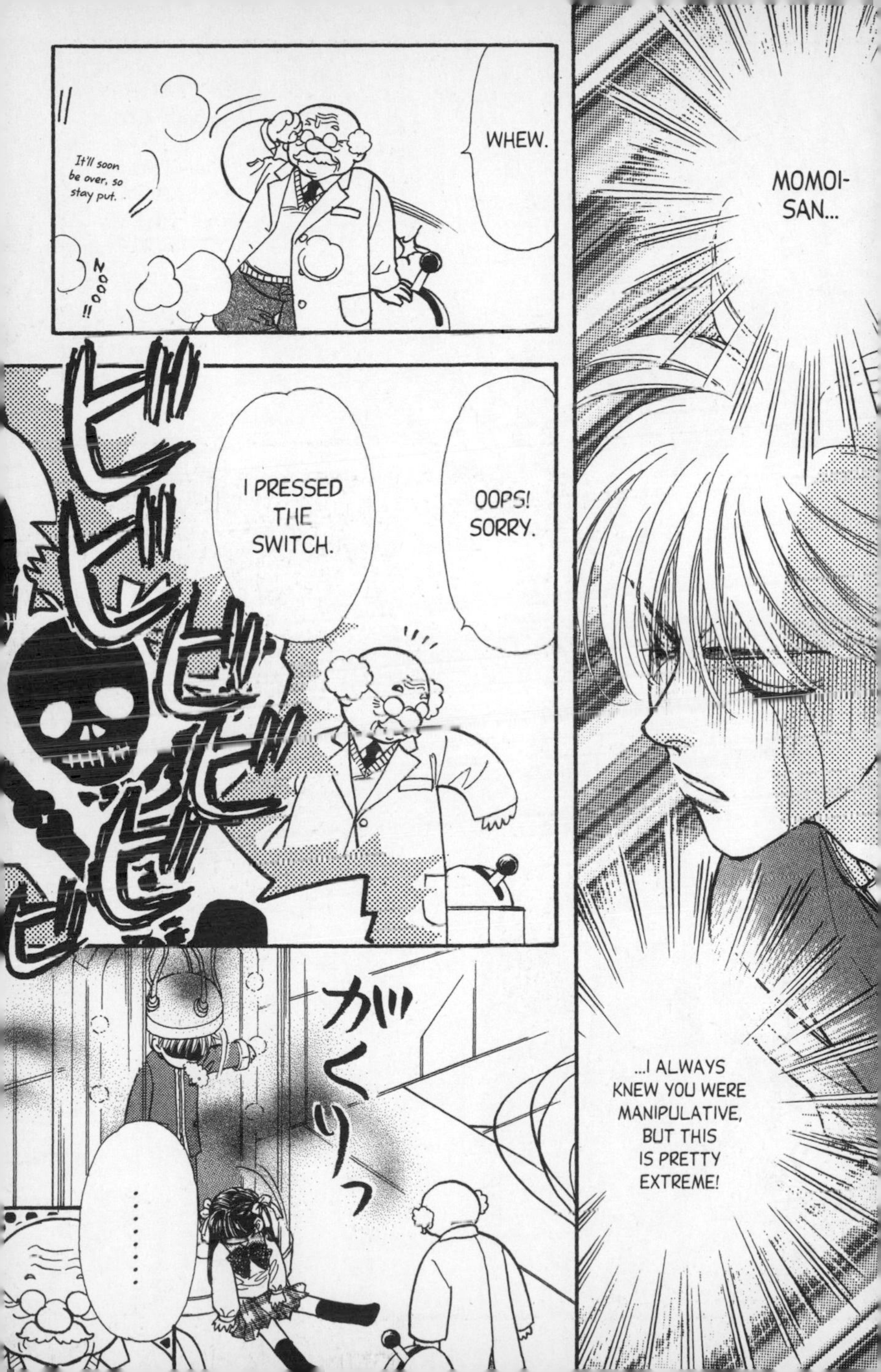
MOMOI-SAN...
...I ALWAYS KNEW YOU WERE MANIPULATIVE, BUT THIS IS PRETTY EXTREME!
WHEW.
It'll soon be over, so stay put.
NOOO!!
OOPS! SORRY.
I PRESSED THE SWITCH.
がくりっ
......

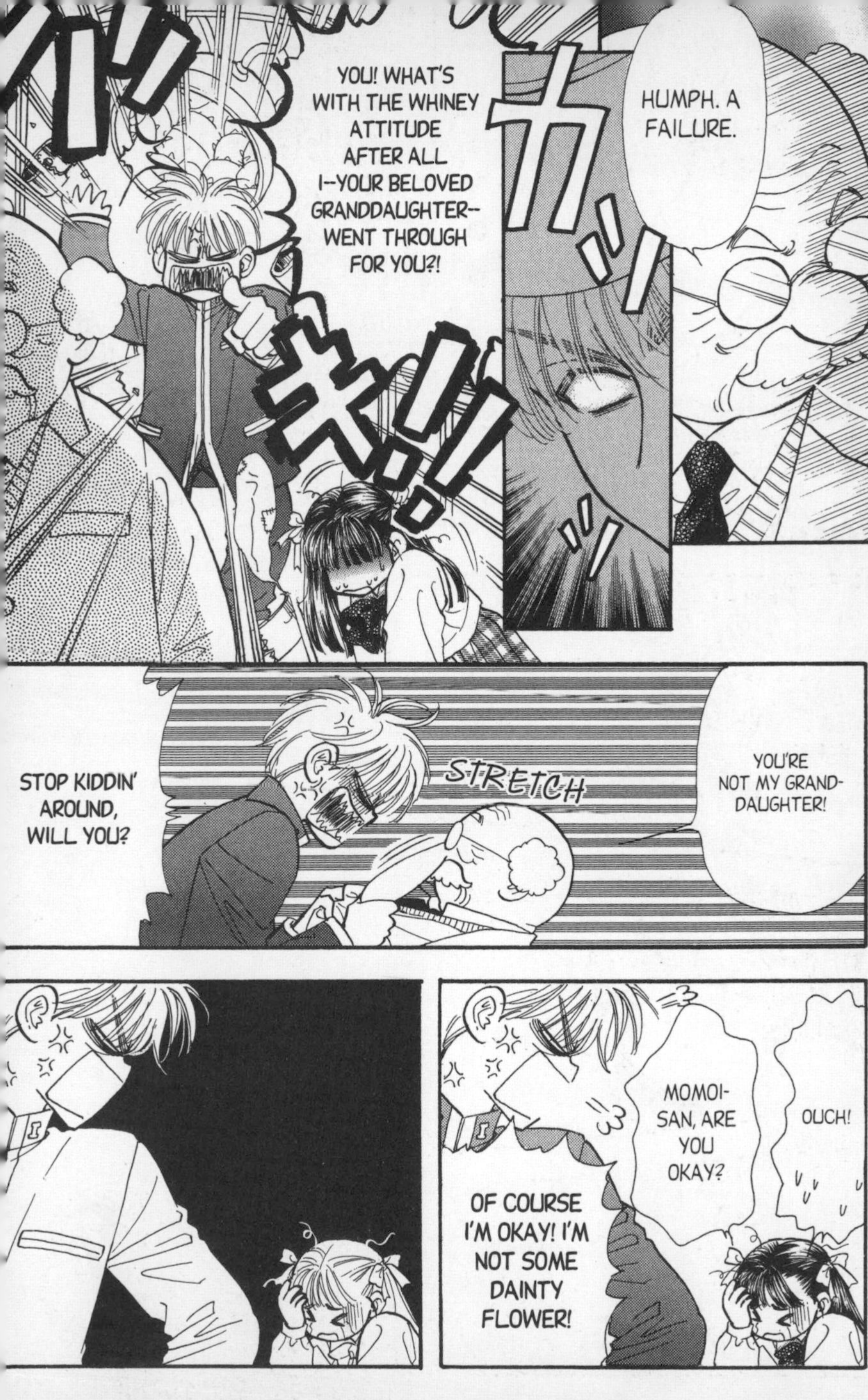
HUMPH. A FAILURE.
YOU! WHAT'S WITH THE WHINEY ATTITUDE AFTER ALL I--YOUR BELOVED GRANDDAUGHTER--WENT THROUGH FOR YOU?!
YOU'RE NOT MY GRAND-DAUGHTER!
STRETCH
STOP KIDDIN' AROUND, WILL YOU?
OUCH!
MOMOI-SAN, ARE YOU OKAY?
OF COURSE I'M OKAY! I'M NOT SOME DAINTY FLOWER!

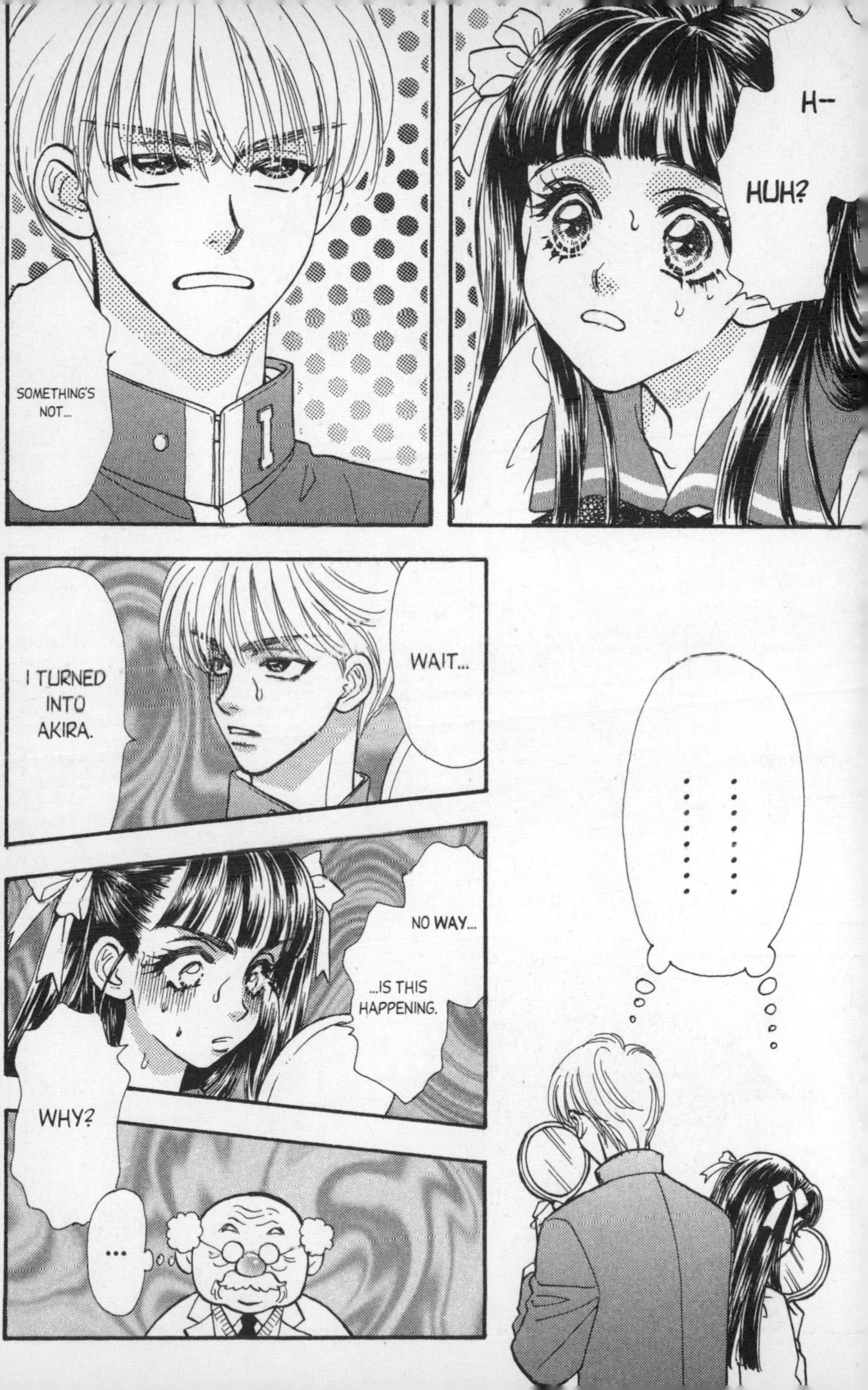
H--
HUH?
SOMETHING'S NOT...
......
WAIT...
I TURNED INTO AKIRA.
NO WAY...
...IS THIS HAPPENING.
WHY?
...

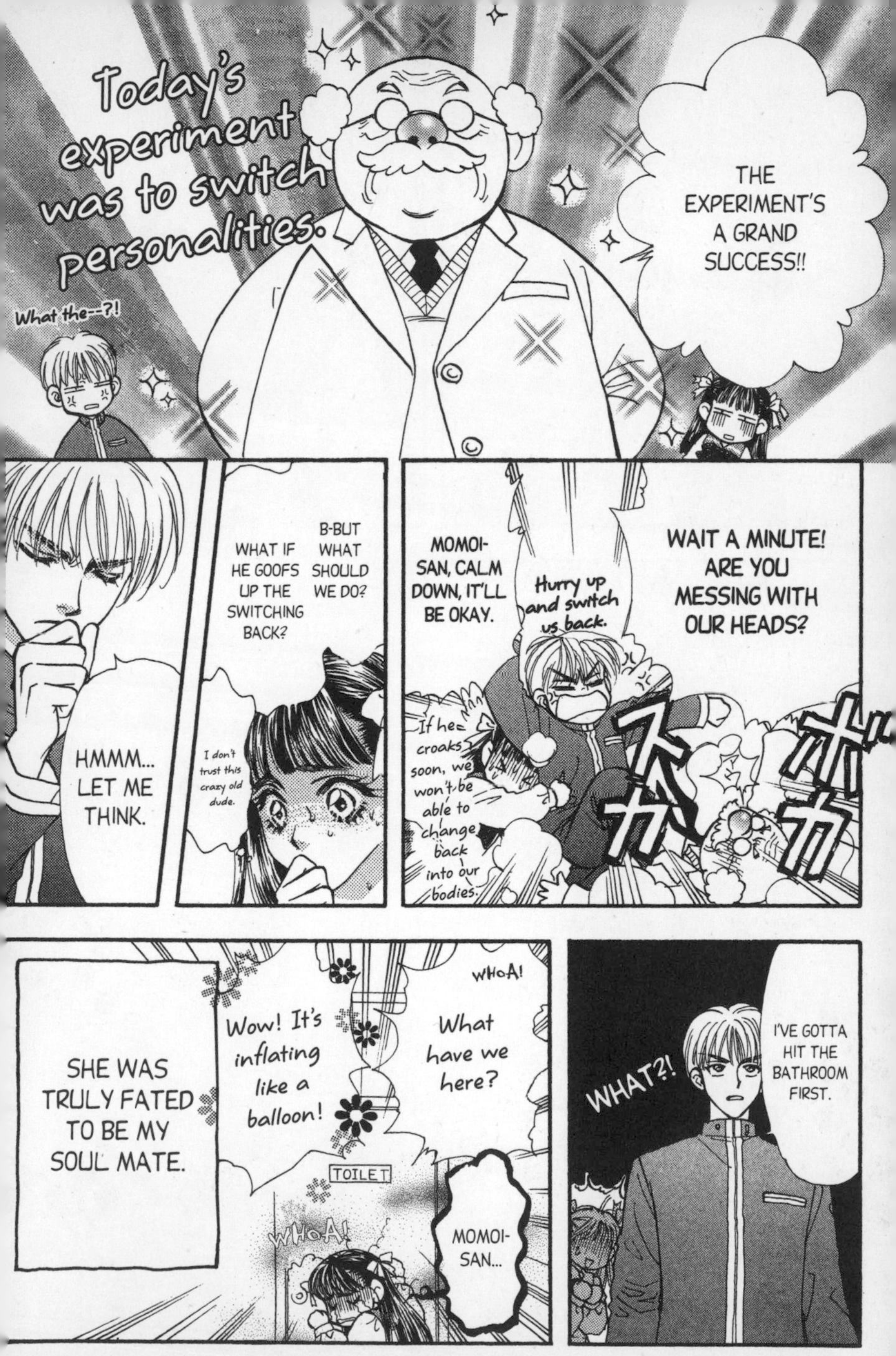
THE EXPERIMENT'S A GRAND SUCCESS!!
Today's experiment was to switch personalities.
What the--?!
WAIT A MINUTE! ARE YOU MESSING WITH OUR HEADS?
Hurry up and switch us back.
ボカ
スカ
MOMOI-SAN, CALM DOWN, IT'LL BE OKAY.
If he croaks soon, we won't be able to change back into our bodies.
B-BUT WHAT SHOULD WE DO?
WHAT IF HE GOOFS UP THE SWITCHING BACK?
I don't trust this crazy old dude.
HMMM... LET ME THINK.
I'VE GOTTA HIT THE BATHROOM FIRST.
WHAT?!
WHOA!
What have we here?
Wow! It's inflating like a balloon!
TOILET
MOMOI-SAN...
WHOA!
SHE WAS TRULY FATED TO BE MY SOUL MATE.

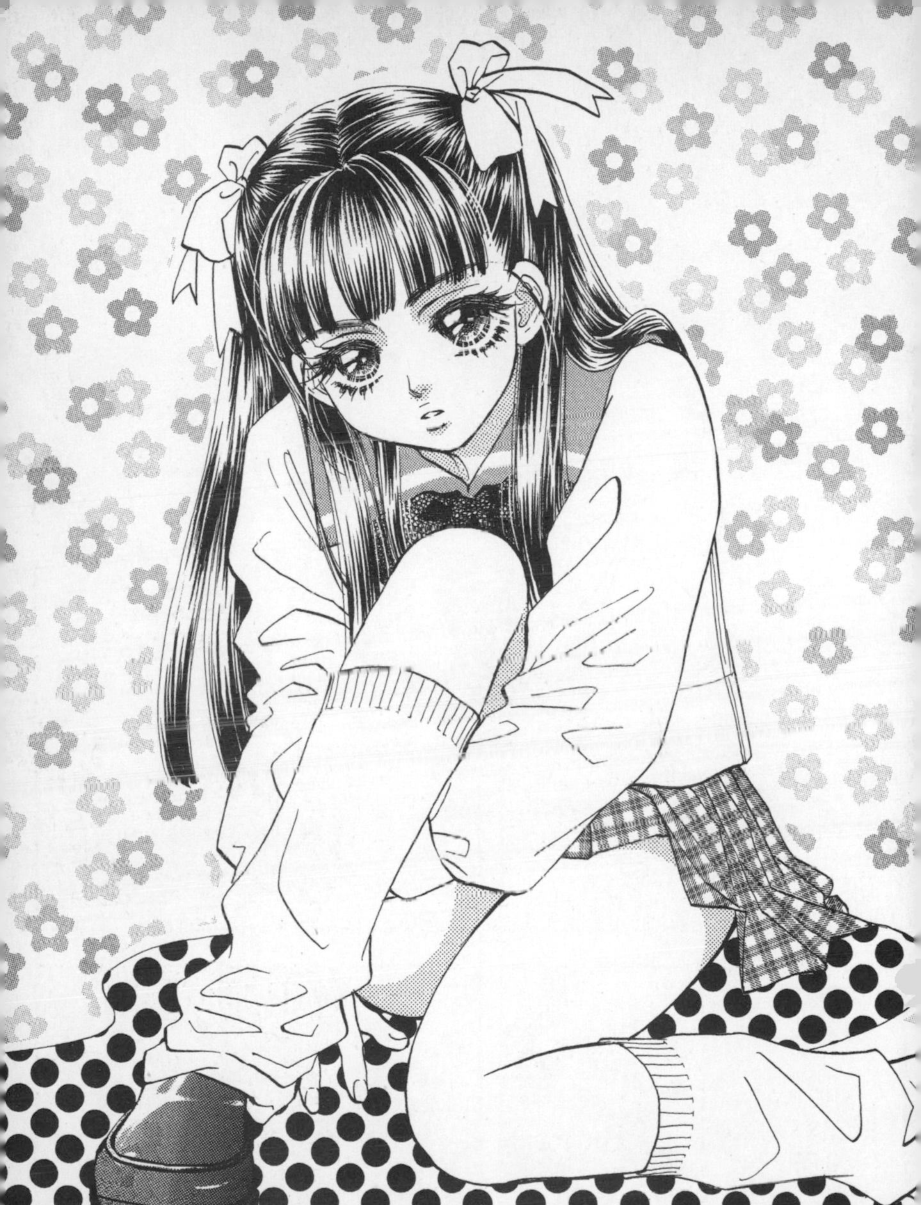

Episode 2
Secretly Exchanged Life

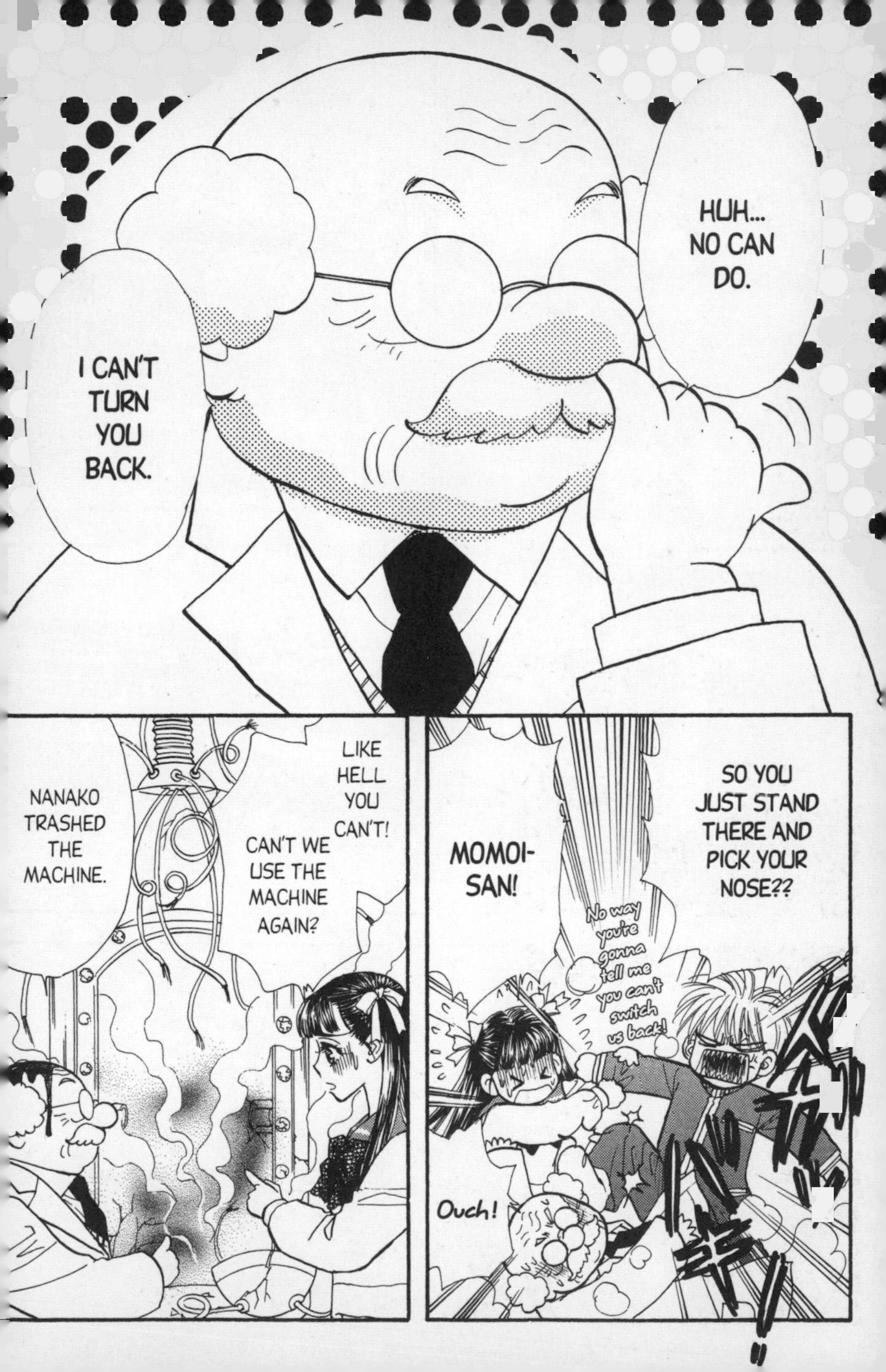
HUH... NO CAN DO.
I CAN'T TURN YOU BACK.
SO YOU JUST STAND THERE AND PICK YOUR NOSE??
MOMOI-SAN!
No way you're gonna tell me you can't switch us back!
Ouch!
LIKE HELL YOU CAN'T!
CAN'T WE USE THE MACHINE AGAIN?
NANAKO TRASHED THE MACHINE.

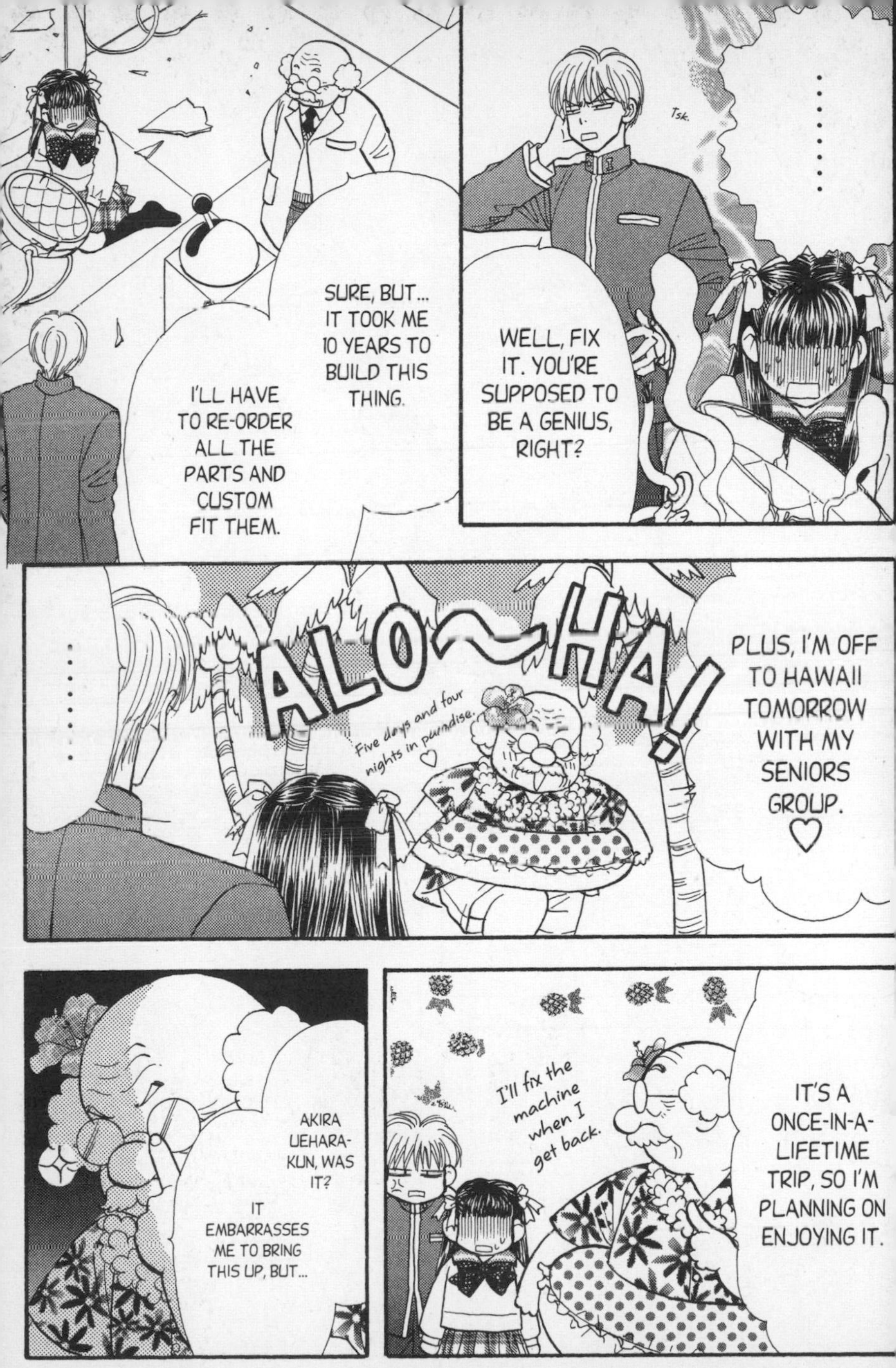
......
Tsk.
WELL, FIX IT. YOU'RE SUPPOSED TO BE A GENIUS, RIGHT?
SURE, BUT... IT TOOK ME 10 YEARS TO BUILD THIS THING.
I'LL HAVE TO RE-ORDER ALL THE PARTS AND CUSTOM FIT THEM.
PLUS, I'M OFF TO HAWAII TOMORROW WITH MY SENIORS GROUP. ♡
ALO~HA!
Five days and four nights in paradise. ♡
......
IT'S A ONCE-IN-A-LIFETIME TRIP, SO I'M PLANNING ON ENJOYING IT.
I'll fix the machine when I get back.
AKIRA UEHARA-KUN, WAS IT?
IT EMBARRASSES ME TO BRING THIS UP, BUT...

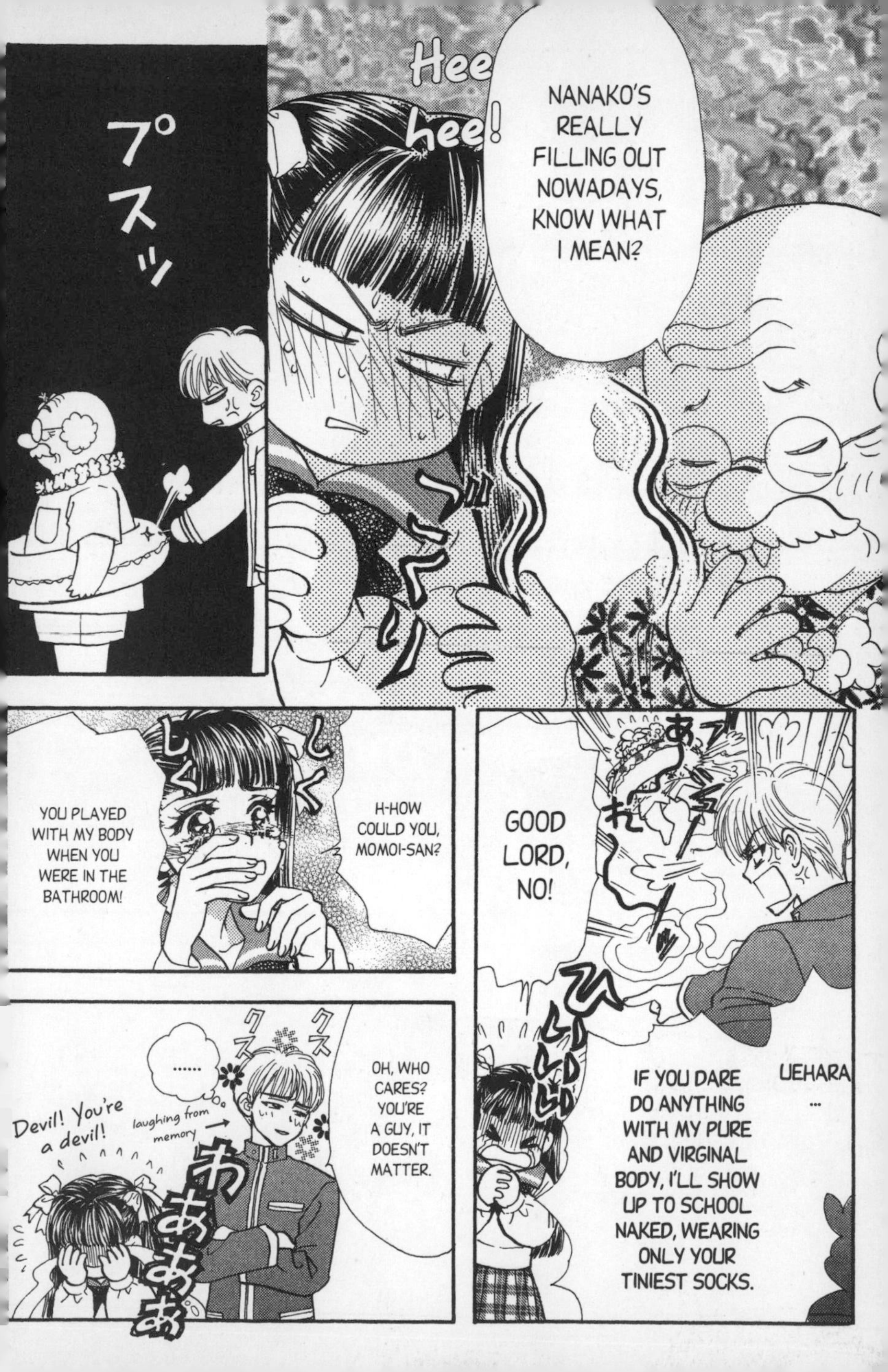

Hee hee!
NANAKO'S REALLY FILLING OUT NOWADAYS, KNOW WHAT I MEAN?
プスッ
GOOD LORD, NO!
UEHARA...
IF YOU DARE DO ANYTHING WITH MY PURE AND VIRGINAL BODY, I'LL SHOW UP TO SCHOOL NAKED, WEARING ONLY YOUR TINIEST SOCKS.
しくしく
H-HOW COULD YOU, MOMOI-SAN?
YOU PLAYED WITH MY BODY WHEN YOU WERE IN THE BATHROOM!
クスクス
OH, WHO CARES? YOU'RE A GUY, IT DOESN'T MATTER.
......
laughing from memory
Devil! You're a devil!

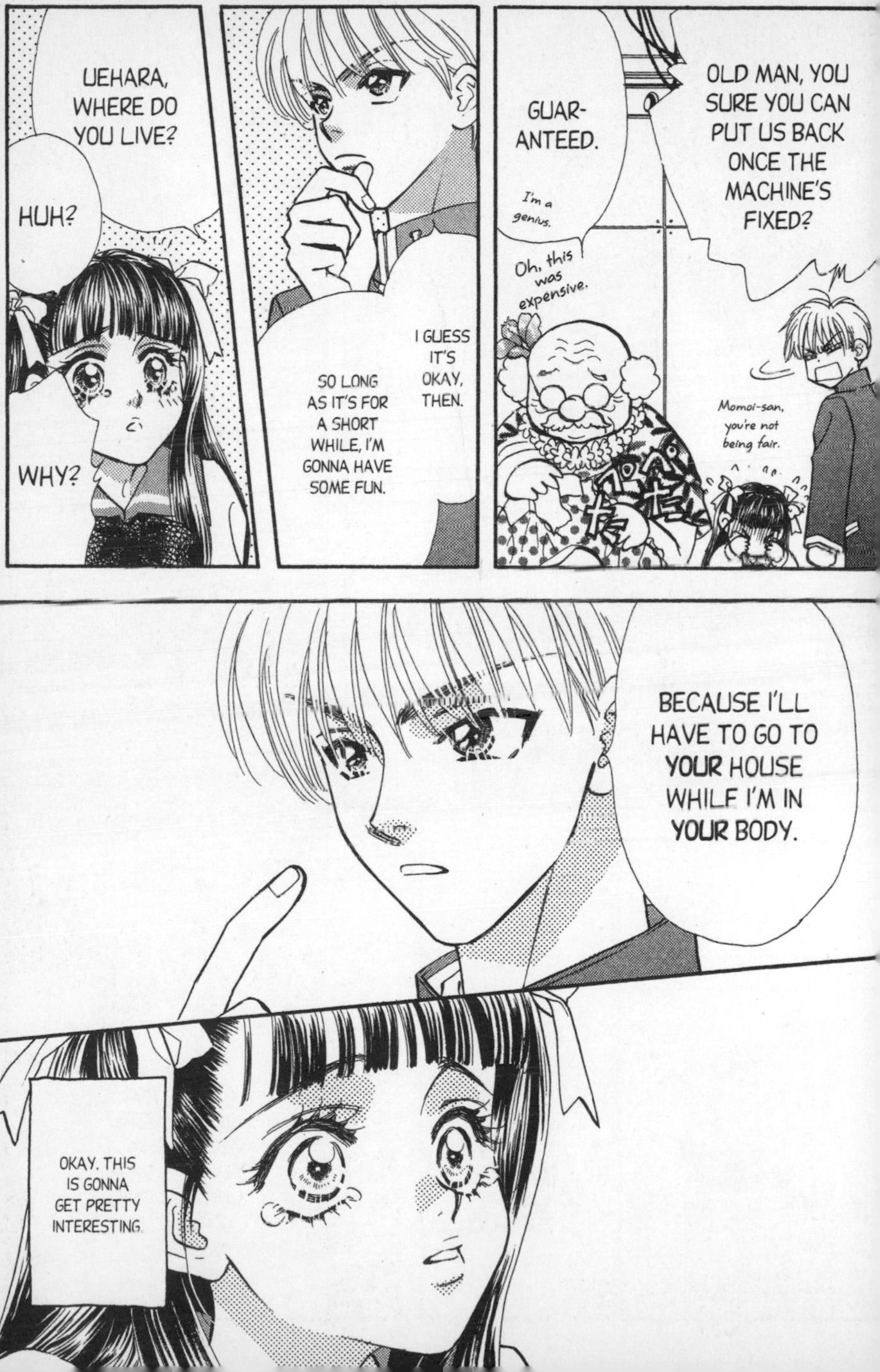
OLD MAN, YOU SURE YOU CAN PUT US BACK ONCE THE MACHINE'S FIXED?
GUAR-ANTEED.
I'm a genius.
Oh, this was expensive.
Momoi-san, you're not being fair.
I GUESS IT'S OKAY, THEN.
SO LONG AS IT'S FOR A SHORT WHILE, I'M GONNA HAVE SOME FUN.
UEHARA, WHERE DO YOU LIVE?
HUH?
WHY?
BECAUSE I'LL HAVE TO GO TO **YOUR** HOUSE WHILE I'M IN **YOUR** BODY.
OKAY. THIS IS GONNA GET PRETTY INTERESTING.

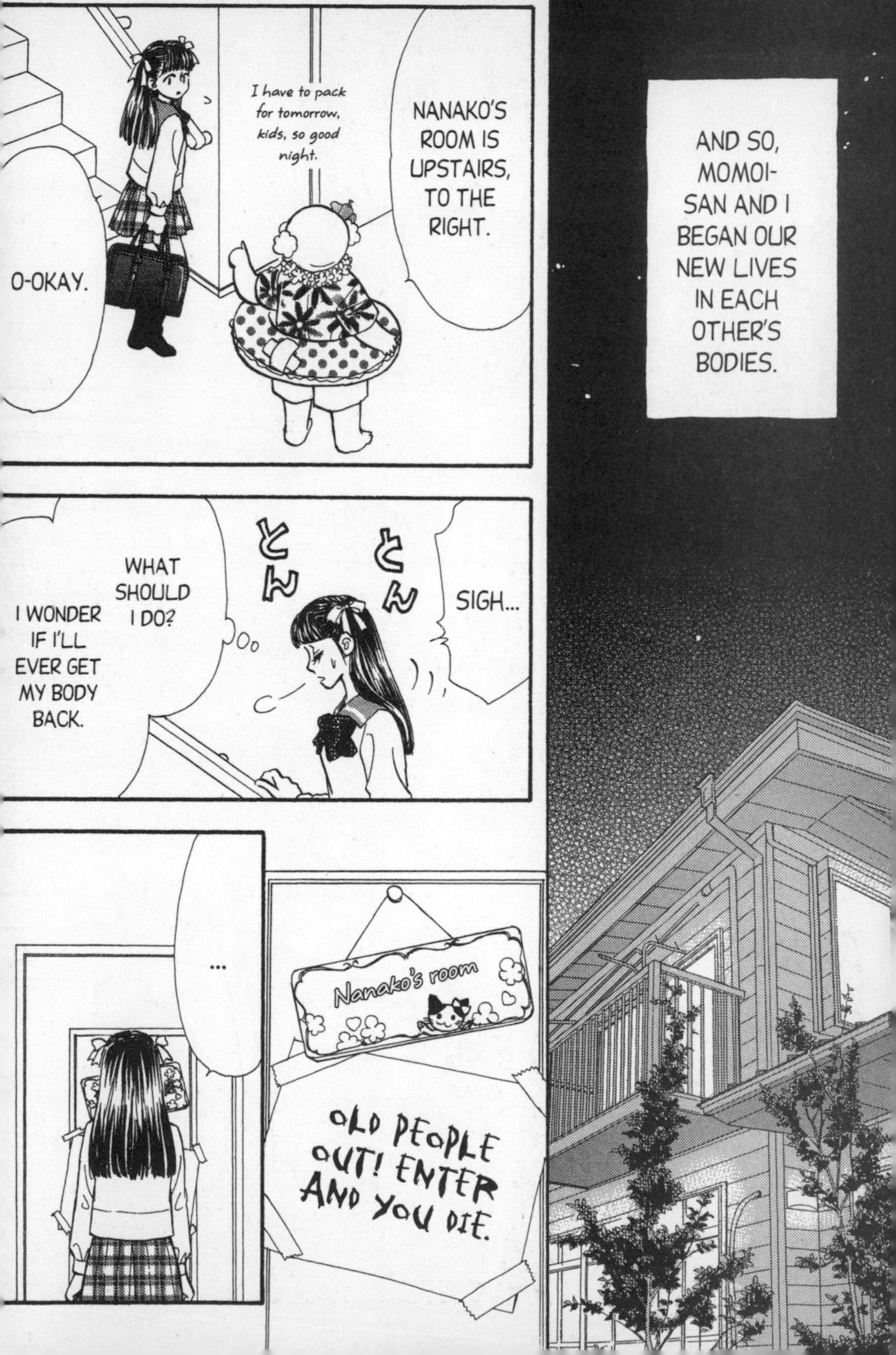
AND SO, MOMOI-SAN AND I BEGAN OUR NEW LIVES IN EACH OTHER'S BODIES.
NANAKO'S ROOM IS UPSTAIRS, TO THE RIGHT.
I have to pack for tomorrow, kids, so good night.
O-OKAY.
SIGH...
とん とん
WHAT SHOULD I DO?
I WONDER IF I'LL EVER GET MY BODY BACK.
Nanako's room
OLD PEOPLE OUT! ENTER AND YOU DIE.
...

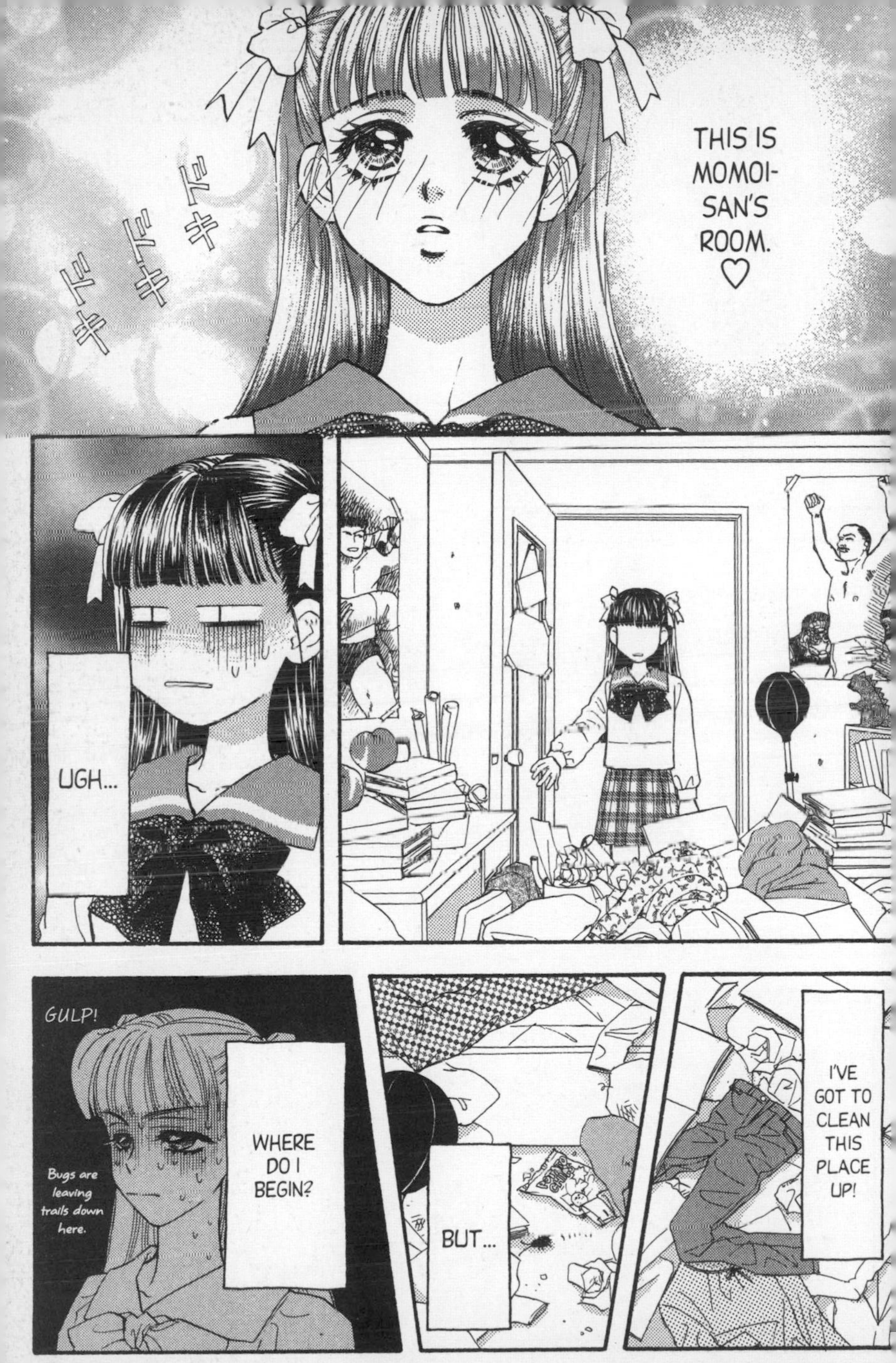
THIS IS MOMOI-SAN'S ROOM. ♡
UGH...
I'VE GOT TO CLEAN THIS PLACE UP!
BUT...
WHERE DO I BEGIN?
GULP!
Bugs are leaving trails down here.

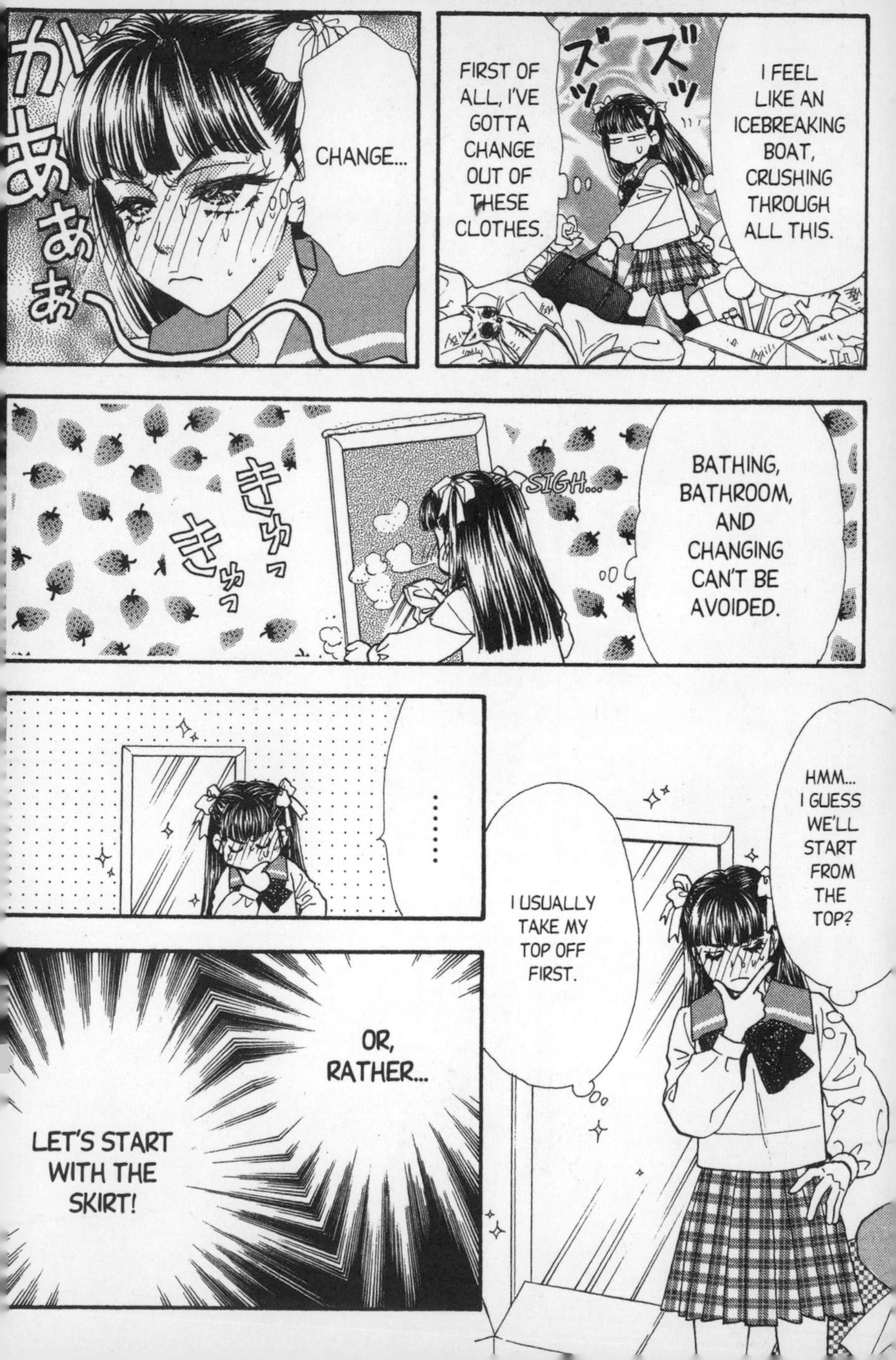
I FEEL LIKE AN ICEBREAKING BOAT, CRUSHING THROUGH ALL THIS.
ズッ ズッ
FIRST OF ALL, I'VE GOTTA CHANGE OUT OF THESE CLOTHES.
CHANGE...
かあぁぁ
BATHING, BATHROOM, AND CHANGING CAN'T BE AVOIDED.
SIGH...
きゅっ きゅっ
HMM... I GUESS WE'LL START FROM THE TOP?
I USUALLY TAKE MY TOP OFF FIRST.
......
OR, RATHER...
LET'S START WITH THE SKIRT!

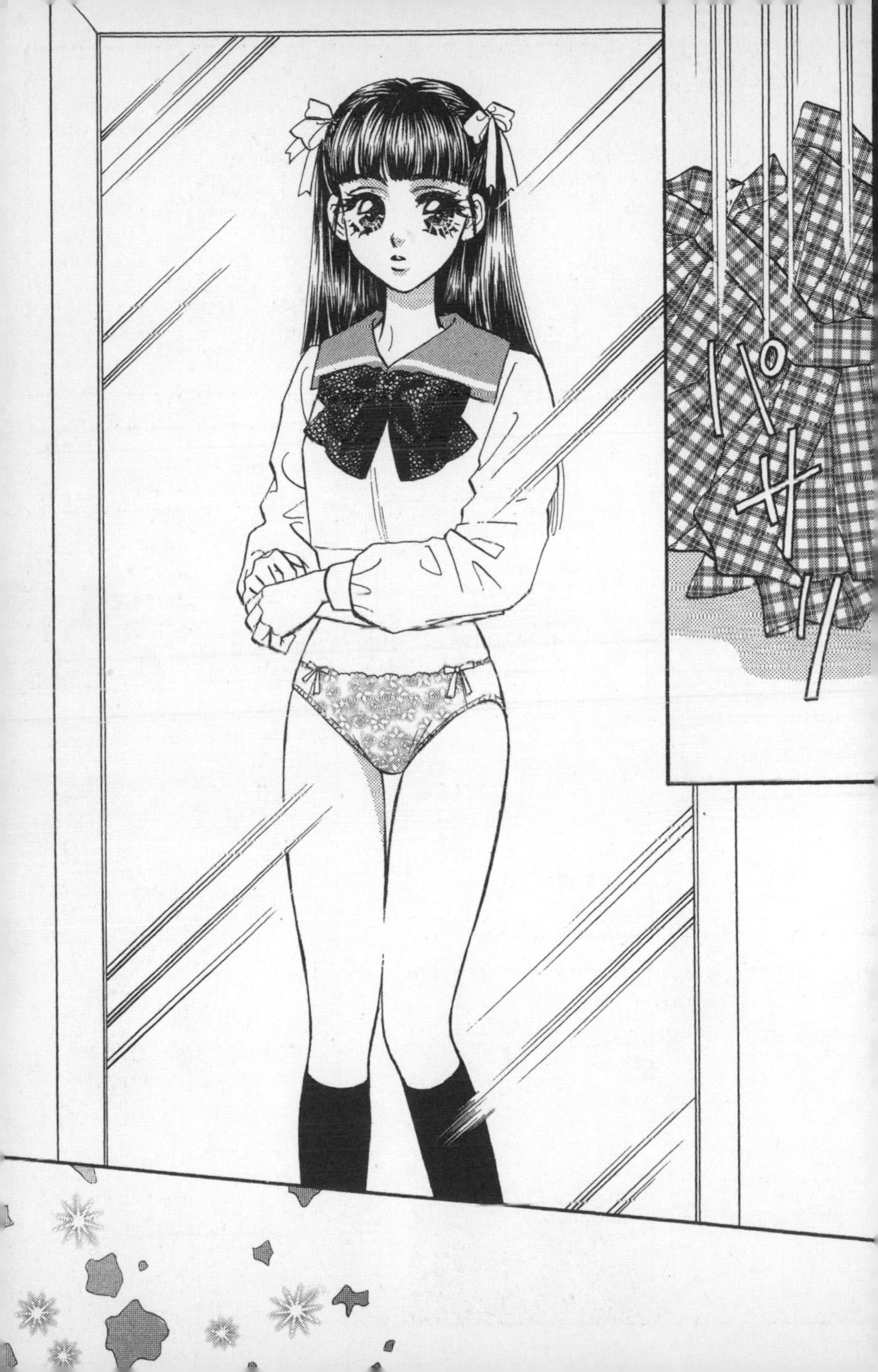
パサ

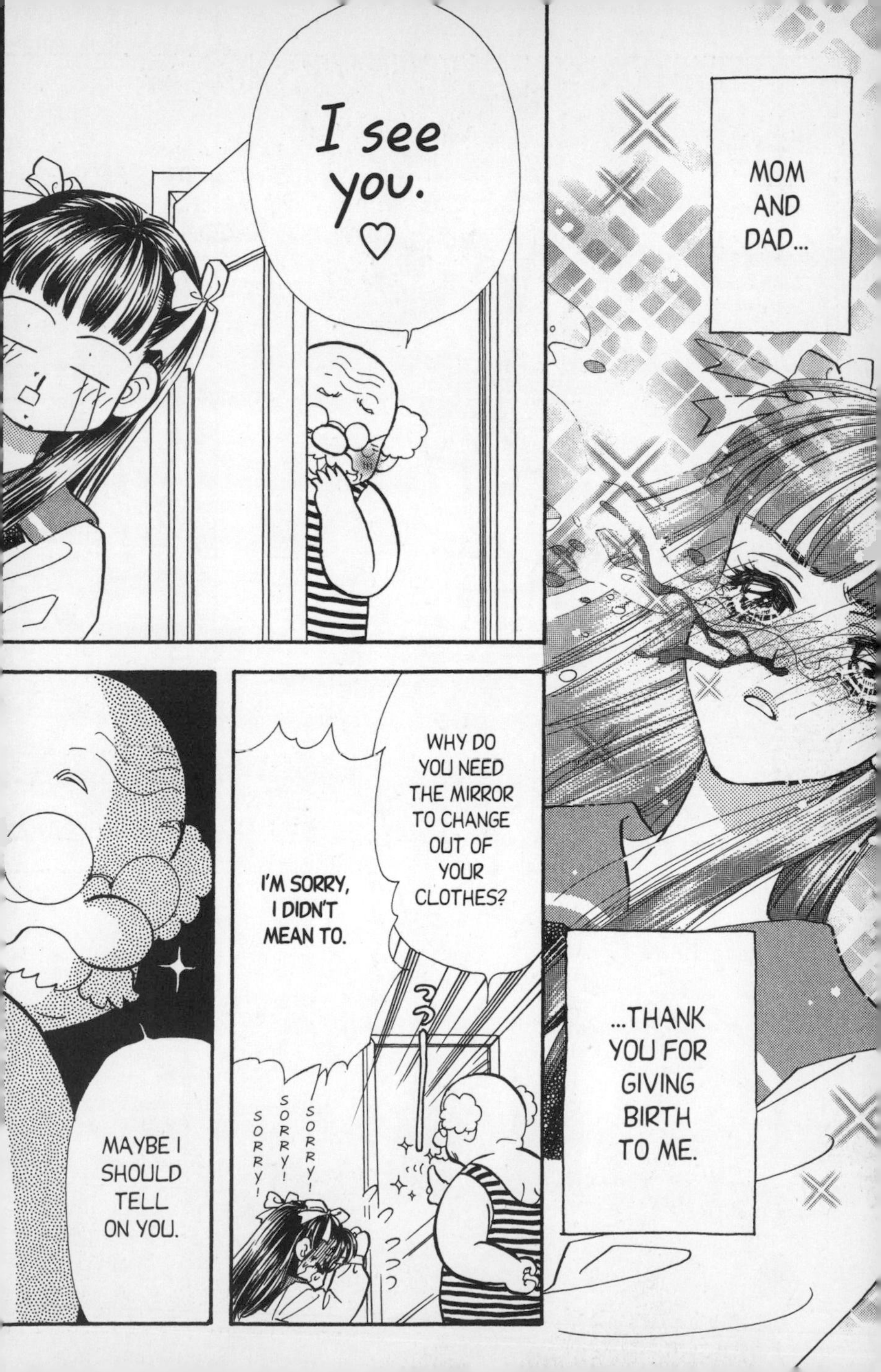
MOM AND DAD...
...THANK YOU FOR GIVING BIRTH TO ME.
I see you. ♡
WHY DO YOU NEED THE MIRROR TO CHANGE OUT OF YOUR CLOTHES?
I'M SORRY, I DIDN'T MEAN TO.
SORRY! SORRY! SORRY!
MAYBE I SHOULD TELL ON YOU.

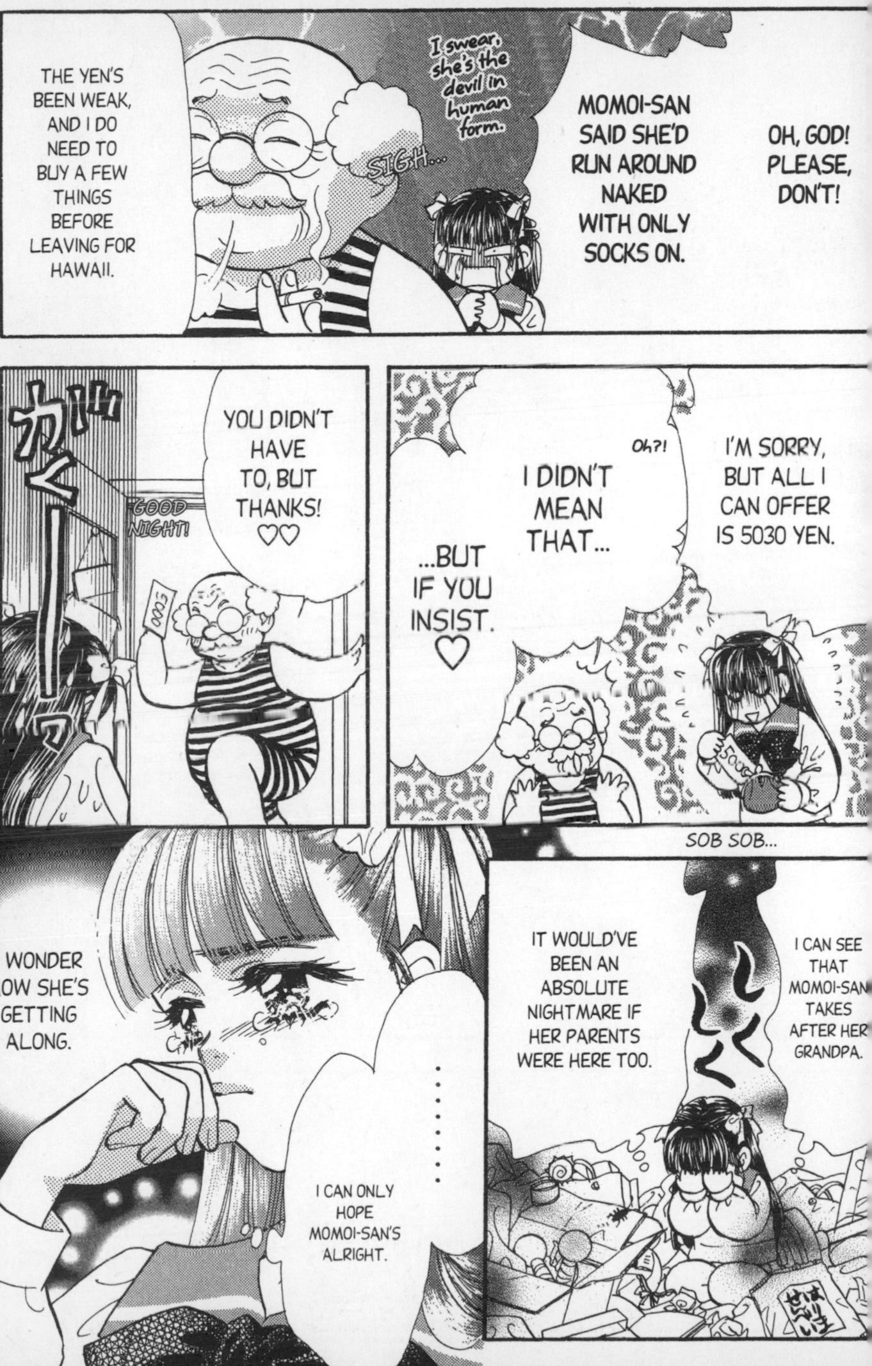
OH, GOD! PLEASE, DON'T!
MOMOI-SAN SAID SHE'D RUN AROUND NAKED WITH ONLY SOCKS ON.
I swear, she's the devil in human form.
SIGH...
THE YEN'S BEEN WEAK, AND I DO NEED TO BUY A FEW THINGS BEFORE LEAVING FOR HAWAII.
I'M SORRY, BUT ALL I CAN OFFER IS 5030 YEN.
Oh?!
I DIDN'T MEAN THAT...
...BUT IF YOU INSIST. ♡
YOU DIDN'T HAVE TO, BUT THANKS! ♡♡
GOOD NIGHT!
SOB SOB...
I CAN SEE THAT MOMOI-SAN TAKES AFTER HER GRANDPA.
IT WOULD'VE BEEN AN ABSOLUTE NIGHTMARE IF HER PARENTS WERE HERE TOO.
I WONDER HOW SHE'S GETTING ALONG.
......
I CAN ONLY HOPE MOMOI-SAN'S ALRIGHT.

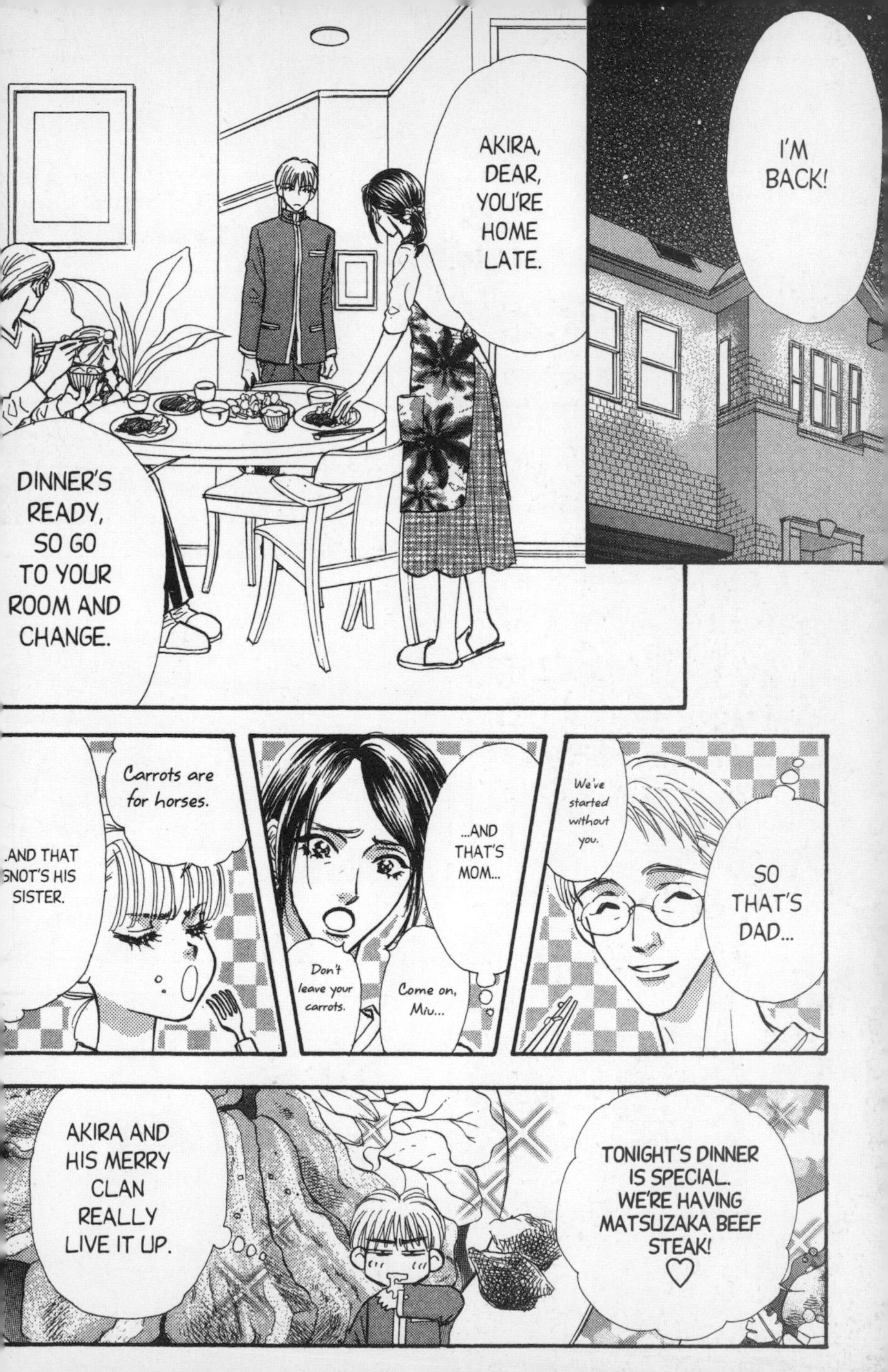
I'M BACK!
AKIRA, DEAR, YOU'RE HOME LATE.
DINNER'S READY, SO GO TO YOUR ROOM AND CHANGE.
We've started without you.
SO THAT'S DAD...
...AND THAT'S MOM...
Come on, Miu...
Don't leave your carrots.
Carrots are for horses.
.AND THAT SNOT'S HIS SISTER.
TONIGHT'S DINNER IS SPECIAL. WE'RE HAVING MATSUZAKA BEEF STEAK! ♡
AKIRA AND HIS MERRY CLAN REALLY LIVE IT UP.

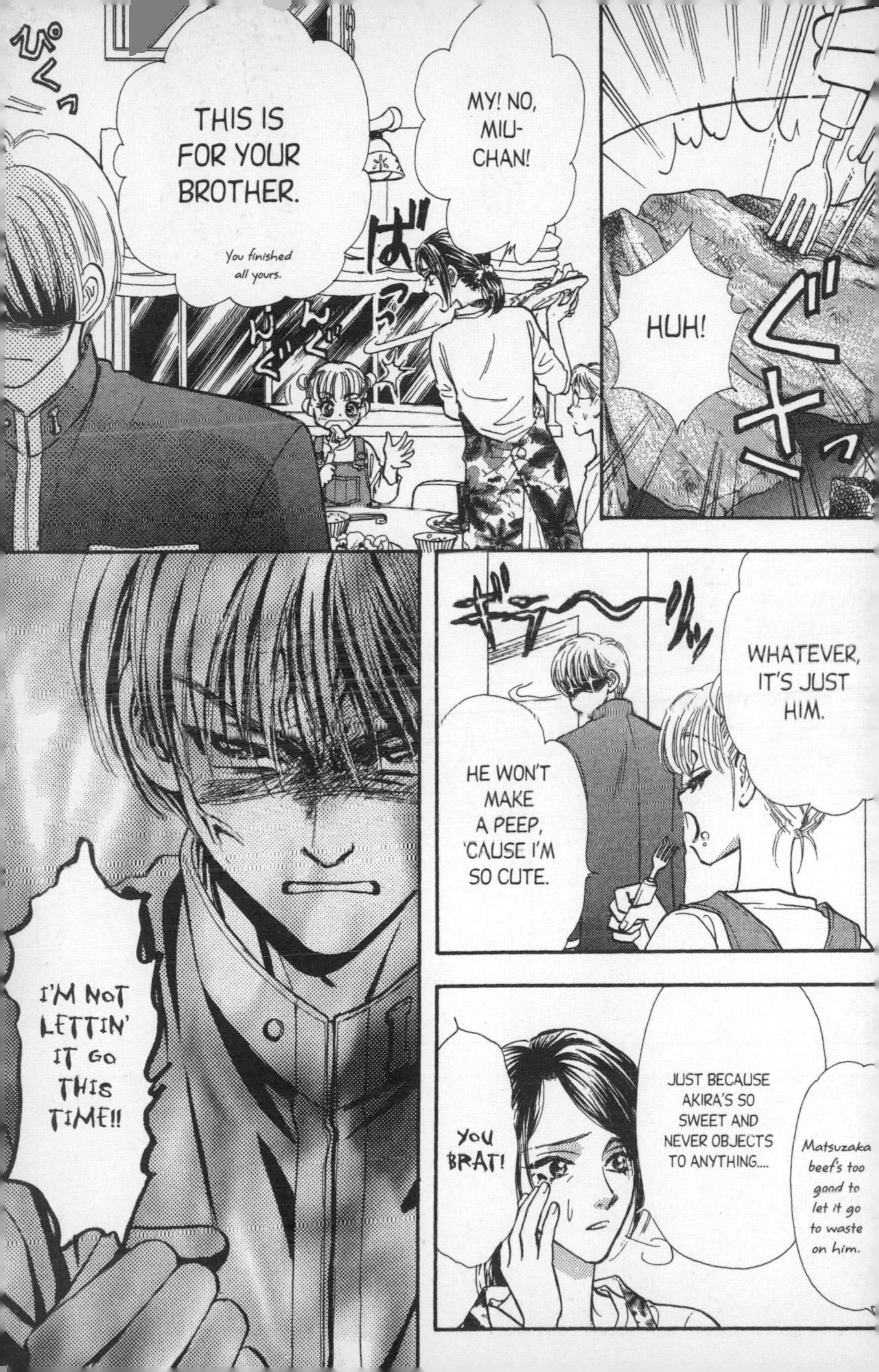
HUH!
MY! NO, MIU-CHAN!
THIS IS FOR YOUR BROTHER.
You finished all yours.
WHATEVER, IT'S JUST HIM.
HE WON'T MAKE A PEEP, 'CAUSE I'M SO CUTE.
Matsuzaka beef's too good to let it go to waste on him.
JUST BECAUSE AKIRA'S SO SWEET AND NEVER OBJECTS TO ANYTHING....
YOU BRAT!
I'M NOT LETTIN' IT GO THIS TIME!!

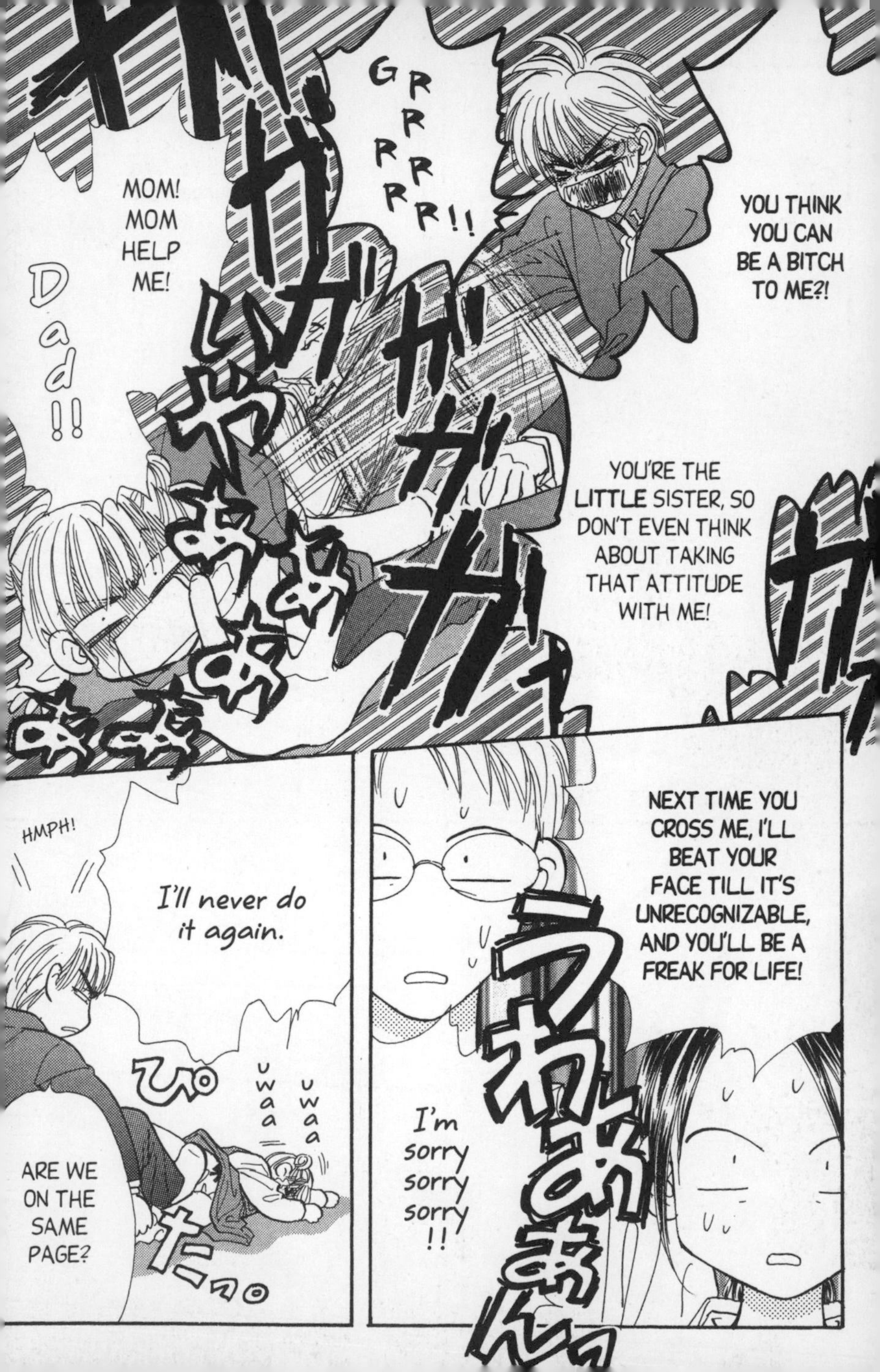
YOU THINK YOU CAN BE A BITCH TO ME?!
GRRRRRR!!
MOM! MOM HELP ME!
Dad!!
YOU'RE THE LITTLE SISTER, SO DON'T EVEN THINK ABOUT TAKING THAT ATTITUDE WITH ME!
NEXT TIME YOU CROSS ME, I'LL BEAT YOUR FACE TILL IT'S UNRECOGNIZABLE, AND YOU'LL BE A FREAK FOR LIFE!
I'm sorry sorry sorry !!
HMPH!
I'll never do it again.
uwaa
uwaa
ARE WE ON THE SAME PAGE?

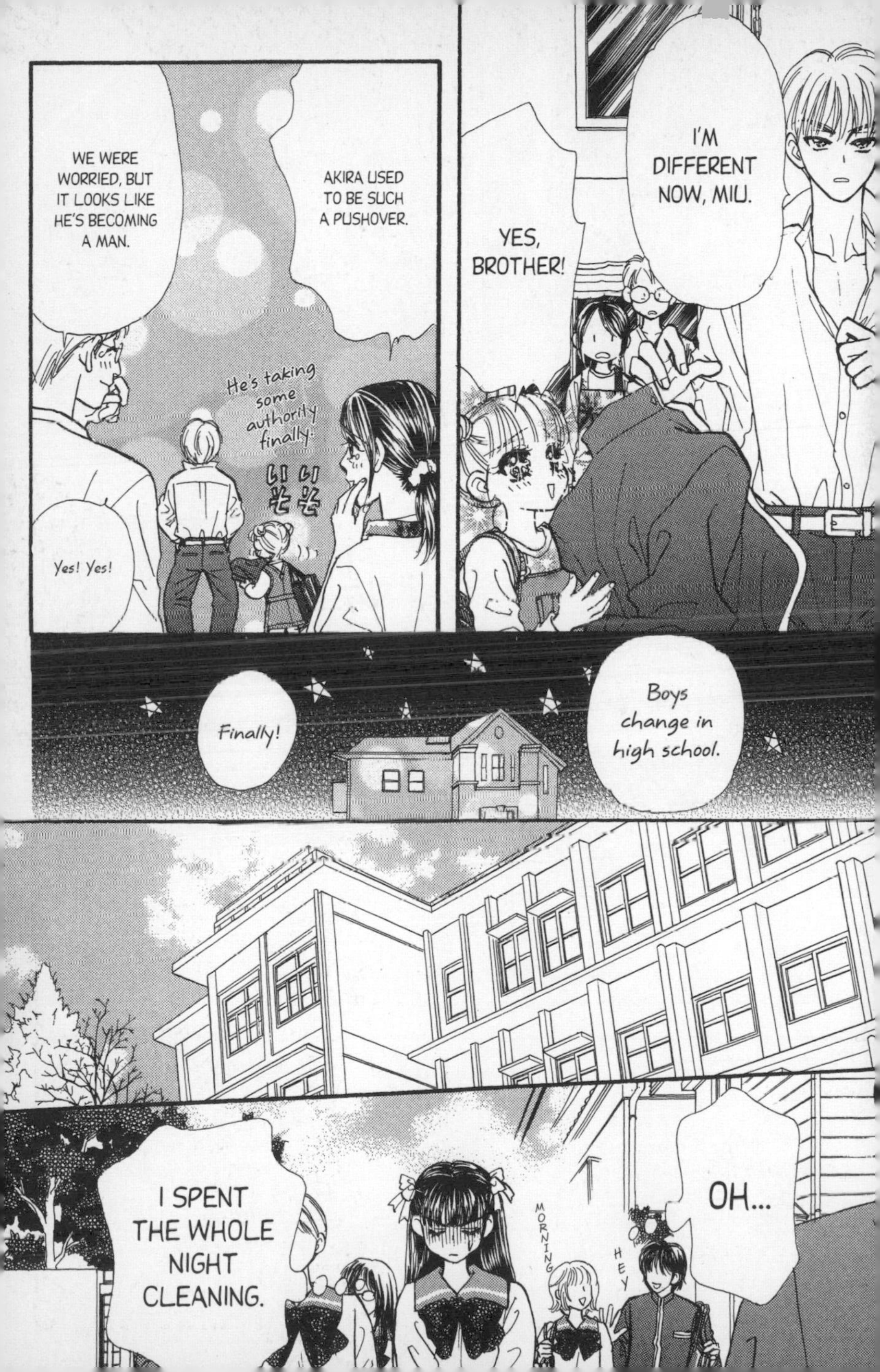
I'M DIFFERENT NOW, MIU.
YES, BROTHER!
AKIRA USED TO BE SUCH A PUSHOVER.
WE WERE WORRIED, BUT IT LOOKS LIKE HE'S BECOMING A MAN.
He's taking some authority finally.
Yes! Yes!
Boys change in high school.
Finally!
OH...
HEY
MORNING
I SPENT THE WHOLE NIGHT CLEANING.

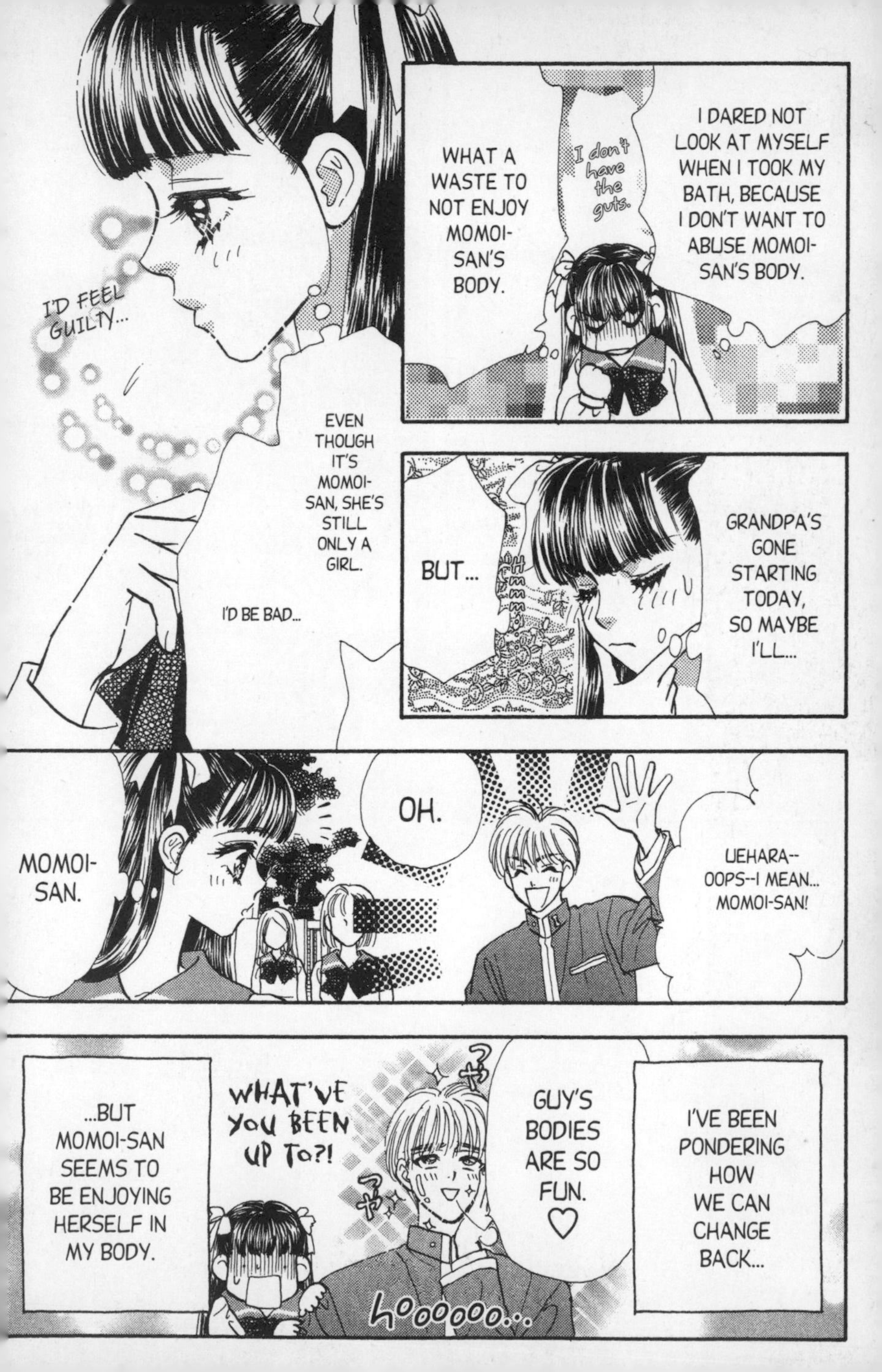
I DARED NOT LOOK AT MYSELF WHEN I TOOK MY BATH, BECAUSE I DON'T WANT TO ABUSE MOMOI-SAN'S BODY.
I don't have the guts.
WHAT A WASTE TO NOT ENJOY MOMOI-SAN'S BODY.
GRANDPA'S GONE STARTING TODAY, SO MAYBE I'LL...
Hmmm...
BUT...
EVEN THOUGH IT'S MOMOI-SAN, SHE'S STILL ONLY A GIRL.
I'D BE BAD...
I'D FEEL GUILTY...
UEHARA--OOPS--I MEAN... MOMOI-SAN!
OH.
MOMOI-SAN.
I'VE BEEN PONDERING HOW WE CAN CHANGE BACK...
GUY'S BODIES ARE SO FUN. ♡
WHAT'VE YOU BEEN UP TO?!
...BUT MOMOI-SAN SEEMS TO BE ENJOYING HERSELF IN MY BODY.
hoooooo...

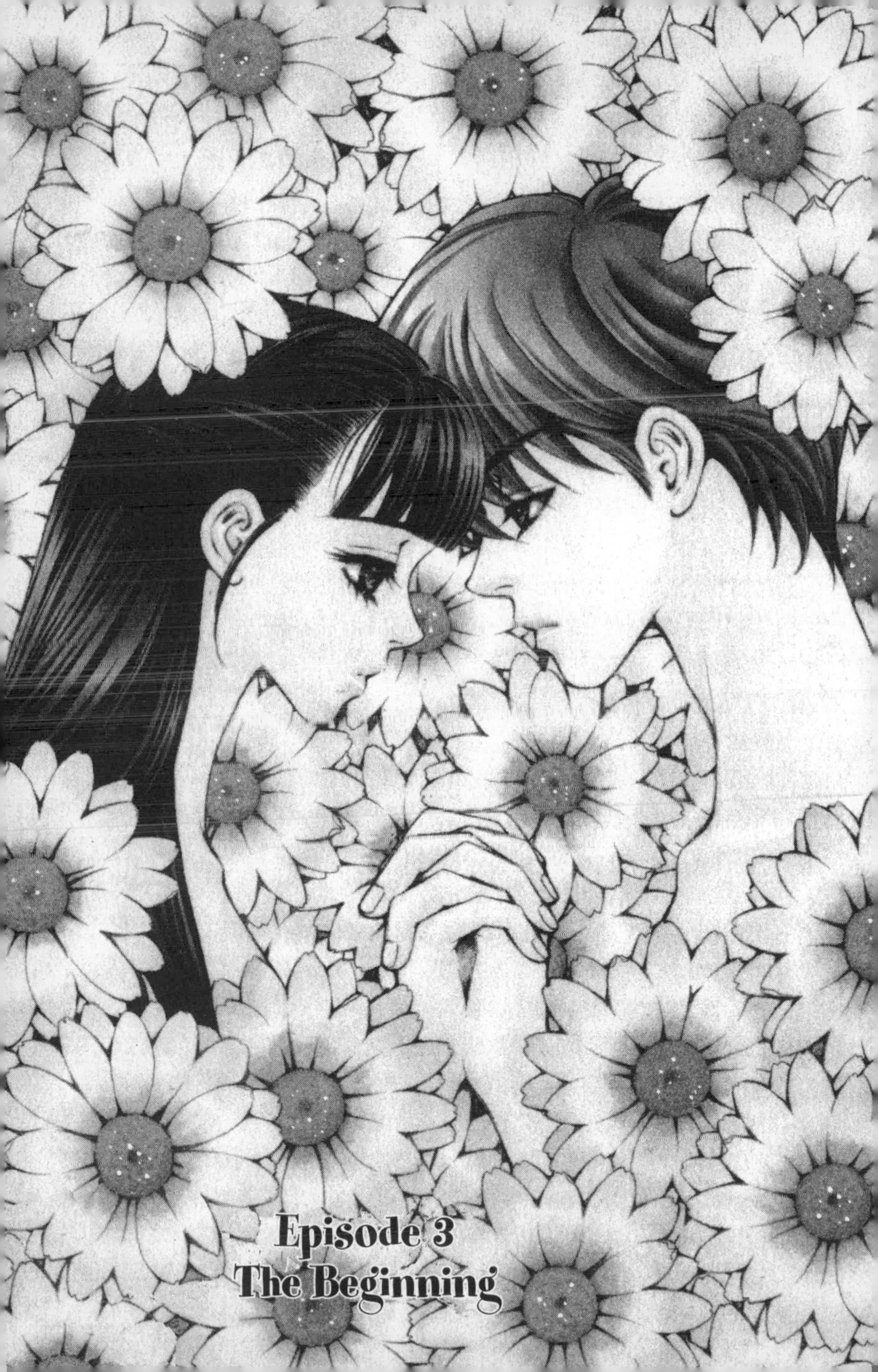
Episode 3
The Beginning

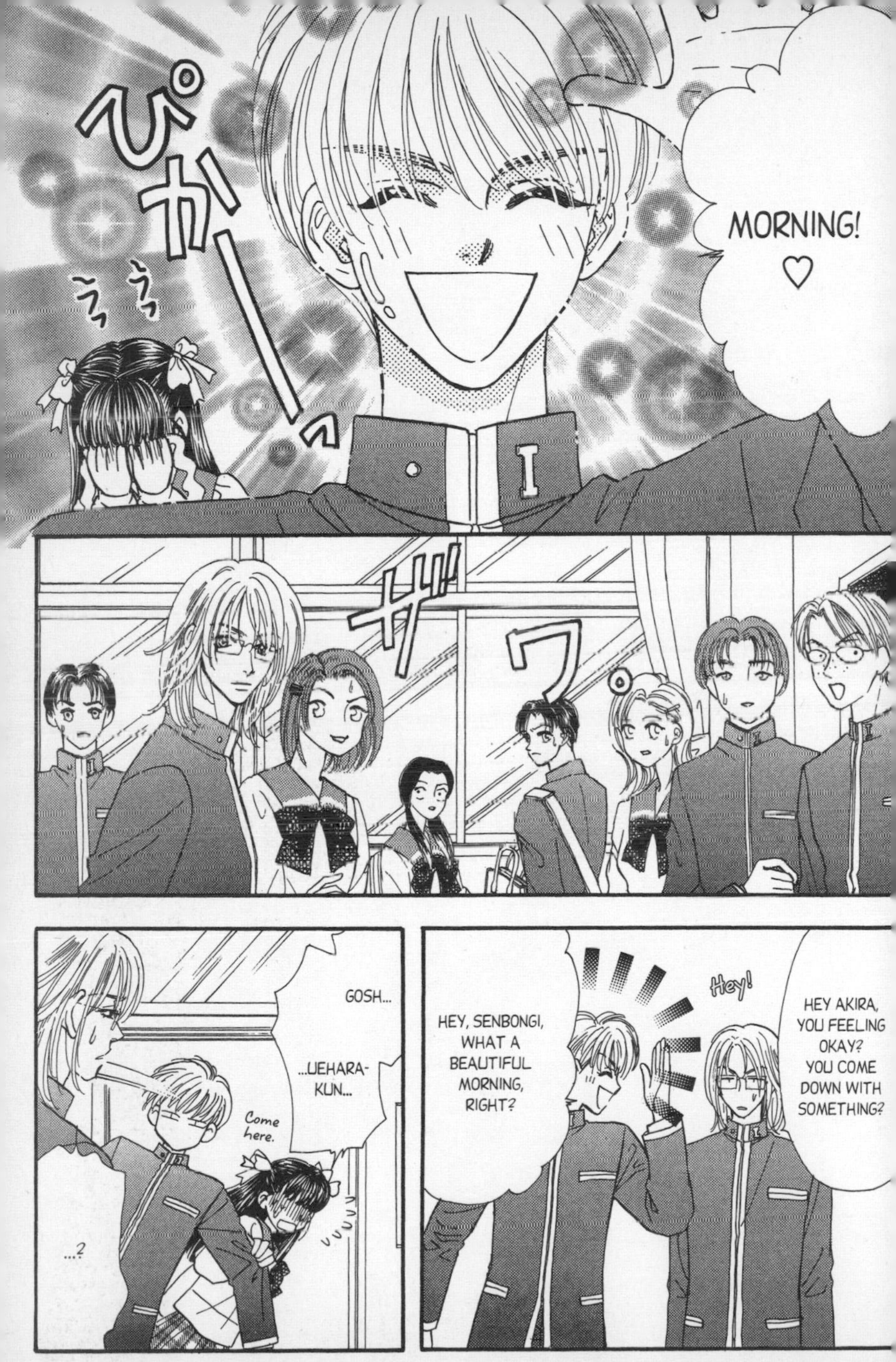
MORNING! ♡
ぴかーっ
うぅ うぅ
ザワ
Hey!
HEY AKIRA, YOU FEELING OKAY? YOU COME DOWN WITH SOMETHING?
HEY, SENBONGI, WHAT A BEAUTIFUL MORNING, RIGHT?
GOSH...
...UEHARA-KUN...
Come here.
...?

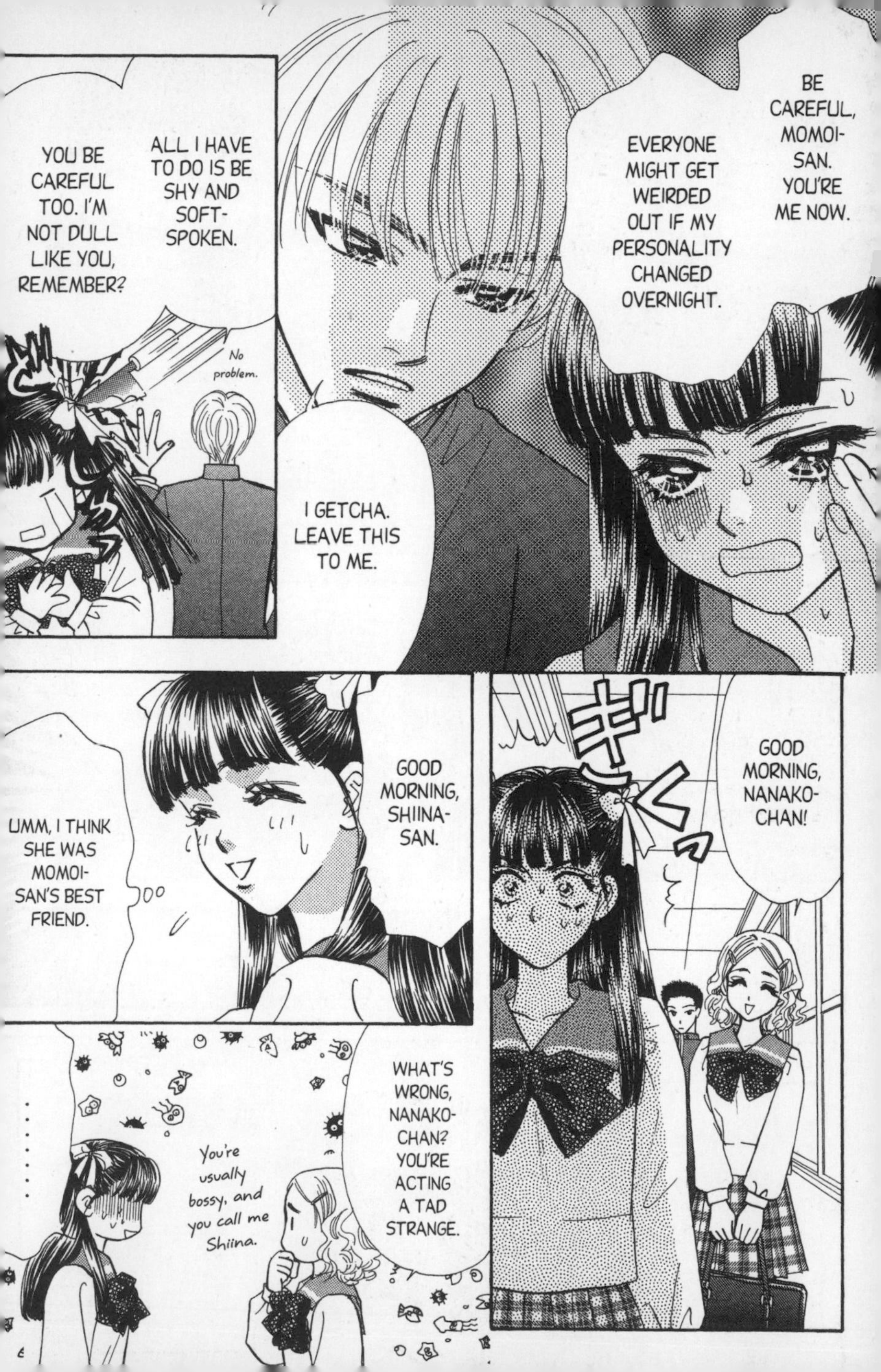
BE CAREFUL, MOMOI-SAN. YOU'RE ME NOW.
EVERYONE MIGHT GET WEIRDED OUT IF MY PERSONALITY CHANGED OVERNIGHT.
I GETCHA. LEAVE THIS TO ME.
ALL I HAVE TO DO IS BE SHY AND SOFT-SPOKEN.
YOU BE CAREFUL TOO. I'M NOT DULL LIKE YOU, REMEMBER?
No problem.
GOOD MORNING, NANAKO-CHAN!
GOOD MORNING, SHIINA-SAN.
UMM, I THINK SHE WAS MOMOI-SAN'S BEST FRIEND.
WHAT'S WRONG, NANAKO-CHAN? YOU'RE ACTING A TAD STRANGE.
You're usually bossy, and you call me Shiina.

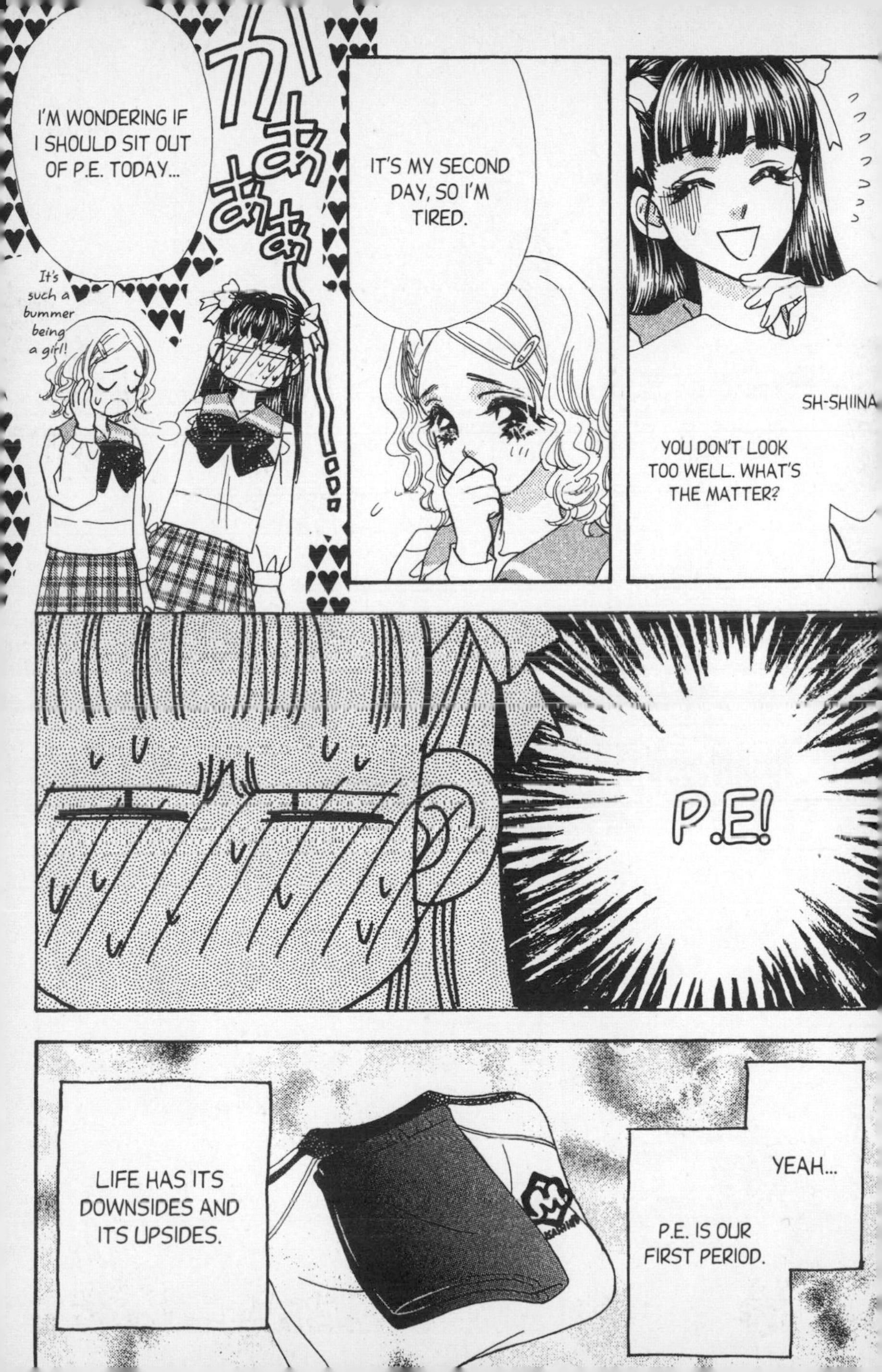
SH-SHIINA
YOU DON'T LOOK TOO WELL. WHAT'S THE MATTER?
IT'S MY SECOND DAY, SO I'M TIRED.
I'M WONDERING IF I SHOULD SIT OUT OF P.E. TODAY...
It's such a bummer being a girl!
P.E!
YEAH...
P.E. IS OUR FIRST PERIOD.
LIFE HAS ITS DOWNSIDES AND ITS UPSIDES.

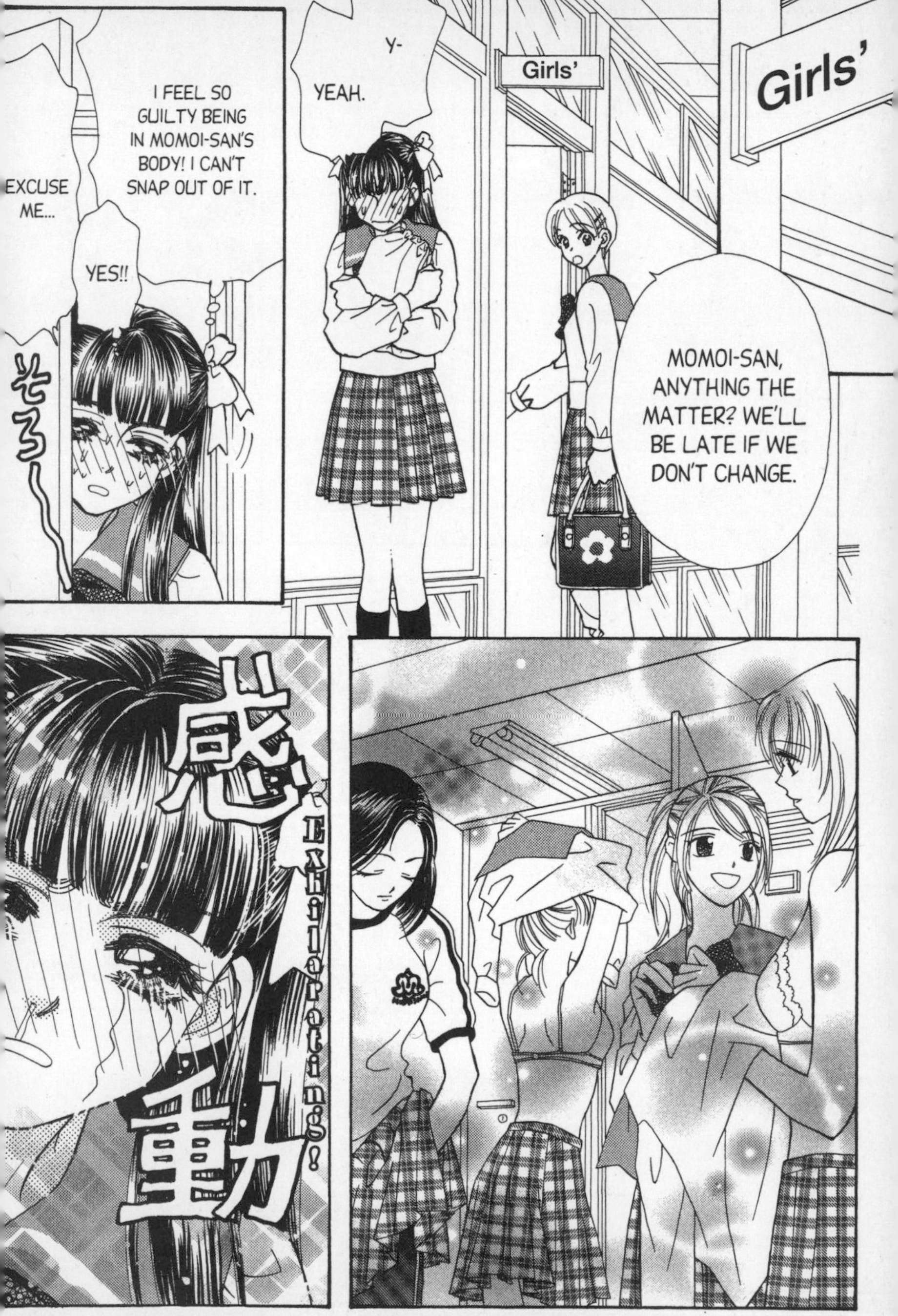
Girls'
Girls'
MOMOI-SAN, ANYTHING THE MATTER? WE'LL BE LATE IF WE DON'T CHANGE.
Y-
YEAH.
I FEEL SO GUILTY BEING IN MOMOI-SAN'S BODY! I CAN'T SNAP OUT OF IT.
EXCUSE ME...
YES!!
そろ〜
感動
Exhilarating!

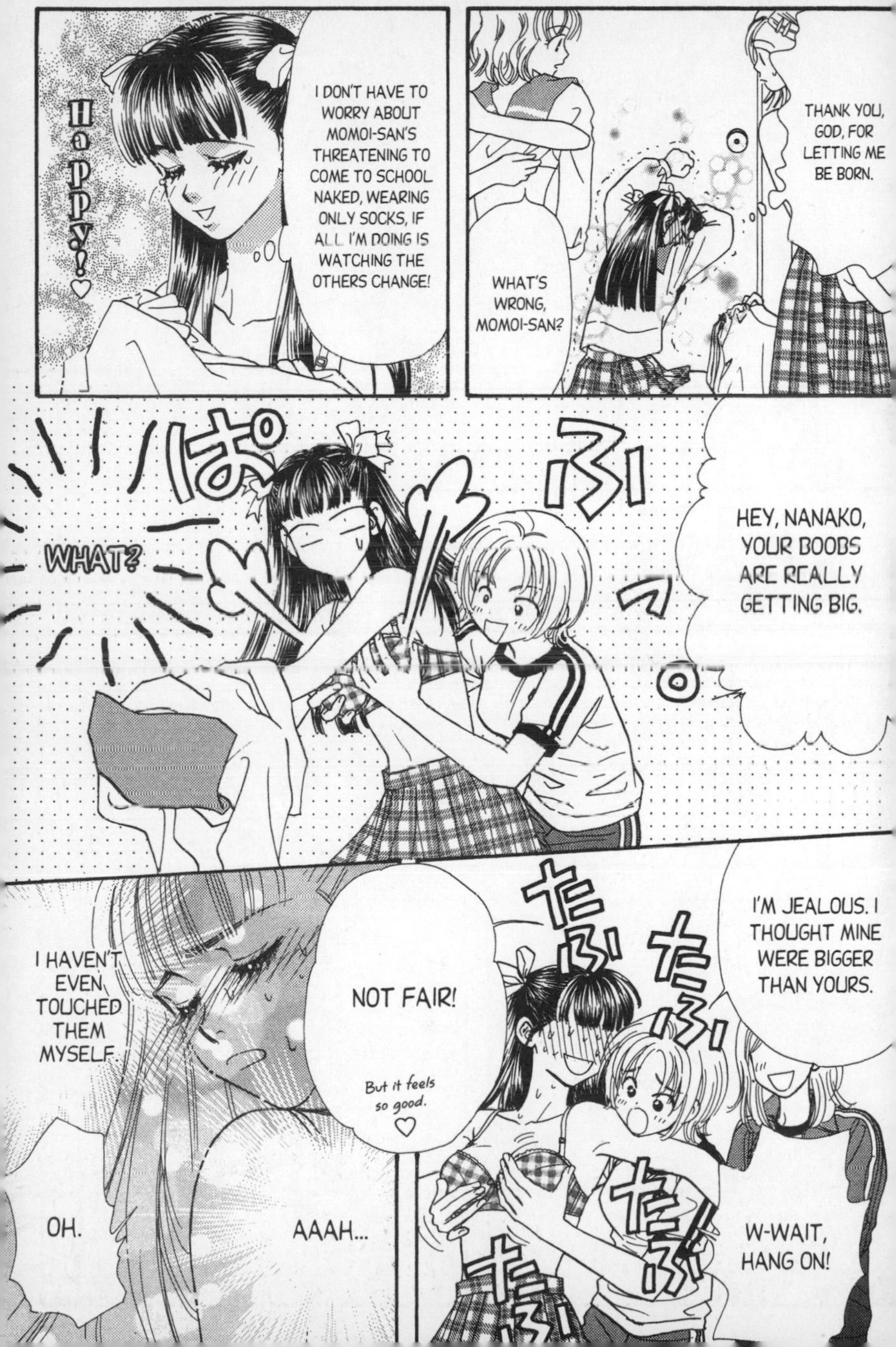
THANK YOU, GOD, FOR LETTING ME BE BORN.
WHAT'S WRONG, MOMOI-SAN?
Happy!♡
I DON'T HAVE TO WORRY ABOUT MOMOI-SAN'S THREATENING TO COME TO SCHOOL NAKED, WEARING ONLY SOCKS, IF ALL I'M DOING IS WATCHING THE OTHERS CHANGE!
HEY, NANAKO, YOUR BOOBS ARE REALLY GETTING BIG.
WHAT?
I'M JEALOUS. I THOUGHT MINE WERE BIGGER THAN YOURS.
W-WAIT, HANG ON!
NOT FAIR!
But it feels so good. ♡
I HAVEN'T EVEN TOUCHED THEM MYSELF.
OH.
AAAH...

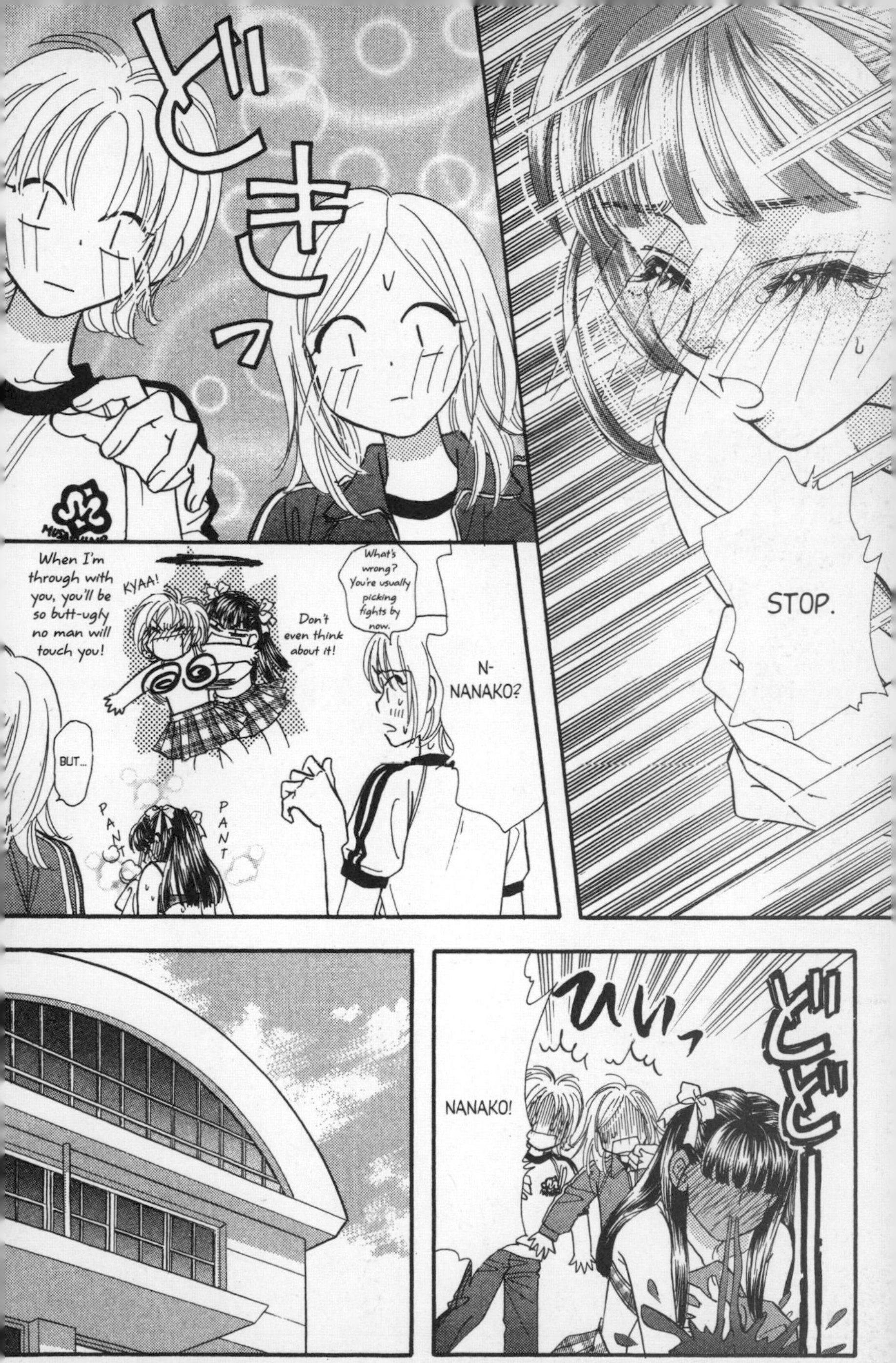

STOP.
どきっ
N-NANAKO?
What's wrong? You're usually picking fights by now.
Don't even think about it!
KYAA!
When I'm through with you, you'll be so butt-ugly no man will touch you!
BUT...
PANT
PANT
どど
ひぃっ
NANAKO!

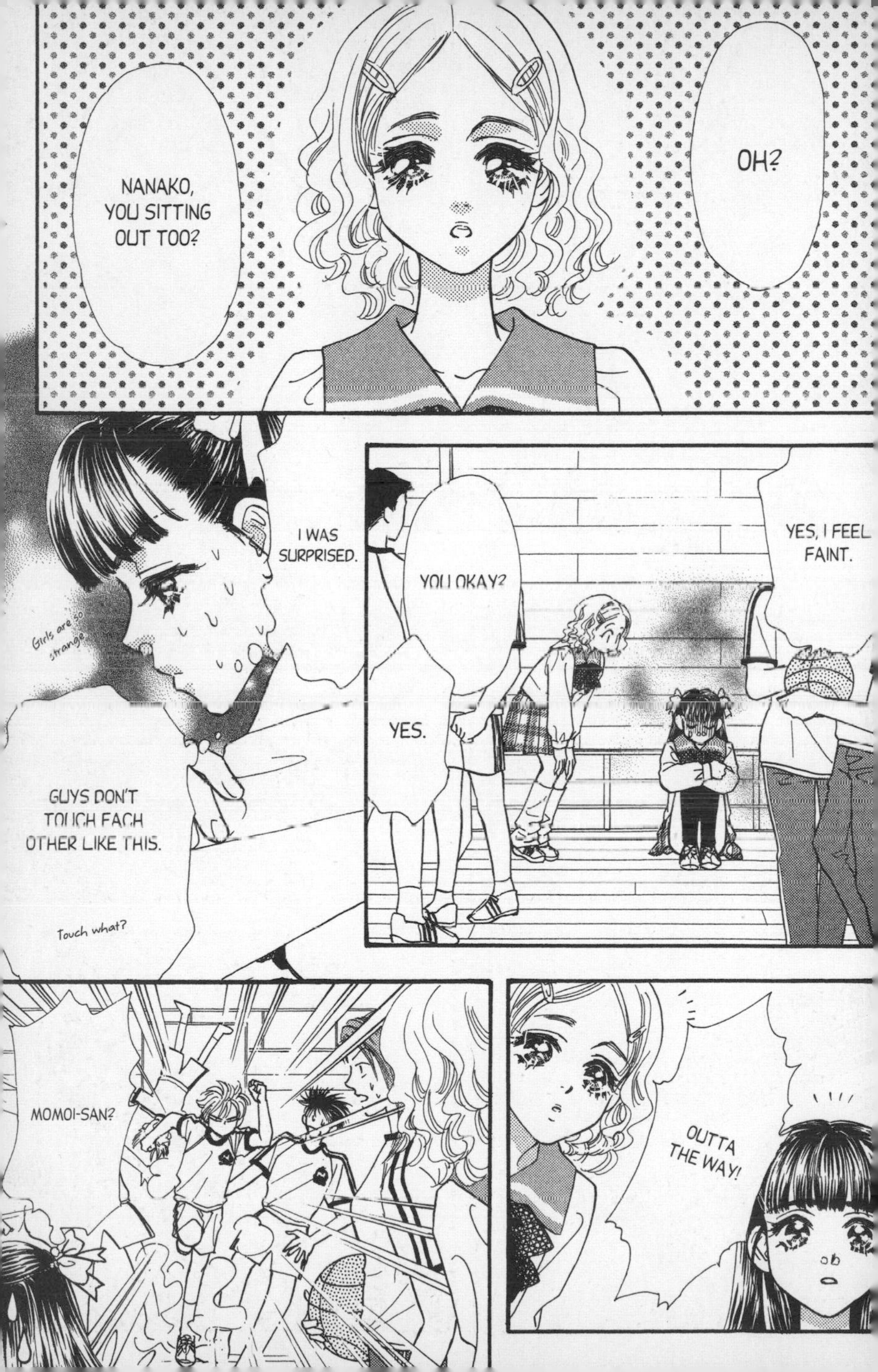
OH?
NANAKO, YOU SITTING OUT TOO?
YES, I FEEL FAINT.
YOU OKAY?
YES.
I WAS SURPRISED.
Girls are so strange
GUYS DON'T TOUCH EACH OTHER LIKE THIS.
Touch what?
OUTTA THE WAY!
MOMOI-SAN?

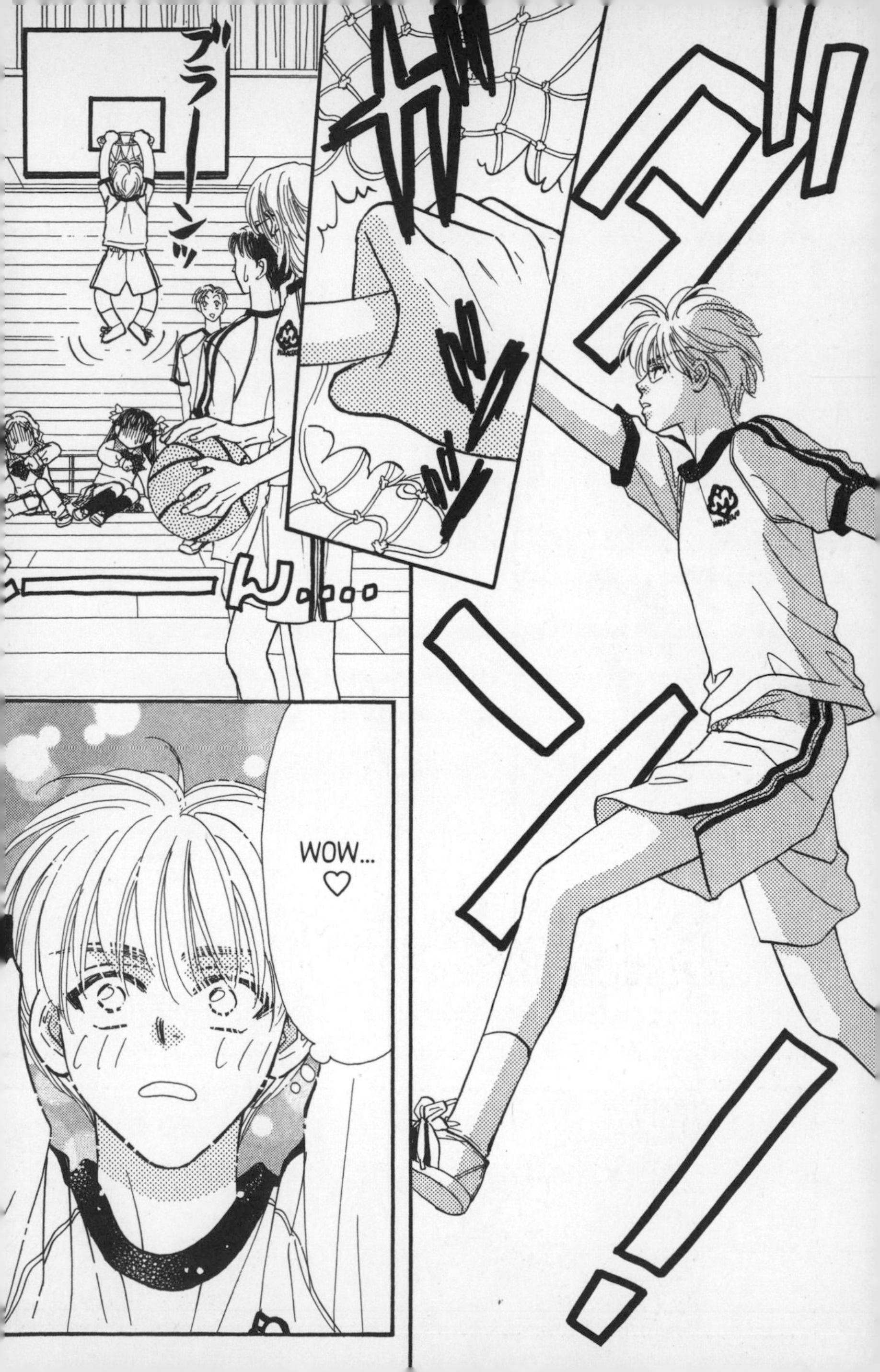
ブラーンッ
WOW... ♡

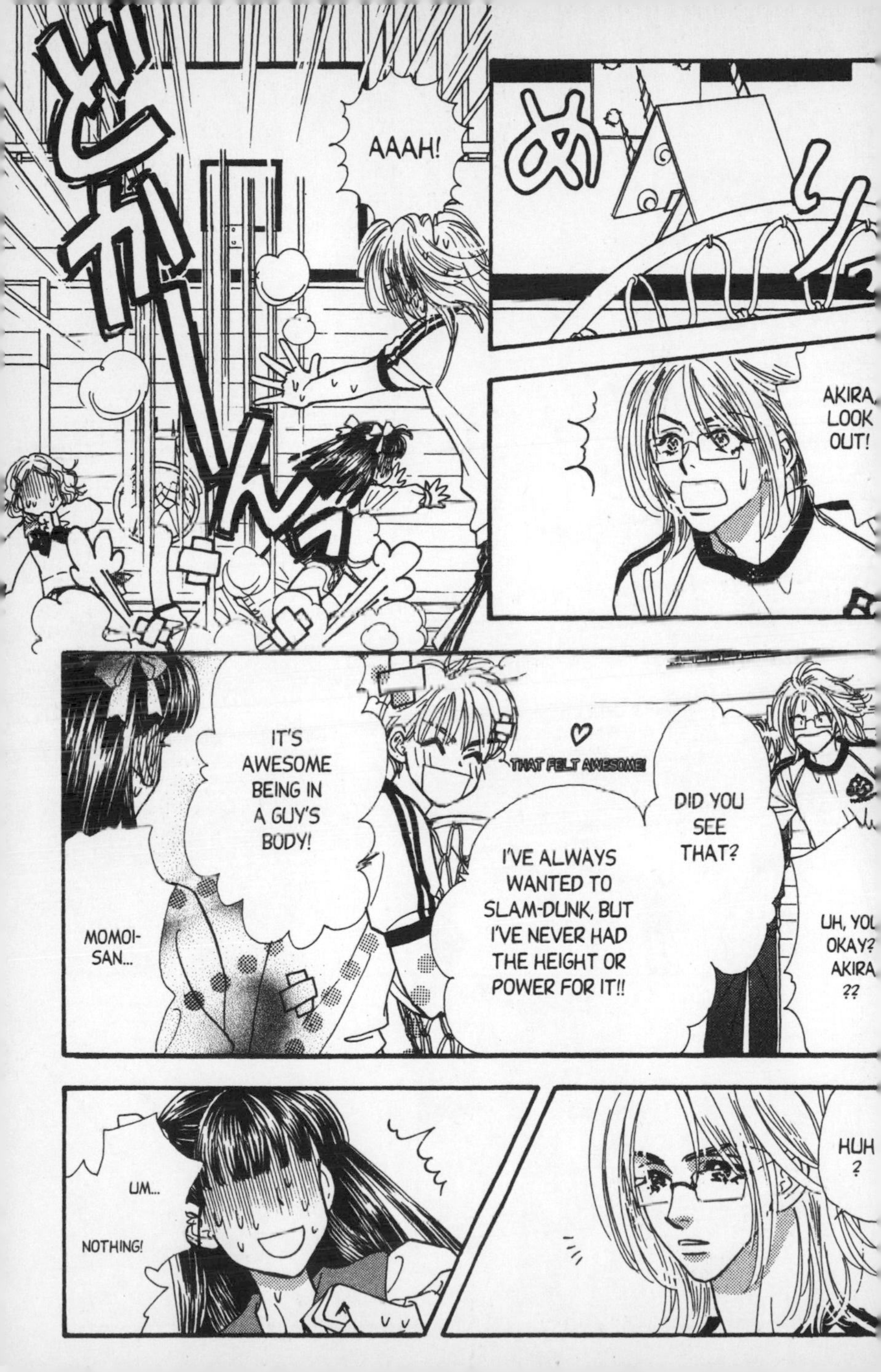
め
AKIRA, LOOK OUT!
AAAH!
どかーん
UH, YOU OKAY? AKIRA ??
DID YOU SEE THAT?
THAT FELT AWESOME!
I'VE ALWAYS WANTED TO SLAM-DUNK, BUT I'VE NEVER HAD THE HEIGHT OR POWER FOR IT!!
IT'S AWESOME BEING IN A GUY'S BODY!
MOMOI-SAN...
HUH ?
UM...
NOTHING!

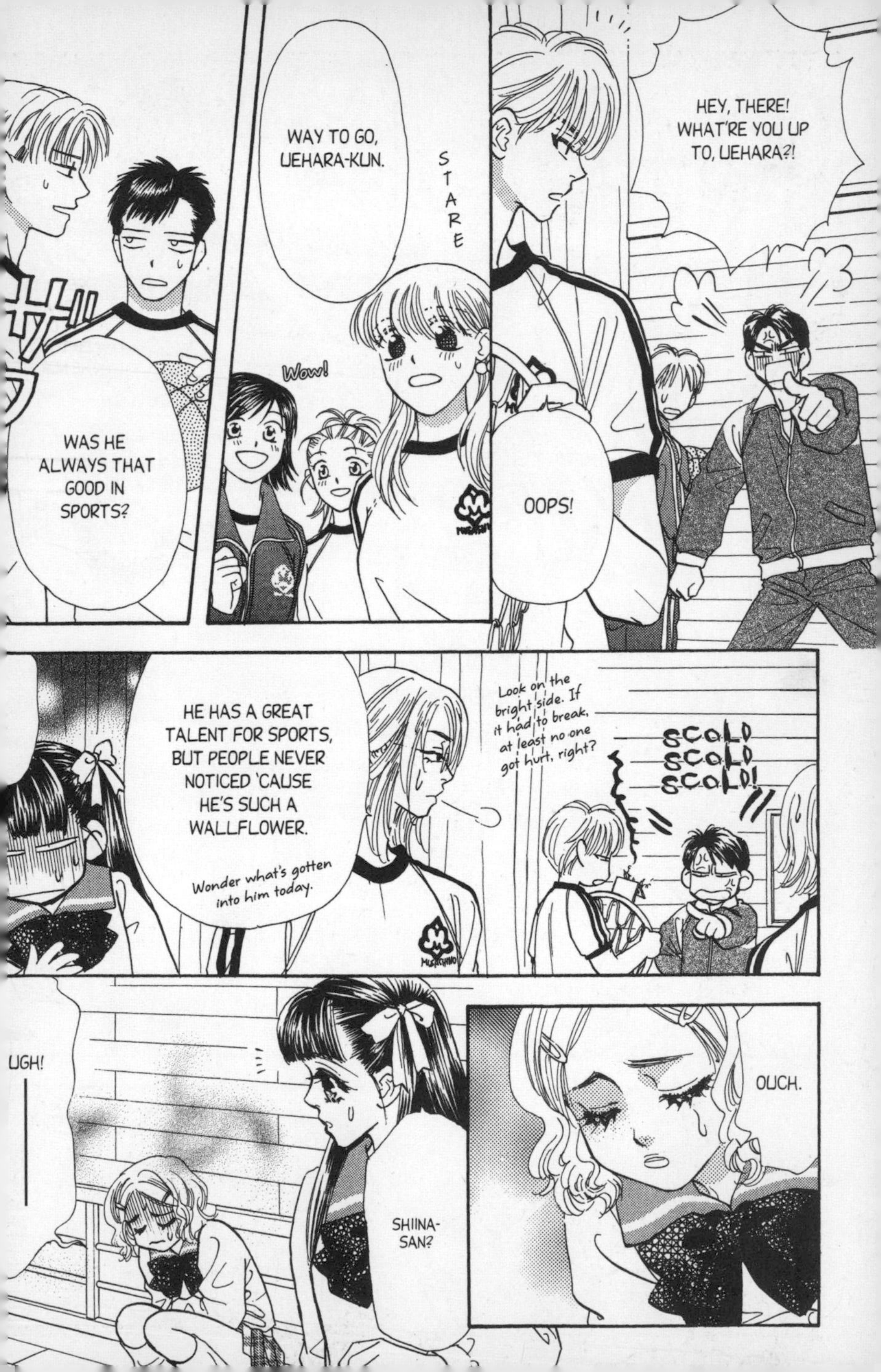
HEY, THERE! WHAT'RE YOU UP TO, UEHARA?!
OOPS!
WAY TO GO, UEHARA-KUN.
STARE
Wow!
WAS HE ALWAYS THAT GOOD IN SPORTS?
Look on the bright side. If it had to break, at least no one got hurt, right?
SCOLD SCOLD SCOLD!
HE HAS A GREAT TALENT FOR SPORTS, BUT PEOPLE NEVER NOTICED 'CAUSE HE'S SUCH A WALLFLOWER.
Wonder what's gotten into him today.
OUCH.
SHIINA-SAN?
UGH!

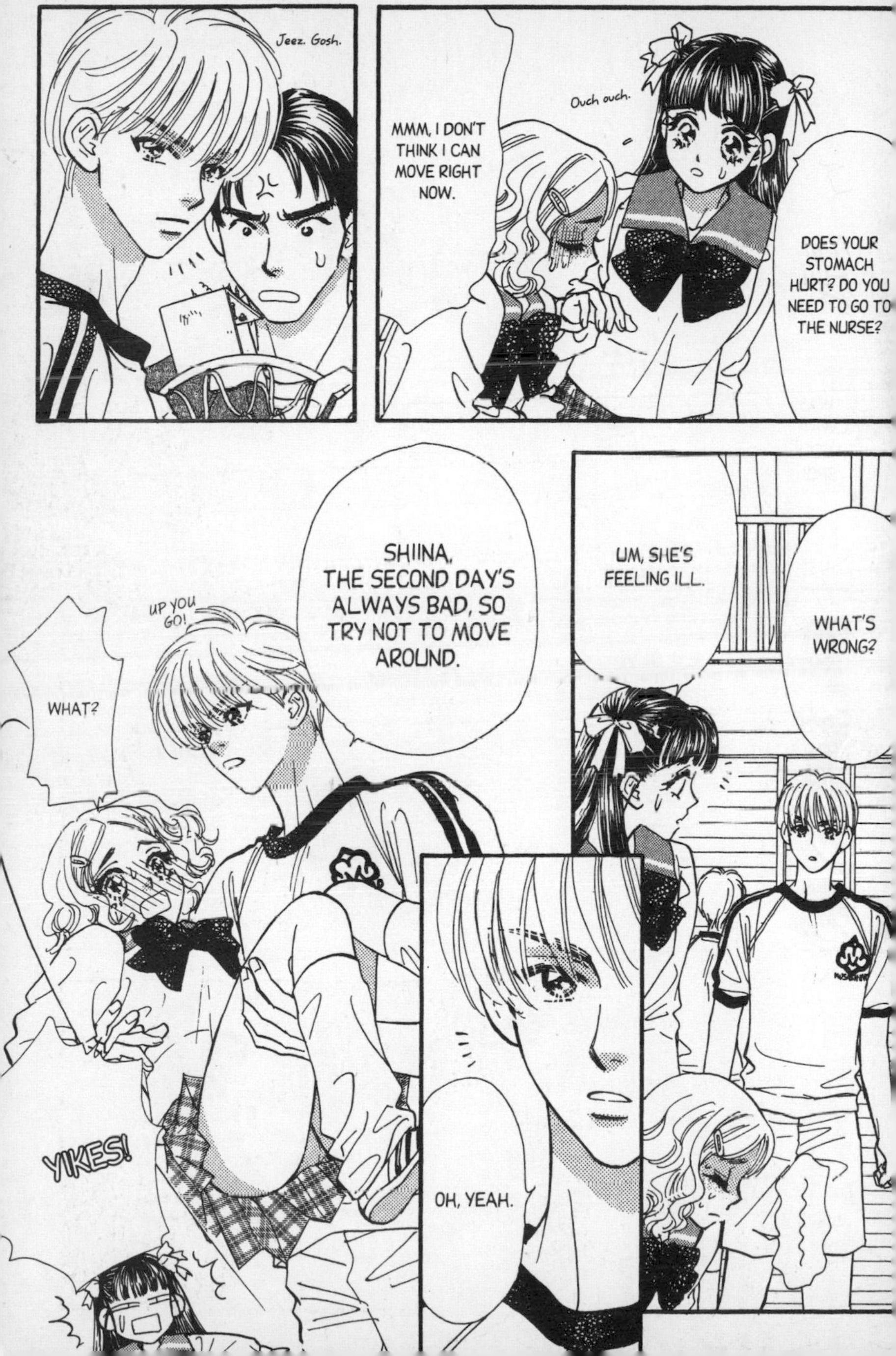
DOES YOUR STOMACH HURT? DO YOU NEED TO GO TO THE NURSE?
Ouch ouch.
MMM, I DON'T THINK I CAN MOVE RIGHT NOW.
Jeez. Gosh.
WHAT'S WRONG?
UM, SHE'S FEELING ILL.
OH, YEAH.
SHIINA, THE SECOND DAY'S ALWAYS BAD, SO TRY NOT TO MOVE AROUND.
UP YOU GO!
WHAT?
YIKES!

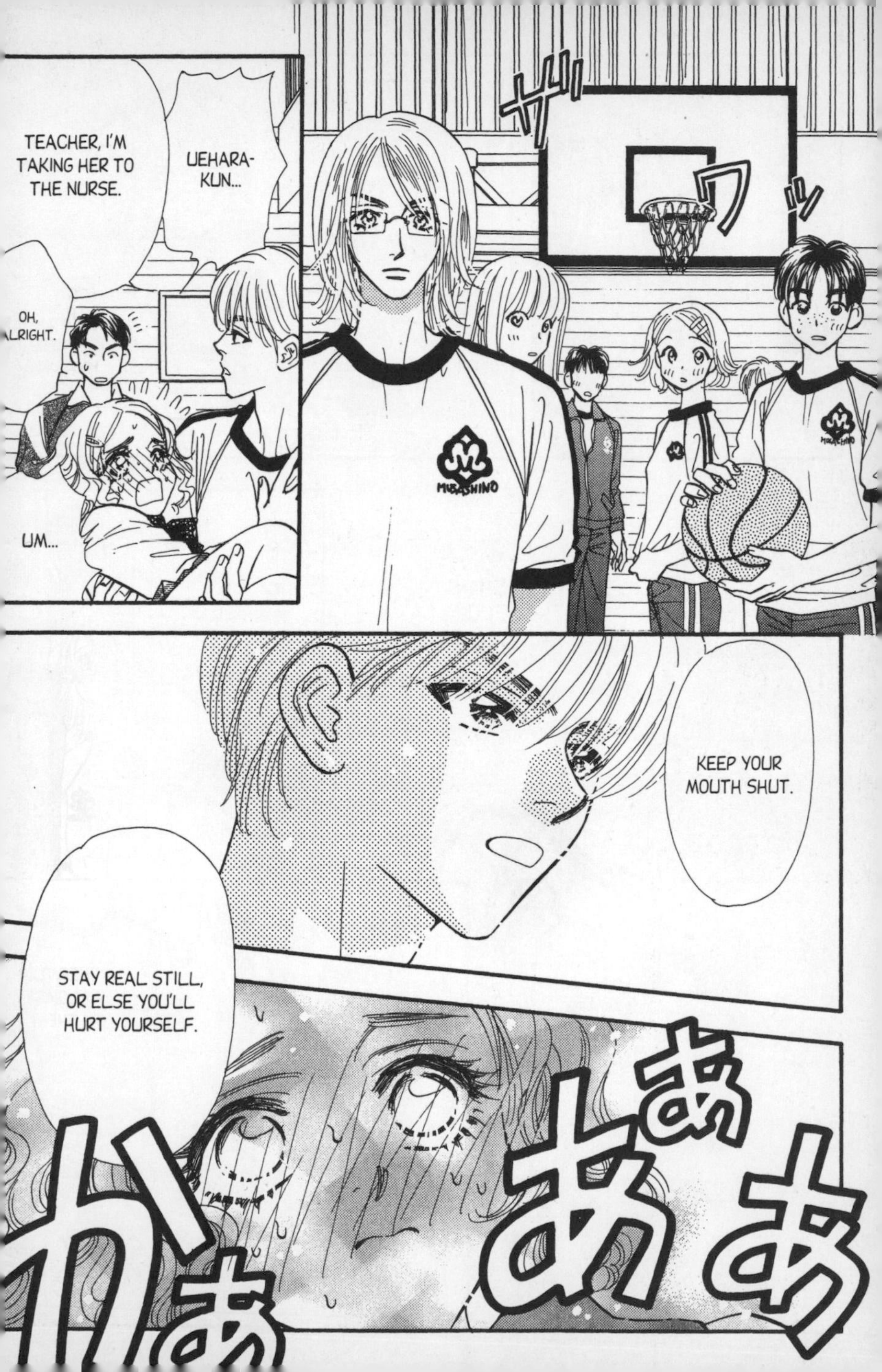
ザワッ
UEHARA-KUN...
TEACHER, I'M TAKING HER TO THE NURSE.
OH, ALRIGHT.
UM...
KEEP YOUR MOUTH SHUT.
STAY REAL STILL, OR ELSE YOU'LL HURT YOURSELF.
あああ

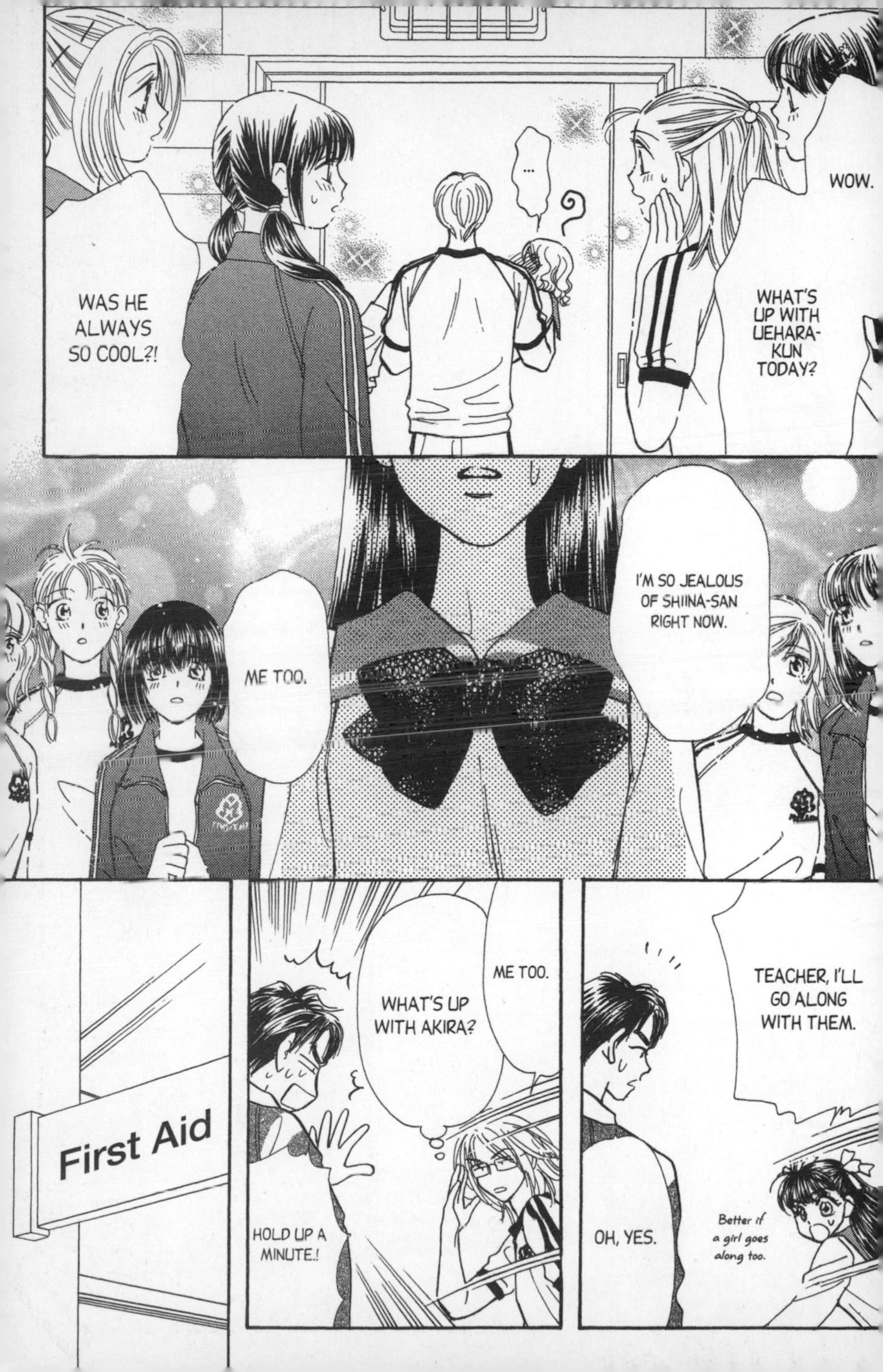
WOW.
WHAT'S UP WITH UEHARA-KUN TODAY?
...
WAS HE ALWAYS SO COOL?!
I'M SO JEALOUS OF SHIINA-SAN RIGHT NOW.
ME TOO.
TEACHER, I'LL GO ALONG WITH THEM.
Better if a girl goes along too.
OH, YES.
ME TOO.
WHAT'S UP WITH AKIRA?
HOLD UP A MINUTE.!
First Aid

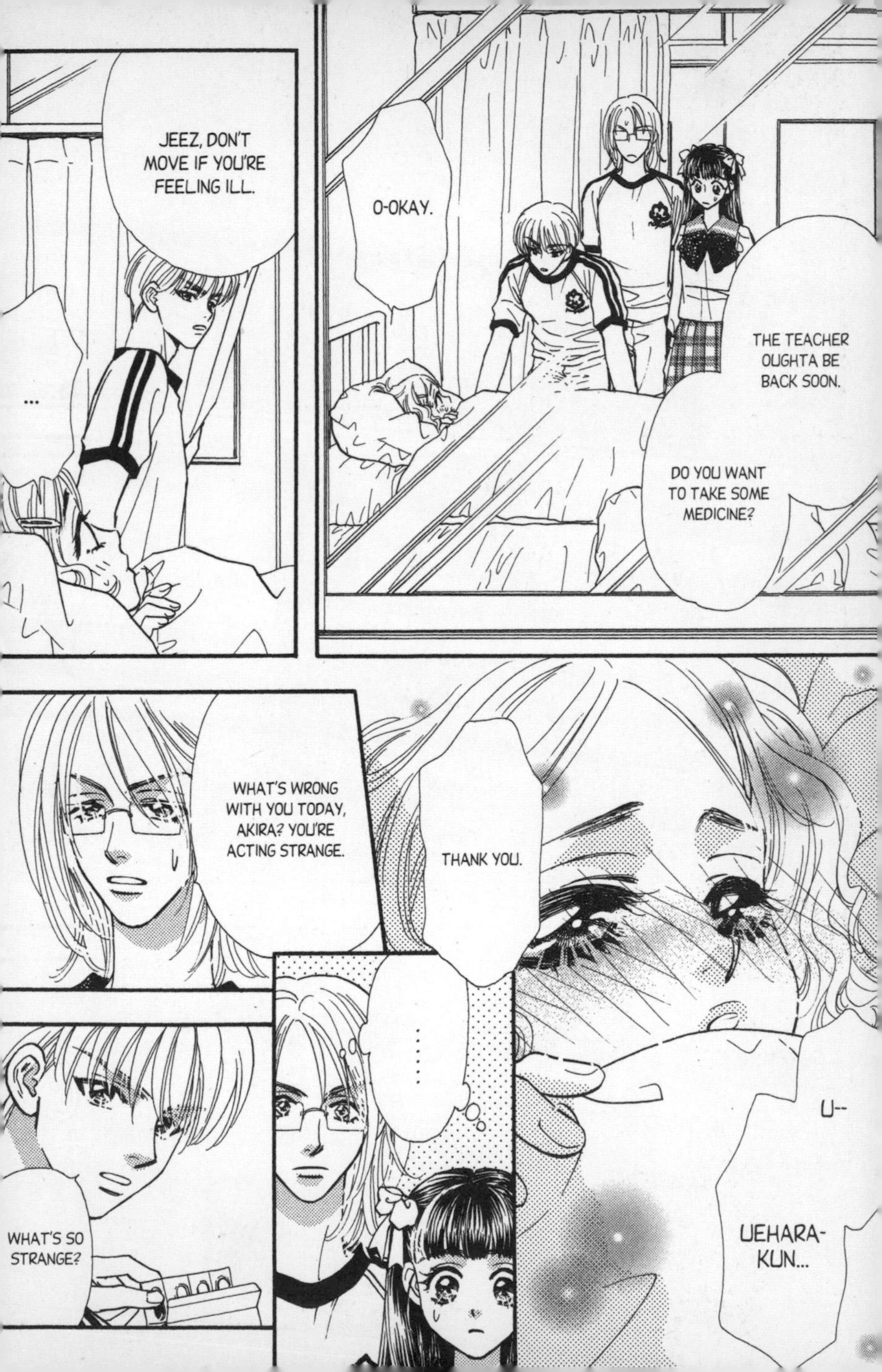
THE TEACHER OUGHTA BE BACK SOON.
DO YOU WANT TO TAKE SOME MEDICINE?
O-OKAY.
JEEZ, DON'T MOVE IF YOU'RE FEELING ILL.
...
U--
UEHARA-KUN...
THANK YOU.
WHAT'S WRONG WITH YOU TODAY, AKIRA? YOU'RE ACTING STRANGE.
......
WHAT'S SO STRANGE?

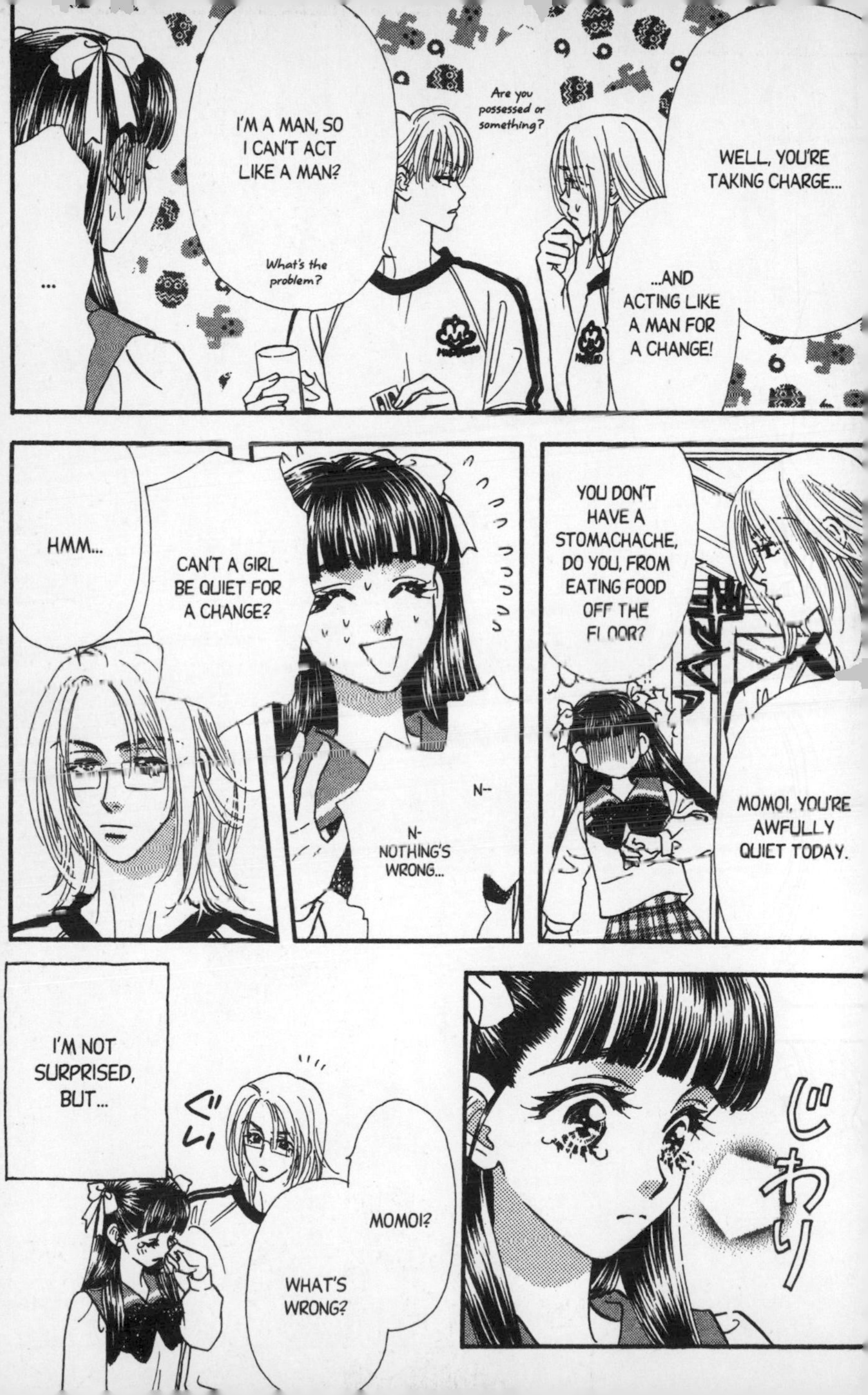
WELL, YOU'RE TAKING CHARGE...
...AND ACTING LIKE A MAN FOR A CHANGE!
Are you possessed or something?
I'M A MAN, SO I CAN'T ACT LIKE A MAN?
What's the problem?
...
MOMOI, YOU'RE AWFULLY QUIET TODAY.
YOU DON'T HAVE A STOMACHACHE, DO YOU, FROM EATING FOOD OFF THE FLOOR?
N--
N- NOTHING'S WRONG...
CAN'T A GIRL BE QUIET FOR A CHANGE?
HMM...
じわり
MOMOI?
WHAT'S WRONG?
ぐい
I'M NOT SURPRISED, BUT...

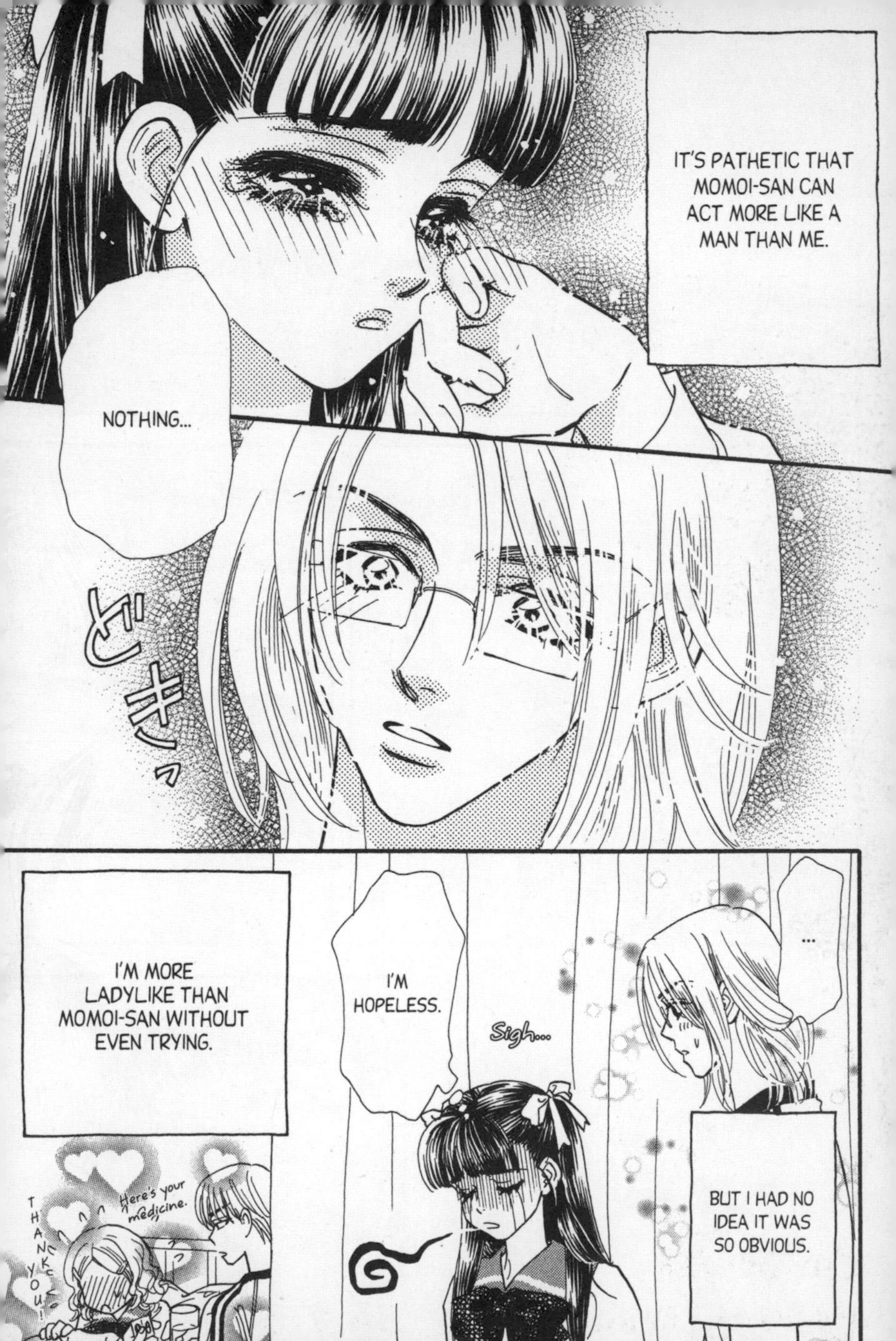
IT'S PATHETIC THAT MOMOI-SAN CAN ACT MORE LIKE A MAN THAN ME.
NOTHING...
どきん
...
BUT I HAD NO IDEA IT WAS SO OBVIOUS.
Sigh...
I'M HOPELESS.
I'M MORE LADYLIKE THAN MOMOI-SAN WITHOUT EVEN TRYING.
Here's your medicine.
THANK YOU!

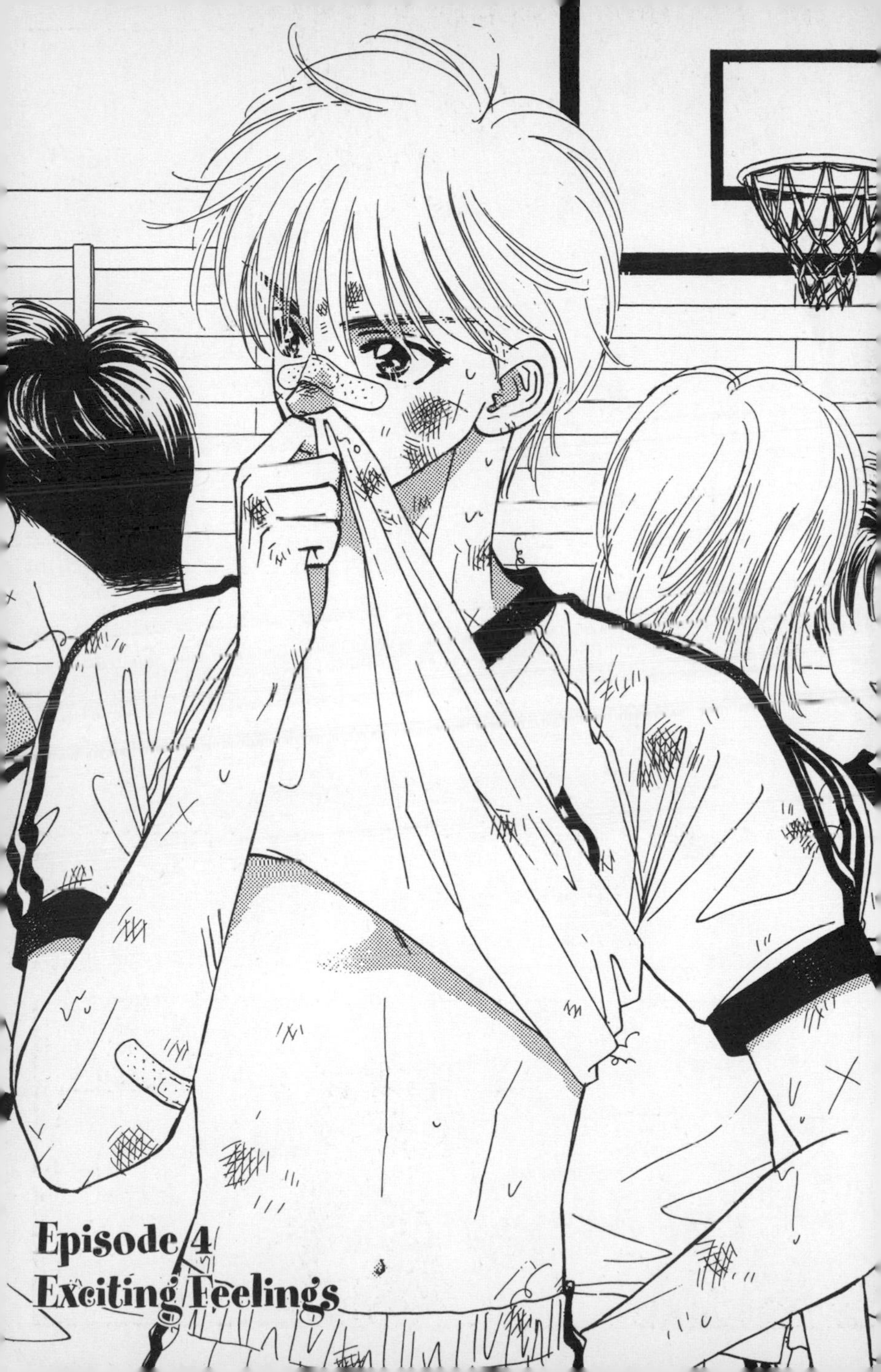
Episode 4
Exciting Feelings

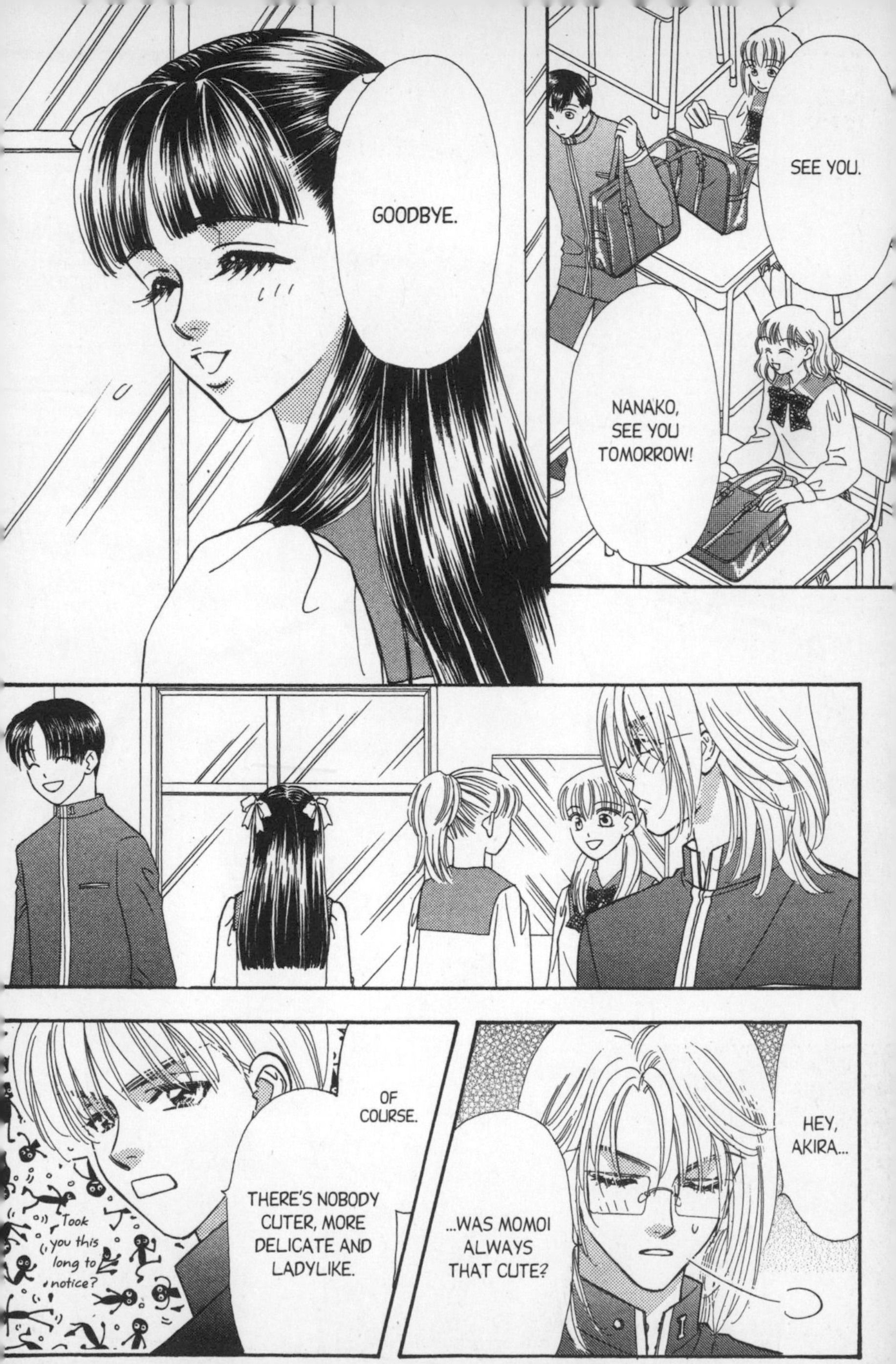
SEE YOU.
NANAKO, SEE YOU TOMORROW!
GOODBYE.
HEY, AKIRA...
...WAS MOMOI ALWAYS THAT CUTE?
OF COURSE.
THERE'S NOBODY CUTER, MORE DELICATE AND LADYLIKE.
Took you this long to notice?

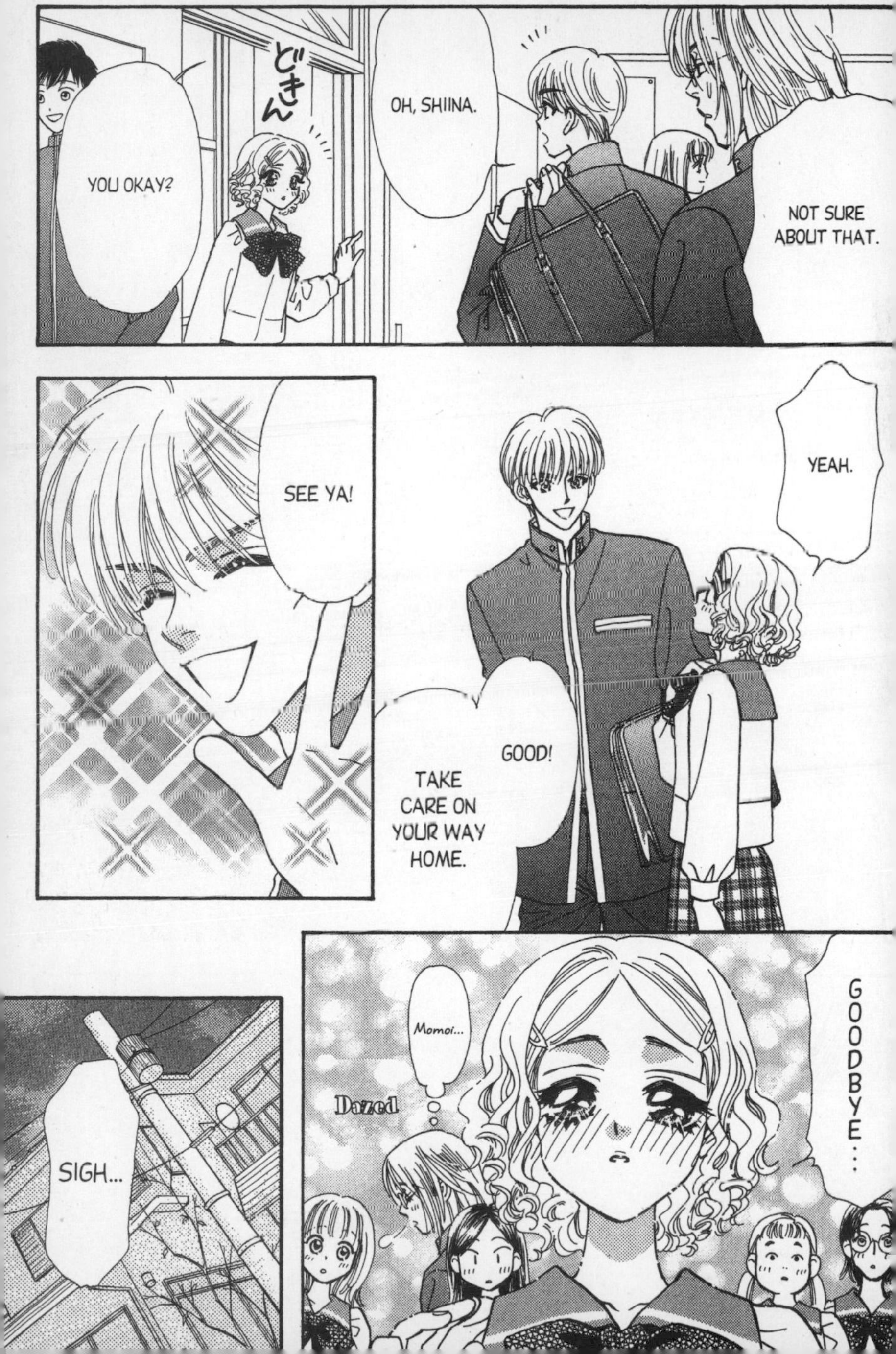
NOT SURE ABOUT THAT.
OH, SHIINA.
どきん
YOU OKAY?
YEAH.
GOOD!
TAKE CARE ON YOUR WAY HOME.
SEE YA!
GOODBYE...
Momoi...
Dazed
SIGH...

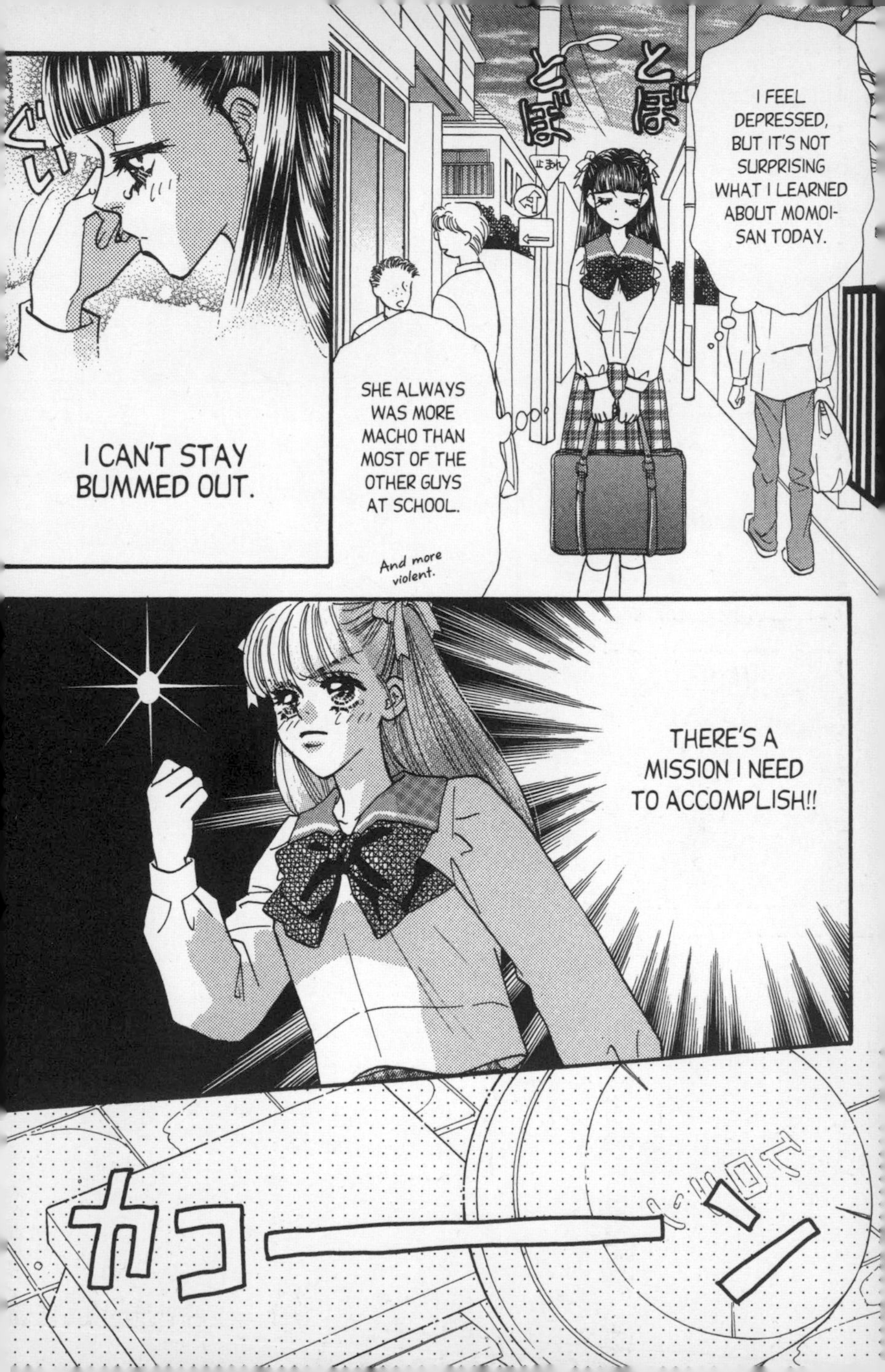
とぼとぼ
I FEEL DEPRESSED, BUT IT'S NOT SURPRISING WHAT I LEARNED ABOUT MOMOI-SAN TODAY.
SHE ALWAYS WAS MORE MACHO THAN MOST OF THE OTHER GUYS AT SCHOOL.
And more violent.
ぐい
I CAN'T STAY BUMMED OUT.
THERE'S A MISSION I NEED TO ACCOMPLISH!!
カコーン

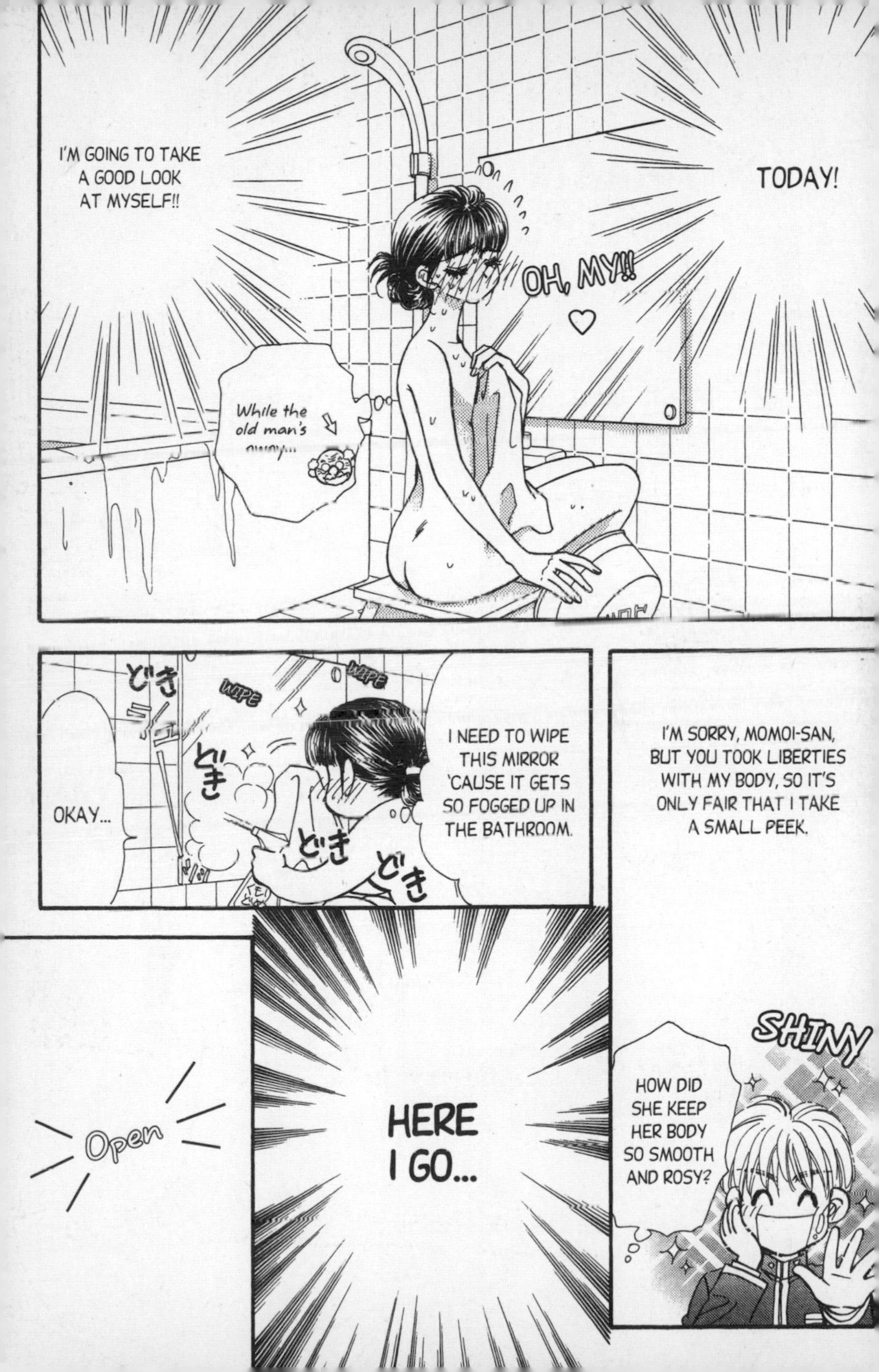
TODAY!
OH, MY!! ♡
I'M GOING TO TAKE A GOOD LOOK AT MYSELF!!
While the old man's away...
I'M SORRY, MOMOI-SAN, BUT YOU TOOK LIBERTIES WITH MY BODY, SO IT'S ONLY FAIR THAT I TAKE A SMALL PEEK.
WIPE
WIPE
I NEED TO WIPE THIS MIRROR 'CAUSE IT GETS SO FOGGED UP IN THE BATHROOM.
どき
どき
どき
どき
OKAY...
SHINY
HOW DID SHE KEEP HER BODY SO SMOOTH AND ROSY?
HERE I GO...
Open

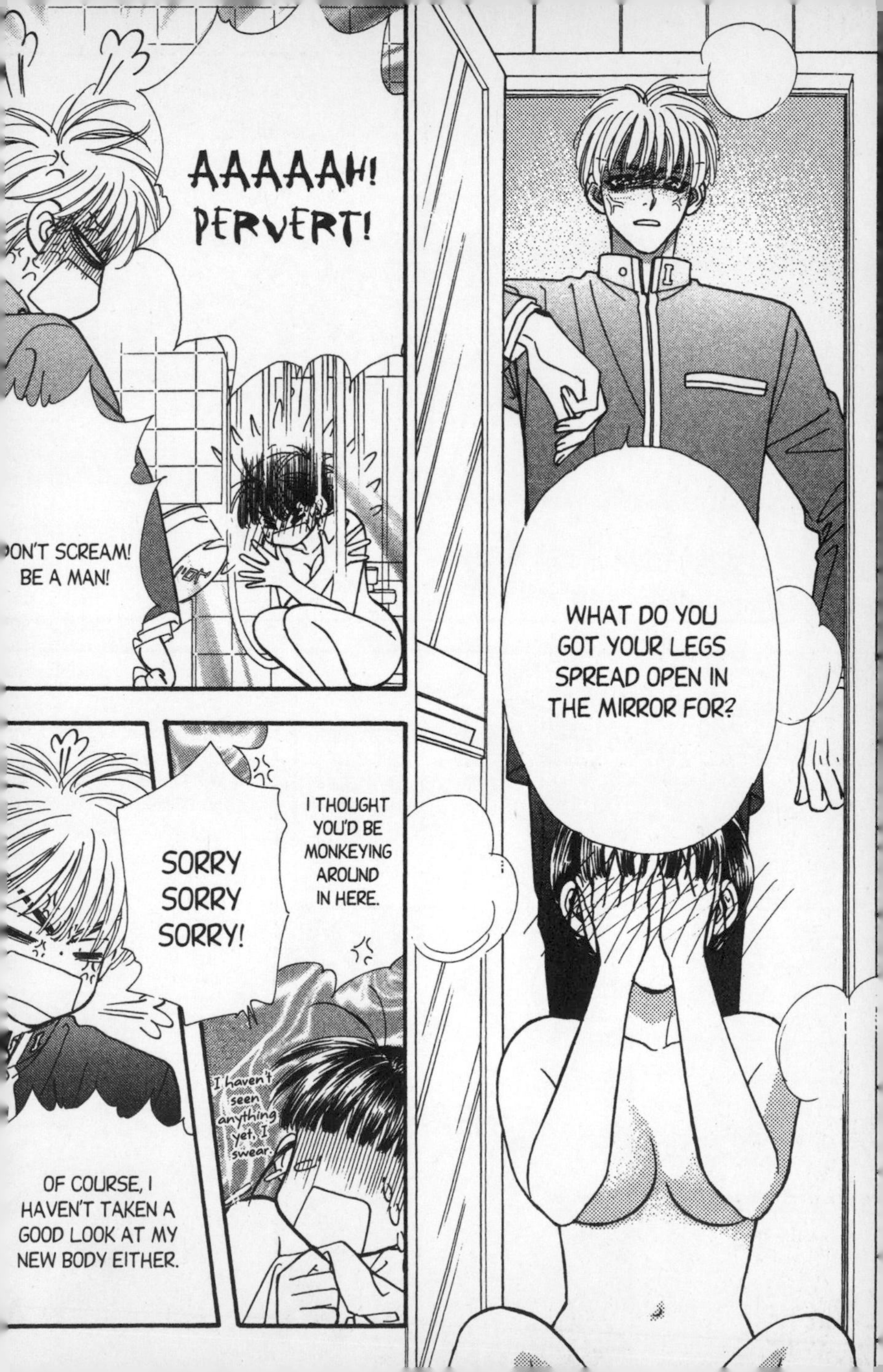
WHAT DO YOU GOT YOUR LEGS SPREAD OPEN IN THE MIRROR FOR?
AAAAAH! PERVERT!
DON'T SCREAM! BE A MAN!
I THOUGHT YOU'D BE MONKEYING AROUND IN HERE.
I haven't seen anything yet, I swear.
SORRY SORRY SORRY!
OF COURSE, I HAVEN'T TAKEN A GOOD LOOK AT MY NEW BODY EITHER.

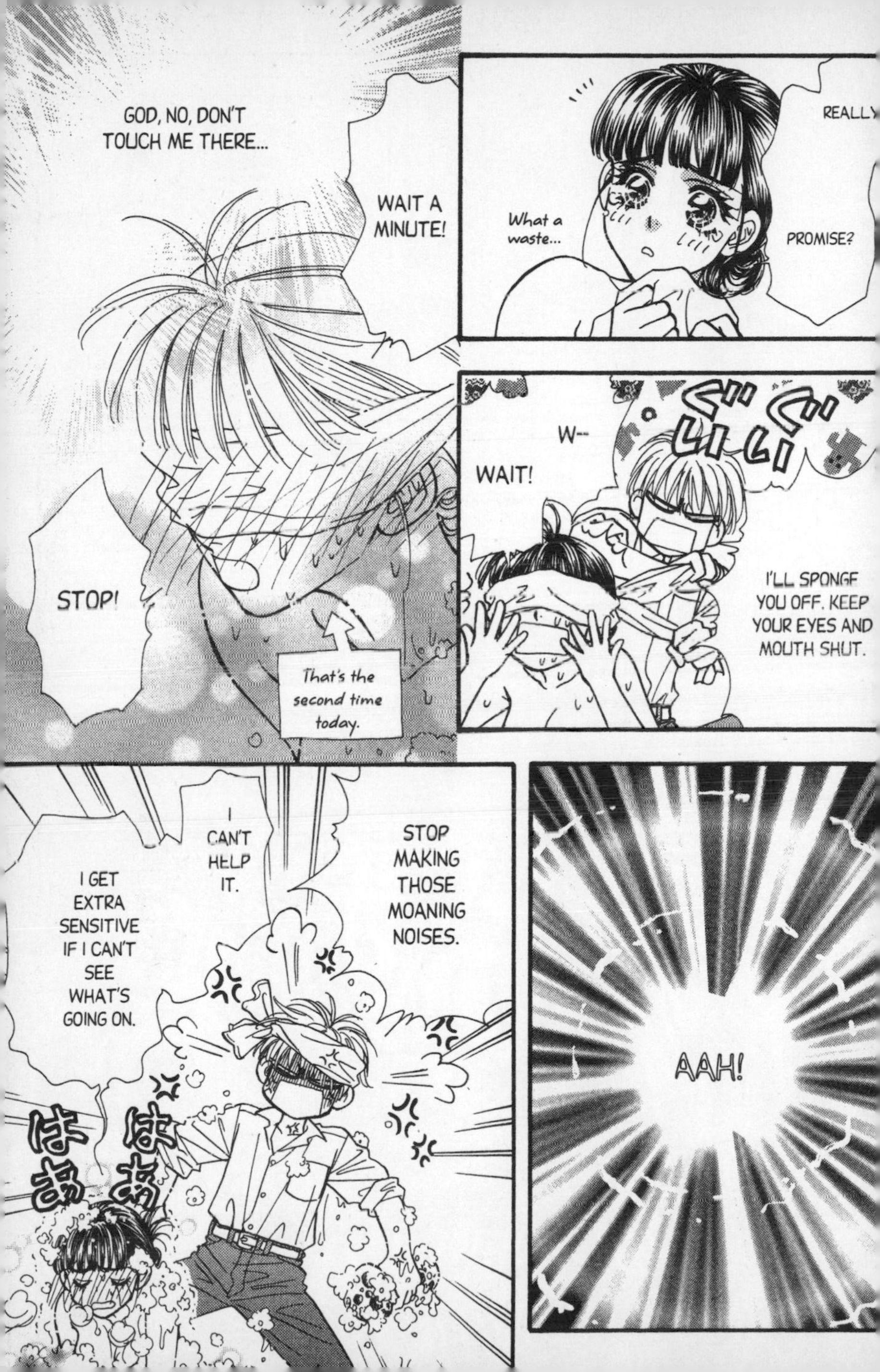
REALLY
PROMISE?
What a waste...
ぐいぐい
I'LL SPONGE YOU OFF. KEEP YOUR EYES AND MOUTH SHUT.
W--
WAIT!
WAIT A MINUTE!
GOD, NO, DON'T TOUCH ME THERE...
STOP!
That's the second time today.
AAH!
STOP MAKING THOSE MOANING NOISES.
I CAN'T HELP IT.
I GET EXTRA SENSITIVE IF I CAN'T SEE WHAT'S GOING ON.
はあはあ

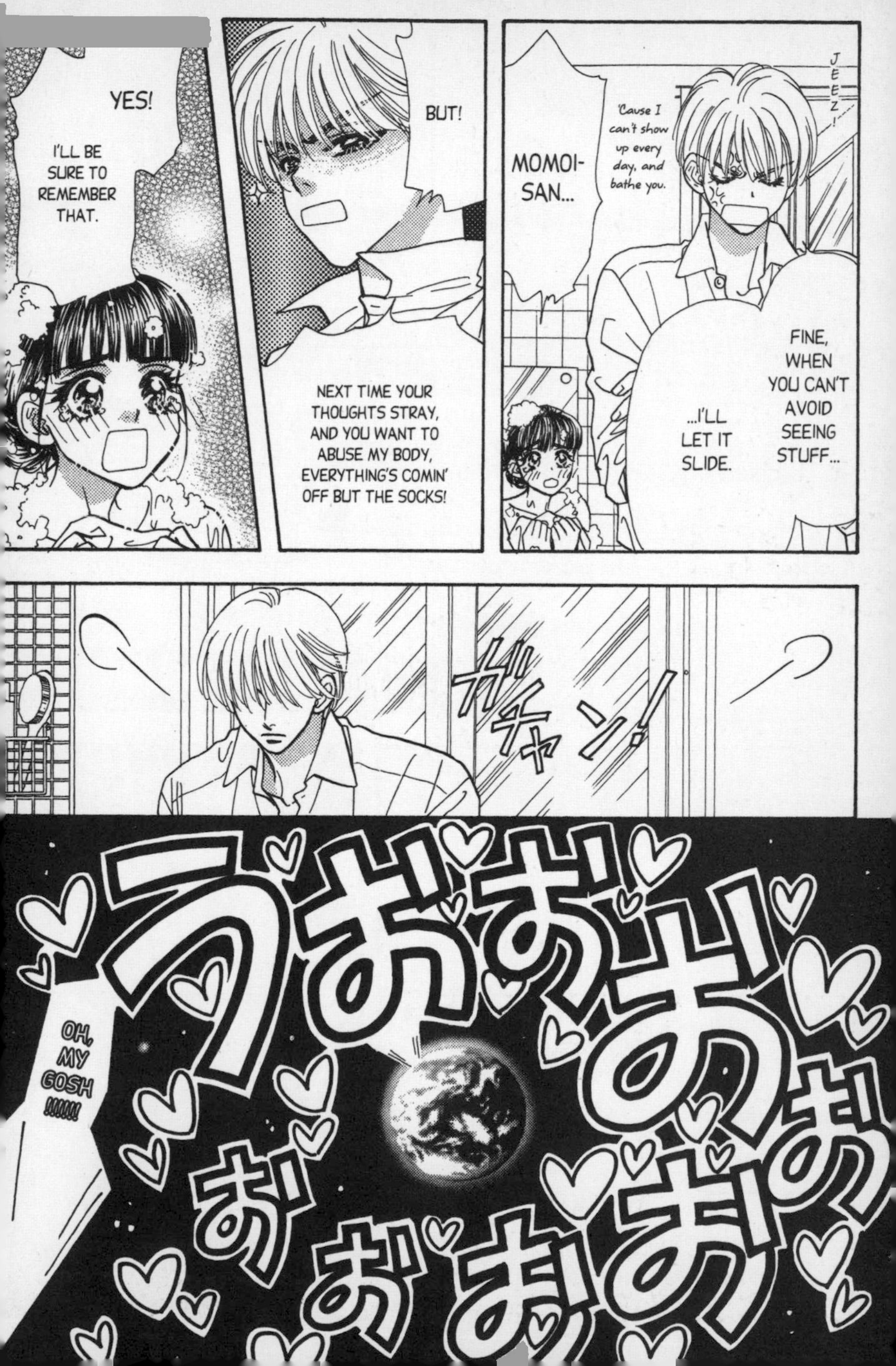
JEEZ!
'Cause I can't show up every day, and bathe you.
MOMOI-SAN...
FINE, WHEN YOU CAN'T AVOID SEEING STUFF...
...I'LL LET IT SLIDE.
BUT!
NEXT TIME YOUR THOUGHTS STRAY, AND YOU WANT TO ABUSE MY BODY, EVERYTHING'S COMIN' OFF BUT THE SOCKS!
YES!
I'LL BE SURE TO REMEMBER THAT.
ガチャン!
うおおおおおおお
OH, MY GOSH!!!!!!

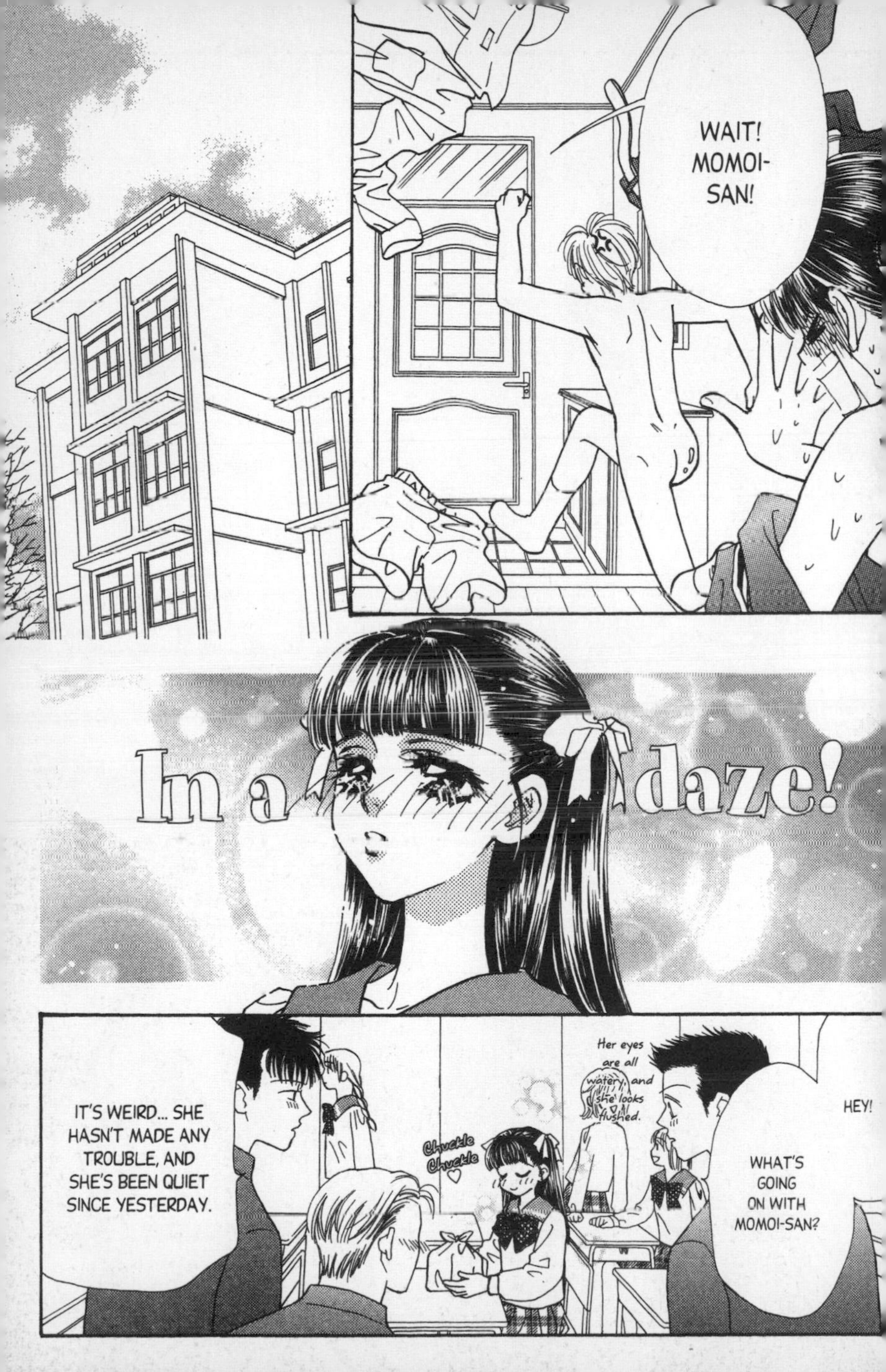
WAIT! MOMOI-SAN!
In a daze!
HEY!
WHAT'S GOING ON WITH MOMOI-SAN?
Her eyes are all watery, and she looks flushed.
Chuckle Chuckle
IT'S WEIRD... SHE HASN'T MADE ANY TROUBLE, AND SHE'S BEEN QUIET SINCE YESTERDAY.

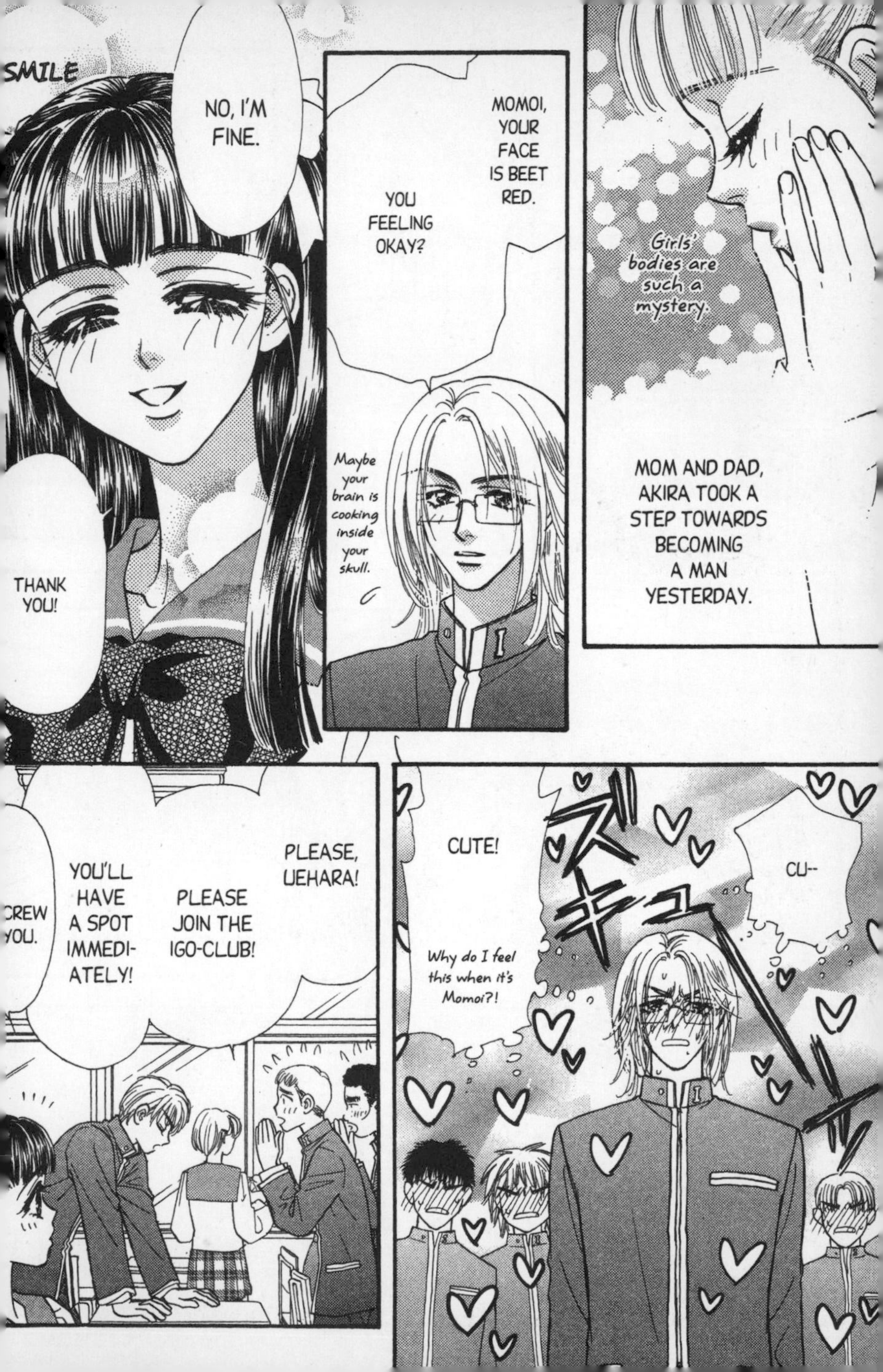
Girls' bodies are such a mystery.
MOM AND DAD, AKIRA TOOK A STEP TOWARDS BECOMING A MAN YESTERDAY.
MOMOI, YOUR FACE IS BEET RED.
YOU FEELING OKAY?
Maybe your brain is cooking inside your skull.
SMILE
NO, I'M FINE.
THANK YOU!
CU--
CUTE!
Why do I feel this when it's Momoi?!
PLEASE, UEHARA!
PLEASE JOIN THE IGO-CLUB!
YOU'LL HAVE A SPOT IMMEDI-ATELY!
CREW YOU.

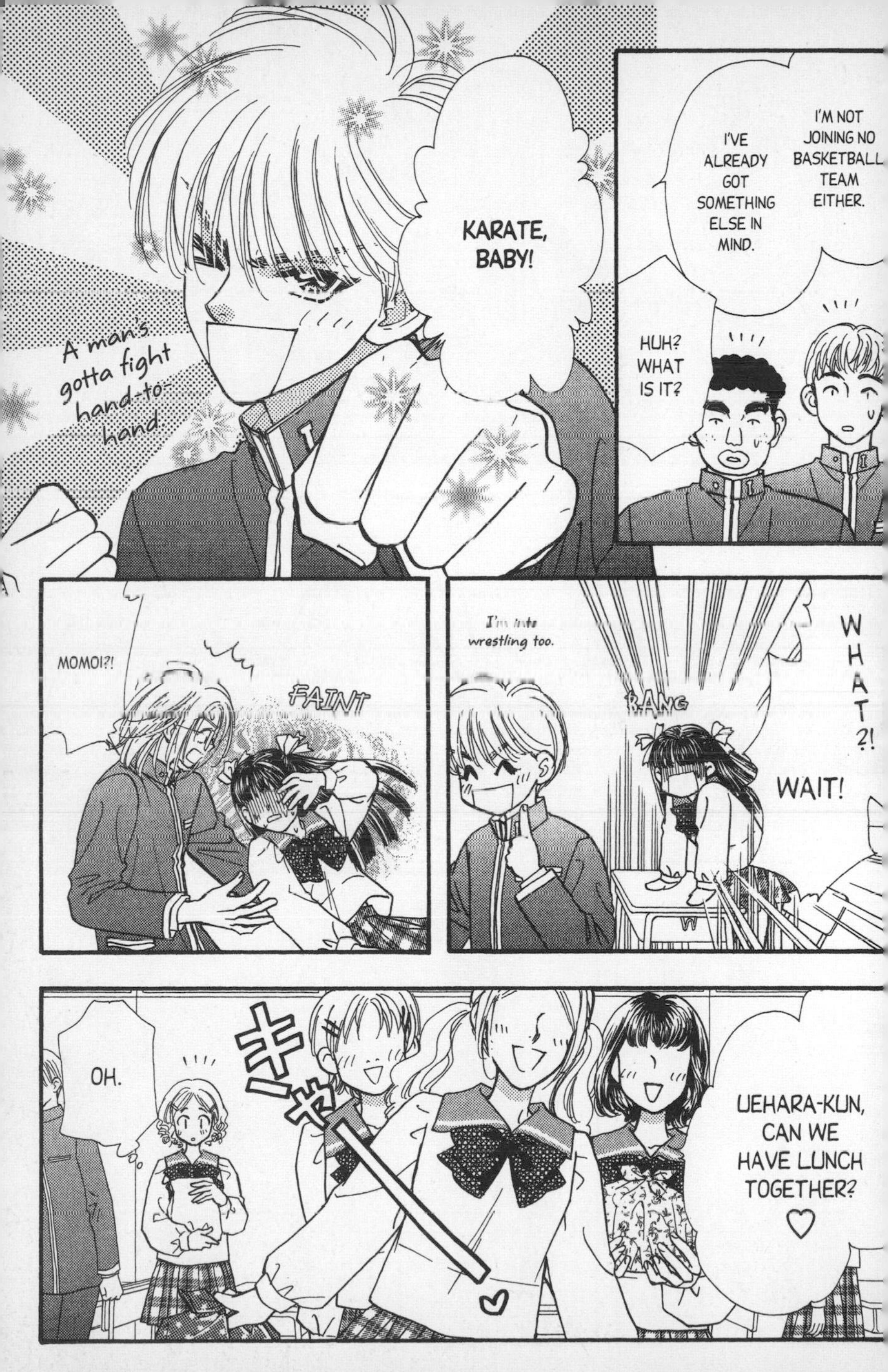
I'M NOT JOINING NO BASKETBALL TEAM EITHER.
I'VE ALREADY GOT SOMETHING ELSE IN MIND.
HUH? WHAT IS IT?
KARATE, BABY!
A man's gotta fight hand-to-hand.
WHAT?!
WAIT!
RANG
I'm into wrestling too.
MOMOI?!
FAINT
UEHARA-KUN, CAN WE HAVE LUNCH TOGETHER? ♡
キャー
OH.

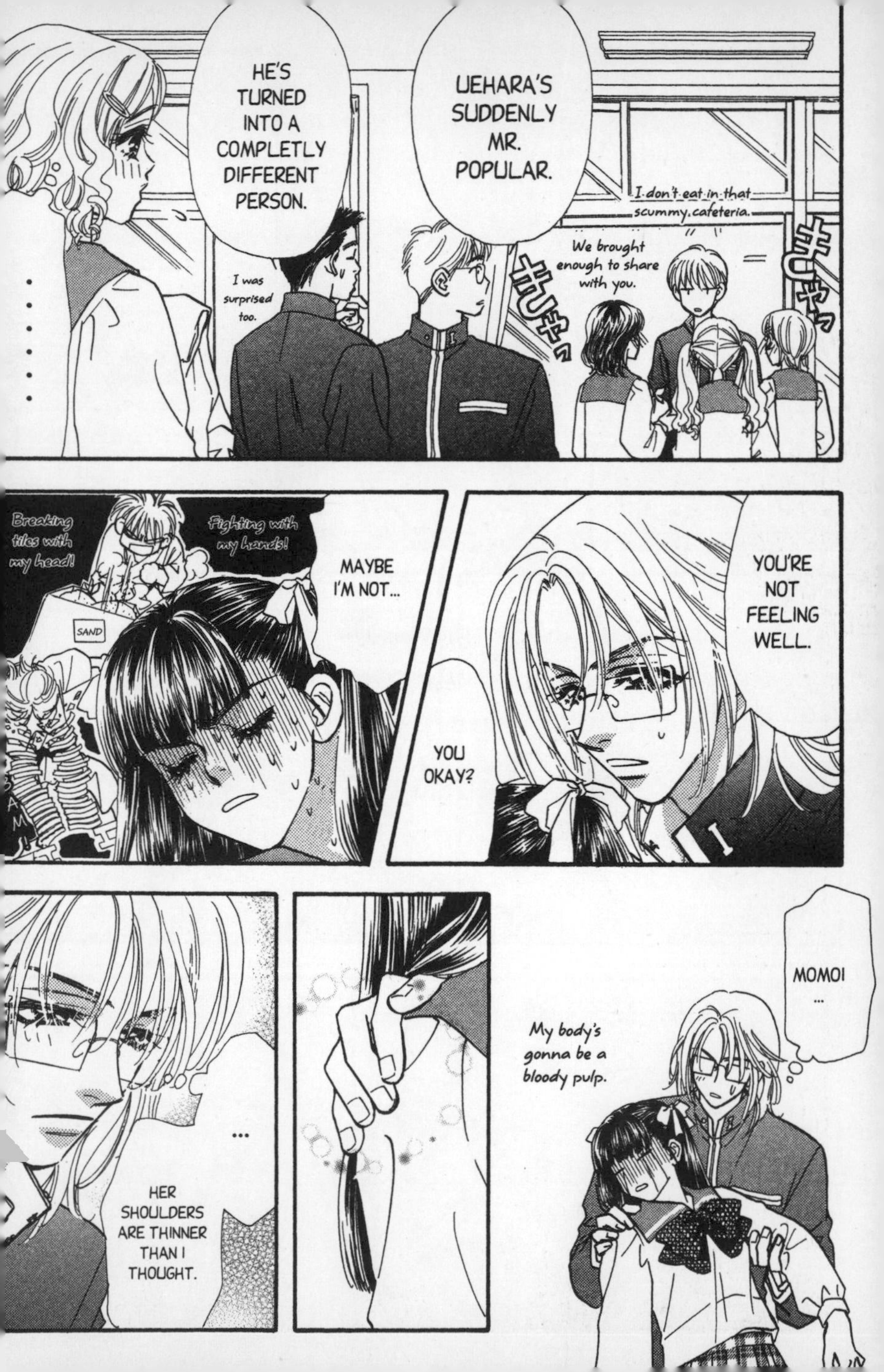
I don't eat in that scummy cafeteria.
We brought enough to share with you.
UEHARA'S SUDDENLY MR. POPULAR.
HE'S TURNED INTO A COMPLETLY DIFFERENT PERSON.
I was surprised too.
......
YOU'RE NOT FEELING WELL.
YOU OKAY?
MAYBE I'M NOT...
Fighting with my hands!
Breaking tiles with my head!
SAND
MOMOI ...
My body's gonna be a bloody pulp.
...
HER SHOULDERS ARE THINNER THAN I THOUGHT.

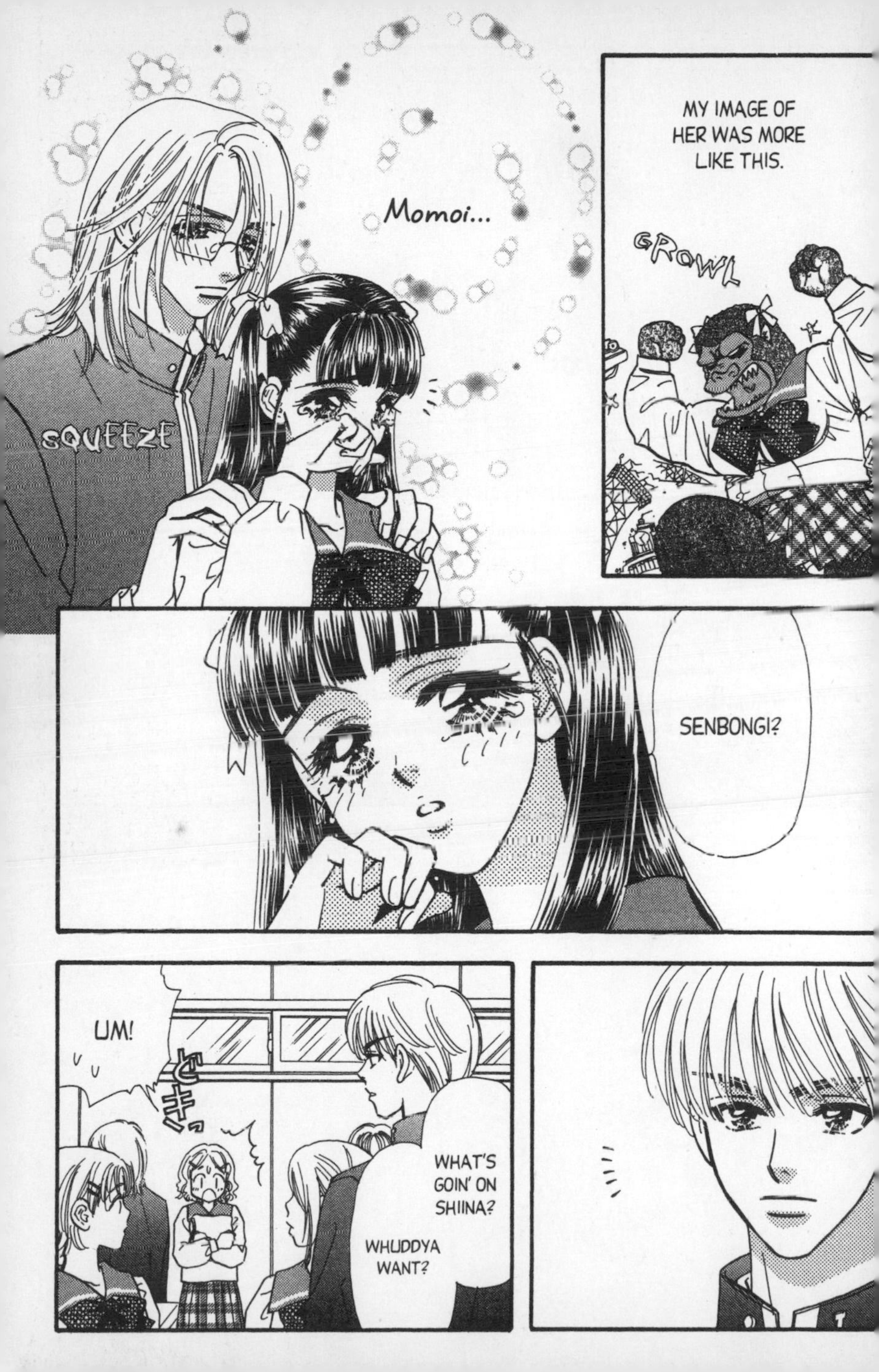
MY IMAGE OF HER WAS MORE LIKE THIS.
GROWL
Momoi...
SQUEEZE
SENBONGI?
UM!
どきっ
WHAT'S GOIN' ON SHIINA?
WHUDDYA WANT?

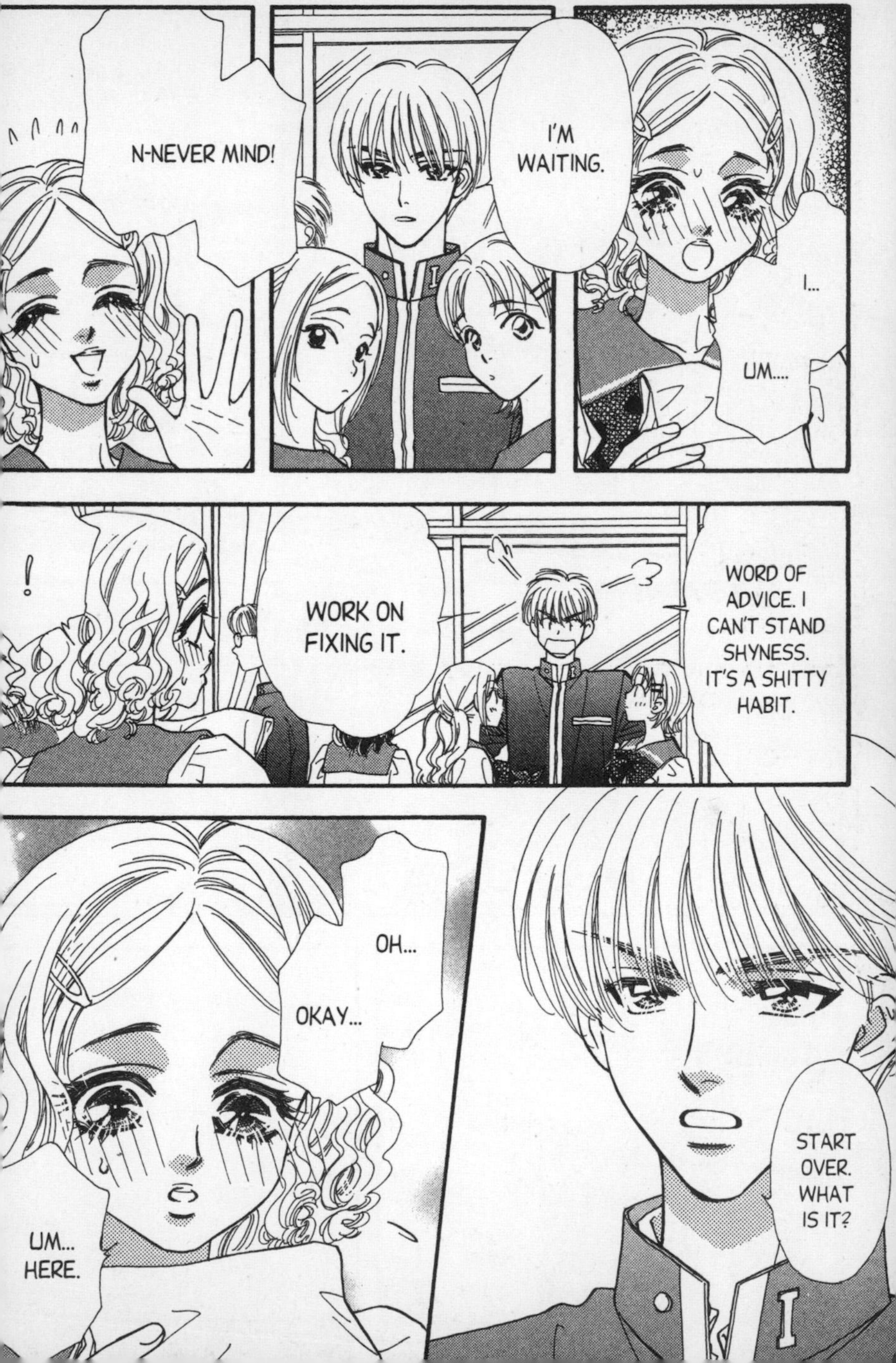
I...
UM....
I'M WAITING.
N-NEVER MIND!
WORD OF ADVICE. I CAN'T STAND SHYNESS. IT'S A SHITTY HABIT.
WORK ON FIXING IT.
!
START OVER. WHAT IS IT?
OH...
OKAY...
UM... HERE.

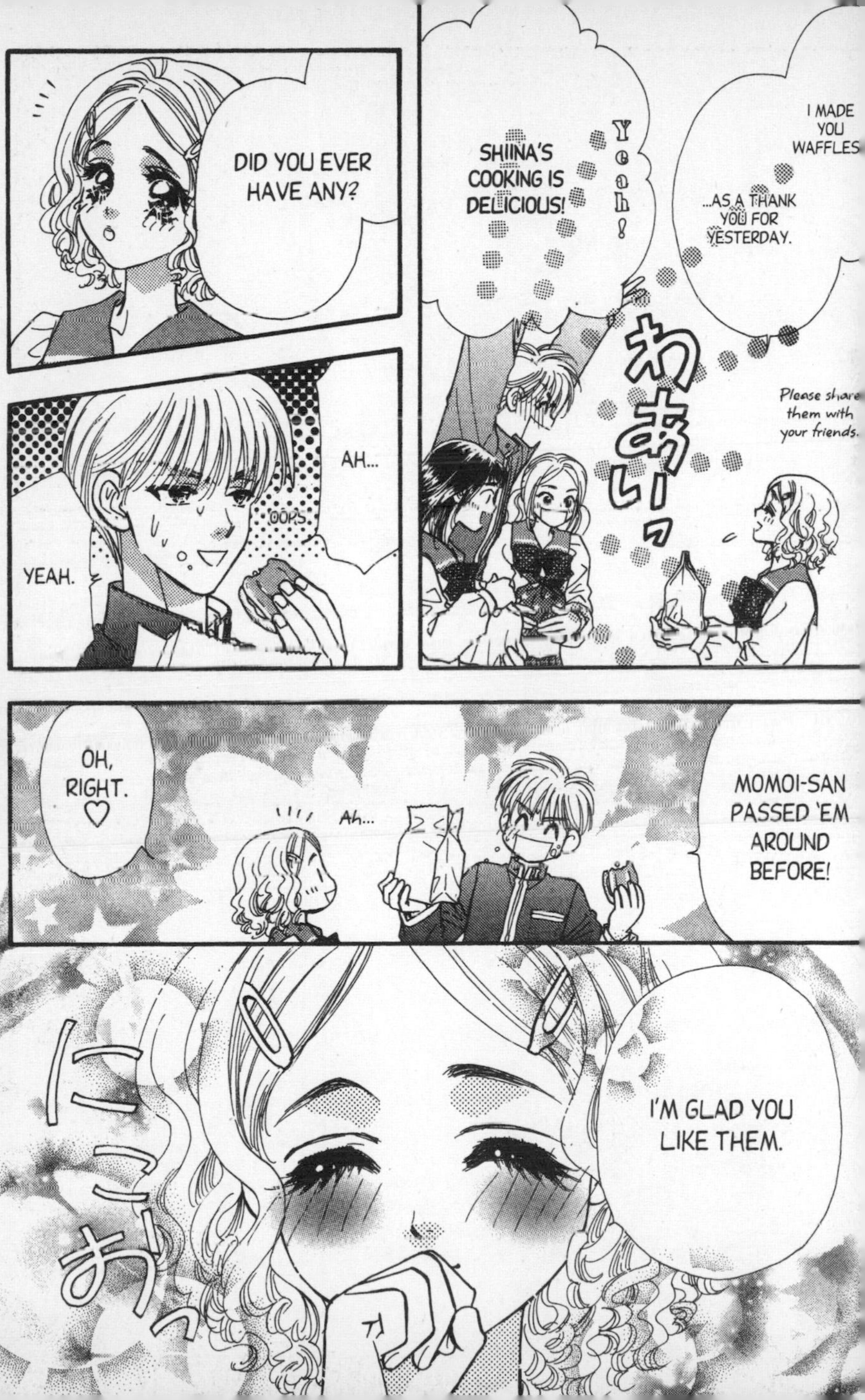

I MADE YOU WAFFLES
...AS A THANK YOU FOR YESTERDAY.
Yeah!
SHIINA'S COOKING IS DELICIOUS!
Please share them with your friends.
わあいっ
DID YOU EVER HAVE ANY?
AH...
OOPS.
YEAH.
MOMOI-SAN PASSED 'EM AROUND BEFORE!
Ah...
OH, RIGHT. ♡
I'M GLAD YOU LIKE THEM.
にこおっ

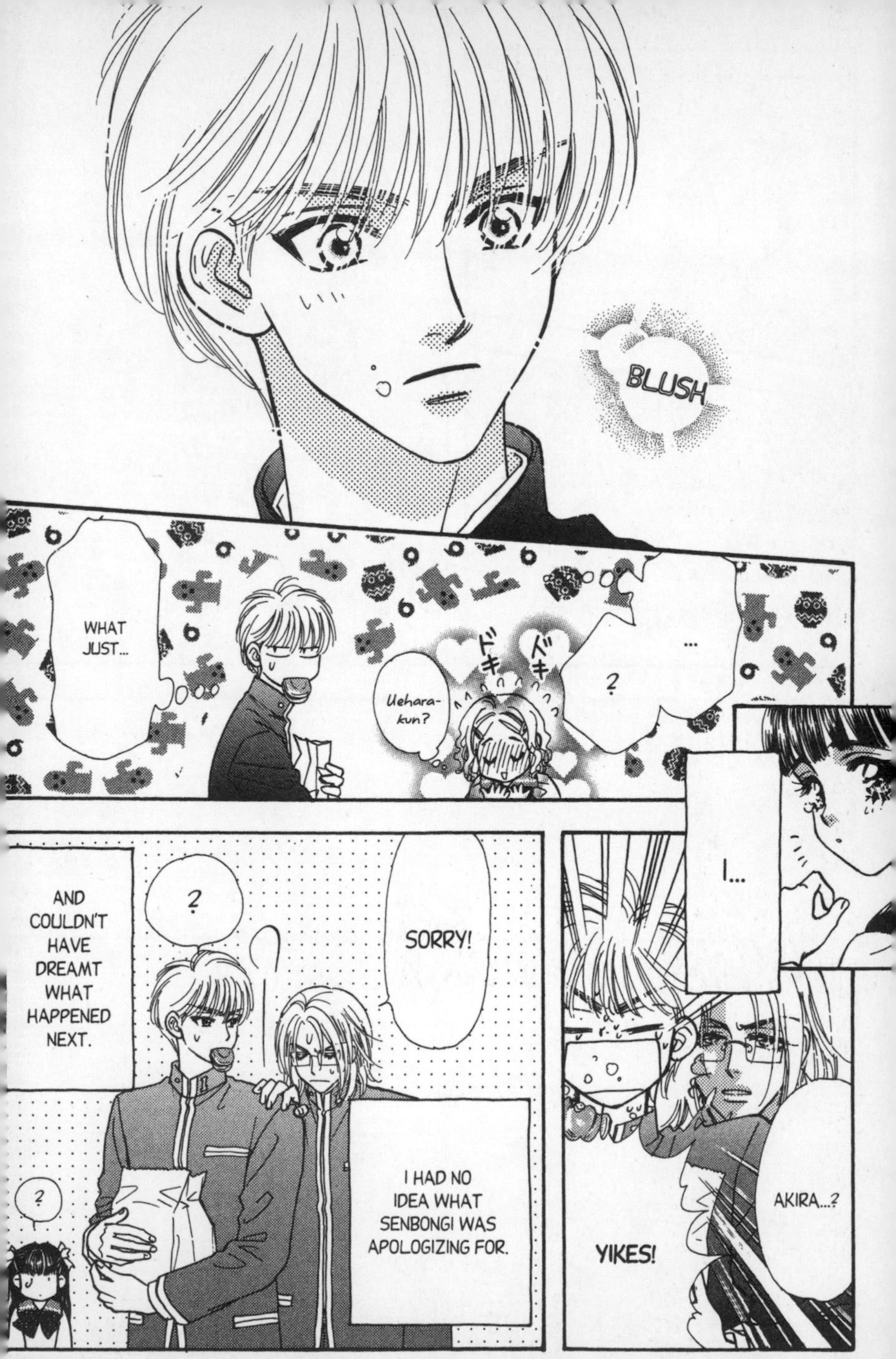
BLUSH
...
?
ドキ ドキ
Uehara-kun?
WHAT JUST...
I...
AKIRA...?
YIKES!
SORRY!
?
I HAD NO IDEA WHAT SENBONGI WAS APOLOGIZING FOR.
AND COULDN'T HAVE DREAMT WHAT HAPPENED NEXT.
?

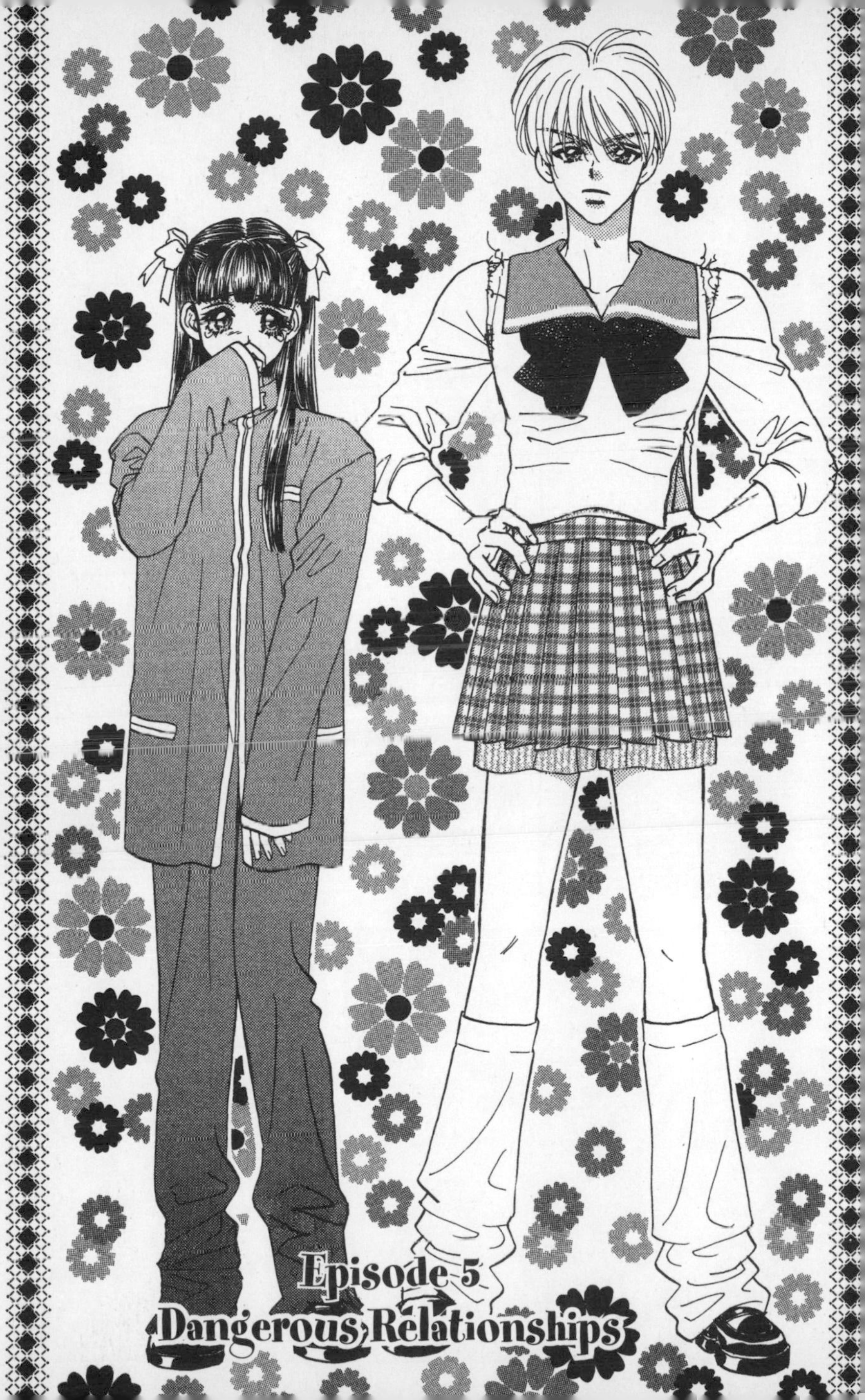
Episode 5
Dangerous Relationships

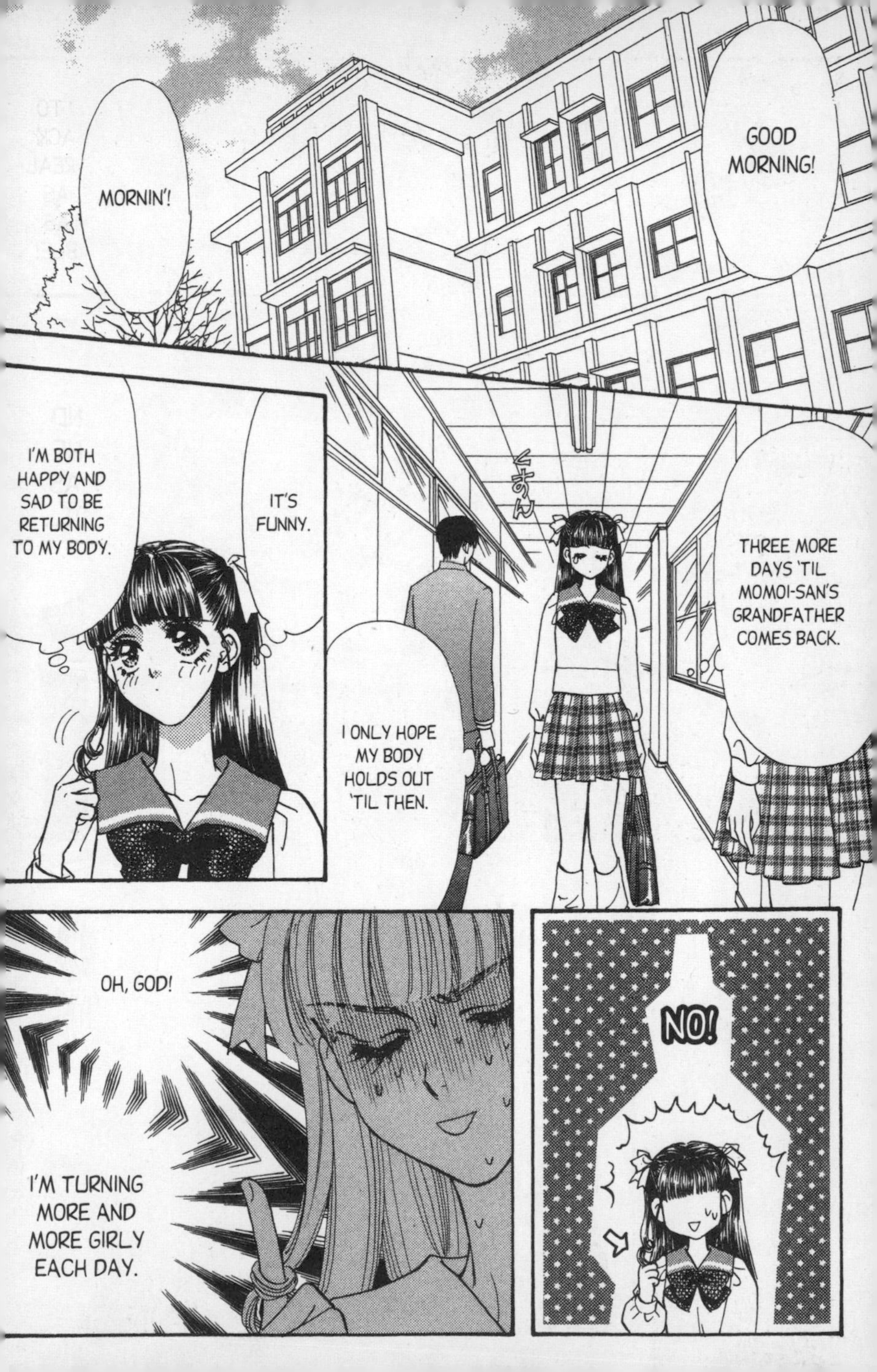
GOOD MORNING!
MORNIN'!
THREE MORE DAYS 'TIL MOMOI-SAN'S GRANDFATHER COMES BACK.
I ONLY HOPE MY BODY HOLDS OUT 'TIL THEN.
IT'S FUNNY.
I'M BOTH HAPPY AND SAD TO BE RETURNING TO MY BODY.
NO!
OH, GOD!
I'M TURNING MORE AND MORE GIRLY EACH DAY.

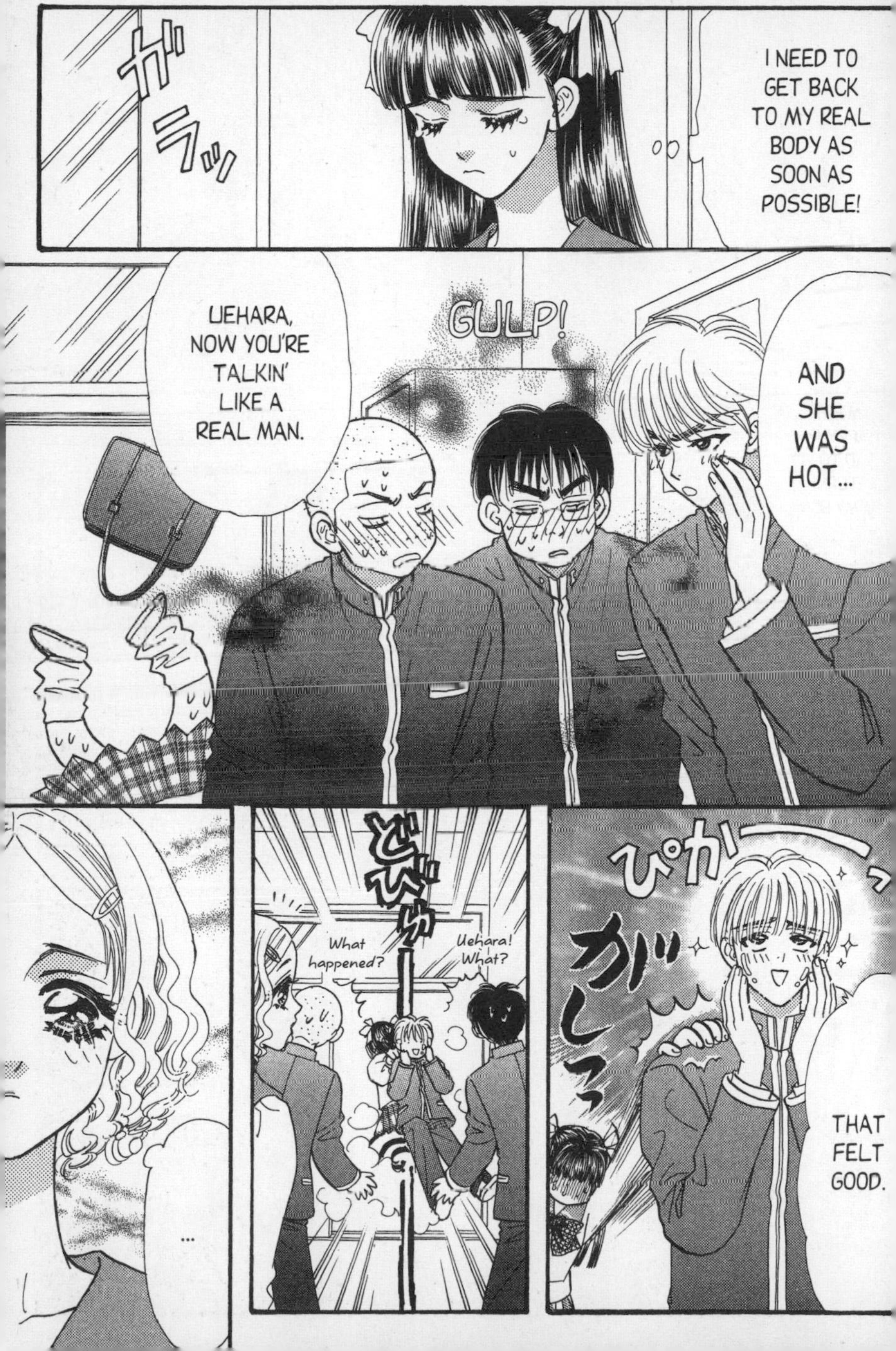

ガラッ
I NEED TO GET BACK TO MY REAL BODY AS SOON AS POSSIBLE!
AND SHE WAS HOT...
GULP!
UEHARA, NOW YOU'RE TALKIN' LIKE A REAL MAN.
ぴかーっ
がしっ
THAT FELT GOOD.
どひゅー
Uehara! What?
What happened?
...

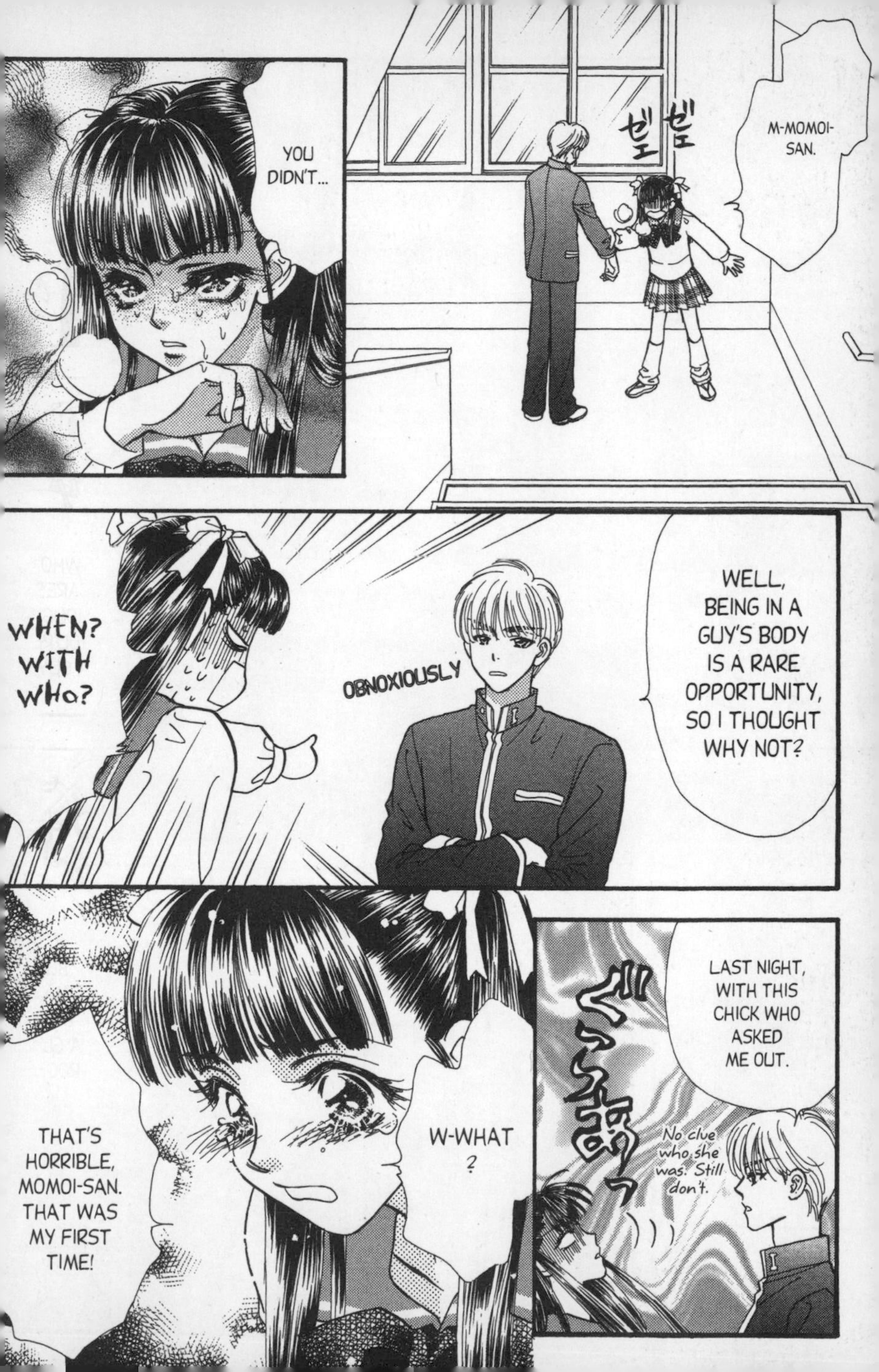
M-MOMOI-SAN.
ゼェゼェ
YOU DIDN'T...
WELL, BEING IN A GUY'S BODY IS A RARE OPPORTUNITY, SO I THOUGHT WHY NOT?
OBNOXIOUSLY
WHEN? WITH WHO?
LAST NIGHT, WITH THIS CHICK WHO ASKED ME OUT.
No clue who she was. Still don't.
W-WHAT?
THAT'S HORRIBLE, MOMOI-SAN. THAT WAS MY FIRST TIME!

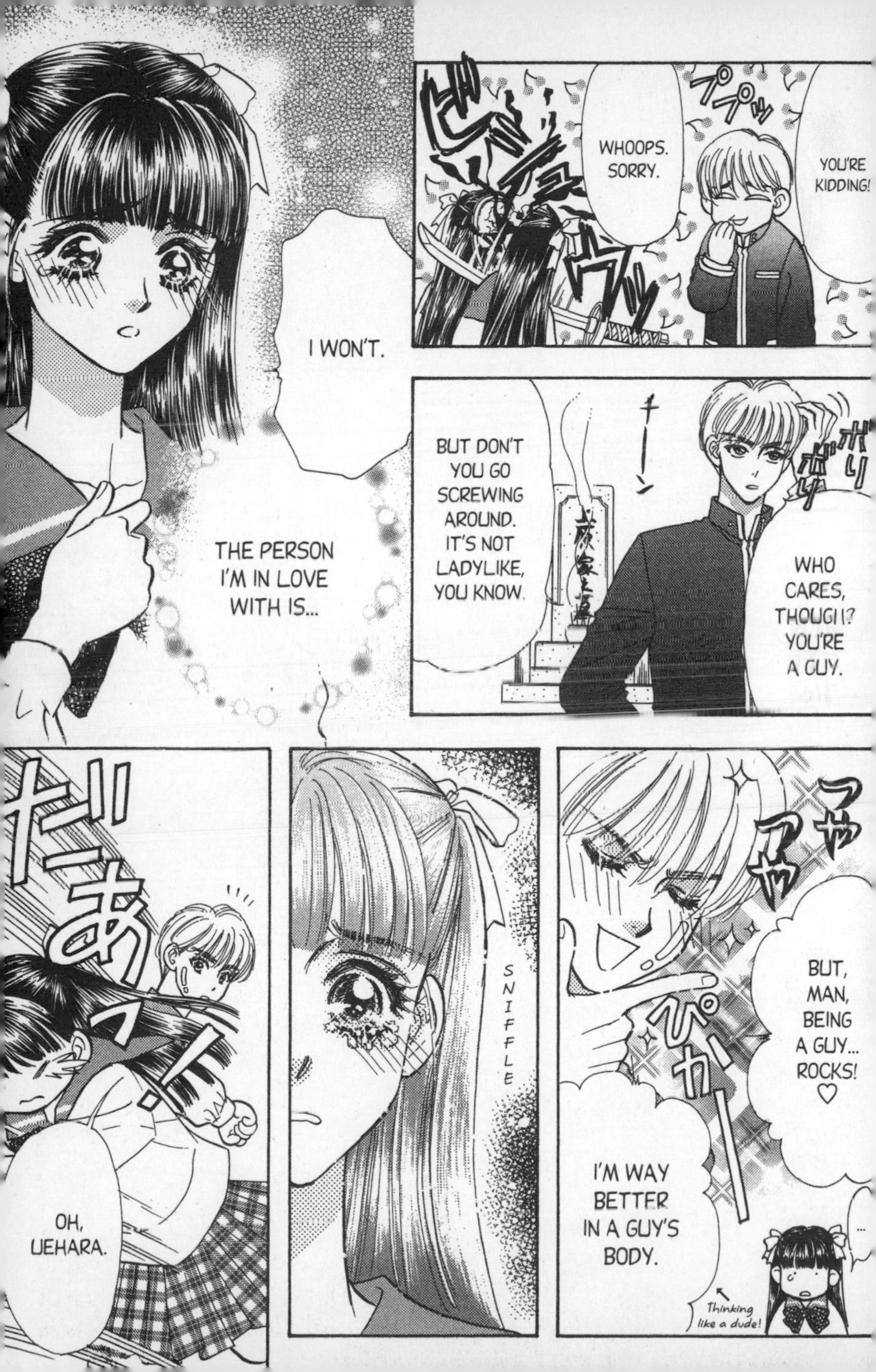
YOU'RE KIDDING!
WHOOPS. SORRY.
WHO CARES, THOUGH? YOU'RE A GUY.
BUT DON'T YOU GO SCREWING AROUND. IT'S NOT LADYLIKE, YOU KNOW.
I WON'T.
THE PERSON I'M IN LOVE WITH IS...
BUT, MAN, BEING A GUY... ROCKS! ♡
I'M WAY BETTER IN A GUY'S BODY.
...
Thinking like a dude!
SNIFFLE
OH, UEHARA.

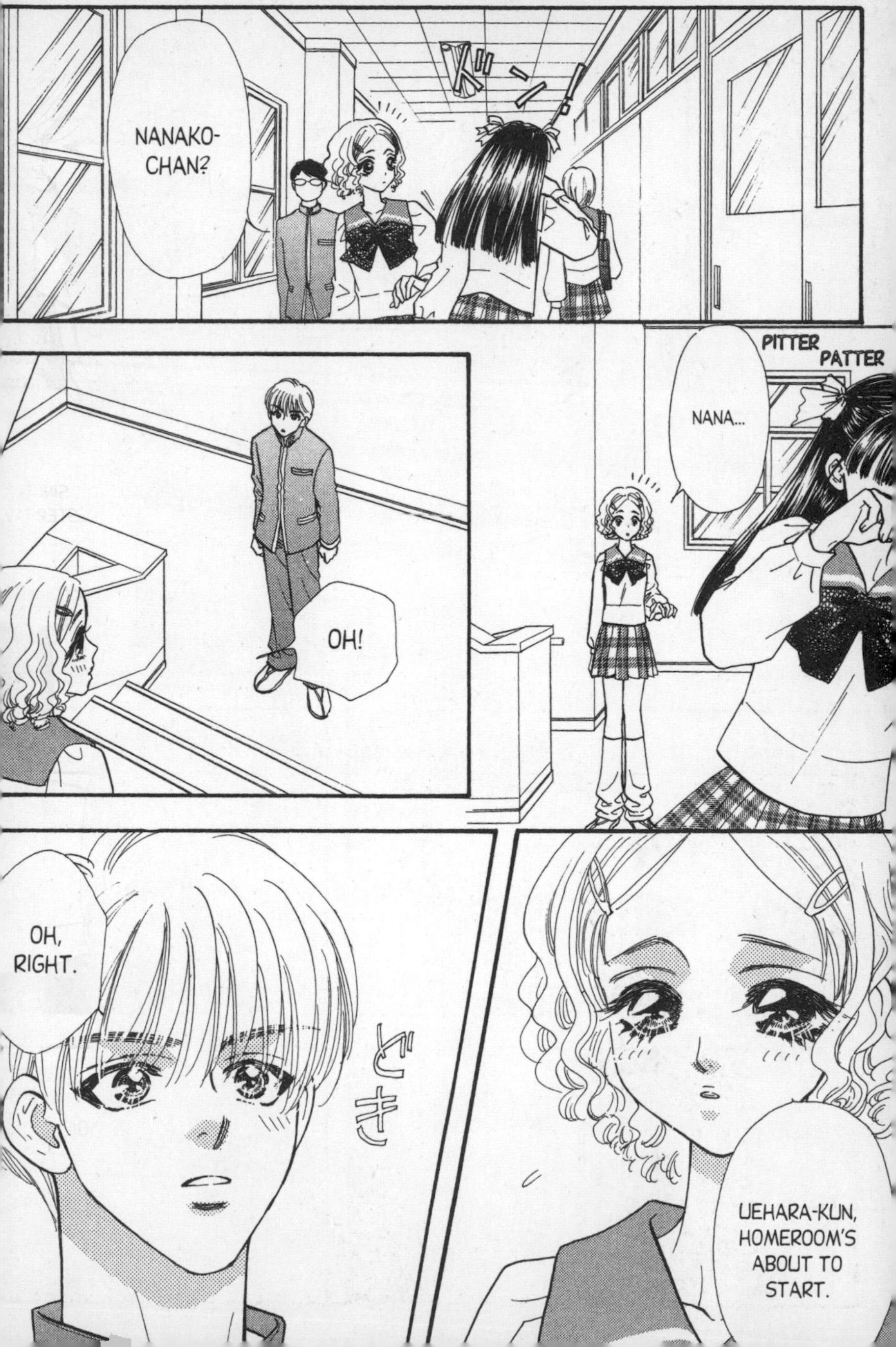
ドーン!
NANAKO-CHAN?
PITTER PATTER
NANA...
OH!
UEHARA-KUN, HOMEROOM'S ABOUT TO START.
どき
OH, RIGHT.

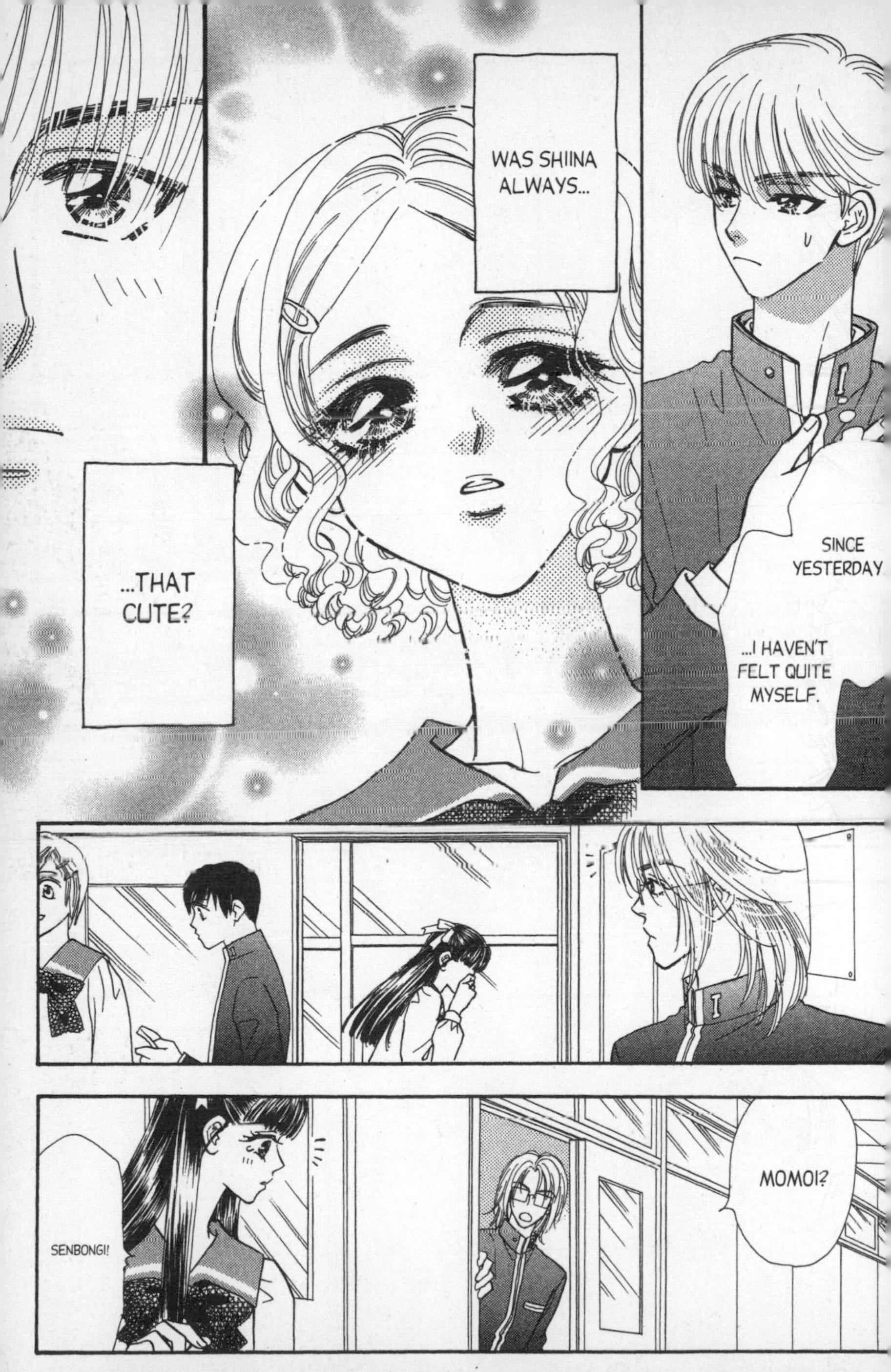
SINCE YESTERDAY
...I HAVEN'T FELT QUITE MYSELF.
WAS SHIINA ALWAYS...
...THAT CUTE?
MOMOI?
SENBONGI!

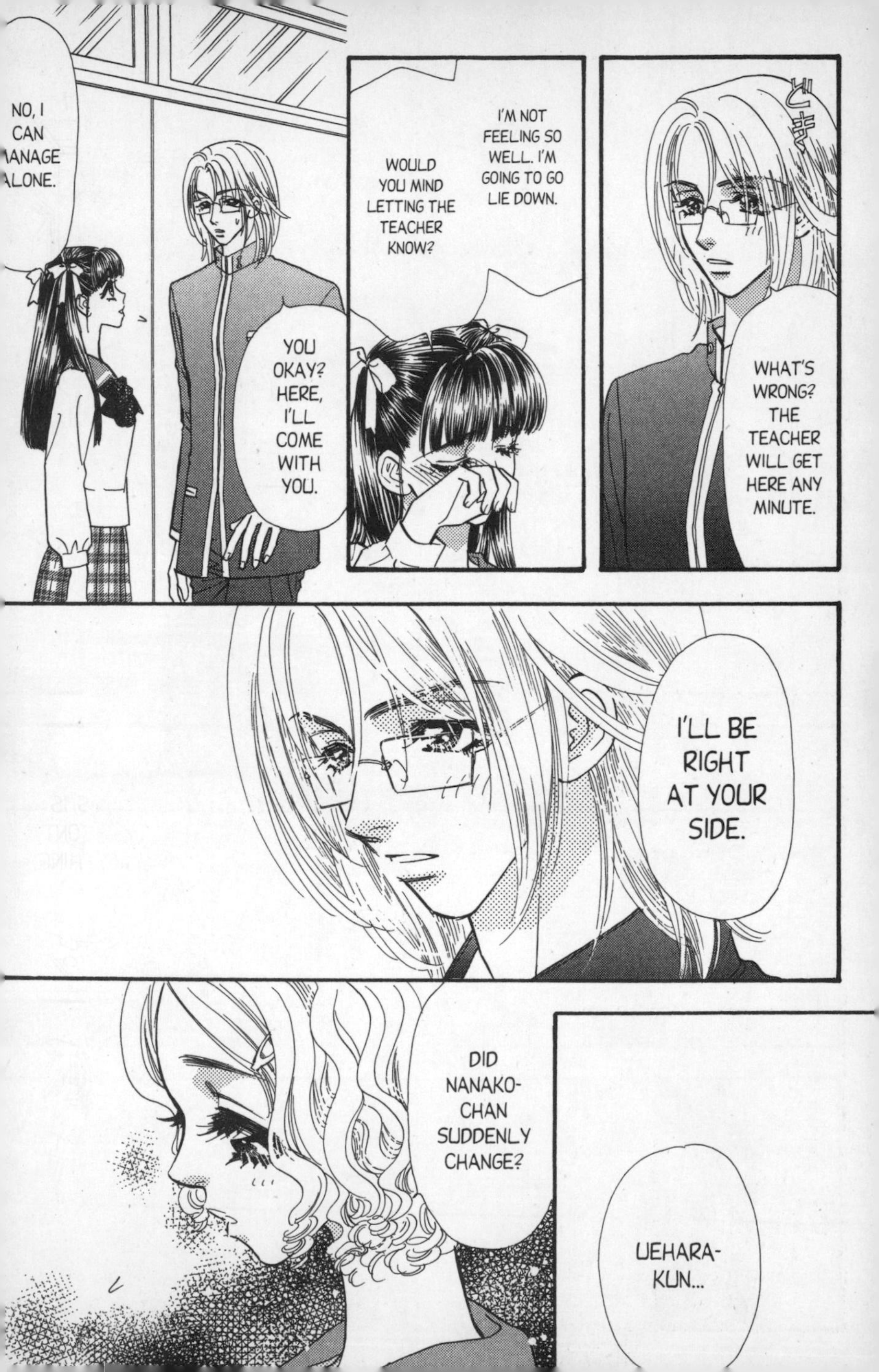
WHAT'S WRONG? THE TEACHER WILL GET HERE ANY MINUTE.
I'M NOT FEELING SO WELL. I'M GOING TO GO LIE DOWN.
WOULD YOU MIND LETTING THE TEACHER KNOW?
YOU OKAY? HERE, I'LL COME WITH YOU.
NO, I CAN MANAGE ALONE.
I'LL BE RIGHT AT YOUR SIDE.
UEHARA-KUN...
DID NANAKO-CHAN SUDDENLY CHANGE?

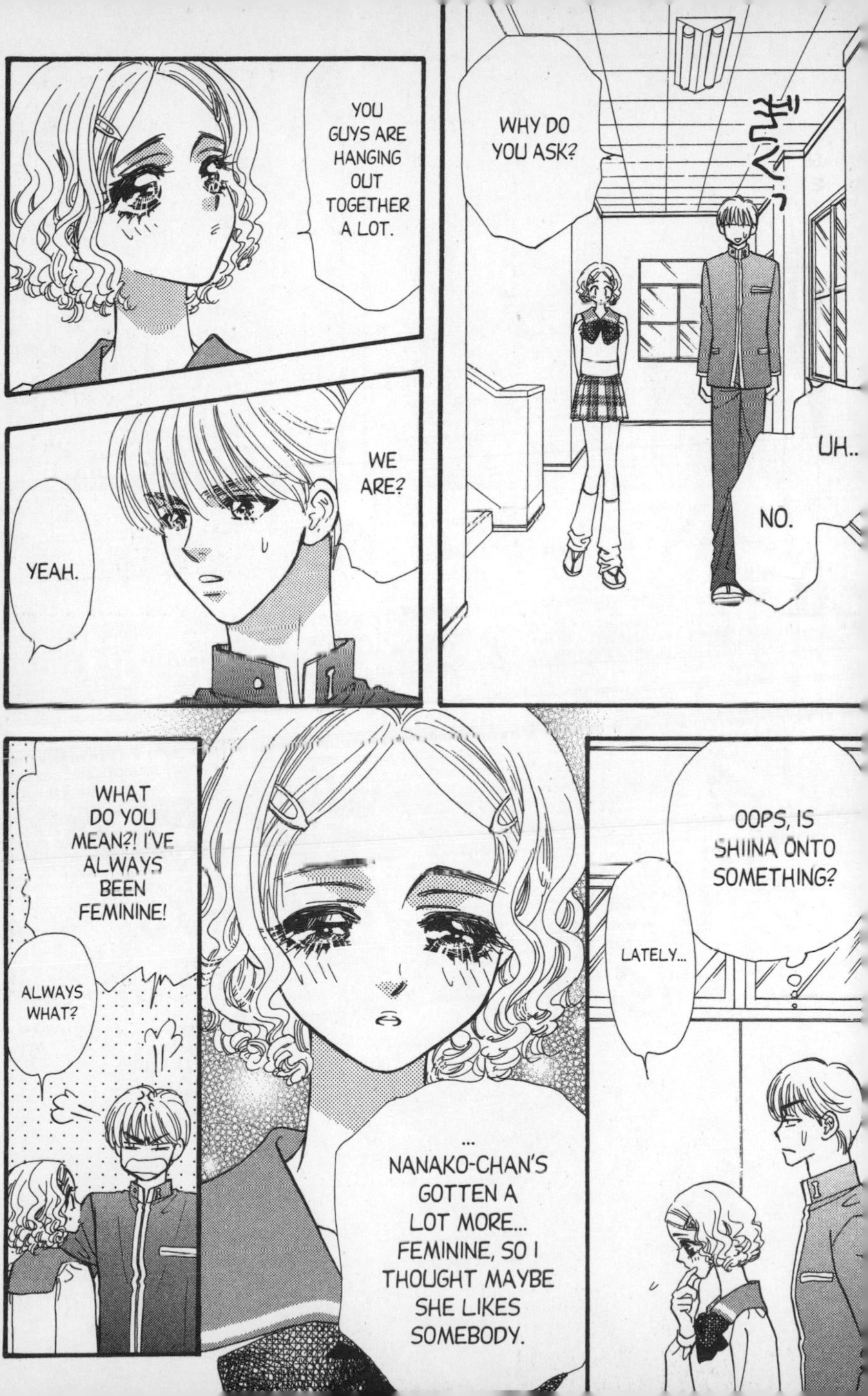

WHY DO YOU ASK?
ぎくっ
UH.. NO.
YOU GUYS ARE HANGING OUT TOGETHER A LOT.
WE ARE?
YEAH.
LATELY...
OOPS, IS SHIINA ONTO SOMETHING?
... NANAKO-CHAN'S GOTTEN A LOT MORE... FEMININE, SO I THOUGHT MAYBE SHE LIKES SOMEBODY.
WHAT DO YOU MEAN?! I'VE ALWAYS BEEN FEMININE!
ALWAYS WHAT?

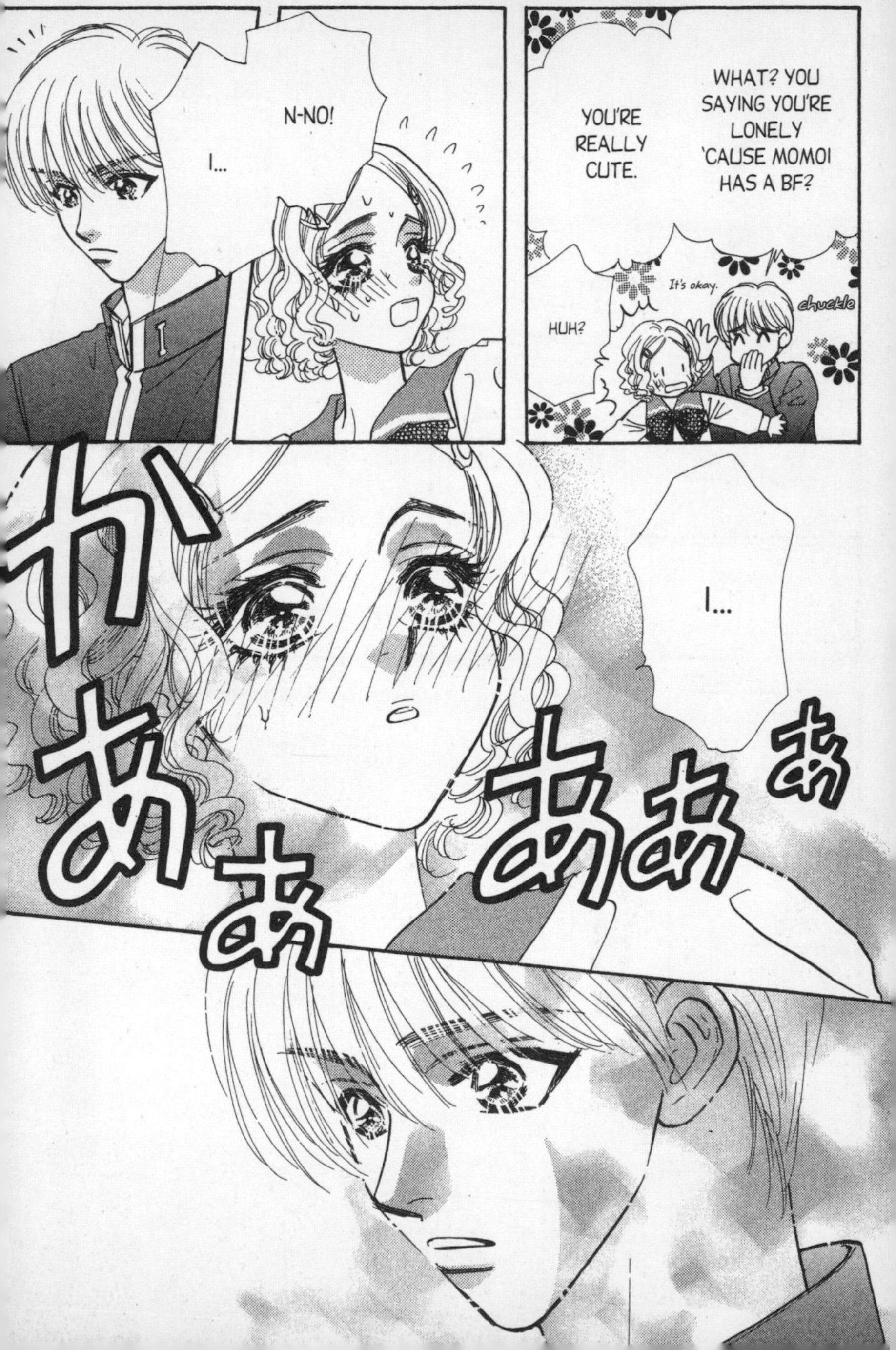
WHAT? YOU SAYING YOU'RE LONELY 'CAUSE MOMOI HAS A BF?
YOU'RE REALLY CUTE.
chuckle
It's okay.
HUH?
N-NO!
I...
I...
かあああああ

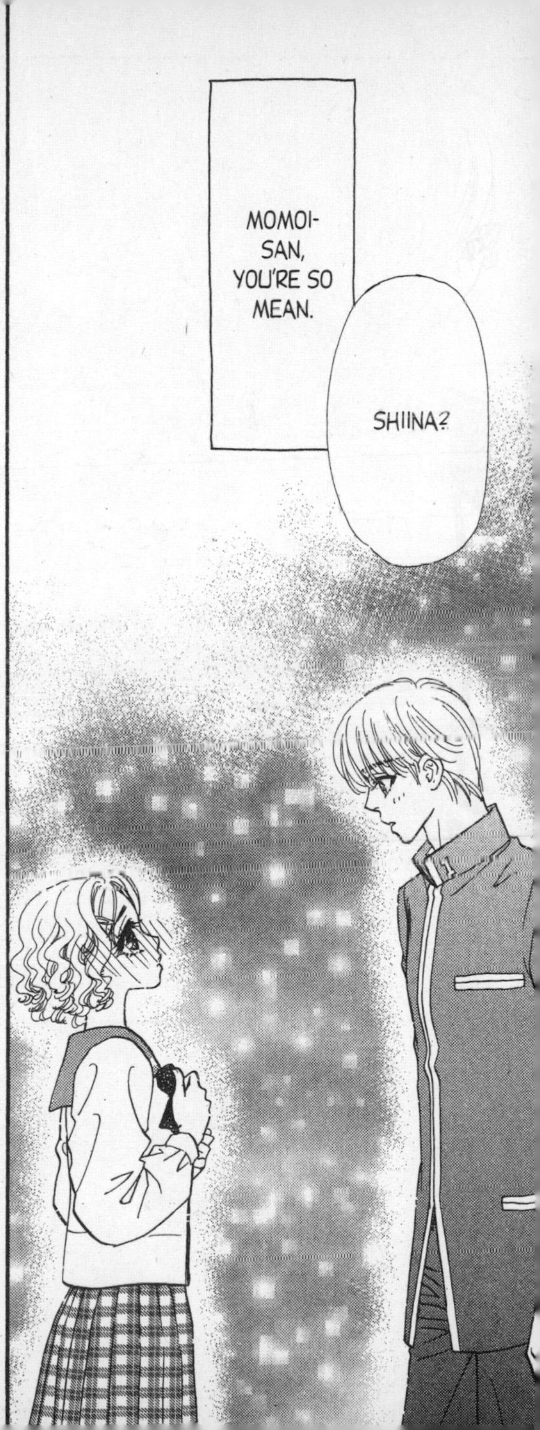
MOMOI-SAN, YOU'RE SO MEAN.
SHIINA?

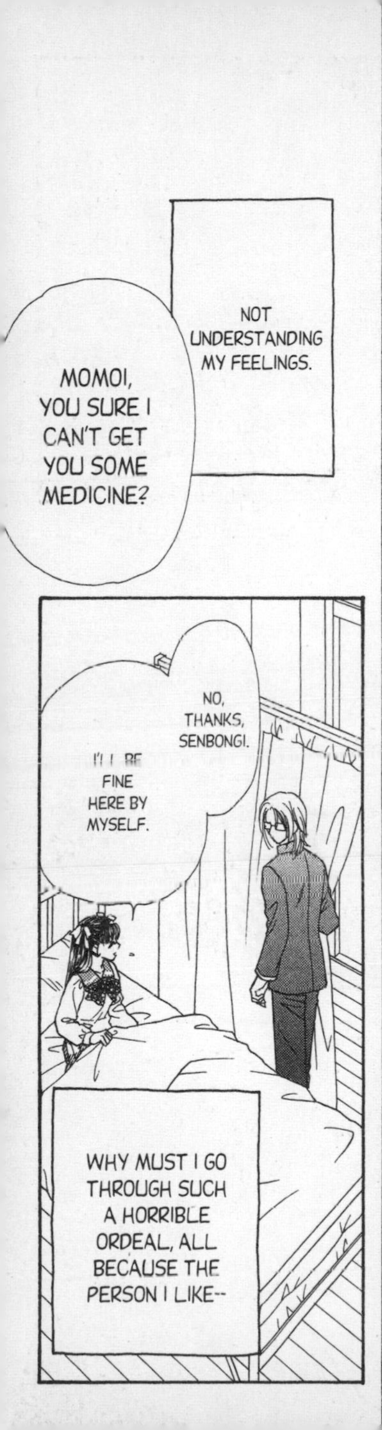
NOT UNDERSTANDING MY FEELINGS.
MOMOI, YOU SURE I CAN'T GET YOU SOME MEDICINE?
NO, THANKS, SENBONGI. I'LL BE FINE HERE BY MYSELF.
WHY MUST I GO THROUGH SUCH A HORRIBLE ORDEAL, ALL BECAUSE THE PERSON I LIKE--

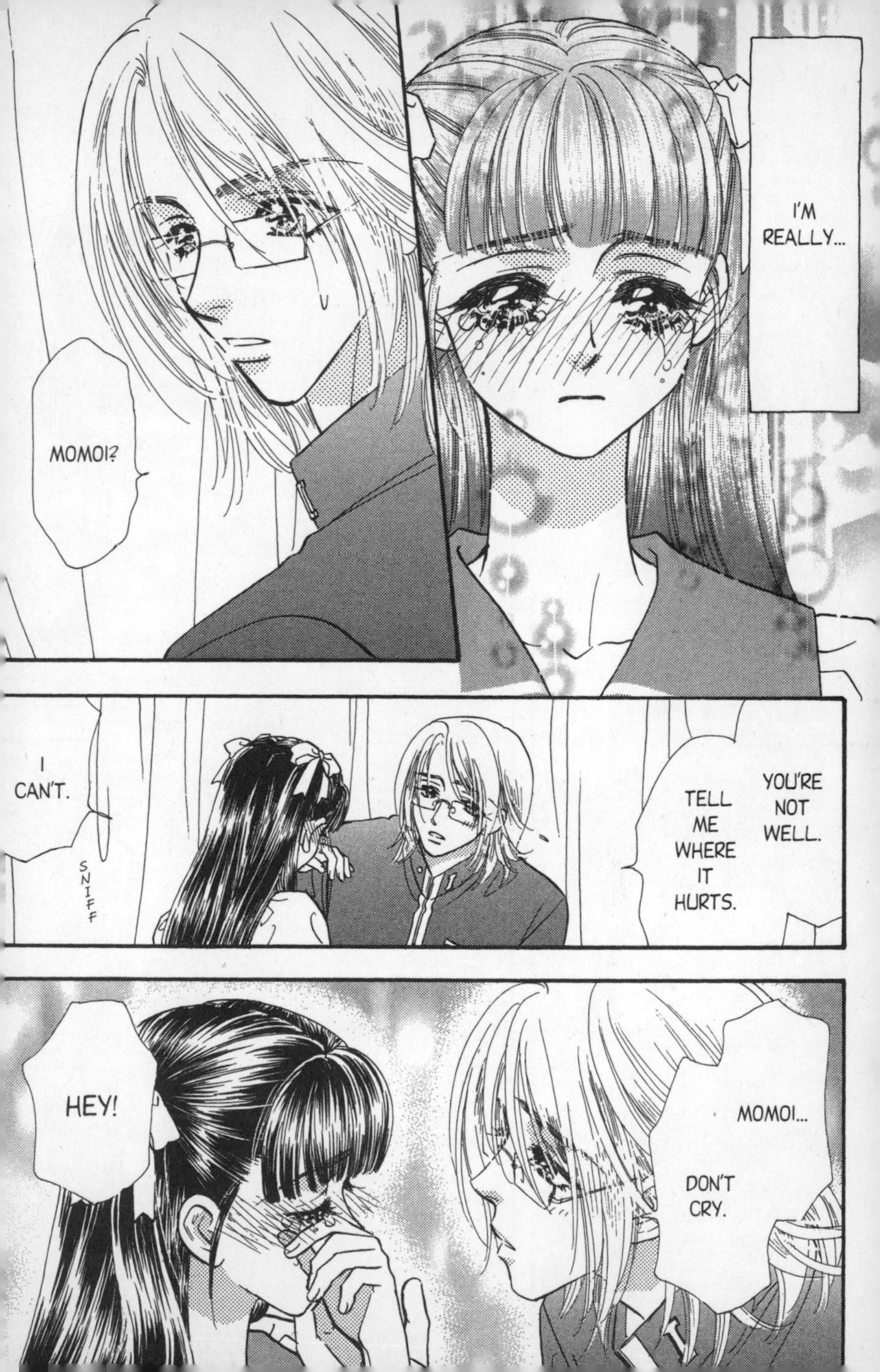

I'M REALLY...
MOMOI?
YOU'RE NOT WELL.
TELL ME WHERE IT HURTS.
SNIFF
I CAN'T.
MOMOI...
DON'T CRY.
HEY!

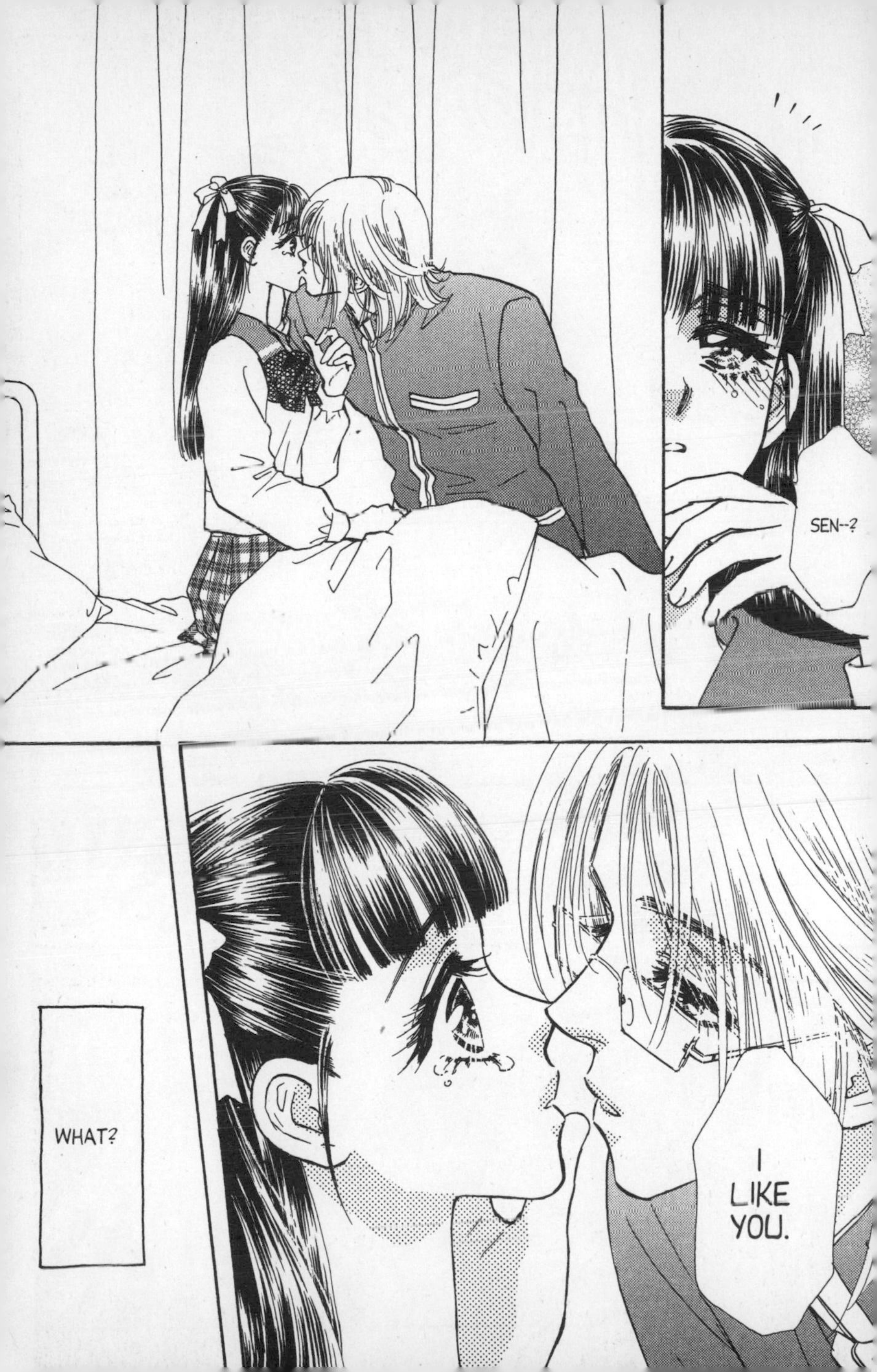
SEN--?
I LIKE YOU.
WHAT?

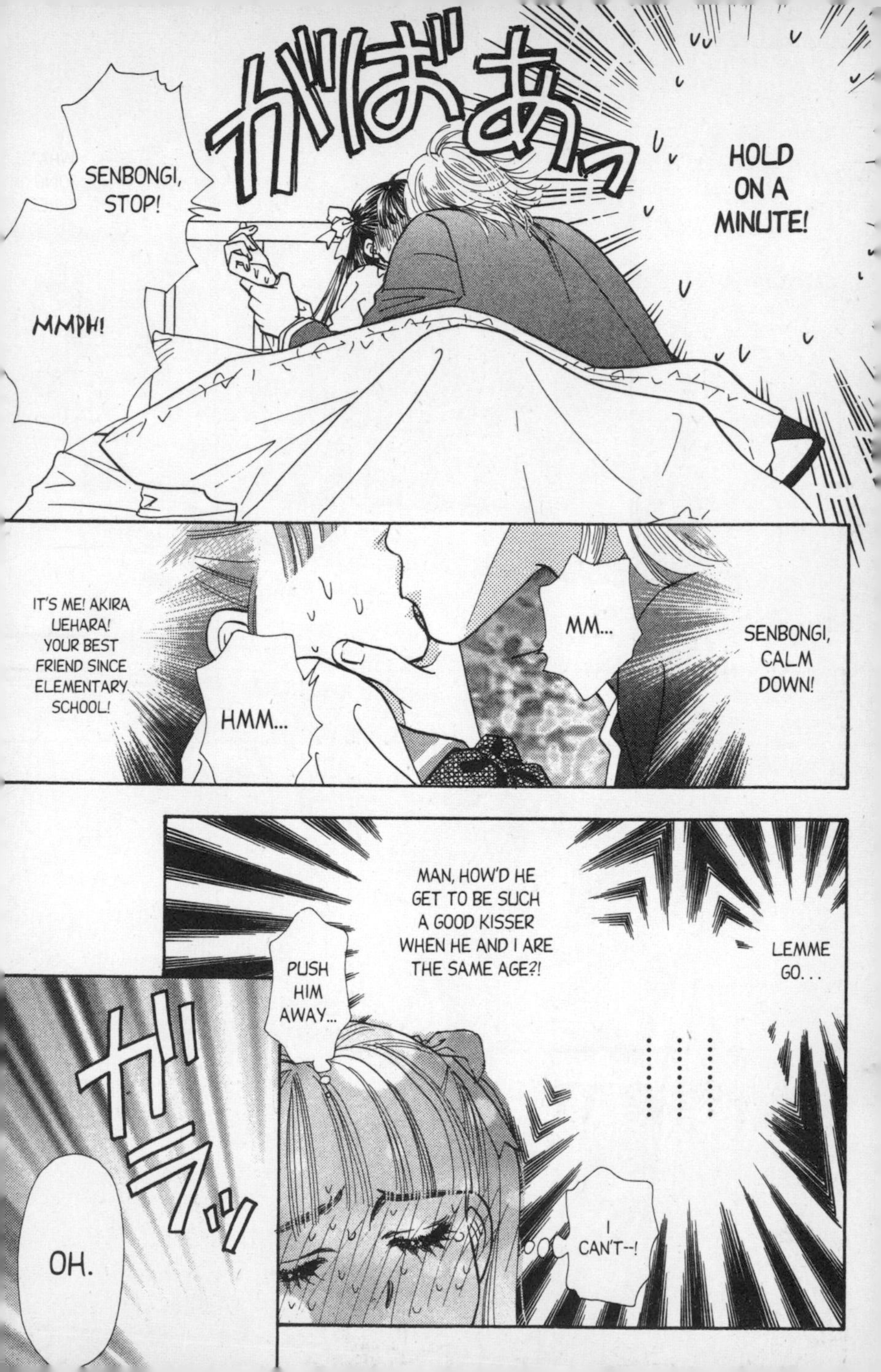
HOLD ON A MINUTE!
がばあっ
SENBONGI, STOP!
MMPH!
SENBONGI, CALM DOWN!
MM...
IT'S ME! AKIRA UEHARA! YOUR BEST FRIEND SINCE ELEMENTARY SCHOOL!
HMM...
LEMME GO. . .
MAN, HOW'D HE GET TO BE SUCH A GOOD KISSER WHEN HE AND I ARE THE SAME AGE?!
PUSH HIM AWAY...
......
I CAN'T--!
ガラッ
OH.

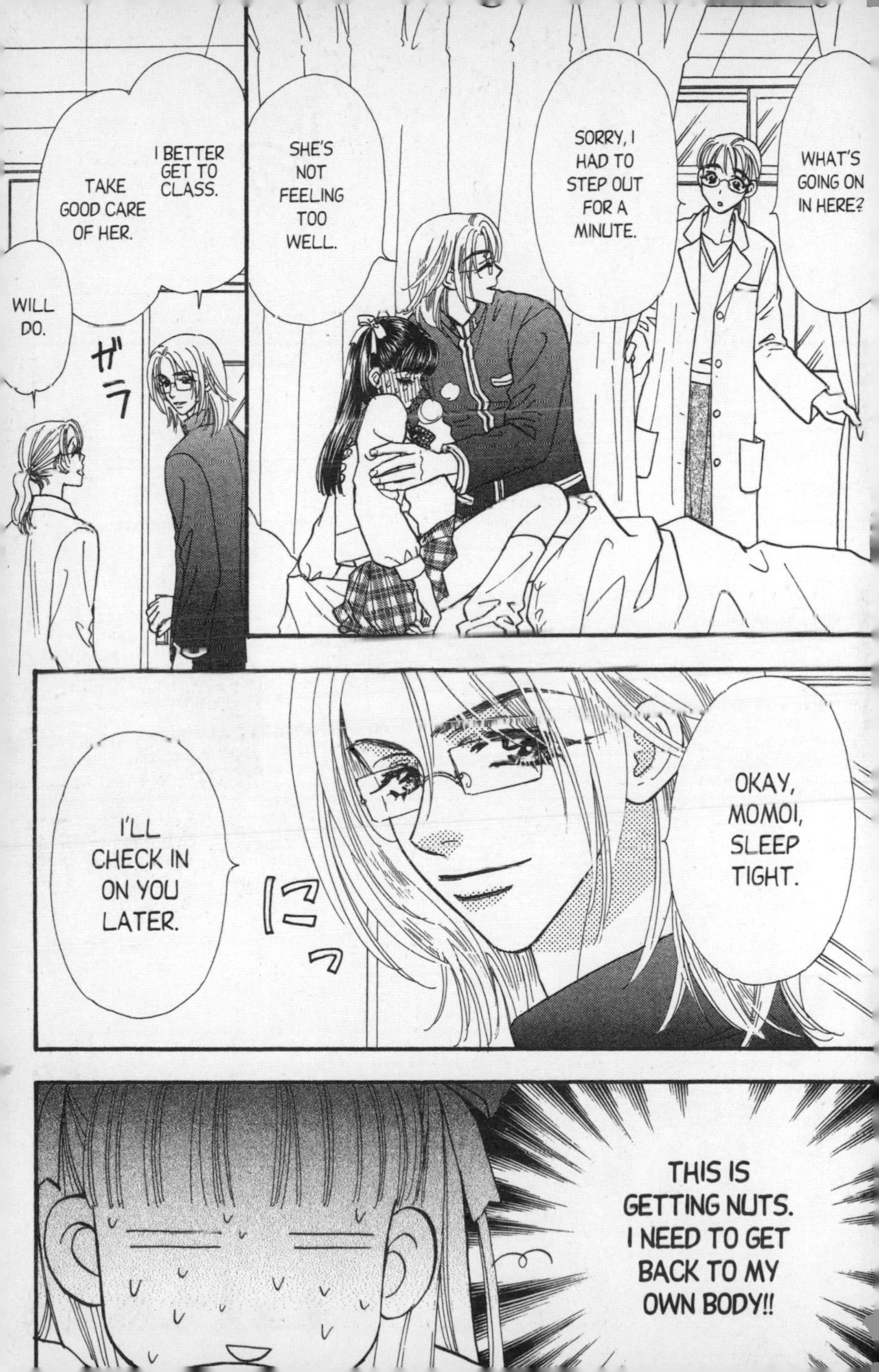
WHAT'S GOING ON IN HERE?
SORRY, I HAD TO STEP OUT FOR A MINUTE.
SHE'S NOT FEELING TOO WELL.
I BETTER GET TO CLASS.
TAKE GOOD CARE OF HER.
ガラ
WILL DO.
OKAY, MOMOI, SLEEP TIGHT.
にこっ
I'LL CHECK IN ON YOU LATER.
THIS IS GETTING NUTS. I NEED TO GET BACK TO MY OWN BODY!!

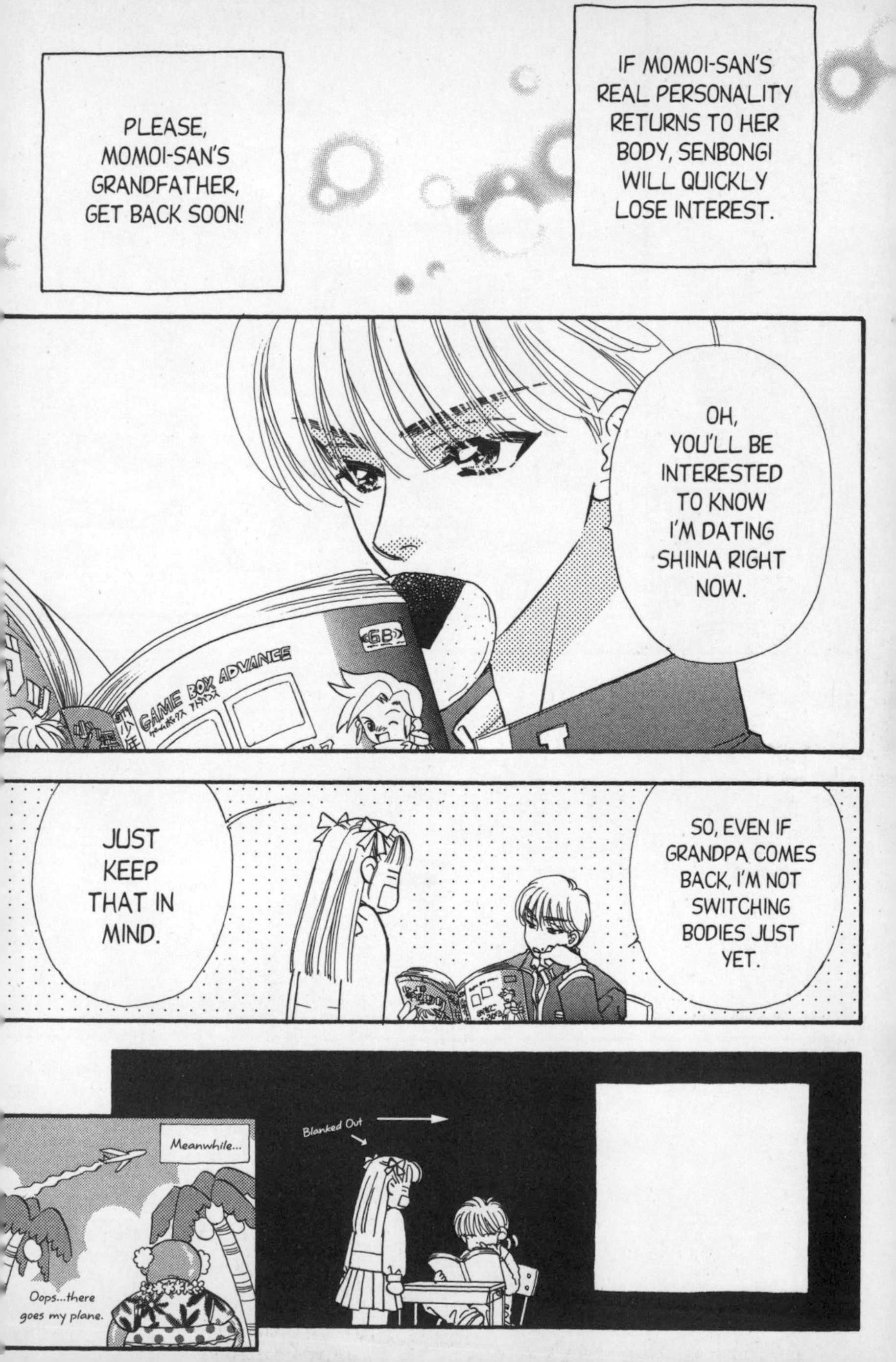
IF MOMOI-SAN'S REAL PERSONALITY RETURNS TO HER BODY, SENBONGI WILL QUICKLY LOSE INTEREST.
PLEASE, MOMOI-SAN'S GRANDFATHER, GET BACK SOON!
OH, YOU'LL BE INTERESTED TO KNOW I'M DATING SHIINA RIGHT NOW.
GB
GAME BOX ADVANCE
SO, EVEN IF GRANDPA COMES BACK, I'M NOT SWITCHING BODIES JUST YET.
JUST KEEP THAT IN MIND.
Blanked Out
Meanwhile...
Oops...there goes my plane.

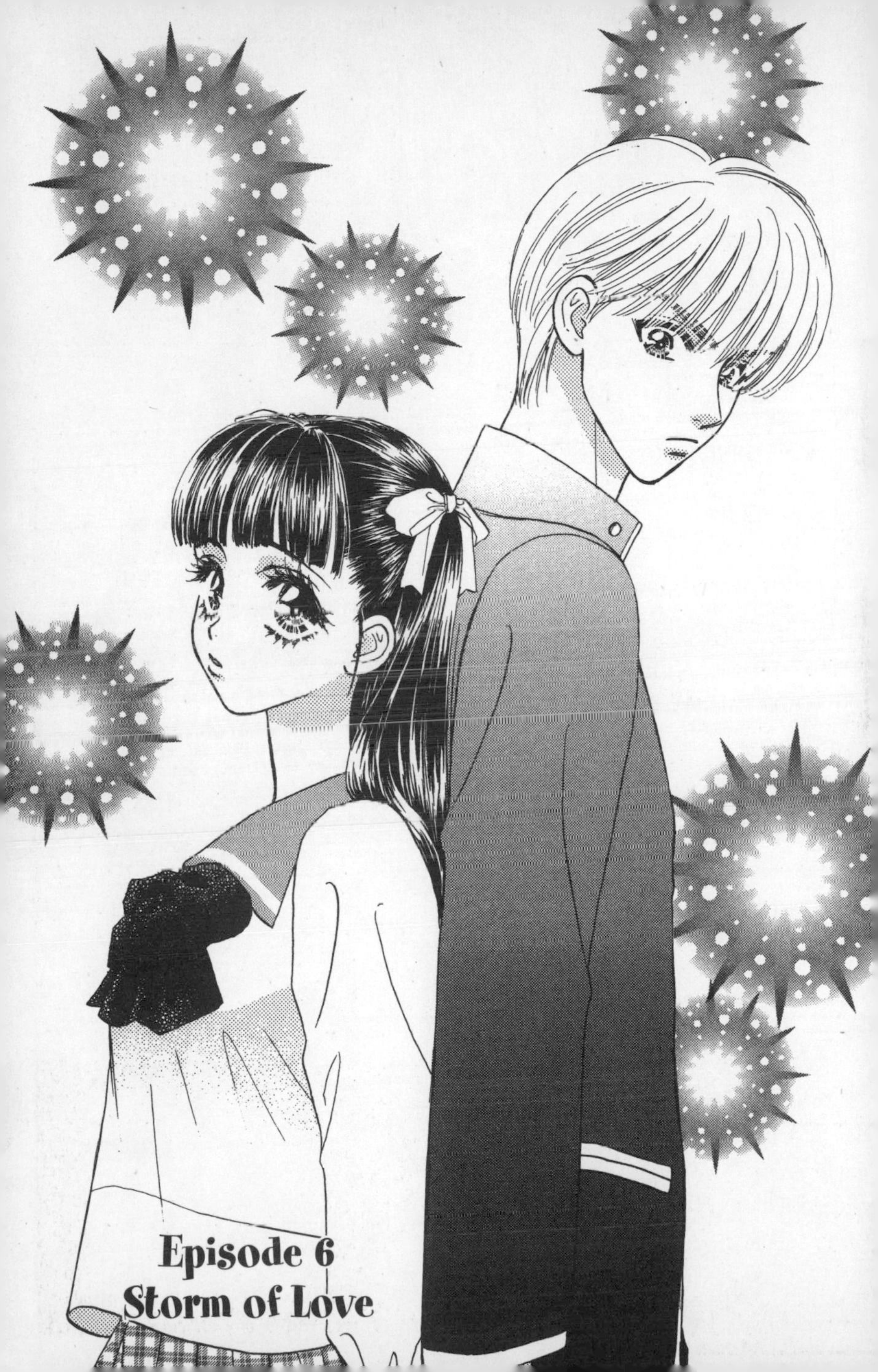
Episode 6
Storm of Love

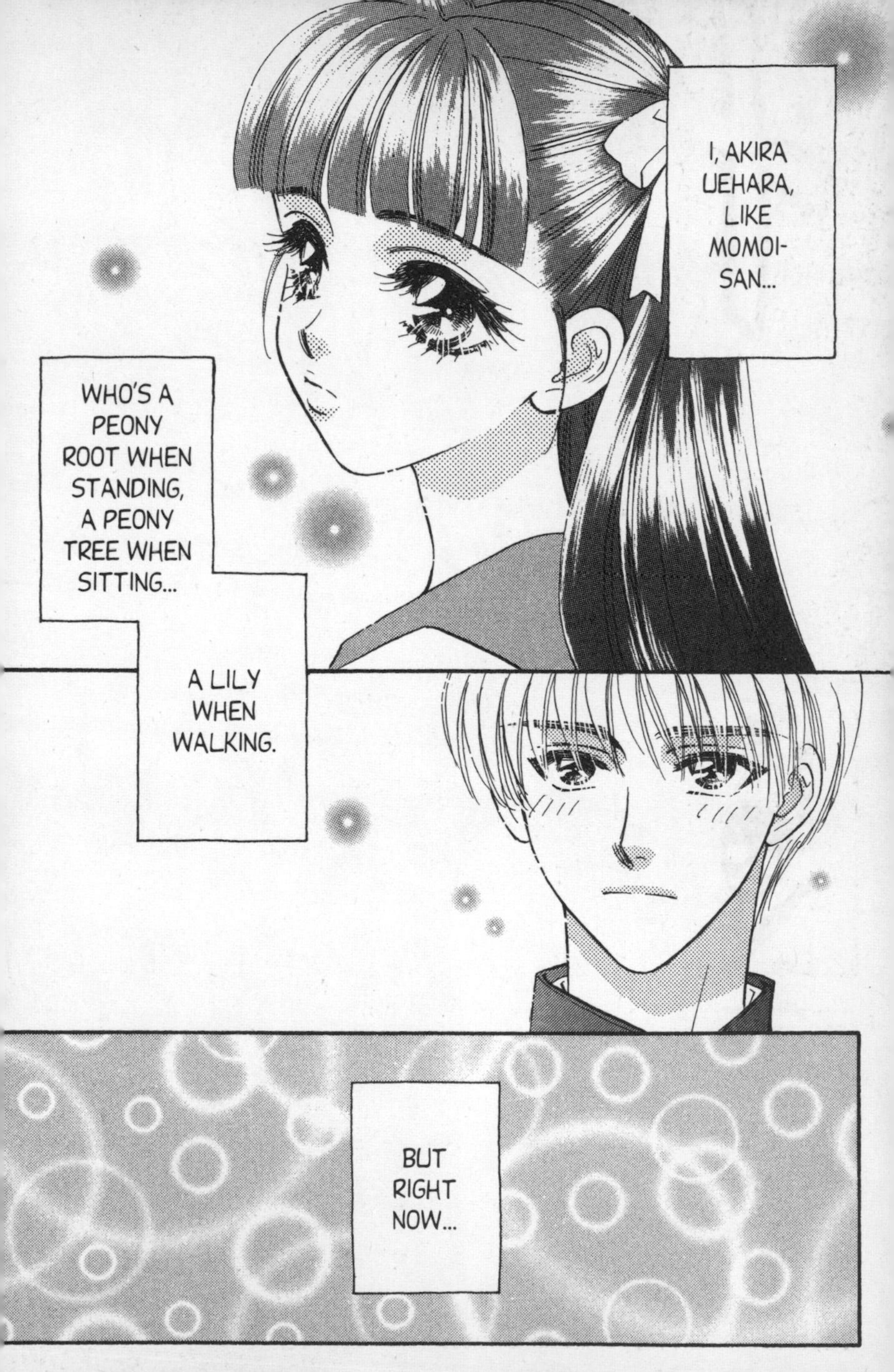
I, AKIRA UEHARA, LIKE MOMOI-SAN...
WHO'S A PEONY ROOT WHEN STANDING, A PEONY TREE WHEN SITTING...
A LILY WHEN WALKING.
BUT RIGHT NOW...

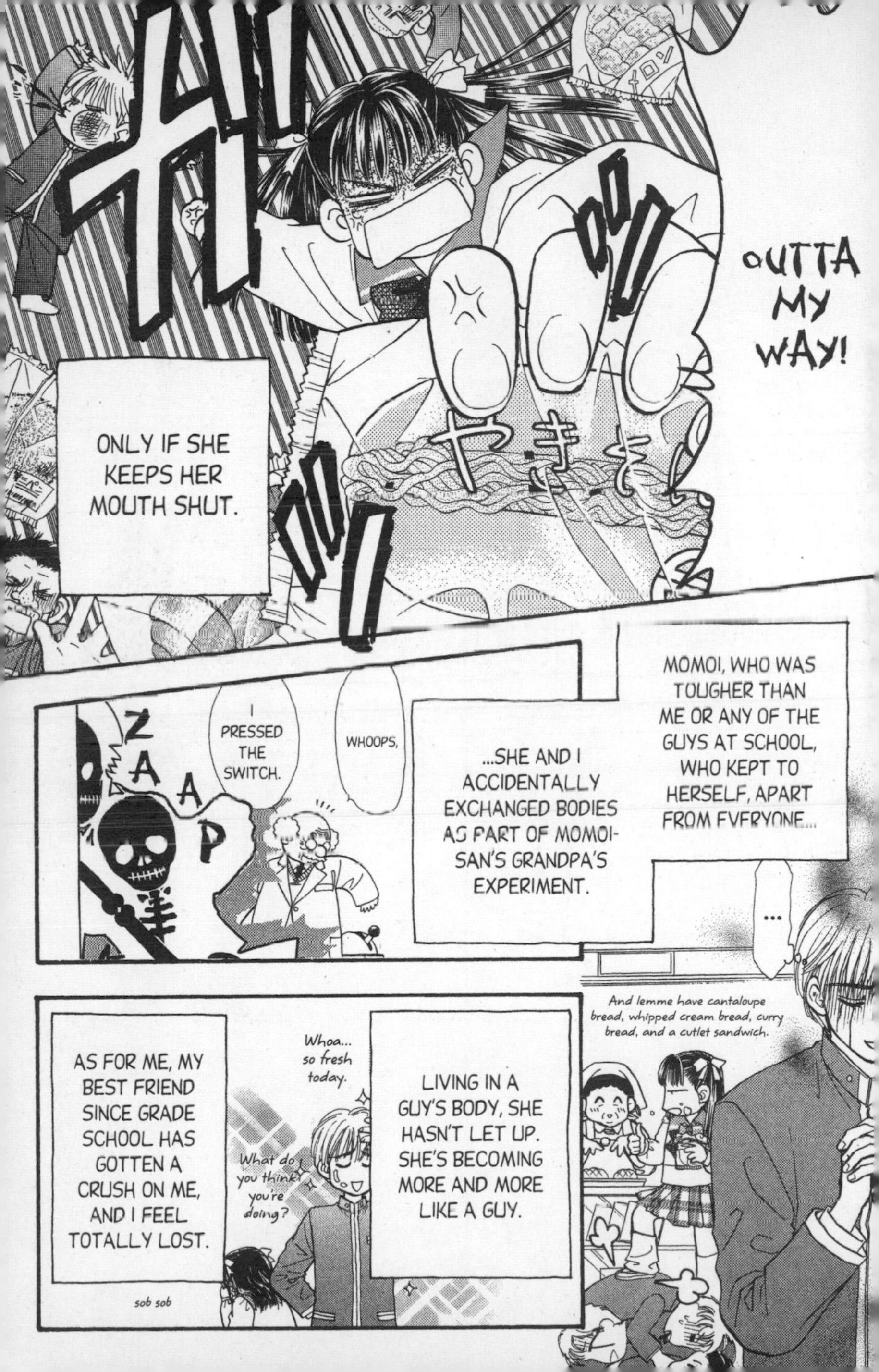
OUTTA MY WAY!
ONLY IF SHE KEEPS HER MOUTH SHUT.
MOMOI, WHO WAS TOUGHER THAN ME OR ANY OF THE GUYS AT SCHOOL, WHO KEPT TO HERSELF, APART FROM EVERYONE...
...
...SHE AND I ACCIDENTALLY EXCHANGED BODIES AS PART OF MOMOI-SAN'S GRANDPA'S EXPERIMENT.
WHOOPS,
I PRESSED THE SWITCH.
ZAAP
And lemme have cantaloupe bread, whipped cream bread, curry bread, and a cutlet sandwich.
LIVING IN A GUY'S BODY, SHE HASN'T LET UP. SHE'S BECOMING MORE AND MORE LIKE A GUY.
Whoa... so fresh today.
What do you think you're doing?
AS FOR ME, MY BEST FRIEND SINCE GRADE SCHOOL HAS GOTTEN A CRUSH ON ME, AND I FEEL TOTALLY LOST.
sob sob

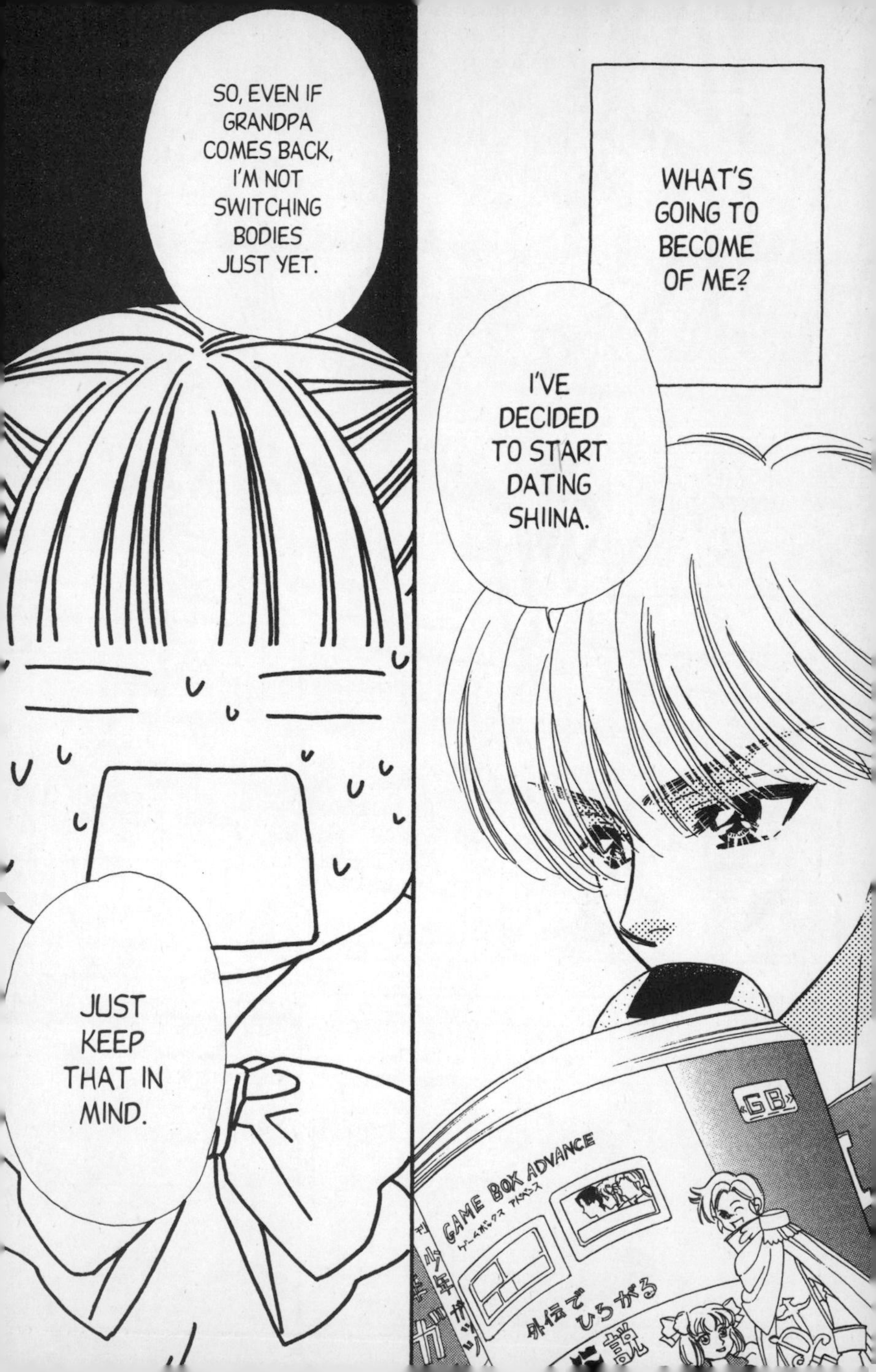
WHAT'S GOING TO BECOME OF ME?
I'VE DECIDED TO START DATING SHIINA.
«GB»
GAME BOX ADVANCE
ゲームボックス アドバンス
外伝で ひろがる
SO, EVEN IF GRANDPA COMES BACK, I'M NOT SWITCHING BODIES JUST YET.
JUST KEEP THAT IN MIND.

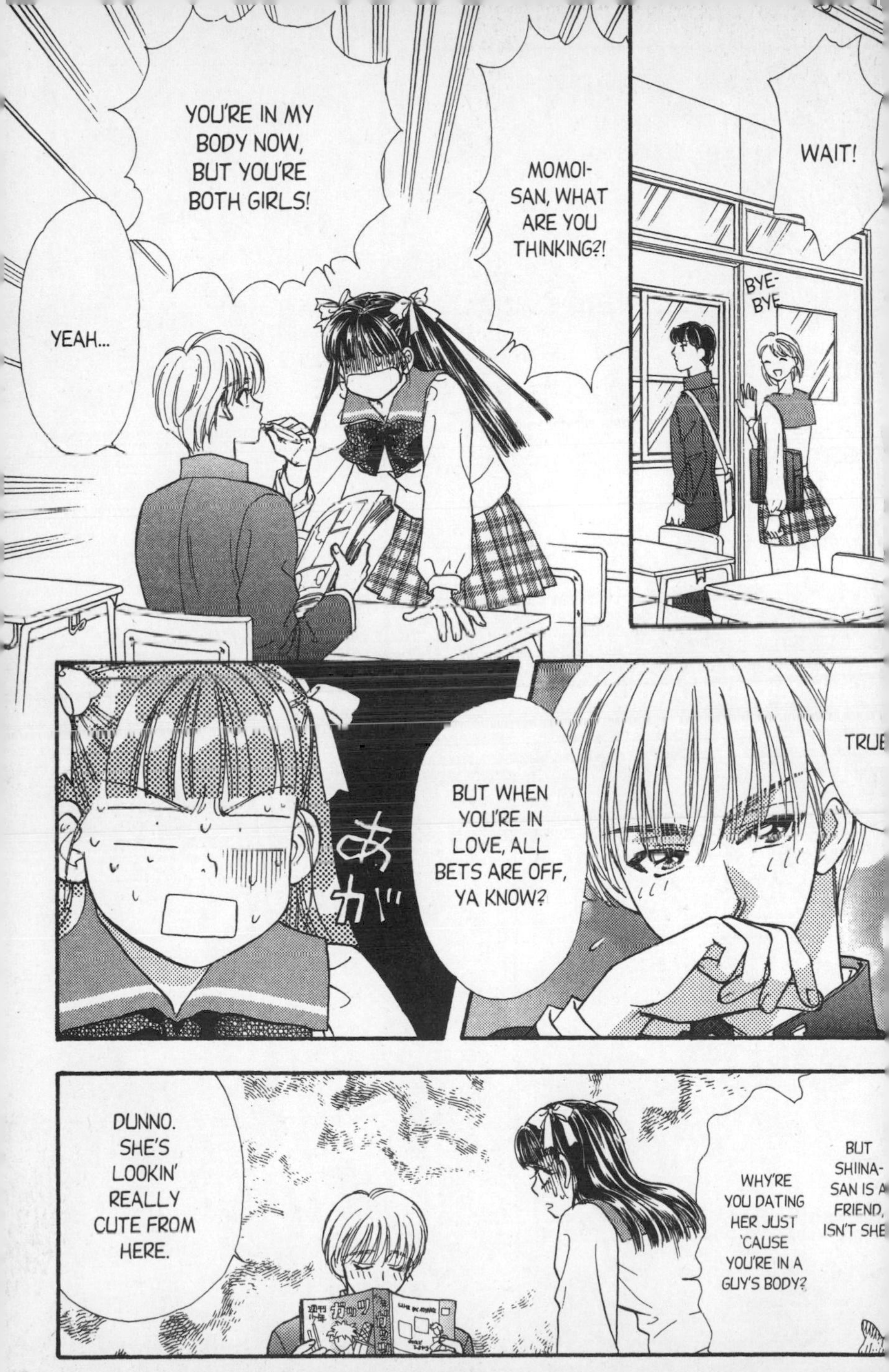
WAIT!
BYE-BYE
MOMOI-SAN, WHAT ARE YOU THINKING?!
YOU'RE IN MY BODY NOW, BUT YOU'RE BOTH GIRLS!
YEAH...
TRUE
BUT WHEN YOU'RE IN LOVE, ALL BETS ARE OFF, YA KNOW?
あガ
BUT SHIINA-SAN IS A FRIEND, ISN'T SHE
WHY'RE YOU DATING HER JUST 'CAUSE YOU'RE IN A GUY'S BODY?
DUNNO. SHE'S LOOKIN' REALLY CUTE FROM HERE.

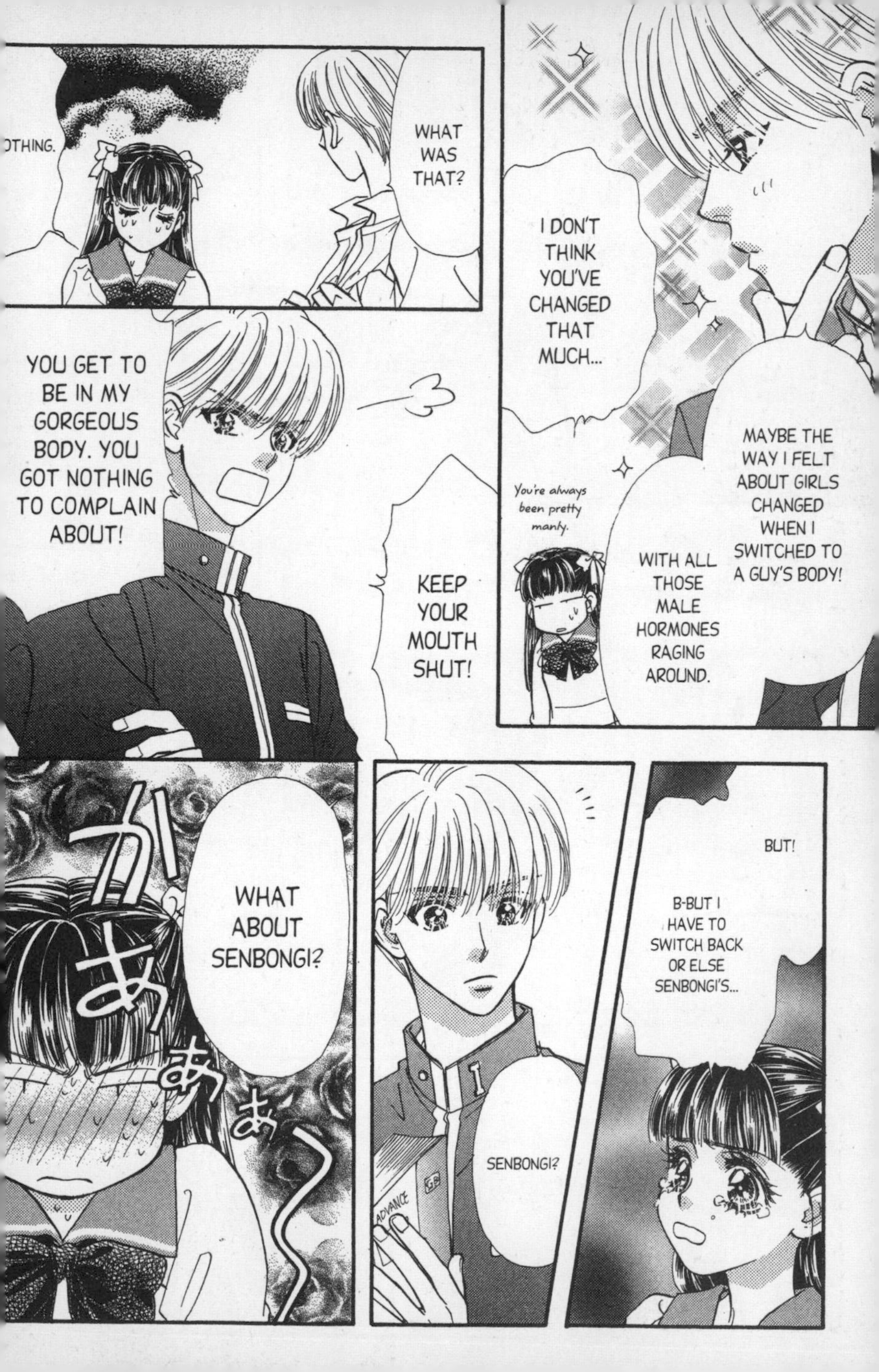

I DON'T THINK YOU'VE CHANGED THAT MUCH...
MAYBE THE WAY I FELT ABOUT GIRLS CHANGED WHEN I SWITCHED TO A GUY'S BODY!
WITH ALL THOSE MALE HORMONES RAGING AROUND.
You're always been pretty manly.
WHAT WAS THAT?
OTHING.
YOU GET TO BE IN MY GORGEOUS BODY. YOU GOT NOTHING TO COMPLAIN ABOUT!
KEEP YOUR MOUTH SHUT!
BUT!
B-BUT I HAVE TO SWITCH BACK OR ELSE SENBONGI'S...
SENBONGI?
WHAT ABOUT SENBONGI?

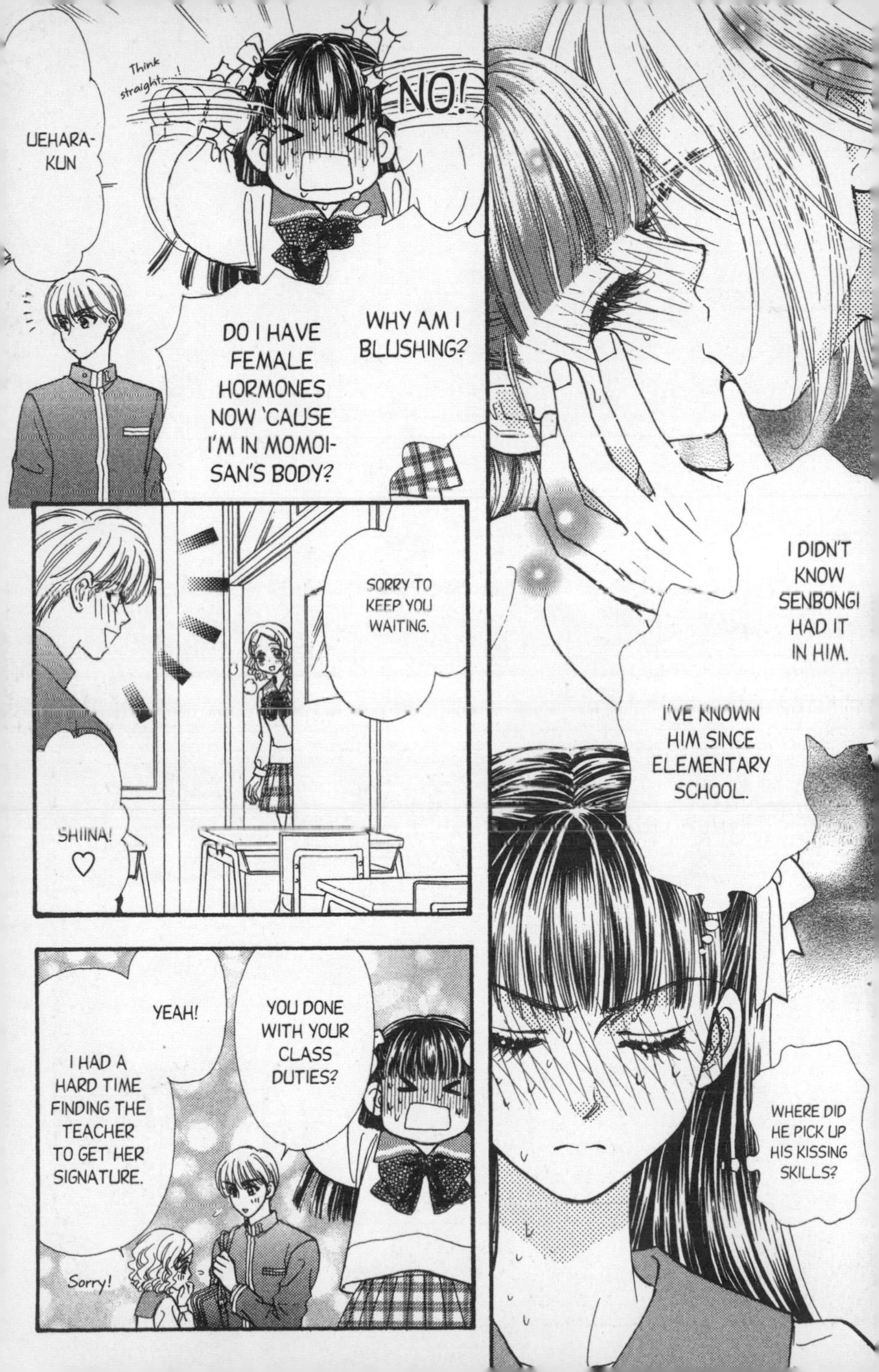
I DIDN'T KNOW SENBONGI HAD IT IN HIM.
I'VE KNOWN HIM SINCE ELEMENTARY SCHOOL.
WHERE DID HE PICK UP HIS KISSING SKILLS?
NO!
Think straight...!
WHY AM I BLUSHING?
DO I HAVE FEMALE HORMONES NOW 'CAUSE I'M IN MOMOI-SAN'S BODY?
UEHARA-KUN
SORRY TO KEEP YOU WAITING.
SHIINA! ♡
YOU DONE WITH YOUR CLASS DUTIES?
YEAH!
I HAD A HARD TIME FINDING THE TEACHER TO GET HER SIGNATURE.
Sorry!

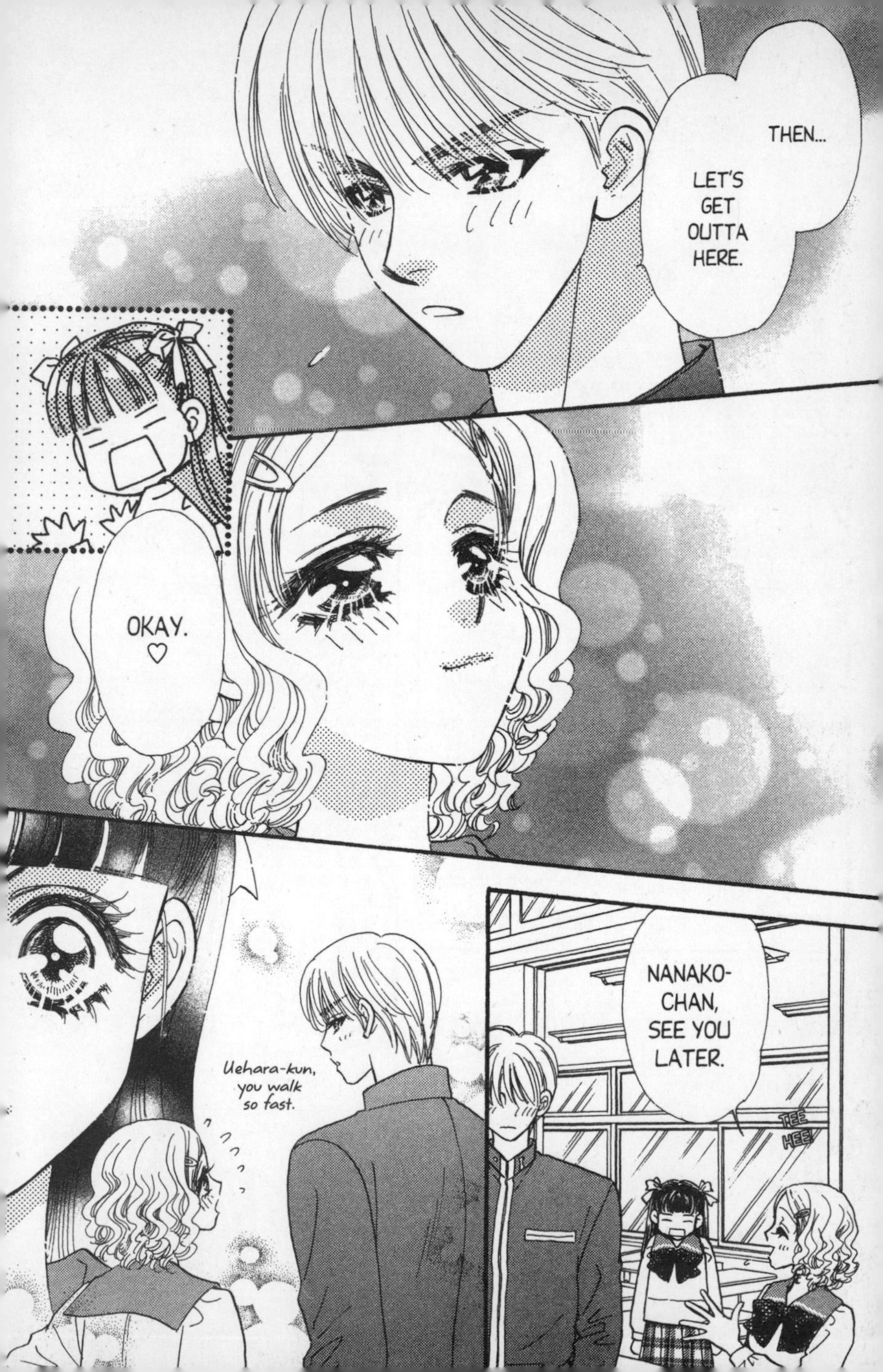
THEN...
LET'S GET OUTTA HERE.
OKAY. ♡
NANAKO-CHAN, SEE YOU LATER.
TEE HEE!
Uehara-kun, you walk so fast.

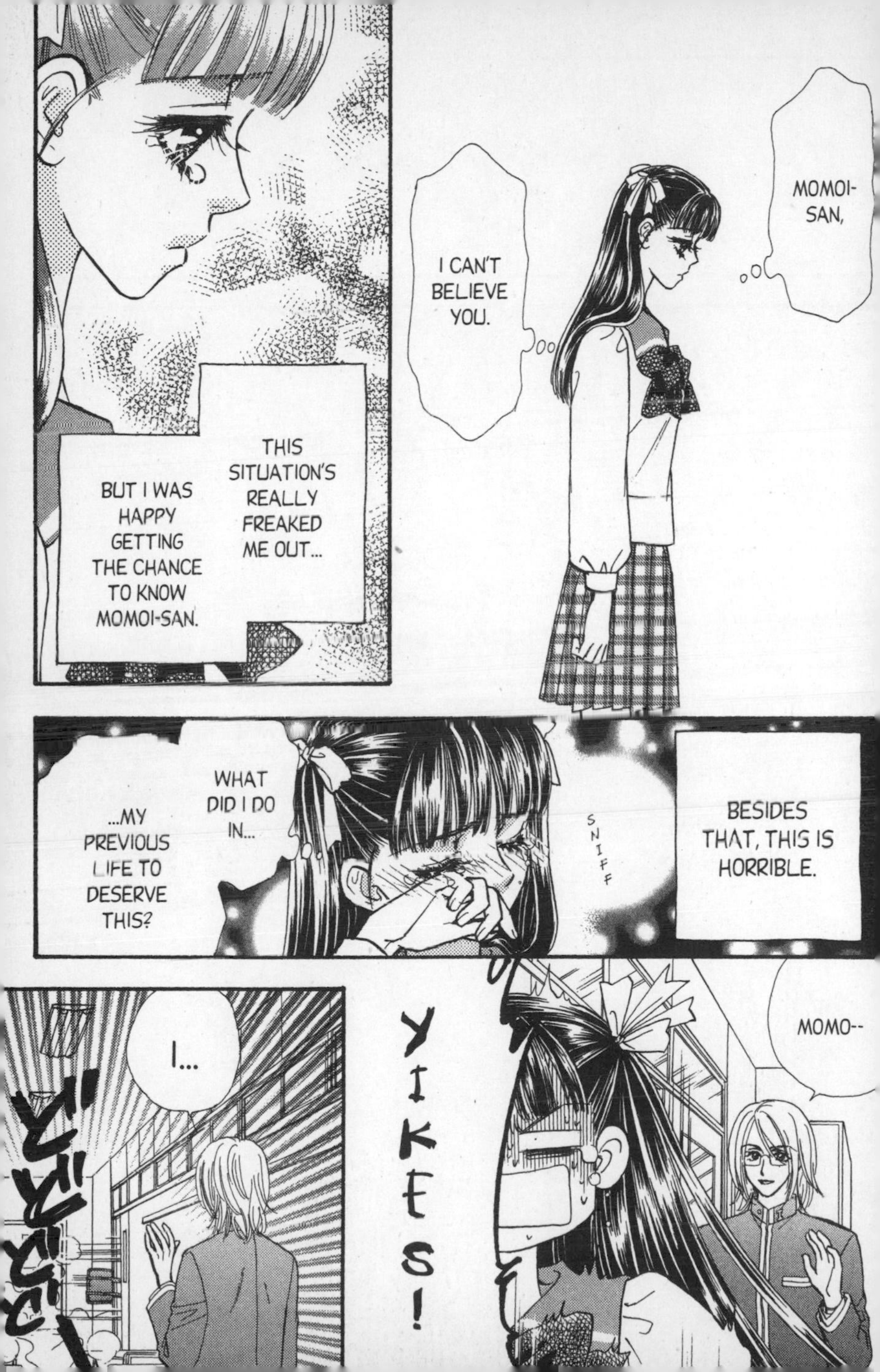
MOMOI-SAN,
I CAN'T BELIEVE YOU.
THIS SITUATION'S REALLY FREAKED ME OUT...
BUT I WAS HAPPY GETTING THE CHANCE TO KNOW MOMOI-SAN.
BESIDES THAT, THIS IS HORRIBLE.
SNIFF
WHAT DID I DO IN...
...MY PREVIOUS LIFE TO DESERVE THIS?
MOMO--
YIKES!
I...

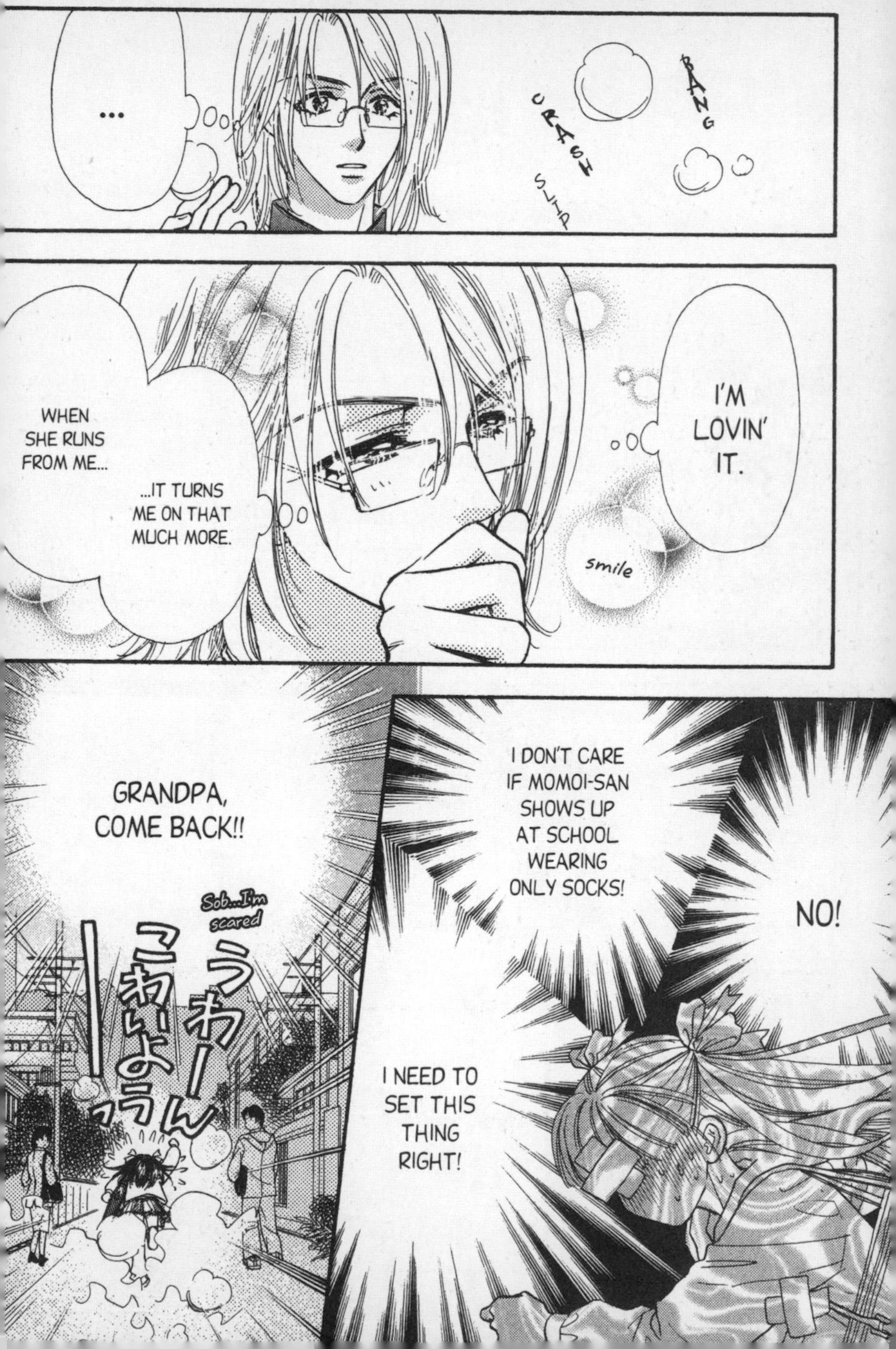
...
BANG
CRASH
SLIP
I'M LOVIN' IT.
smile
WHEN SHE RUNS FROM ME...
...IT TURNS ME ON THAT MUCH MORE.
I DON'T CARE IF MOMOI-SAN SHOWS UP AT SCHOOL WEARING ONLY SOCKS!
NO!
I NEED TO SET THIS THING RIGHT!
GRANDPA, COME BACK!!
Sob...I'm scared
うわーん
こわいよう

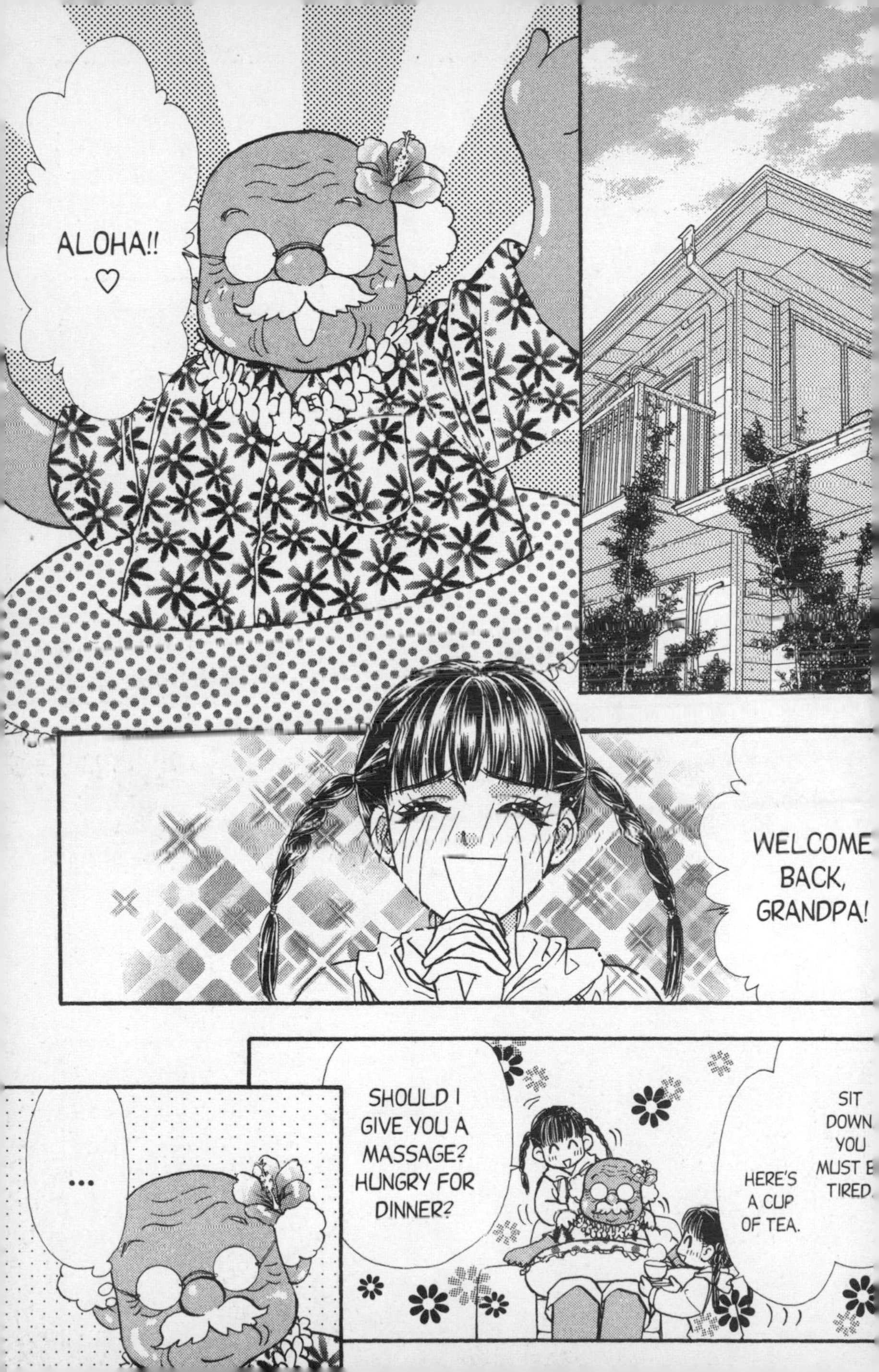
ALOHA!! ♡
WELCOME BACK, GRANDPA!
SIT DOWN YOU MUST B TIRED.
HERE'S A CUP OF TEA.
SHOULD I GIVE YOU A MASSAGE? HUNGRY FOR DINNER?
...

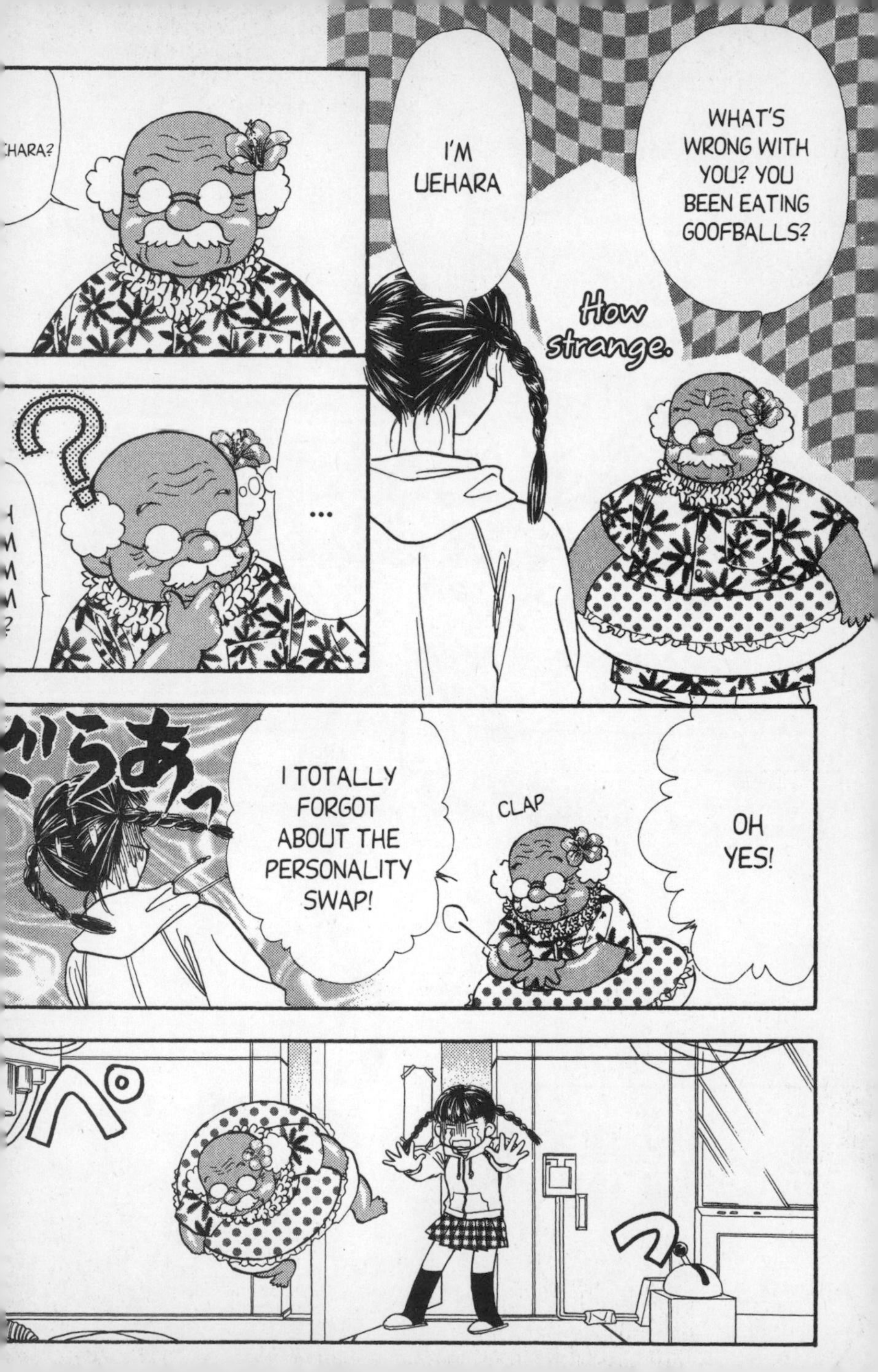
WHAT'S WRONG WITH YOU? YOU BEEN EATING GOOFBALLS?
I'M UEHARA
How strange.
HARA?
...
HMMMM?
OH YES!
CLAP
I TOTALLY FORGOT ABOUT THE PERSONALITY SWAP!
からあっ
ぺ
へ

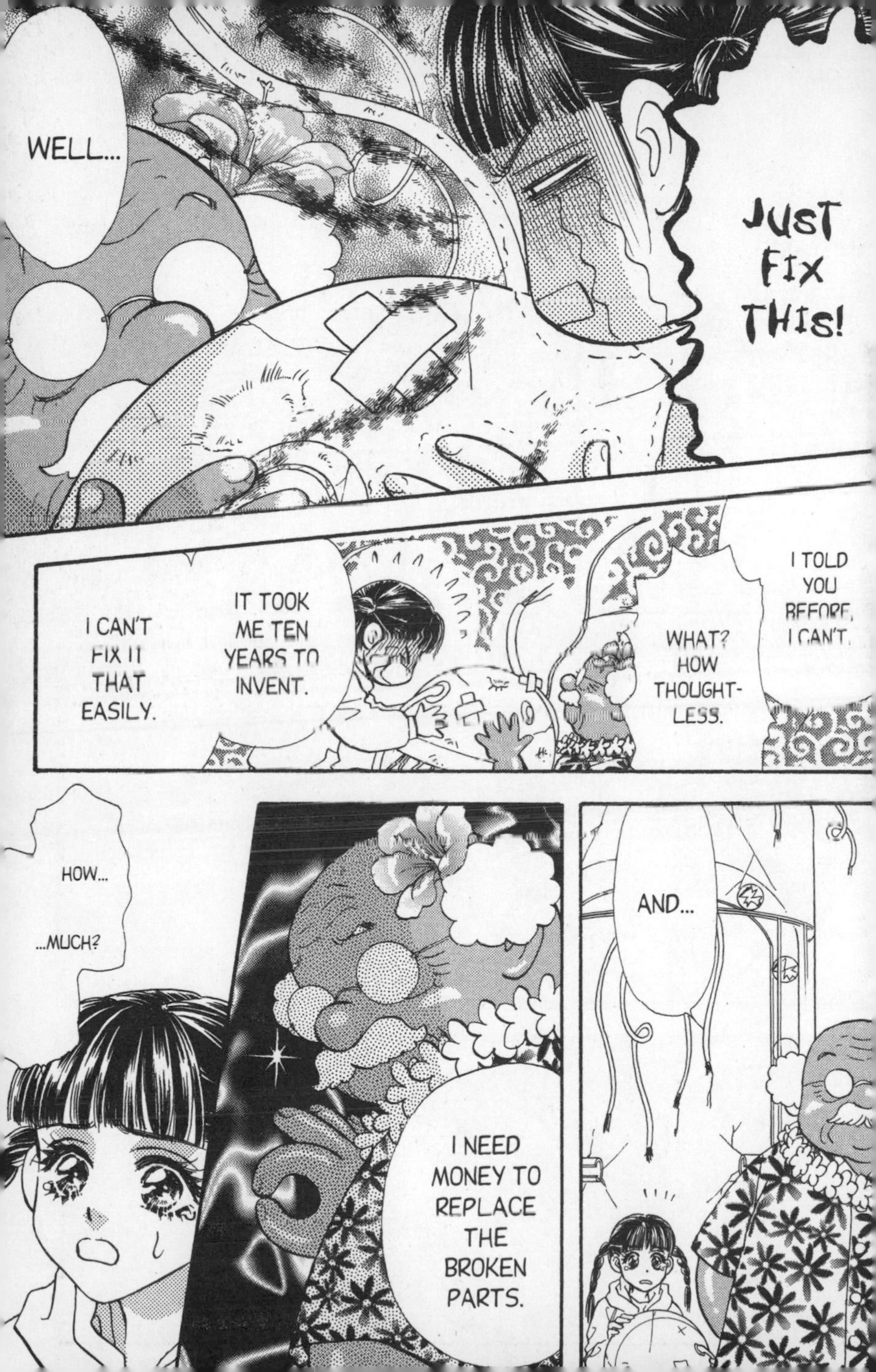
JUST FIX THIS!
WELL...
I TOLD YOU BEFORE, I CAN'T.
WHAT? HOW THOUGHTLESS.
I CAN'T FIX IT THAT EASILY. IT TOOK ME TEN YEARS TO INVENT.
AND...
I NEED MONEY TO REPLACE THE BROKEN PARTS.
HOW...
...MUCH?

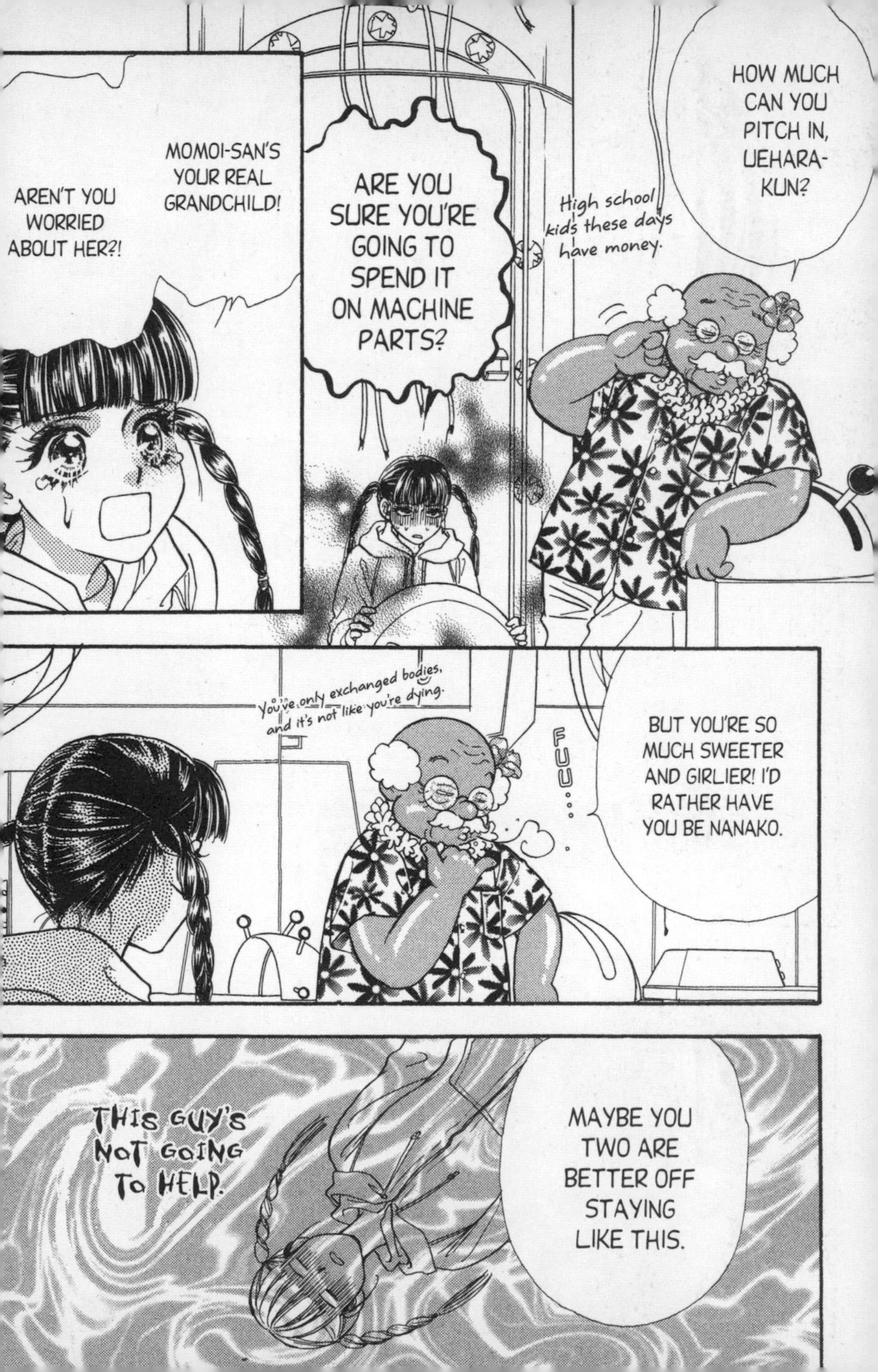
HOW MUCH CAN YOU PITCH IN, UEHARA-KUN?
High school kids these days have money.
ARE YOU SURE YOU'RE GOING TO SPEND IT ON MACHINE PARTS?
MOMOI-SAN'S YOUR REAL GRANDCHILD!
AREN'T YOU WORRIED ABOUT HER?!
BUT YOU'RE SO MUCH SWEETER AND GIRLIER! I'D RATHER HAVE YOU BE NANAKO.
FUU...
You've only exchanged bodies, and it's not like you're dying.
MAYBE YOU TWO ARE BETTER OFF STAYING LIKE THIS.
THIS GUY'S NOT GOING TO HELP.

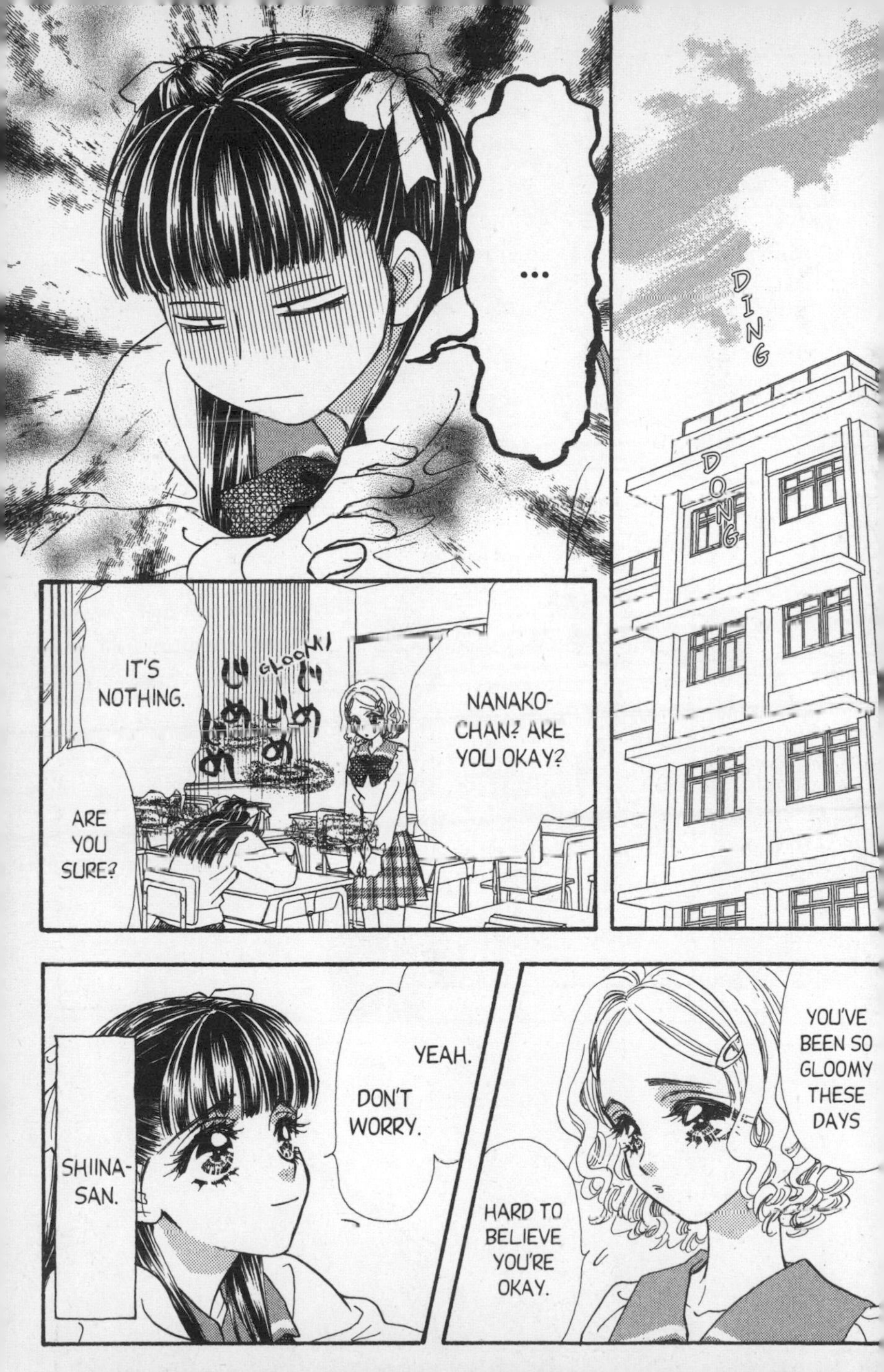
DING
DONG
...
NANAKO-CHAN? ARE YOU OKAY?
IT'S NOTHING.
GLOOM!
ARE YOU SURE?
YOU'VE BEEN SO GLOOMY THESE DAYS
HARD TO BELIEVE YOU'RE OKAY.
YEAH.
DON'T WORRY.
SHIINA-SAN.

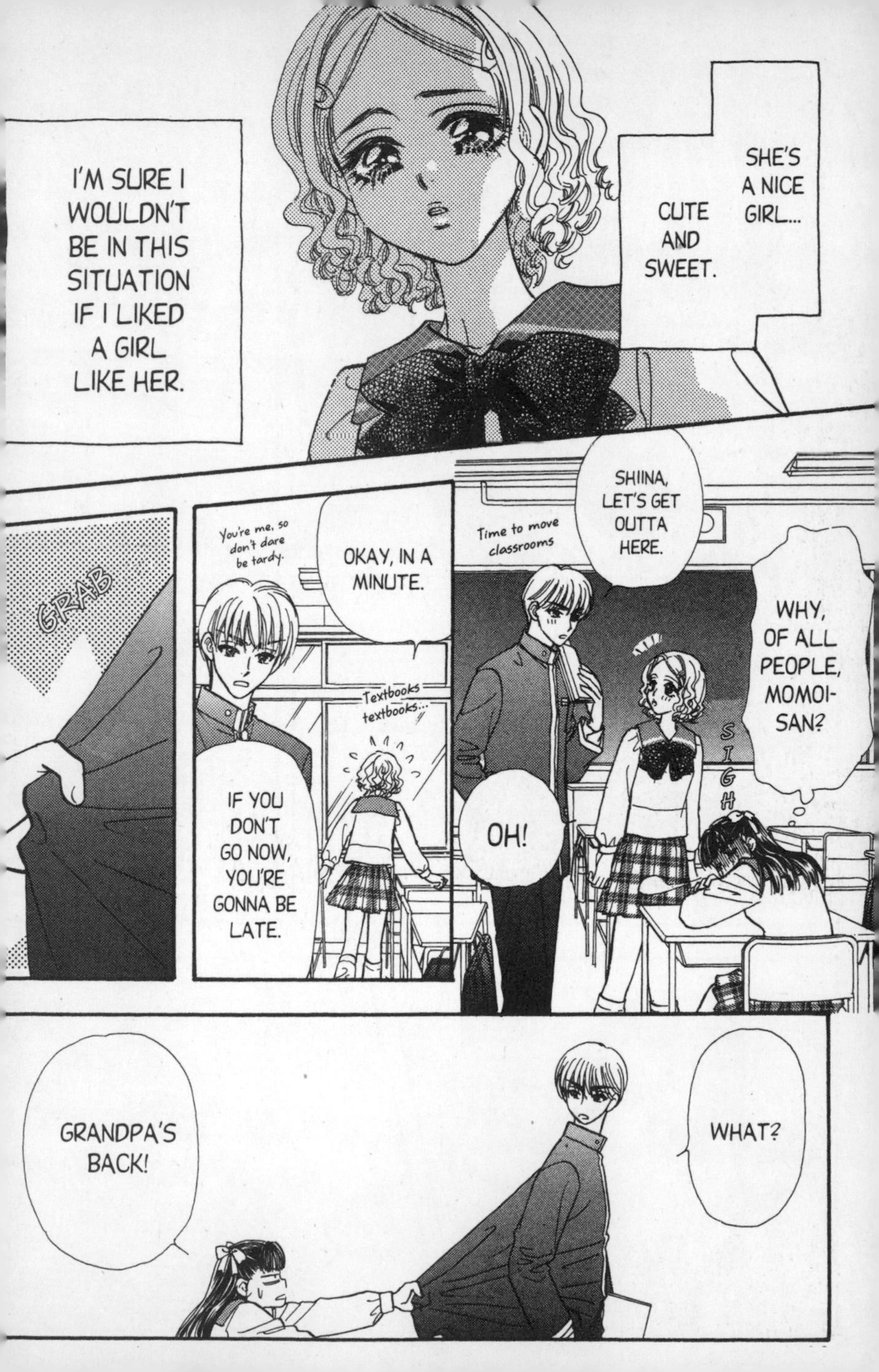
SHE'S A NICE GIRL...
CUTE AND SWEET.
I'M SURE I WOULDN'T BE IN THIS SITUATION IF I LIKED A GIRL LIKE HER.
SHIINA, LET'S GET OUTTA HERE.
Time to move classrooms
WHY, OF ALL PEOPLE, MOMOI-SAN?
SIGH
OH!
OKAY, IN A MINUTE.
You're me, so don't dare be tardy.
Textbooks textbooks...
IF YOU DON'T GO NOW, YOU'RE GONNA BE LATE.
GRAB
WHAT?
GRANDPA'S BACK!

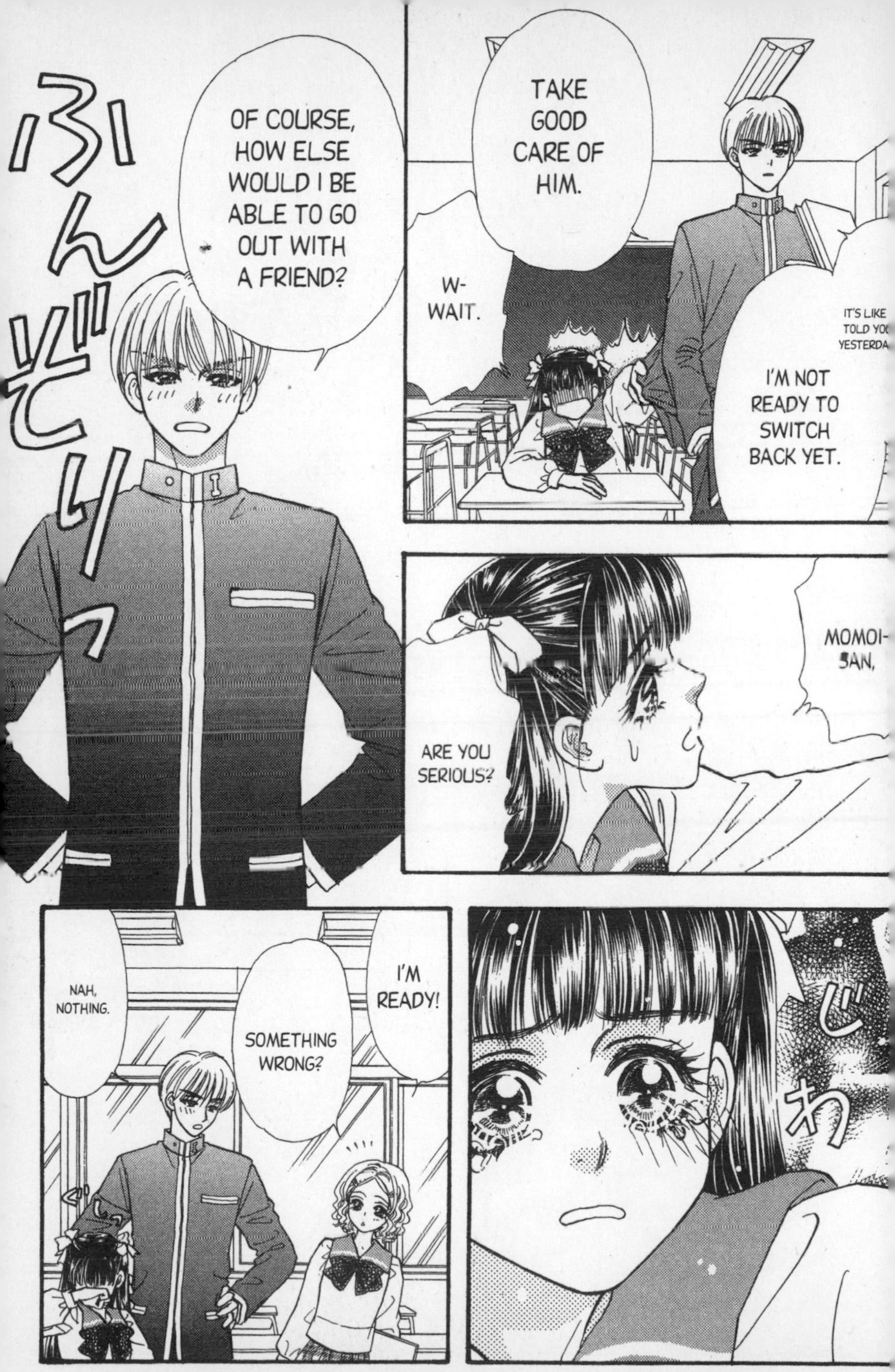

IT'S LIKE TOLD YOU YESTERDA
I'M NOT READY TO SWITCH BACK YET.
TAKE GOOD CARE OF HIM.
W-WAIT.
MOMOI-SAN,
ARE YOU SERIOUS?
OF COURSE, HOW ELSE WOULD I BE ABLE TO GO OUT WITH A FRIEND?
ふんぞりっ
じわ
I'M READY!
SOMETHING WRONG?
NAH, NOTHING.

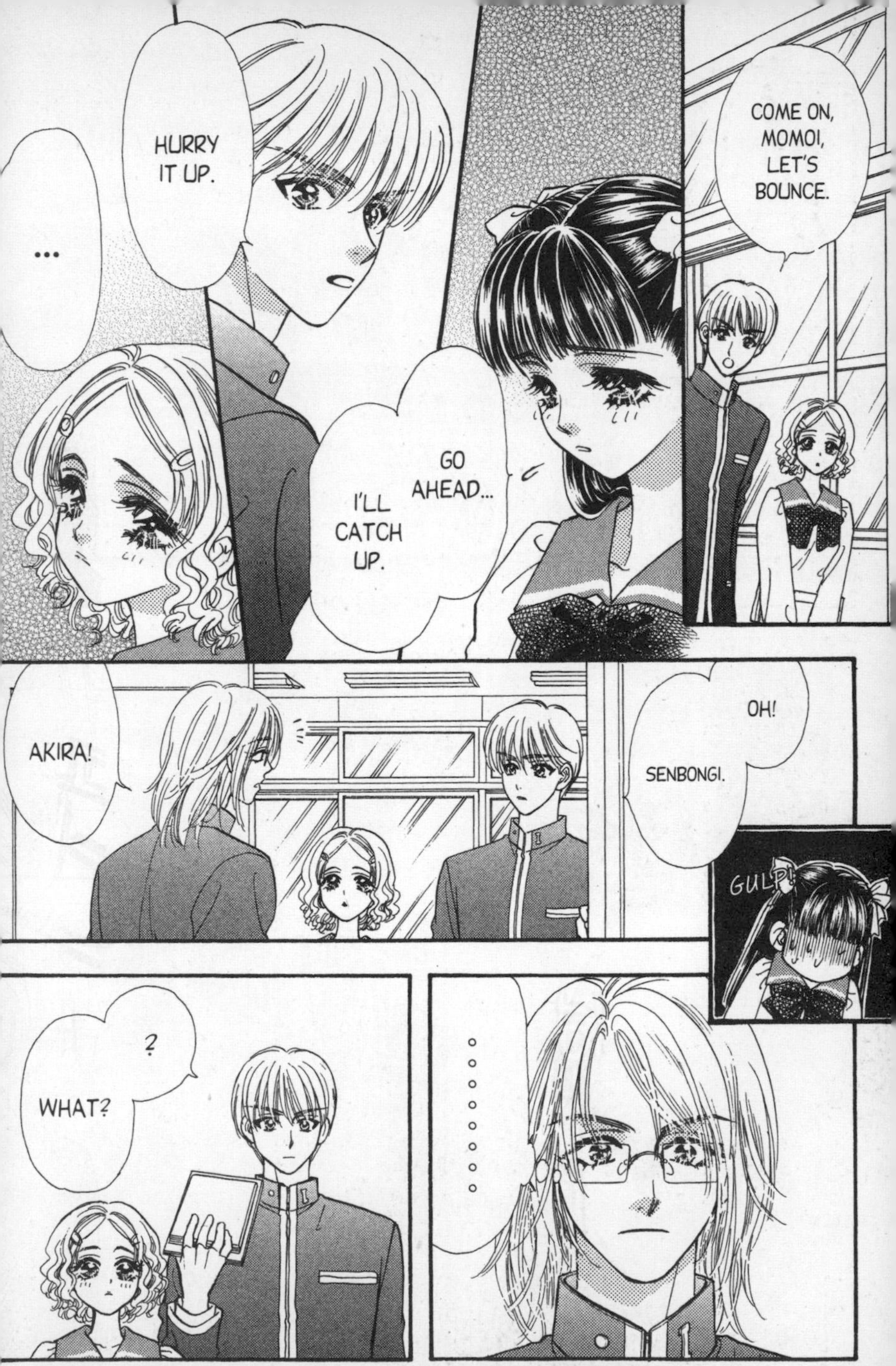
COME ON, MOMOI, LET'S BOUNCE.
GO AHEAD... I'LL CATCH UP.
HURRY IT UP.
...
OH! SENBONGI.
AKIRA!
GULP!
....
?
WHAT?

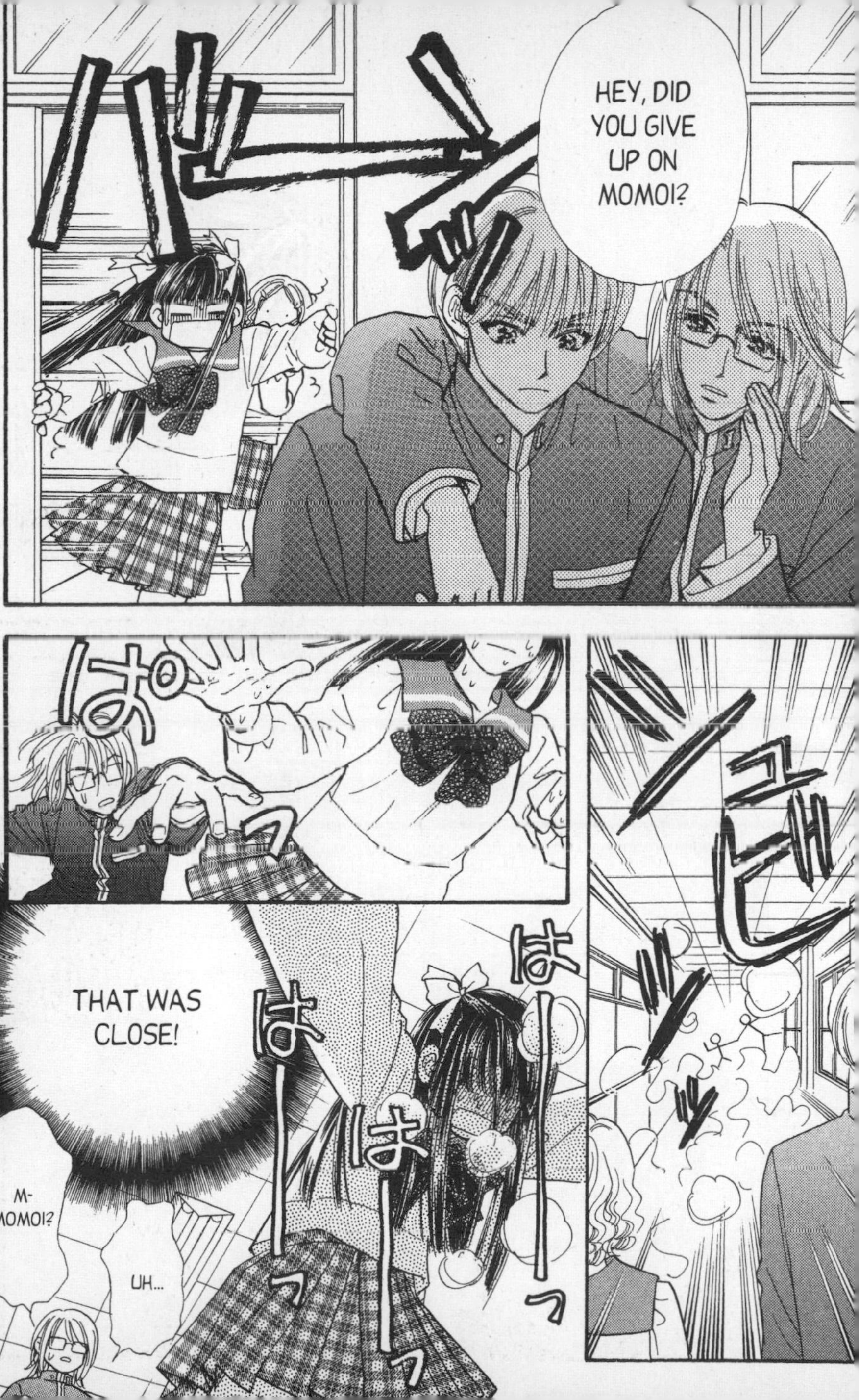
HEY, DID YOU GIVE UP ON MOMOI?
THAT WAS CLOSE!
M-MOMOI?
UH...

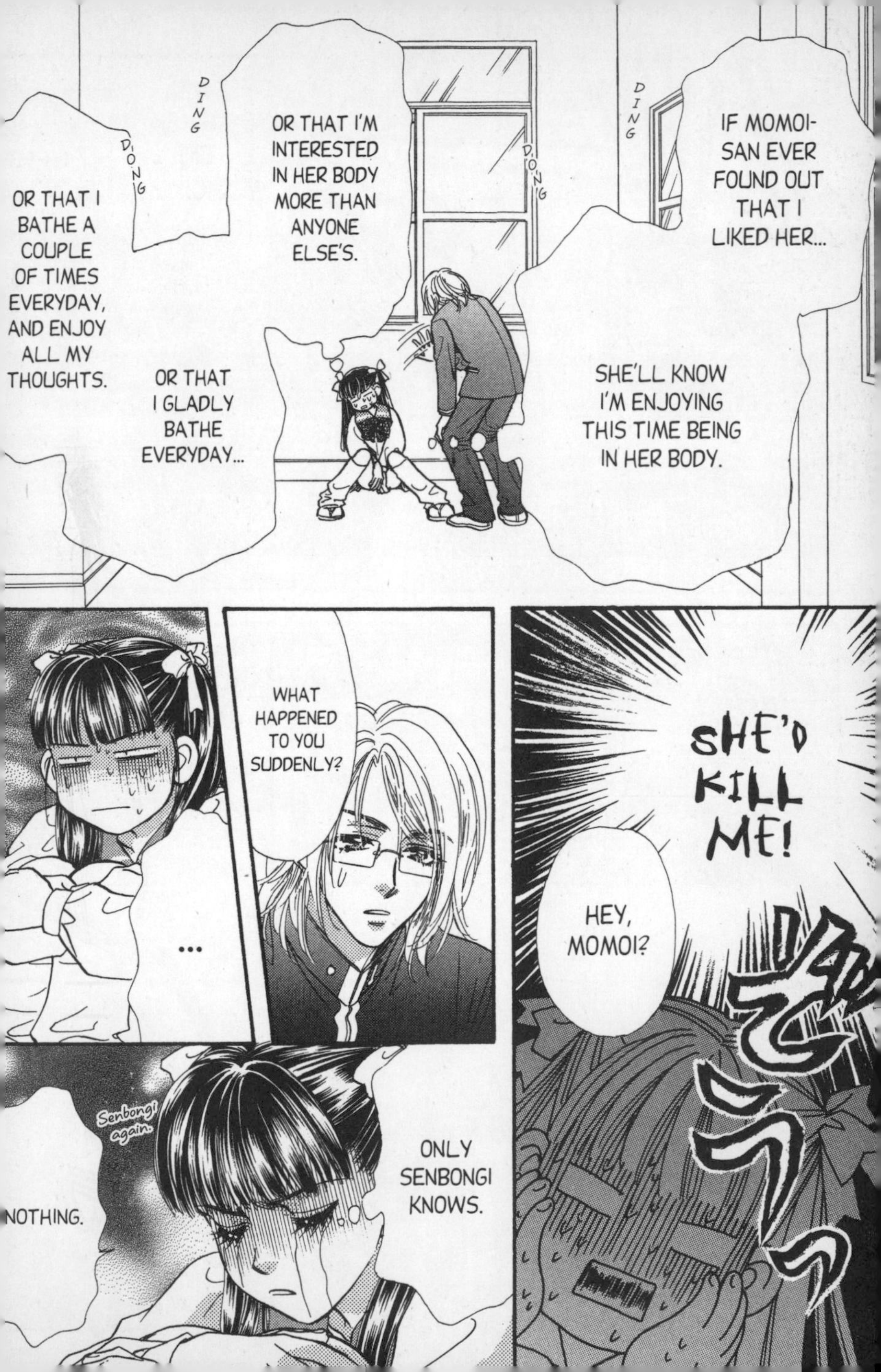
IF MOMOI-SAN EVER FOUND OUT THAT I LIKED HER...
DING
DONG
SHE'LL KNOW I'M ENJOYING THIS TIME BEING IN HER BODY.
OR THAT I'M INTERESTED IN HER BODY MORE THAN ANYONE ELSE'S.
DING
DONG
OR THAT I GLADLY BATHE EVERYDAY...
OR THAT I BATHE A COUPLE OF TIMES EVERYDAY, AND ENJOY ALL MY THOUGHTS.
SHE'D KILL ME!
HEY, MOMOI?
WHAT HAPPENED TO YOU SUDDENLY?
...
ONLY SENBONGI KNOWS.
Senbongi again.
NOTHING.

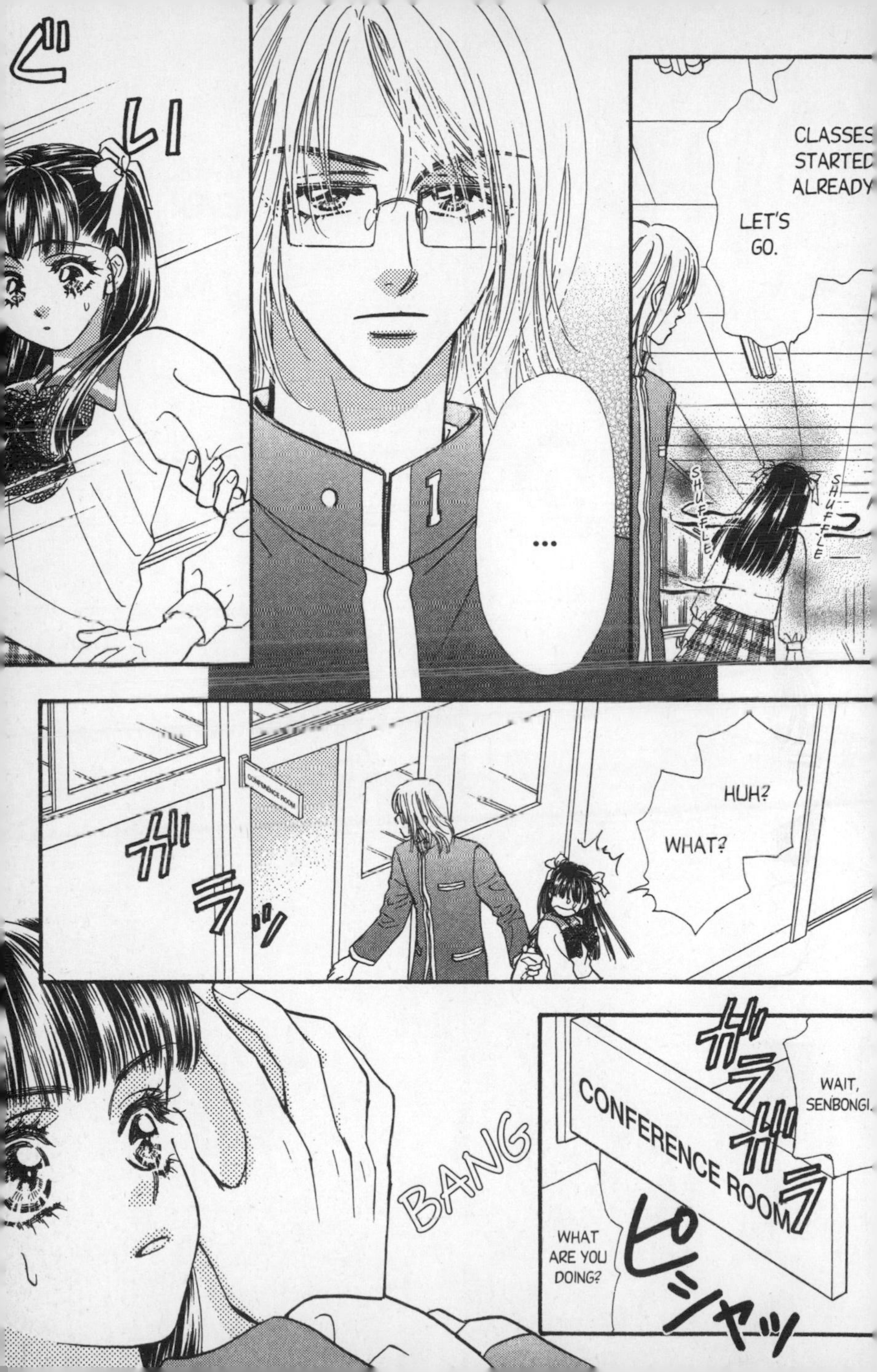

CLASSES STARTED ALREADY
LET'S GO.
SHUFFLE
SHUFFLE
...
ぐい
HUH?
WHAT?
CONFERENCE ROOM
ガラッ
ガラガラ
WAIT, SENBONGI.
CONFERENCE ROOM
WHAT ARE YOU DOING?
ピシャッ
BANG

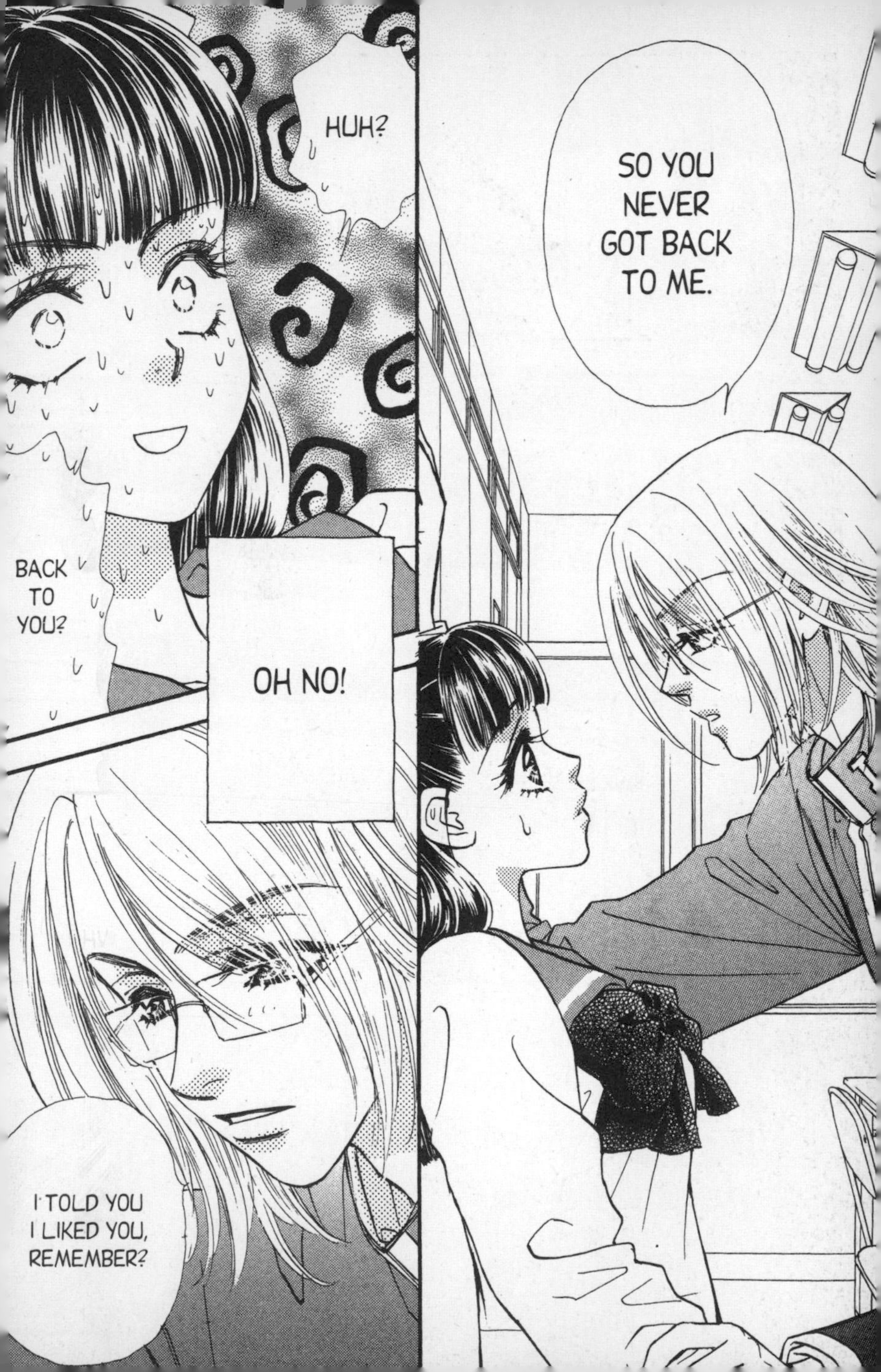
SO YOU NEVER GOT BACK TO ME.
HUH?
BACK TO YOU?
OH NO!
I TOLD YOU I LIKED YOU, REMEMBER?

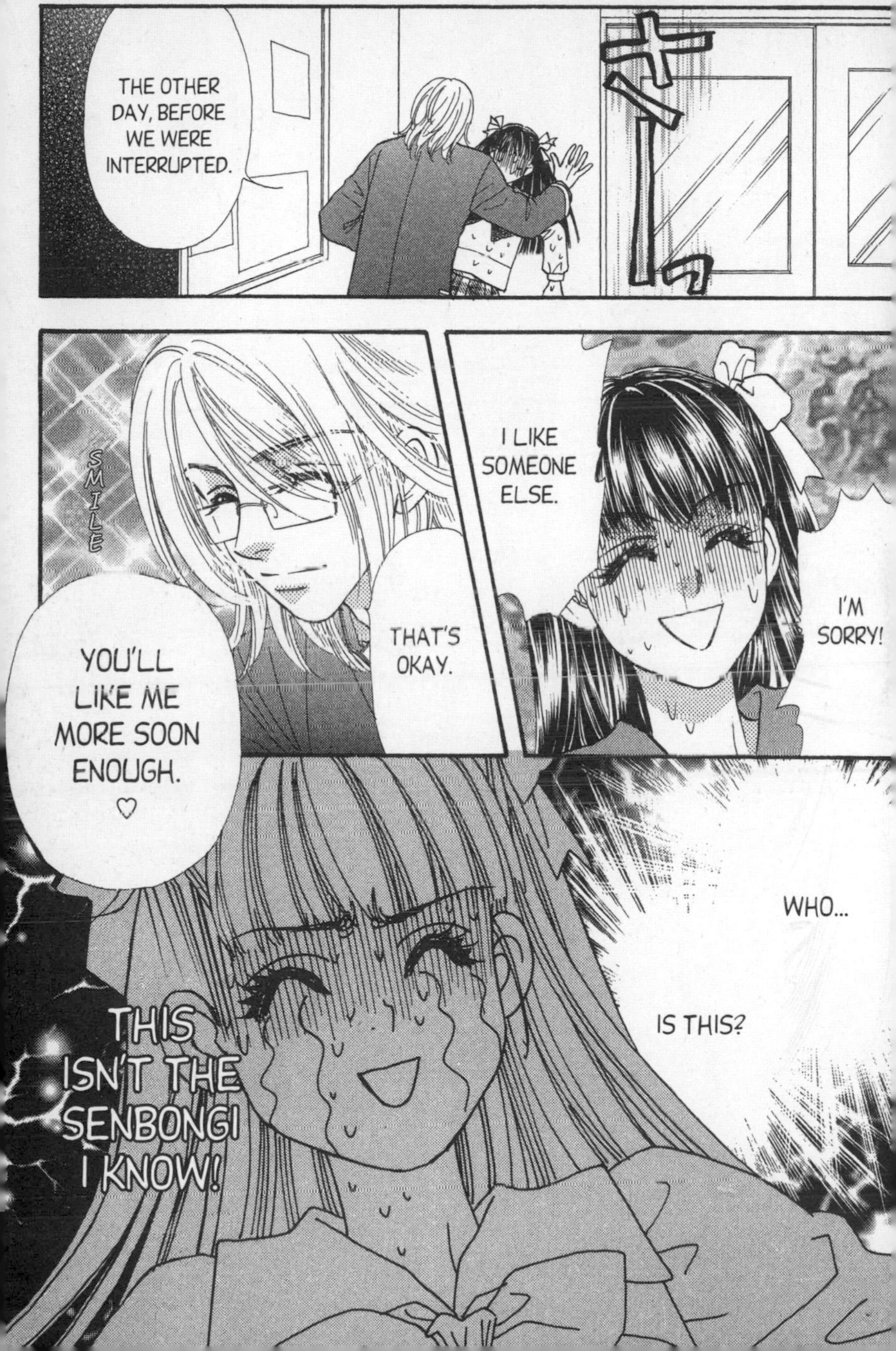
THE OTHER DAY, BEFORE WE WERE INTERRUPTED.
I LIKE SOMEONE ELSE.
I'M SORRY!
SMILE
THAT'S OKAY.
YOU'LL LIKE ME MORE SOON ENOUGH. ♡
WHO...
IS THIS?
THIS ISN'T THE SENBONGI I KNOW!

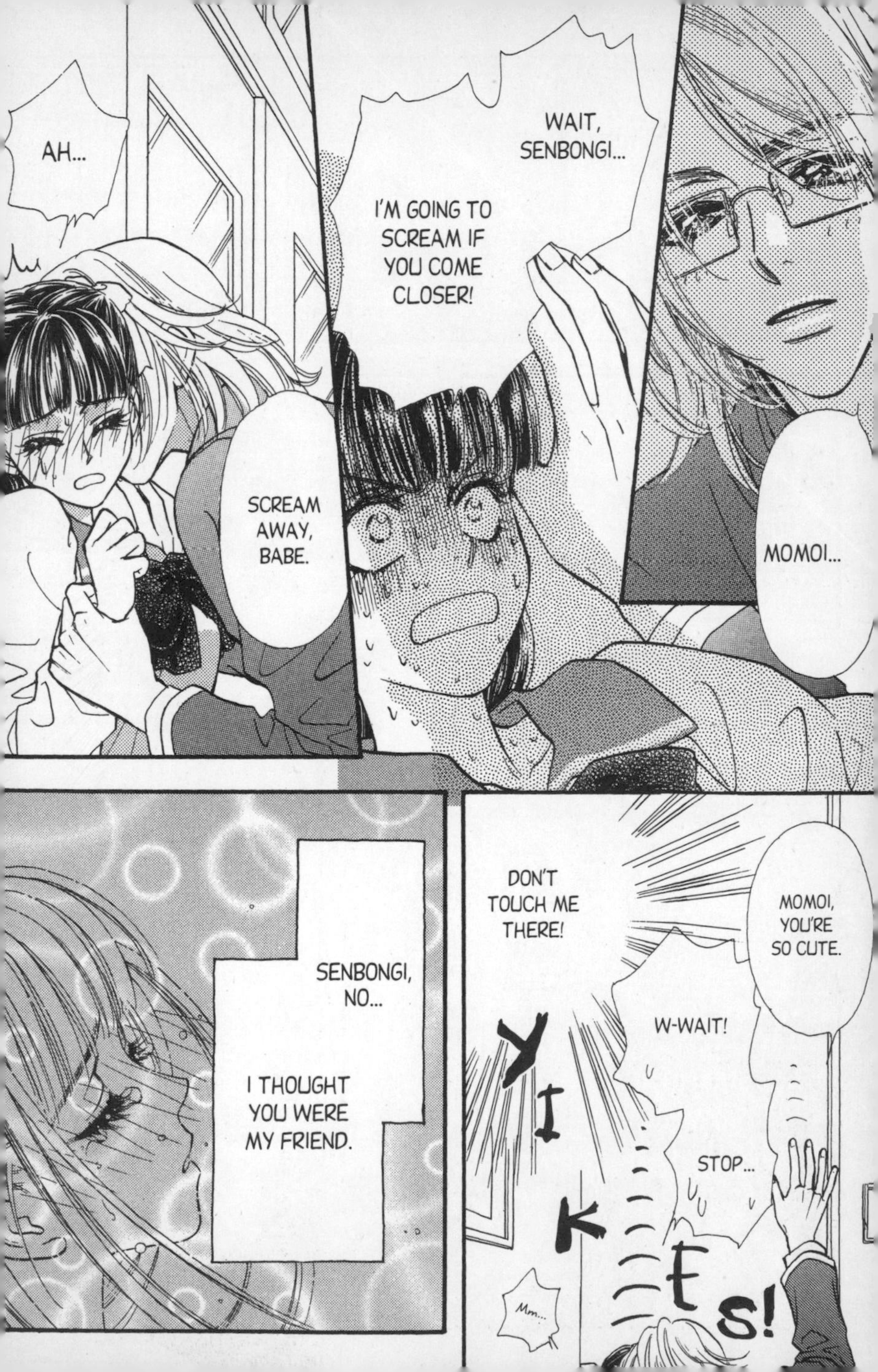
WAIT, SENBONGI...
I'M GOING TO SCREAM IF YOU COME CLOSER!
MOMOI...
SCREAM AWAY, BABE.
AH...
MOMOI, YOU'RE SO CUTE.
DON'T TOUCH ME THERE!
W-WAIT!
STOP...
YIKES!
Mm...
SENBONGI, NO...
I THOUGHT YOU WERE MY FRIEND.

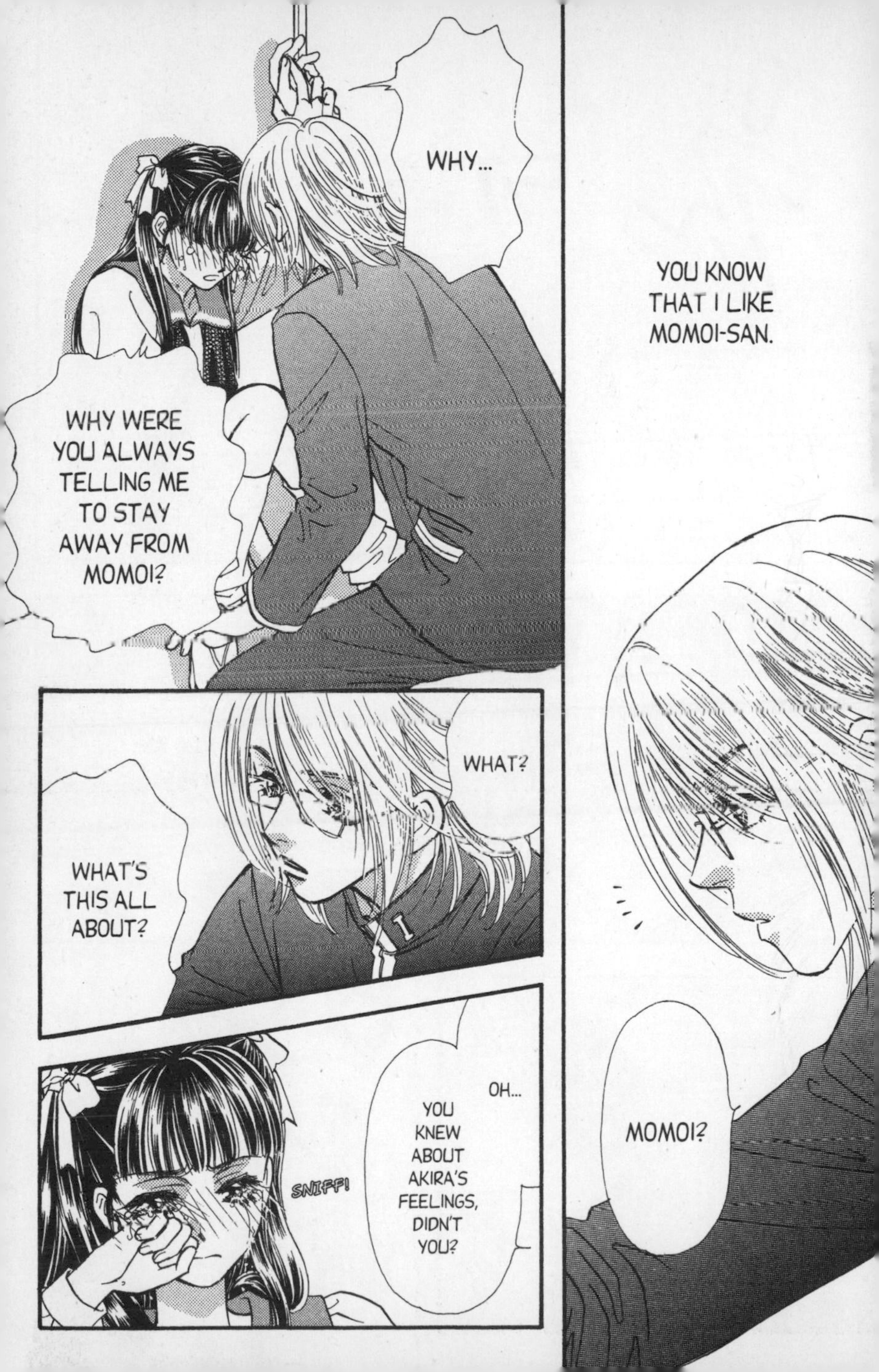
YOU KNOW THAT I LIKE MOMOI-SAN.
MOMOI?
WHY...
WHY WERE YOU ALWAYS TELLING ME TO STAY AWAY FROM MOMOI?
WHAT?
WHAT'S THIS ALL ABOUT?
OH...
YOU KNEW ABOUT AKIRA'S FEELINGS, DIDN'T YOU?
SNIFF!

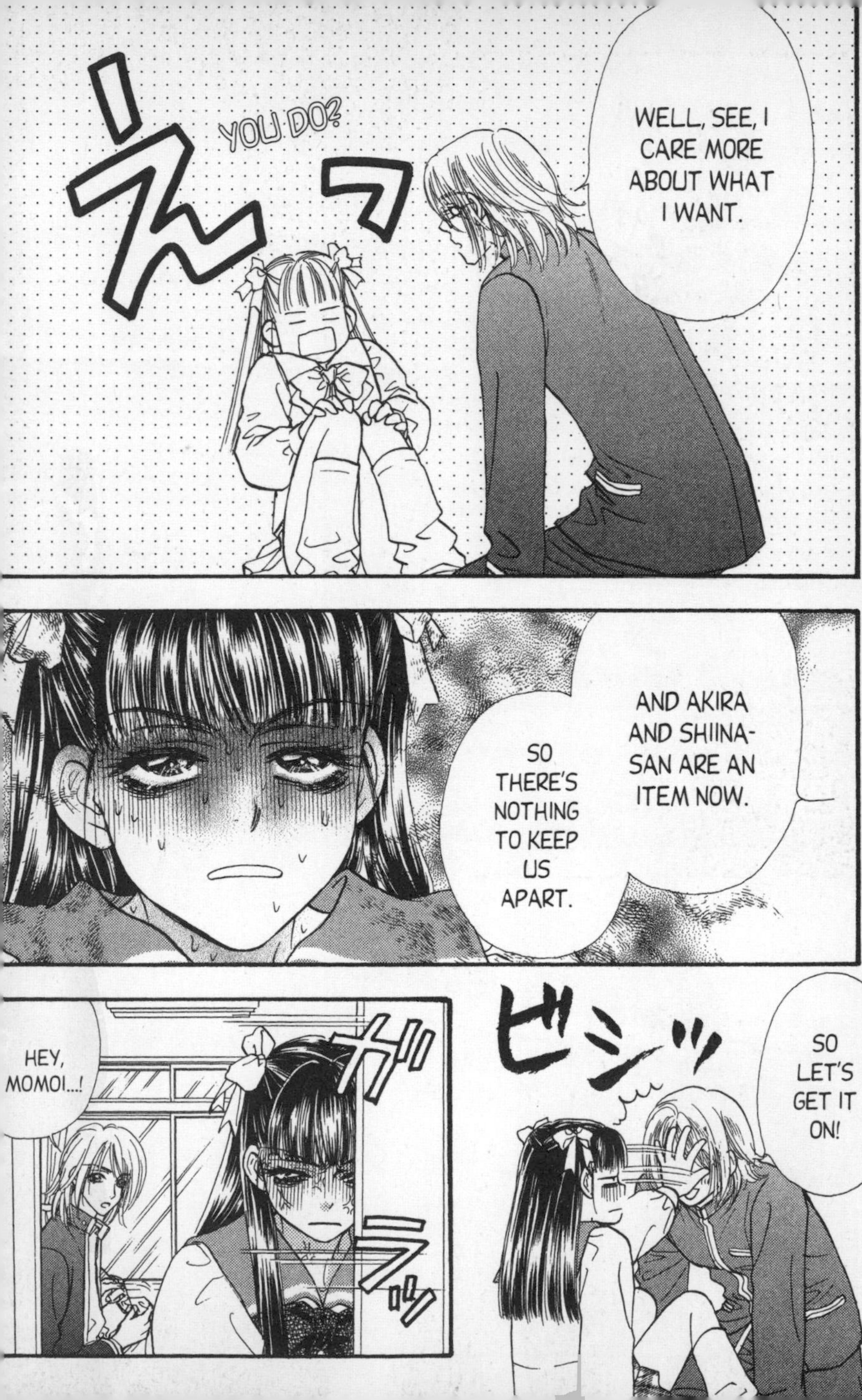
WELL, SEE, I CARE MORE ABOUT WHAT I WANT.
えっ
YOU DO?
AND AKIRA AND SHIINA-SAN ARE AN ITEM NOW.
SO THERE'S NOTHING TO KEEP US APART.
SO LET'S GET IT ON!
ビシッ
ガラッ
HEY, MOMOI...!

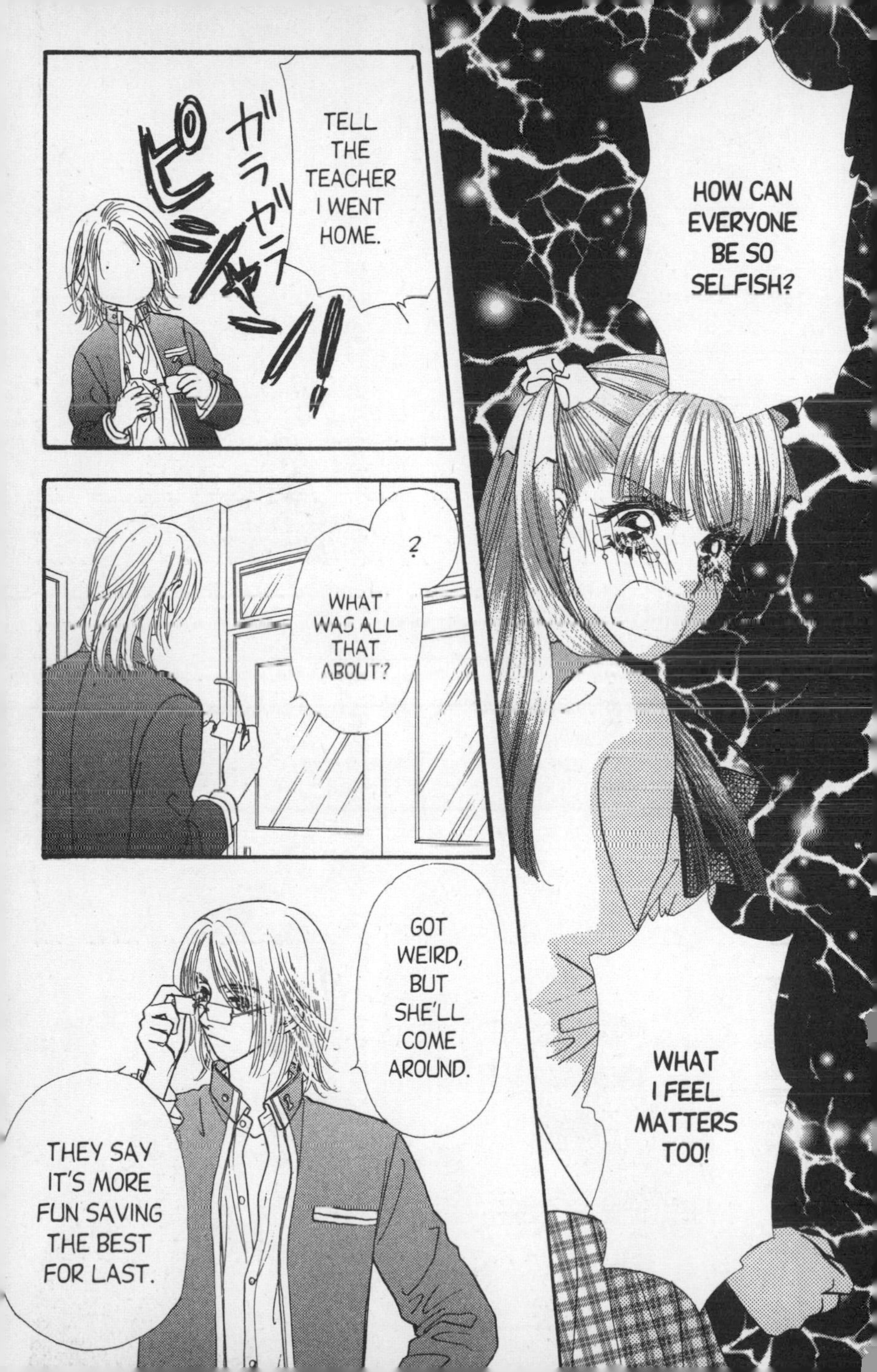
HOW CAN EVERYONE BE SO SELFISH?
WHAT I FEEL MATTERS TOO!
TELL THE TEACHER I WENT HOME.
ガラガラ
ピシャー!!
?
WHAT WAS ALL THAT ABOUT?
GOT WEIRD, BUT SHE'LL COME AROUND.
THEY SAY IT'S MORE FUN SAVING THE BEST FOR LAST.

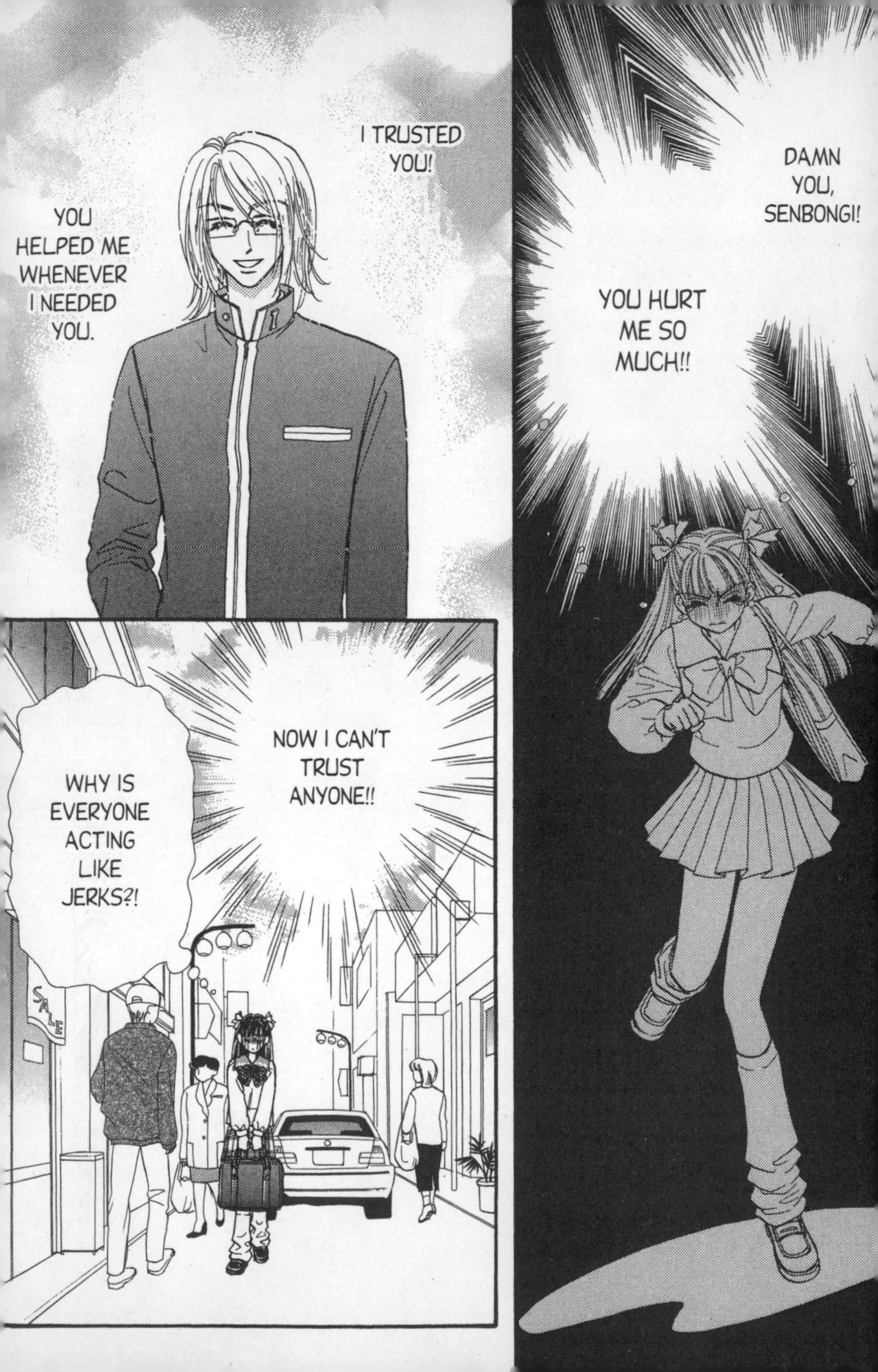
DAMN YOU, SENBONGI!
YOU HURT ME SO MUCH!!
I TRUSTED YOU!
YOU HELPED ME WHENEVER I NEEDED YOU.
NOW I CAN'T TRUST ANYONE!!
WHY IS EVERYONE ACTING LIKE JERKS?!
SALE

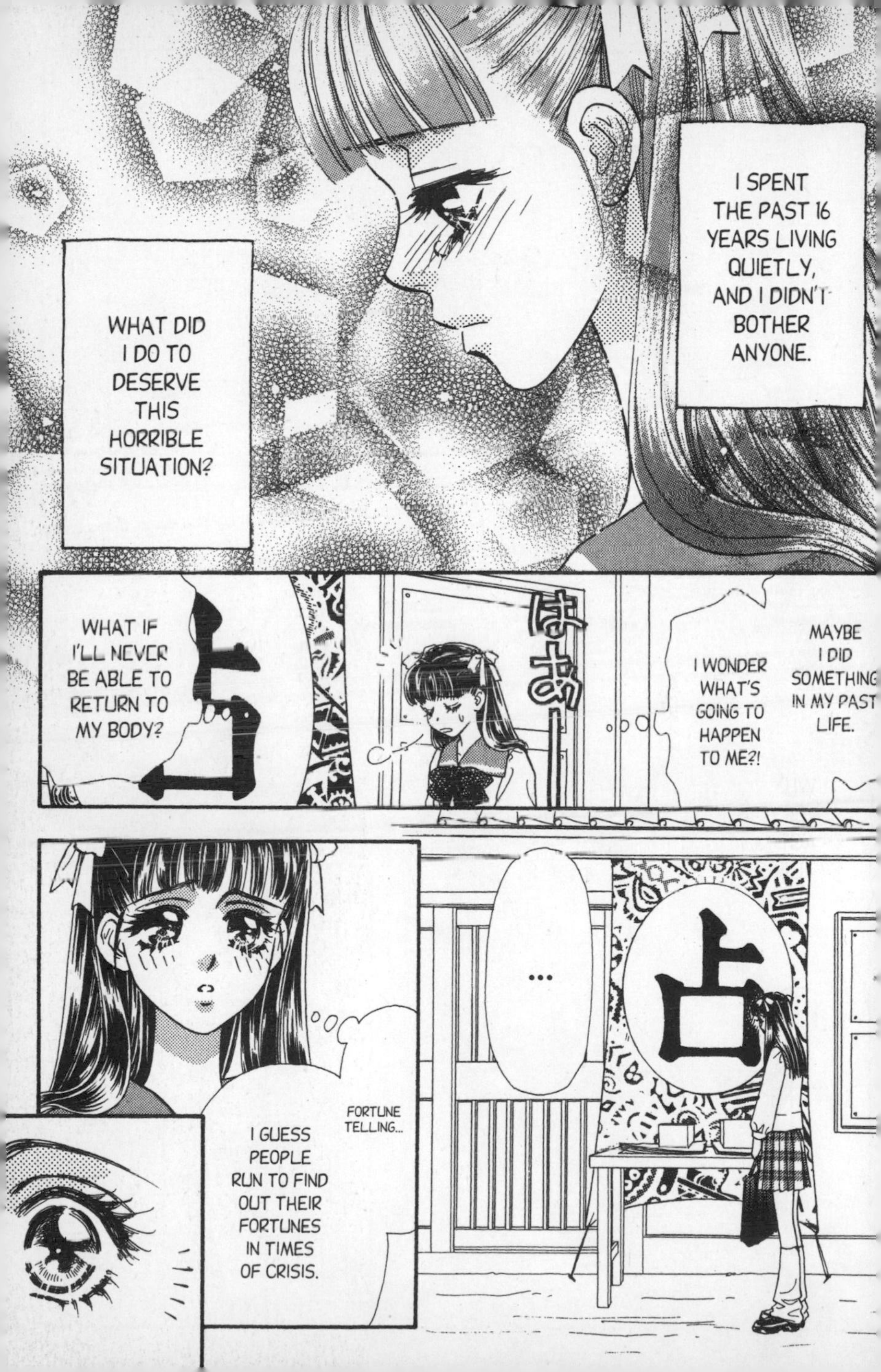
I SPENT THE PAST 16 YEARS LIVING QUIETLY, AND I DIDN'T BOTHER ANYONE.
WHAT DID I DO TO DESERVE THIS HORRIBLE SITUATION?
MAYBE I DID SOMETHING IN MY PAST LIFE.
I WONDER WHAT'S GOING TO HAPPEN TO ME?!
はぁ
占
WHAT IF I'LL NEVER BE ABLE TO RETURN TO MY BODY?
占
...
FORTUNE TELLING...
I GUESS PEOPLE RUN TO FIND OUT THEIR FORTUNES IN TIMES OF CRISIS.

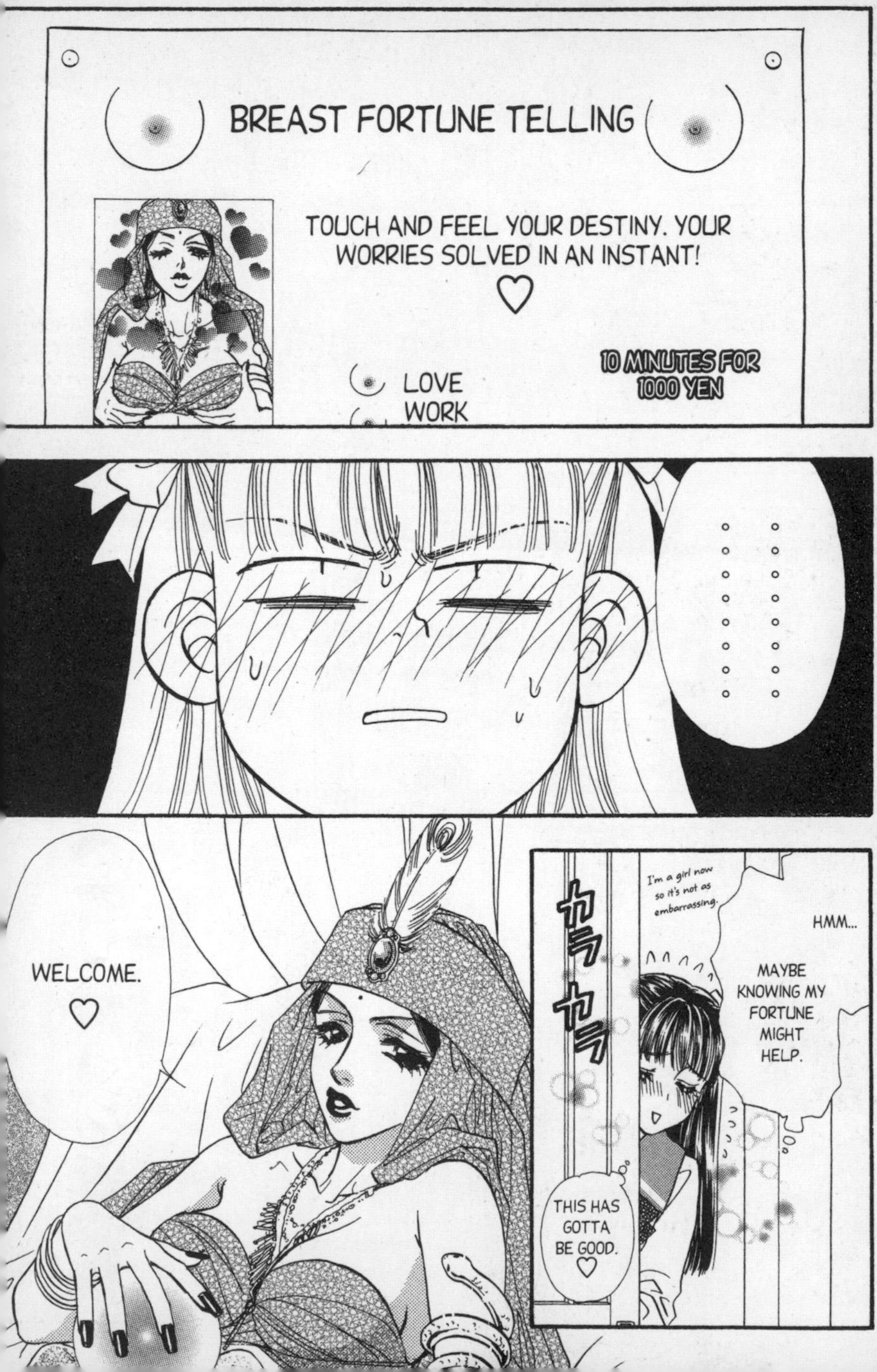
BREAST FORTUNE TELLING
TOUCH AND FEEL YOUR DESTINY. YOUR WORRIES SOLVED IN AN INSTANT! ♡
10 MINUTES FOR 1000 YEN
LOVE
WORK
HMM... MAYBE KNOWING MY FORTUNE MIGHT HELP.
I'm a girl now so it's not as embarrassing.
カラカラ
THIS HAS GOTTA BE GOOD. ♡
WELCOME. ♡

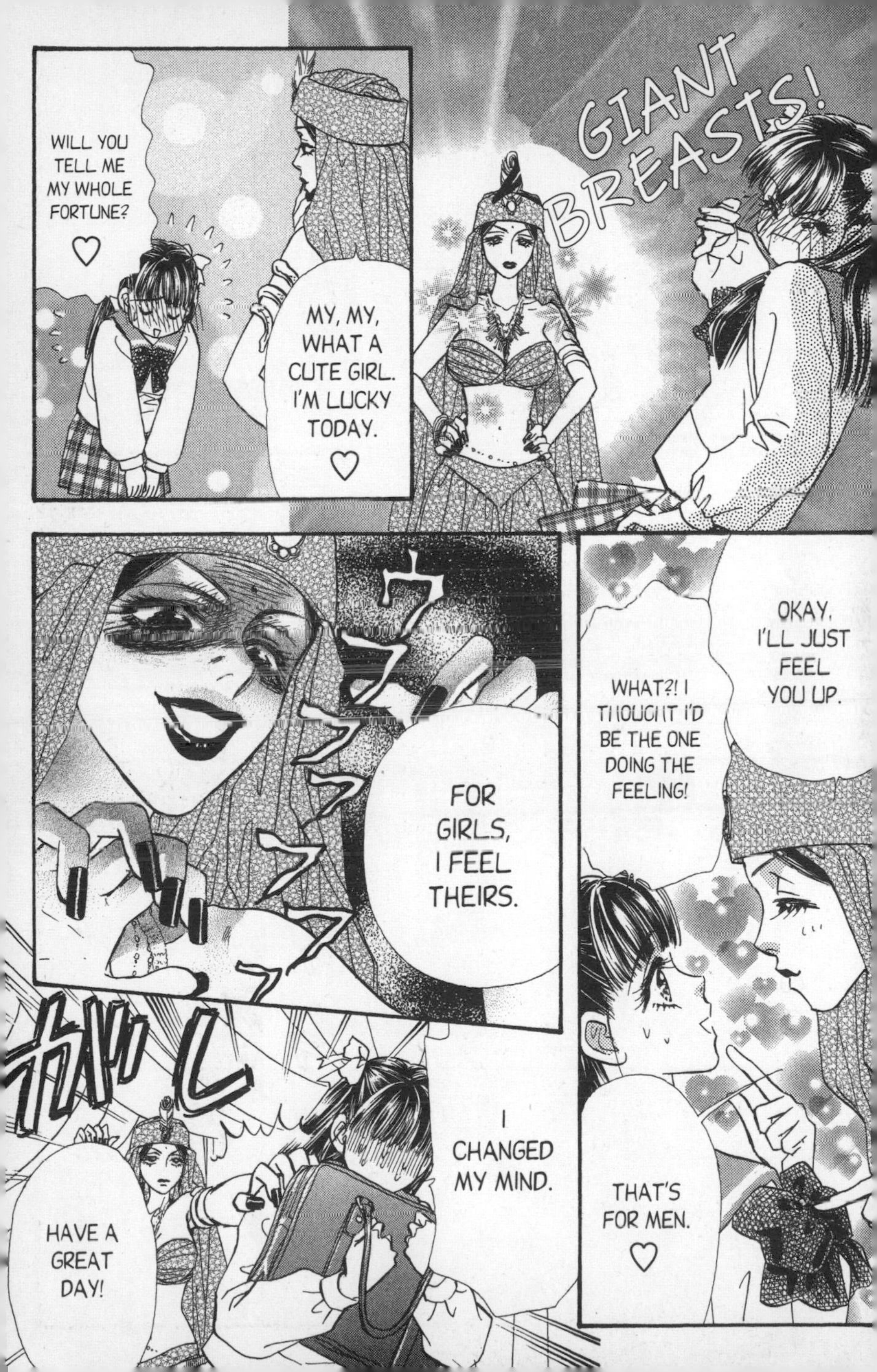
GIANT BREASTS!
WILL YOU TELL ME MY WHOLE FORTUNE? ♡
MY, MY, WHAT A CUTE GIRL. I'M LUCKY TODAY. ♡
OKAY, I'LL JUST FEEL YOU UP.
WHAT?! I THOUGHT I'D BE THE ONE DOING THE FEELING!
THAT'S FOR MEN. ♡
FOR GIRLS, I FEEL THEIRS.
I CHANGED MY MIND.
HAVE A GREAT DAY!

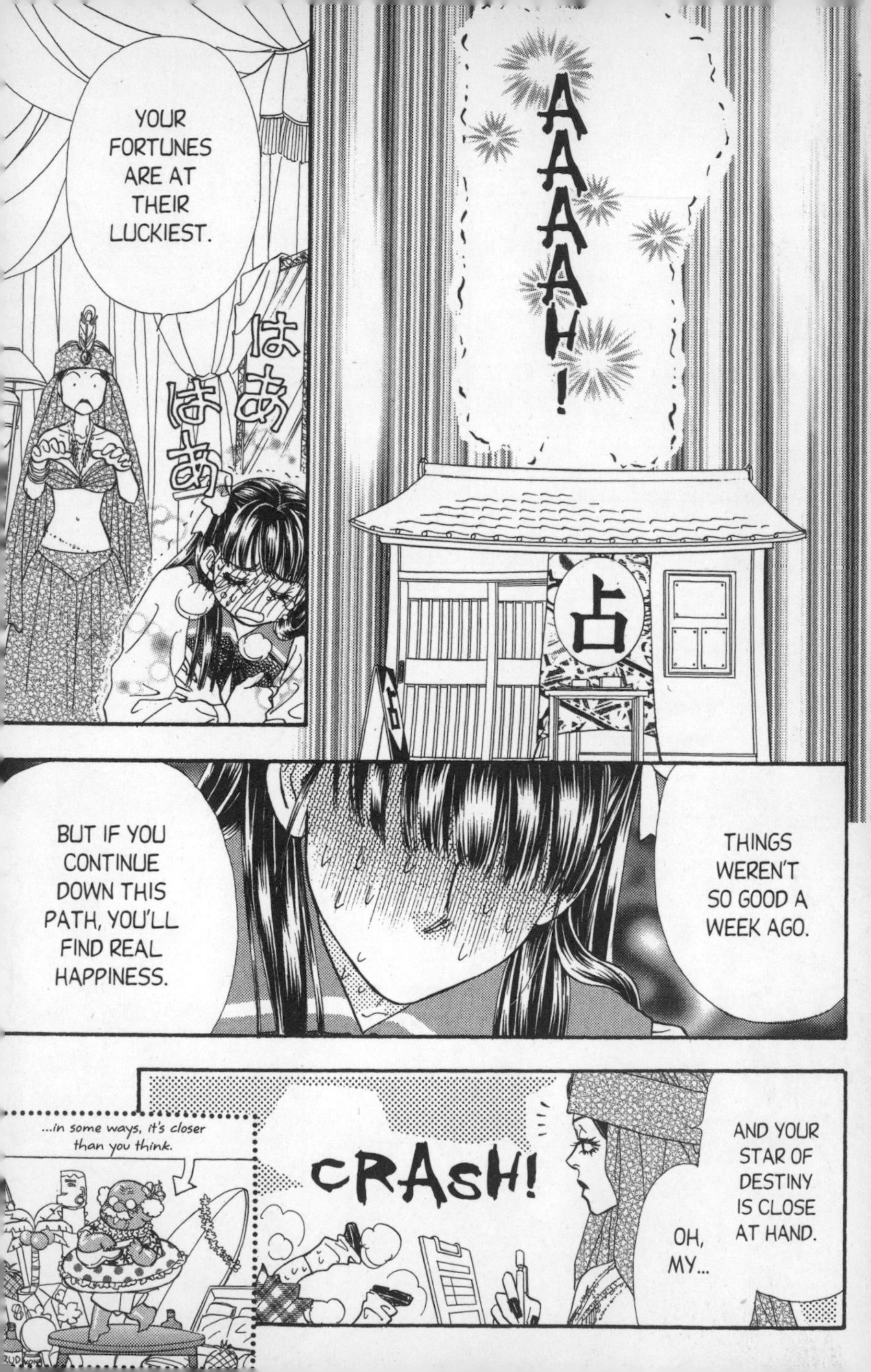
AAAAH!
占
YOUR FORTUNES ARE AT THEIR LUCKIEST.
はあはあ
THINGS WEREN'T SO GOOD A WEEK AGO.
BUT IF YOU CONTINUE DOWN THIS PATH, YOU'LL FIND REAL HAPPINESS.
AND YOUR STAR OF DESTINY IS CLOSE AT HAND.
OH, MY...
CRASH!
...in some ways, it's closer than you think.

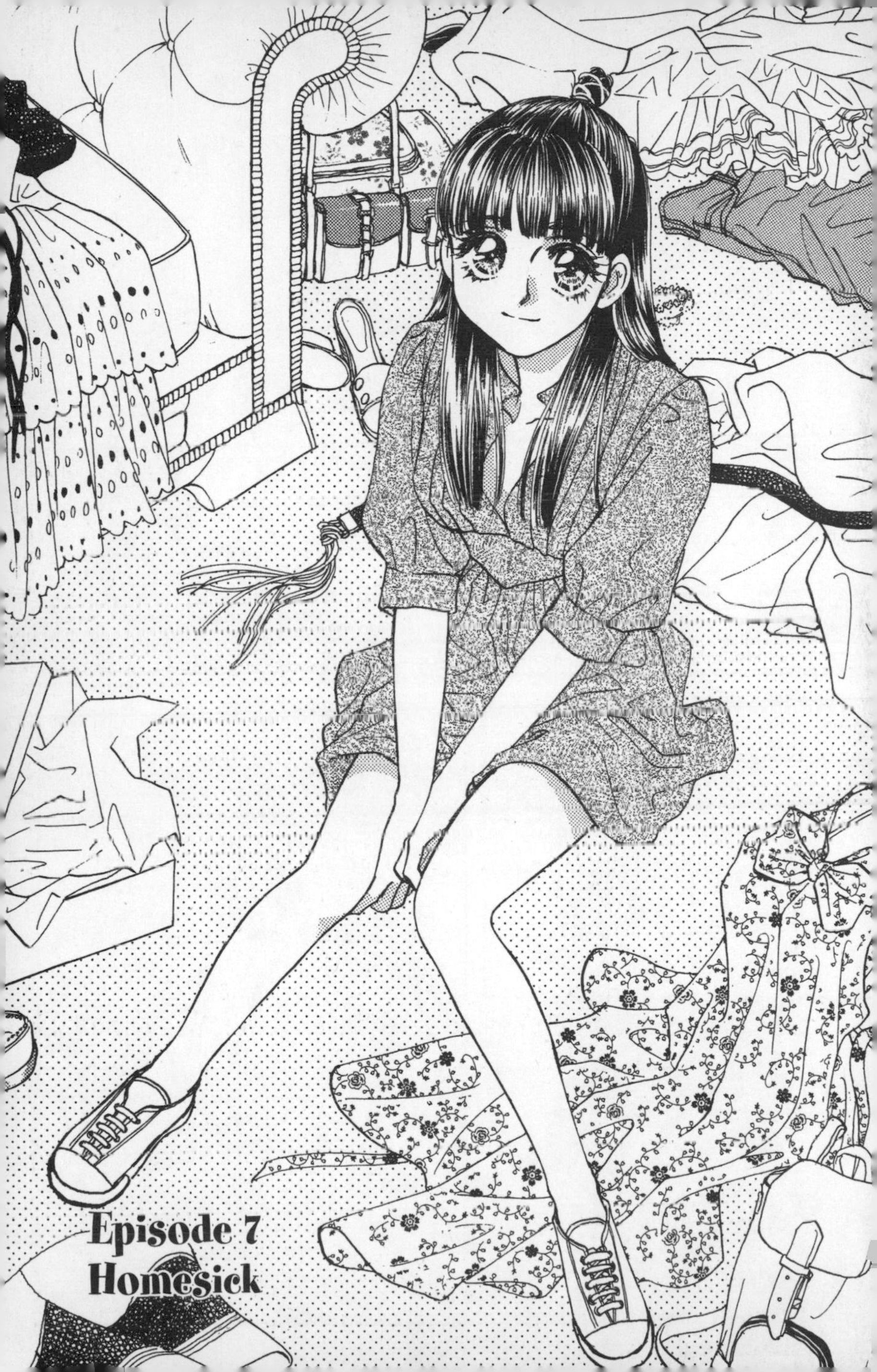
Episode 7
Homesick

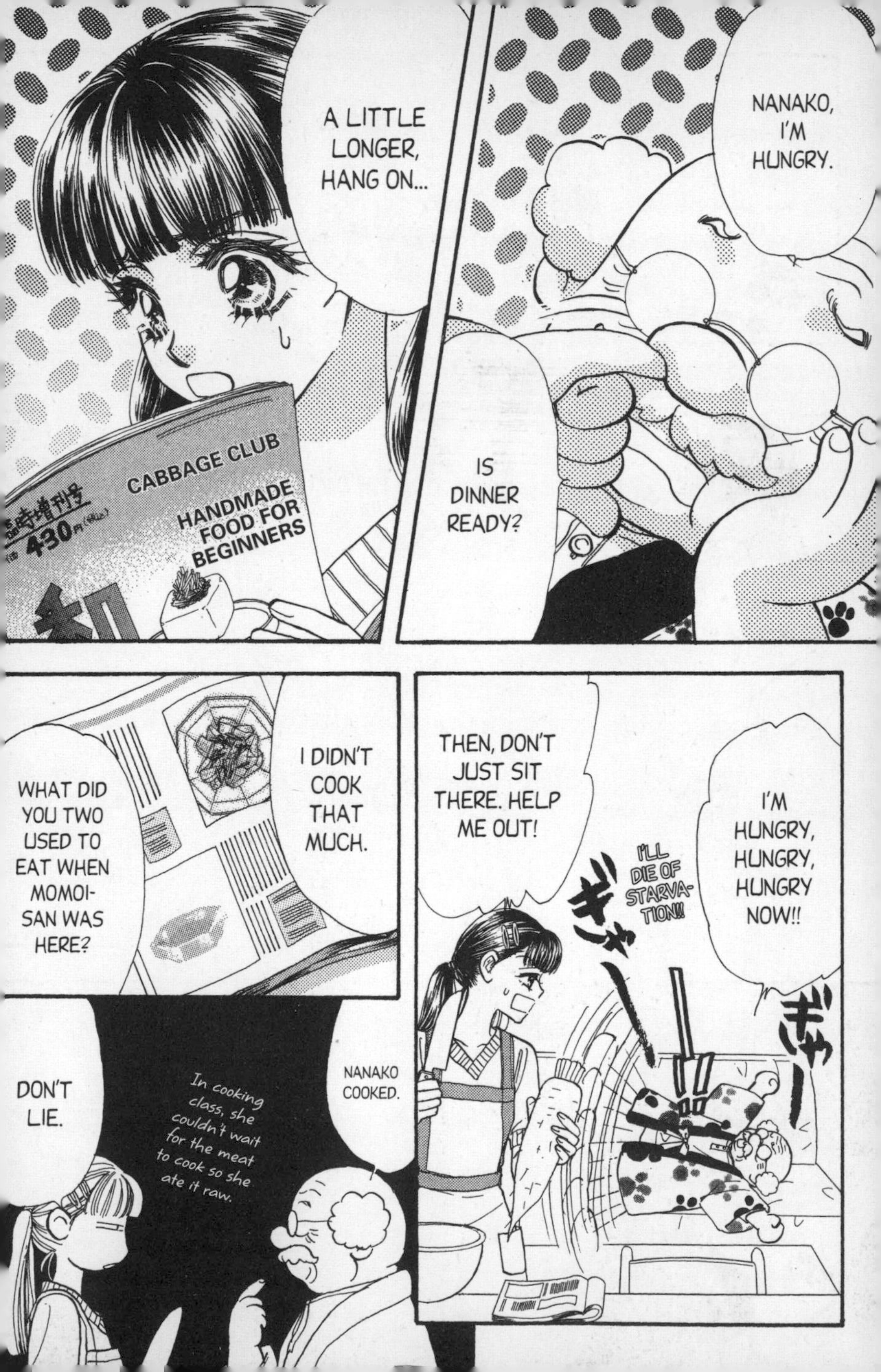
NANAKO, I'M HUNGRY.
IS DINNER READY?
A LITTLE LONGER, HANG ON...
CABBAGE CLUB
HANDMADE FOOD FOR BEGINNERS
430
I'M HUNGRY, HUNGRY, HUNGRY NOW!!
ぎゃー
I'LL DIE OF STARVATION!!
ギャー
THEN, DON'T JUST SIT THERE. HELP ME OUT!
I DIDN'T COOK THAT MUCH.
WHAT DID YOU TWO USED TO EAT WHEN MOMOI-SAN WAS HERE?
NANAKO COOKED.
In cooking class, she couldn't wait for the meat to cook so she ate it raw.
DON'T LIE.

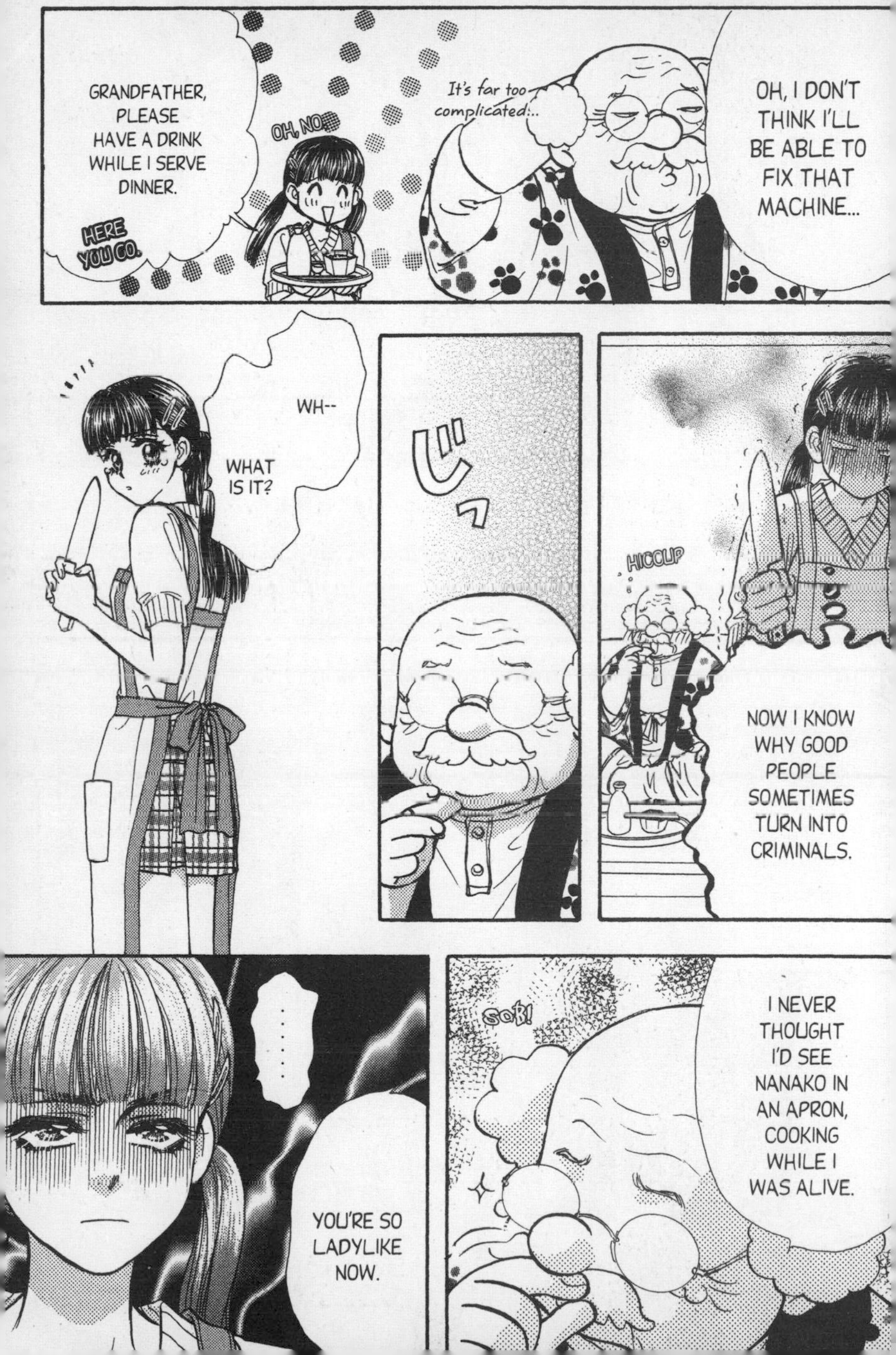
OH, I DON'T THINK I'LL BE ABLE TO FIX THAT MACHINE...
It's far too complicated...
OH, NO!
GRANDFATHER, PLEASE HAVE A DRINK WHILE I SERVE DINNER.
HERE YOU GO.
HICCUP
NOW I KNOW WHY GOOD PEOPLE SOMETIMES TURN INTO CRIMINALS.
WH--
WHAT IS IT?
SOB!
I NEVER THOUGHT I'D SEE NANAKO IN AN APRON, COOKING WHILE I WAS ALIVE.
YOU'RE SO LADYLIKE NOW.
......

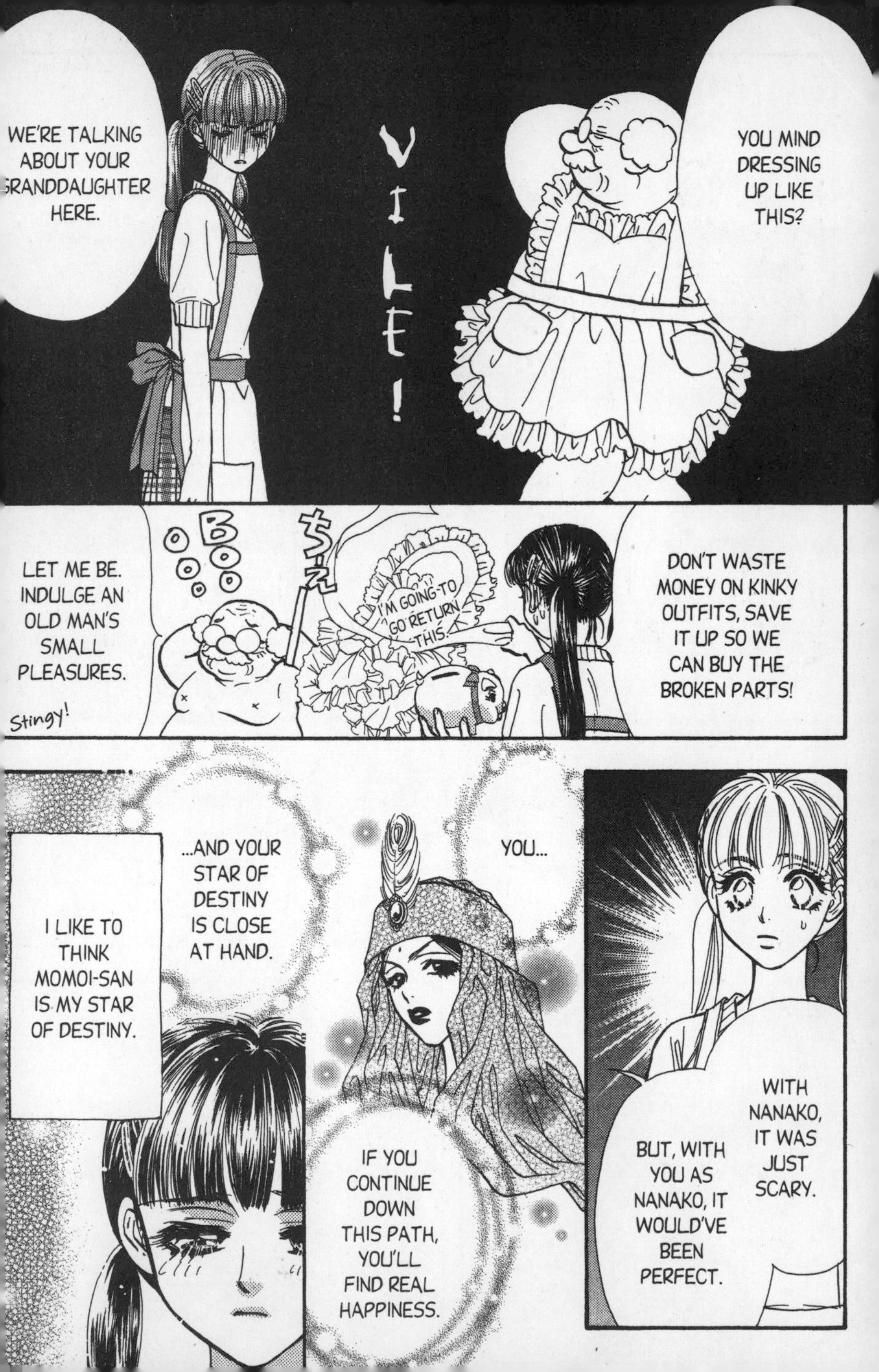

YOU MIND DRESSING UP LIKE THIS?
VILE!
WE'RE TALKING ABOUT YOUR GRANDDAUGHTER HERE.
DON'T WASTE MONEY ON KINKY OUTFITS, SAVE IT UP SO WE CAN BUY THE BROKEN PARTS!
I'M GOING TO GO RETURN THIS.
ちぇ
BOO
LET ME BE. INDULGE AN OLD MAN'S SMALL PLEASURES.
Stingy!
WITH NANAKO, IT WAS JUST SCARY.
BUT, WITH YOU AS NANAKO, IT WOULD'VE BEEN PERFECT.
YOU...
...AND YOUR STAR OF DESTINY IS CLOSE AT HAND.
I LIKE TO THINK MOMOI-SAN IS MY STAR OF DESTINY.
IF YOU CONTINUE DOWN THIS PATH, YOU'LL FIND REAL HAPPINESS.

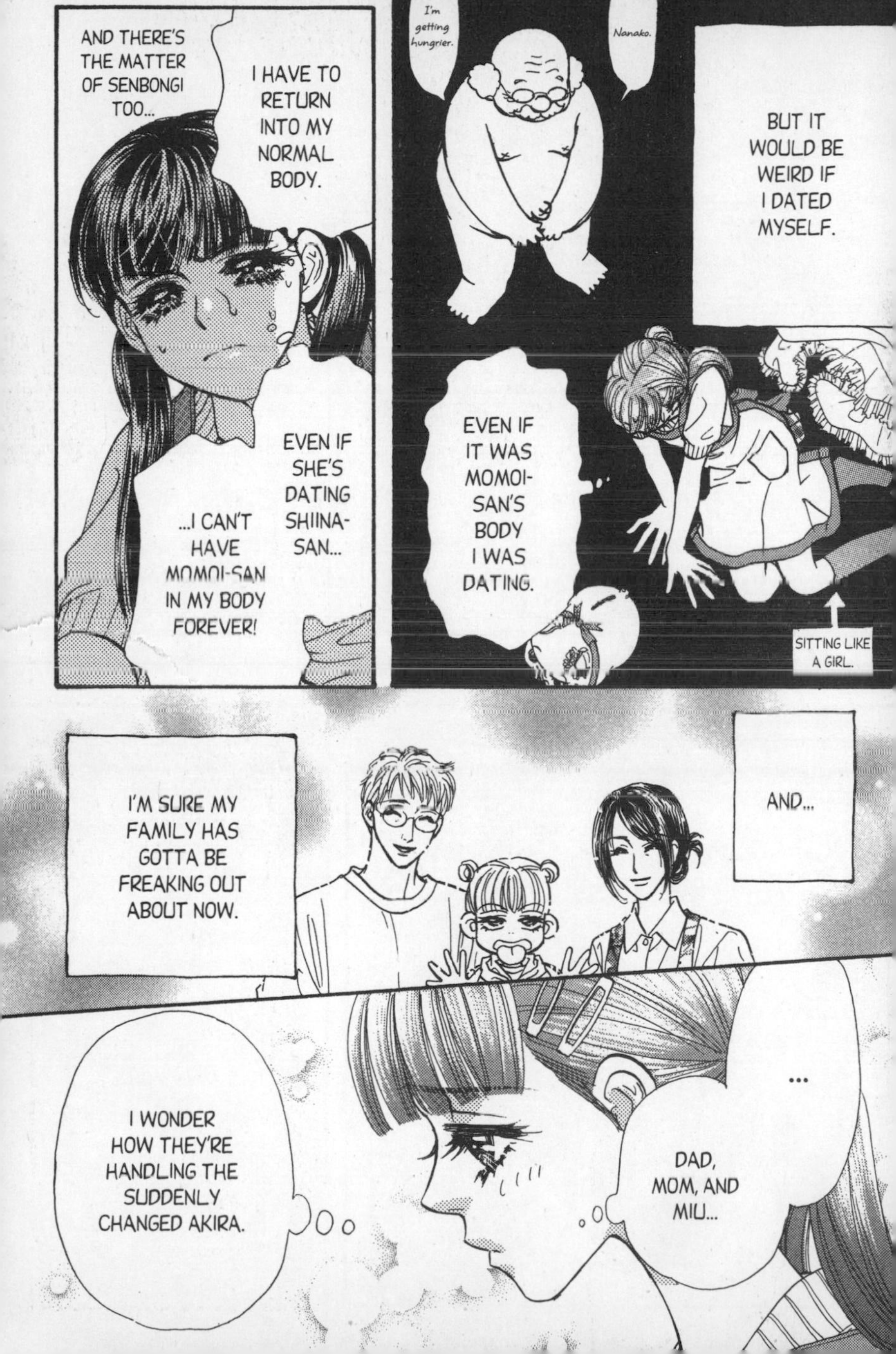
BUT IT WOULD BE WEIRD IF I DATED MYSELF.
Nanako.
I'm getting hungrier.
EVEN IF IT WAS MOMOI-SAN'S BODY I WAS DATING.
SITTING LIKE A GIRL.
I HAVE TO RETURN INTO MY NORMAL BODY.
AND THERE'S THE MATTER OF SENBONGI TOO...
EVEN IF SHE'S DATING SHIINA-SAN...
...I CAN'T HAVE MOMOI-SAN IN MY BODY FOREVER!
AND...
I'M SURE MY FAMILY HAS GOTTA BE FREAKING OUT ABOUT NOW.
...
DAD, MOM, AND MIU...
I WONDER HOW THEY'RE HANDLING THE SUDDENLY CHANGED AKIRA.

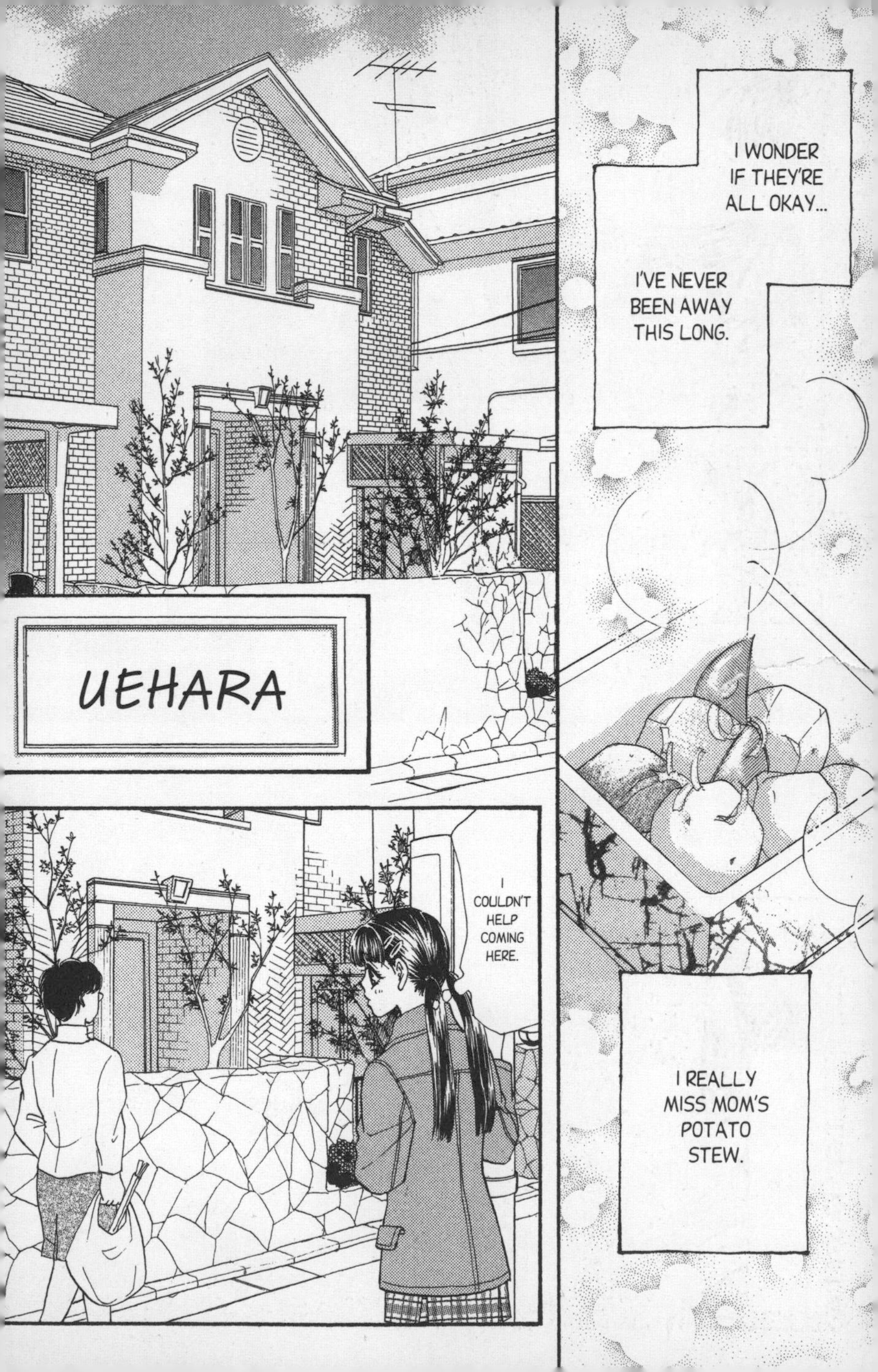
I WONDER IF THEY'RE ALL OKAY...
I'VE NEVER BEEN AWAY THIS LONG.
I REALLY MISS MOM'S POTATO STEW.
UEHARA
I COULDN'T HELP COMING HERE.

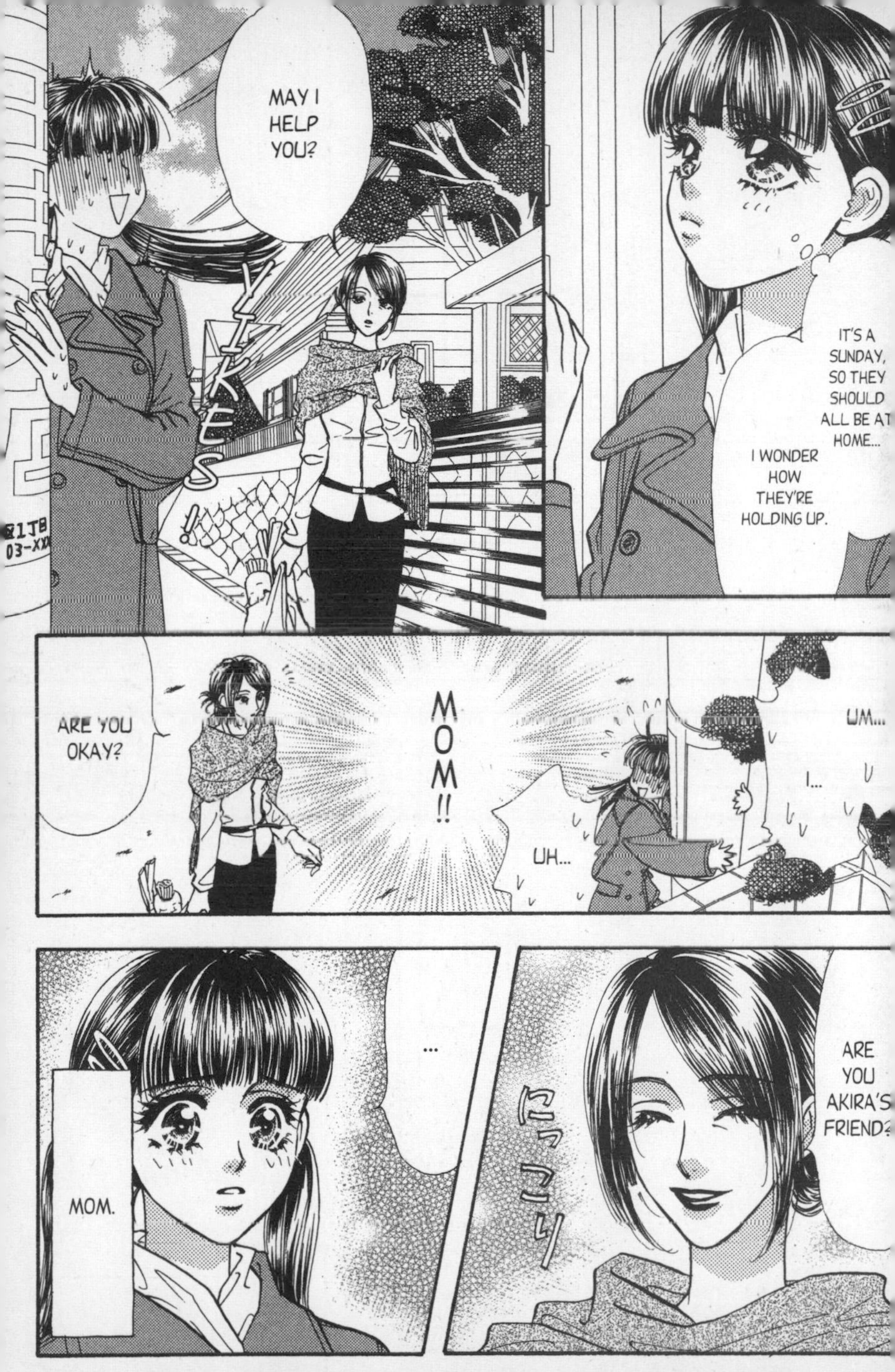
IT'S A SUNDAY, SO THEY SHOULD ALL BE AT HOME...
I WONDER HOW THEY'RE HOLDING UP.
MAY I HELP YOU?
YIKES!
UM...
I...
UH...
MOM!!
ARE YOU OKAY?
ARE YOU AKIRA'S FRIEND?
にっこり
...
MOM.

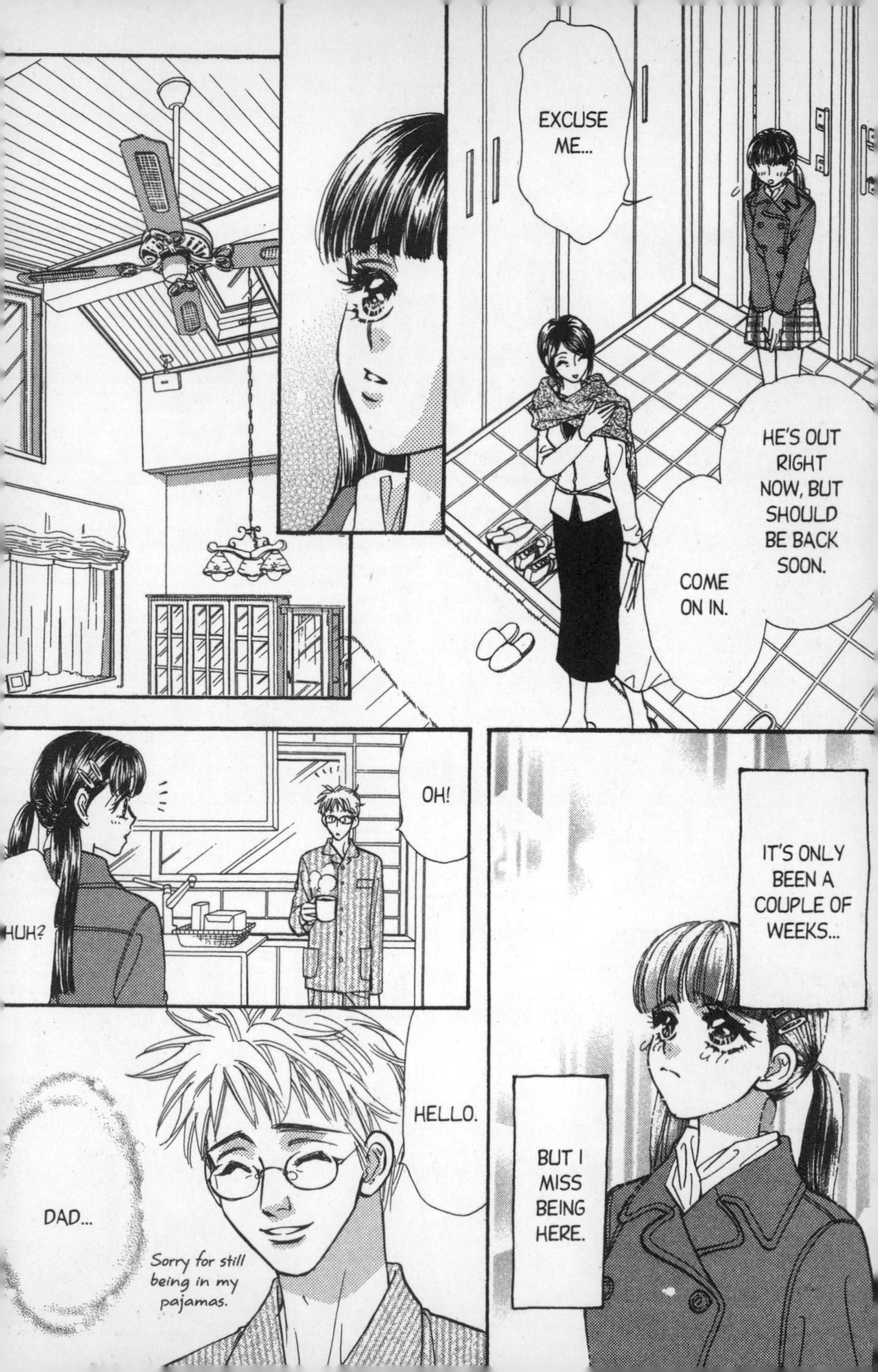
EXCUSE ME...
HE'S OUT RIGHT NOW, BUT SHOULD BE BACK SOON.
COME ON IN.
IT'S ONLY BEEN A COUPLE OF WEEKS...
BUT I MISS BEING HERE.
OH!
HUH?
HELLO.
DAD...
Sorry for still being in my pajamas.

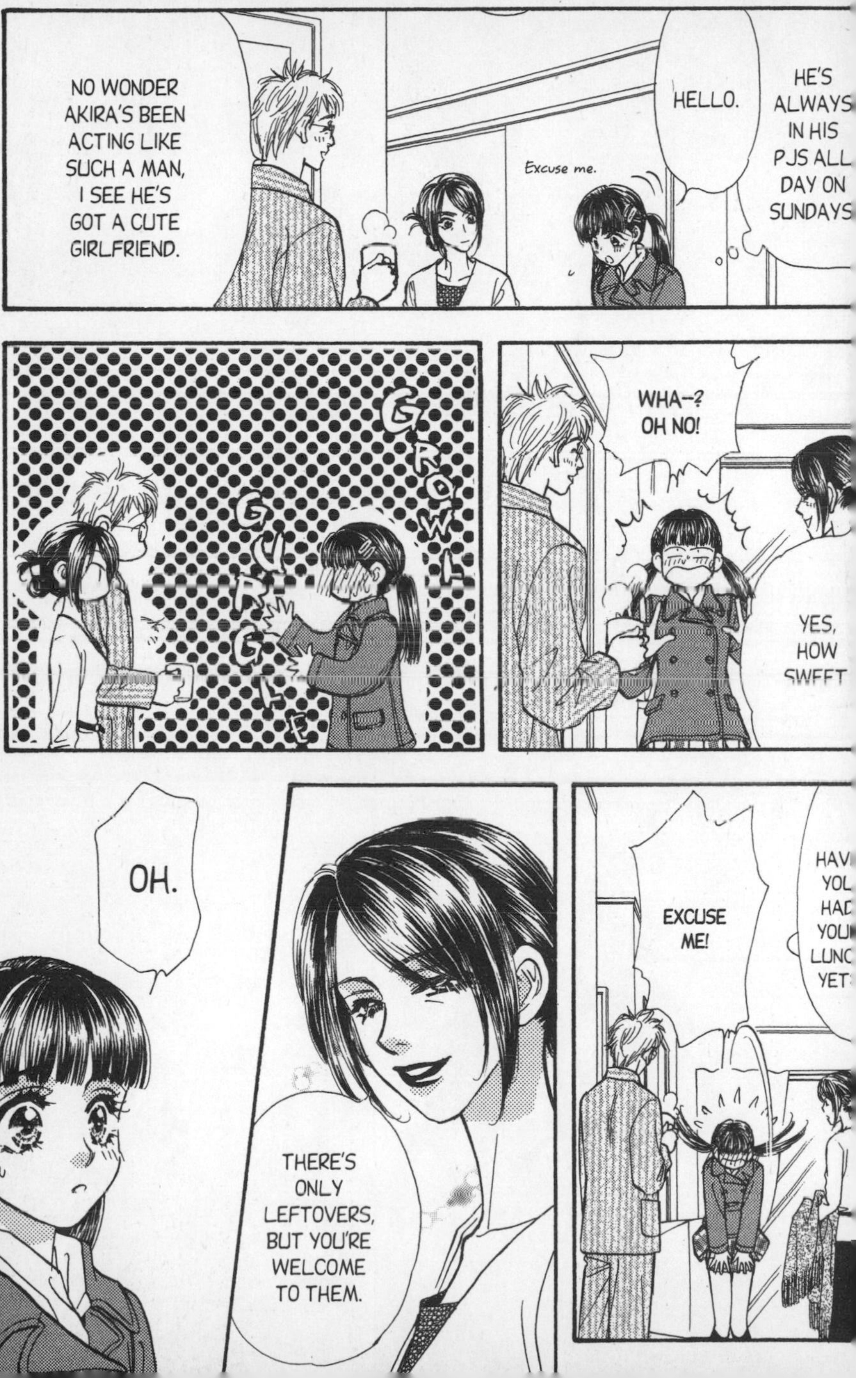
HE'S ALWAYS IN HIS PJS ALL DAY ON SUNDAYS
HELLO.
Excuse me.
NO WONDER AKIRA'S BEEN ACTING LIKE SUCH A MAN, I SEE HE'S GOT A CUTE GIRLFRIEND.
WHA--? OH NO!
YES, HOW SWEET
GROWL
GURGLE
HAV YOU HAD YOU LUNC YET
EXCUSE ME!
THERE'S ONLY LEFTOVERS, BUT YOU'RE WELCOME TO THEM.
OH.

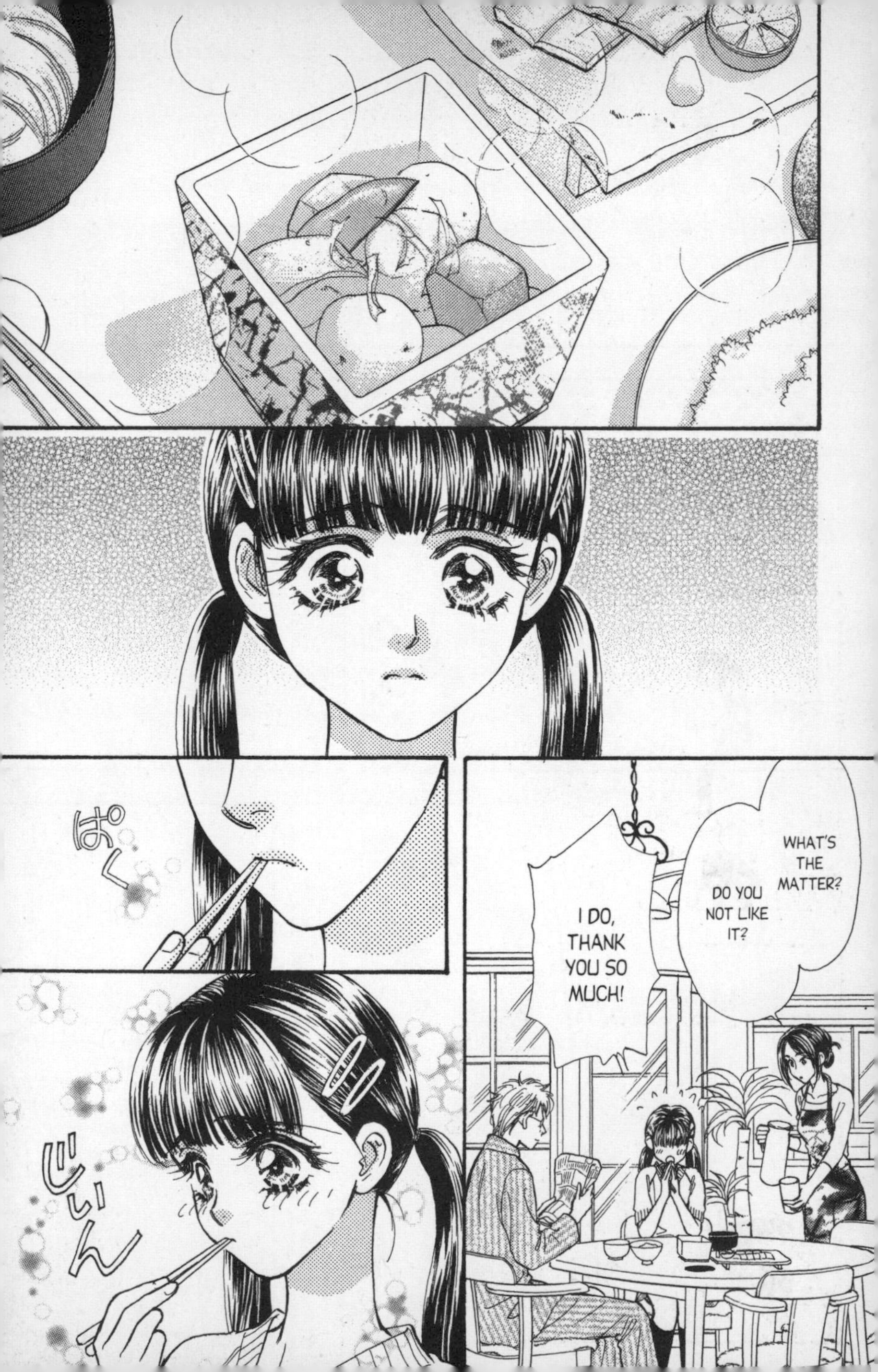
WHAT'S THE MATTER?
DO YOU NOT LIKE IT?
I DO, THANK YOU SO MUCH!
ぱく
じいん

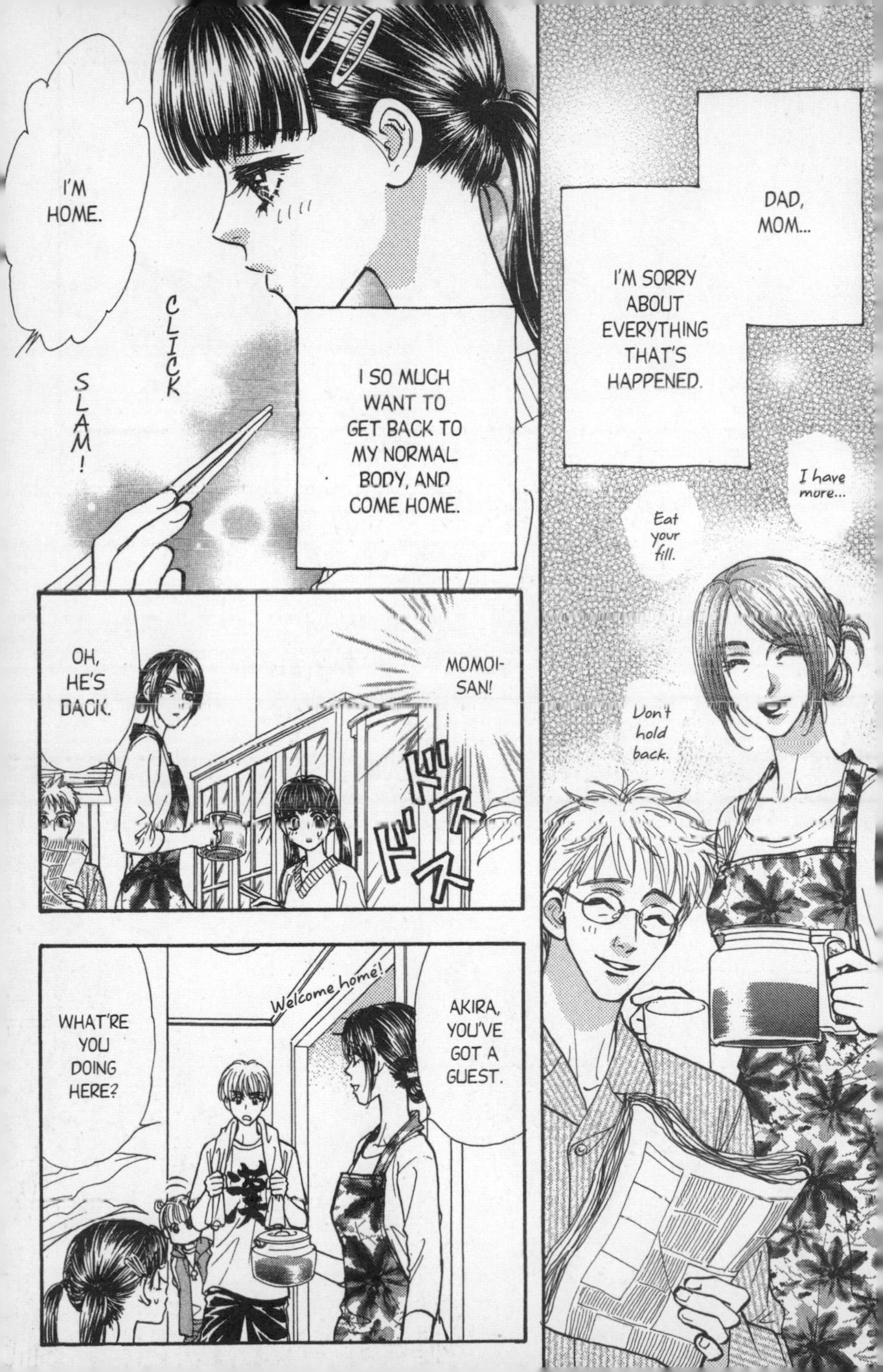
DAD, MOM...
I'M SORRY ABOUT EVERYTHING THAT'S HAPPENED.
I have more...
Eat your fill.
Don't hold back.
I SO MUCH WANT TO GET BACK TO MY NORMAL BODY, AND COME HOME.
CLICK
I'M HOME.
SLAM!
MOMOI-SAN!
ドスドス
OH, HE'S BACK.
AKIRA, YOU'VE GOT A GUEST.
Welcome home!
WHAT'RE YOU DOING HERE?

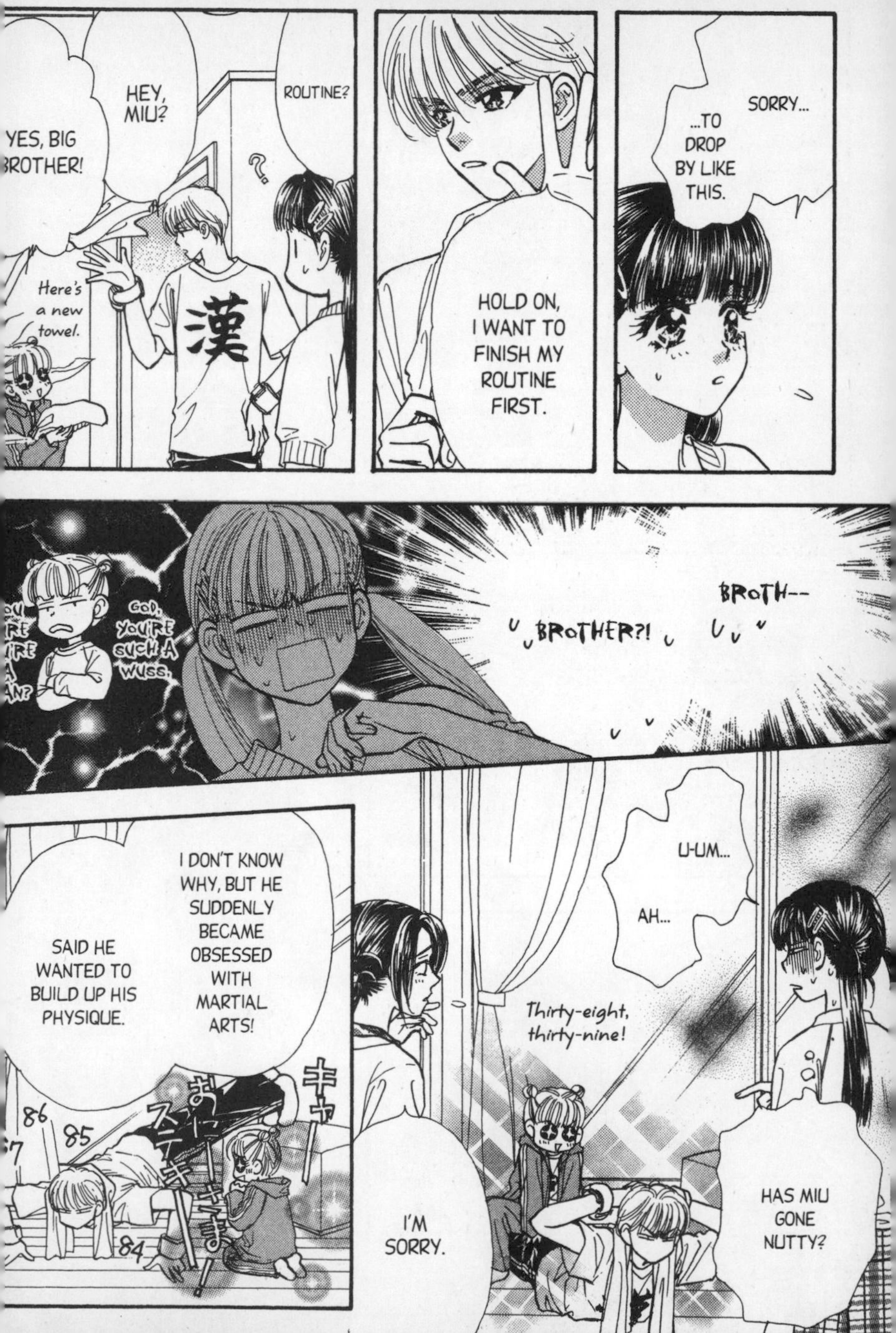
SORRY...
...TO DROP BY LIKE THIS.
HOLD ON, I WANT TO FINISH MY ROUTINE FIRST.
ROUTINE?
HEY, MIU?
YES, BIG BROTHER!
Here's a new towel.
BROTH--
BROTHER?!
GOD, YOU'RE SUCH A WUSS.
U-UM...
AH...
HAS MIU GONE NUTTY?
Thirty-eight, thirty-nine!
I'M SORRY.
I DON'T KNOW WHY, BUT HE SUDDENLY BECAME OBSESSED WITH MARTIAL ARTS!
SAID HE WANTED TO BUILD UP HIS PHYSIQUE.
キャー
86
85
84

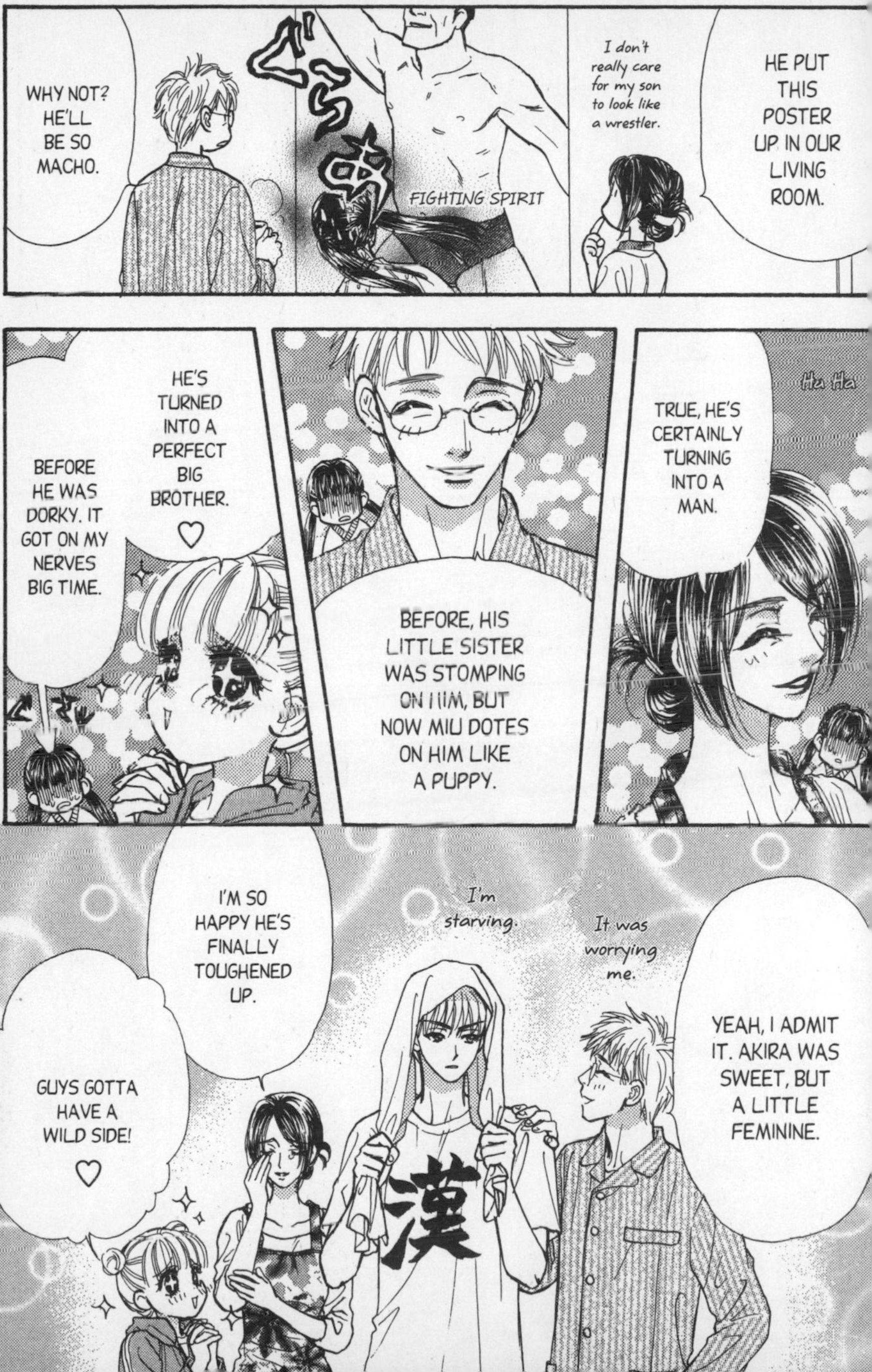
HE PUT THIS POSTER UP IN OUR LIVING ROOM.
I don't really care for my son to look like a wrestler.
FIGHTING SPIRIT
WHY NOT? HE'LL BE SO MACHO.
Ha Ha
TRUE, HE'S CERTAINLY TURNING INTO A MAN.
BEFORE, HIS LITTLE SISTER WAS STOMPING ON HIM, BUT NOW MIU DOTES ON HIM LIKE A PUPPY.
HE'S TURNED INTO A PERFECT BIG BROTHER. ♡
BEFORE HE WAS DORKY. IT GOT ON MY NERVES BIG TIME.
YEAH, I ADMIT IT. AKIRA WAS SWEET, BUT A LITTLE FEMININE.
It was worrying me.
I'm starving.
漢
I'M SO HAPPY HE'S FINALLY TOUGHENED UP.
GUYS GOTTA HAVE A WILD SIDE! ♡

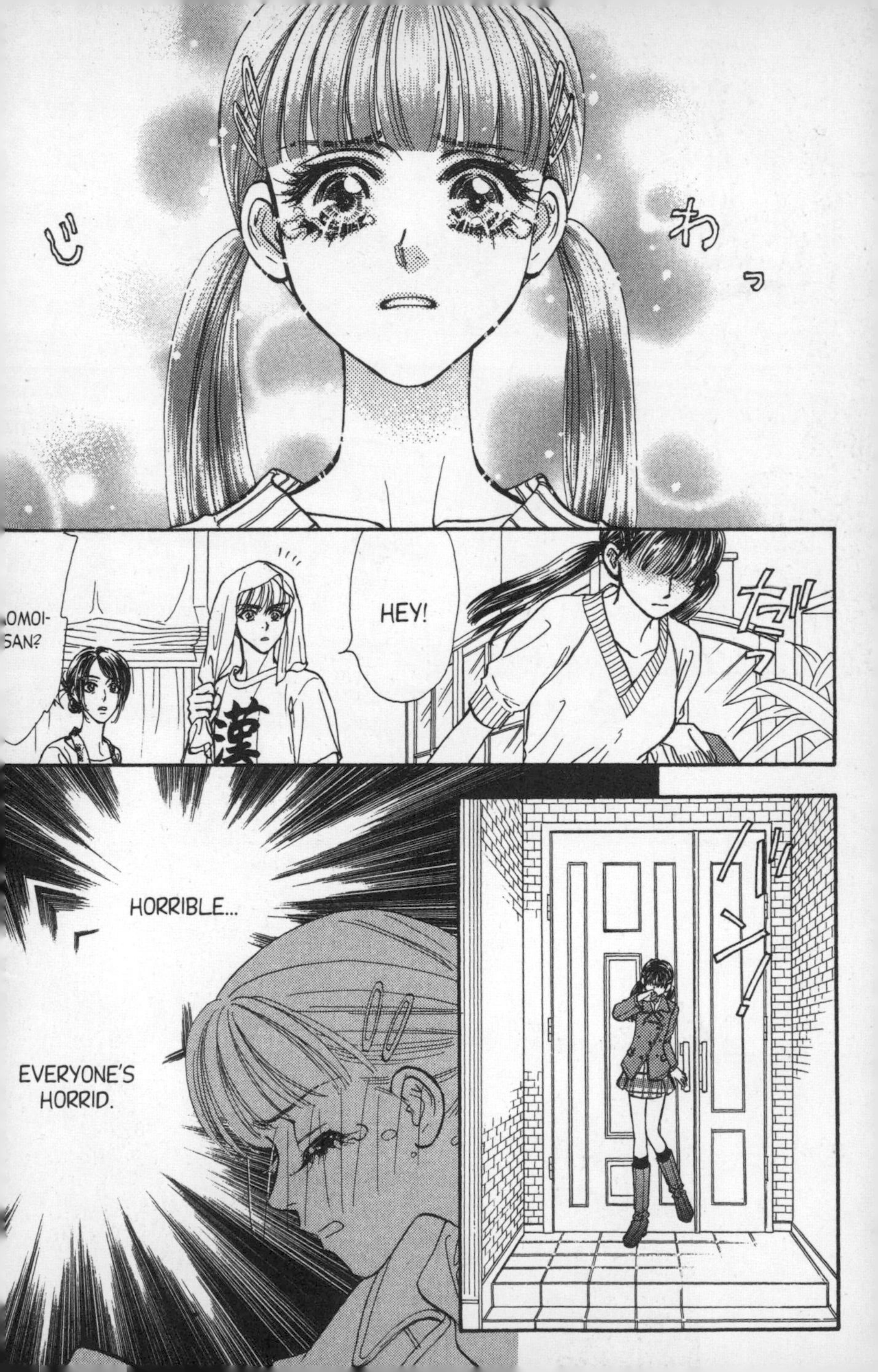
じ
わっ
だッ
HEY!
OMOI-
SAN?
バタン
HORRIBLE...
EVERYONE'S HORRID.

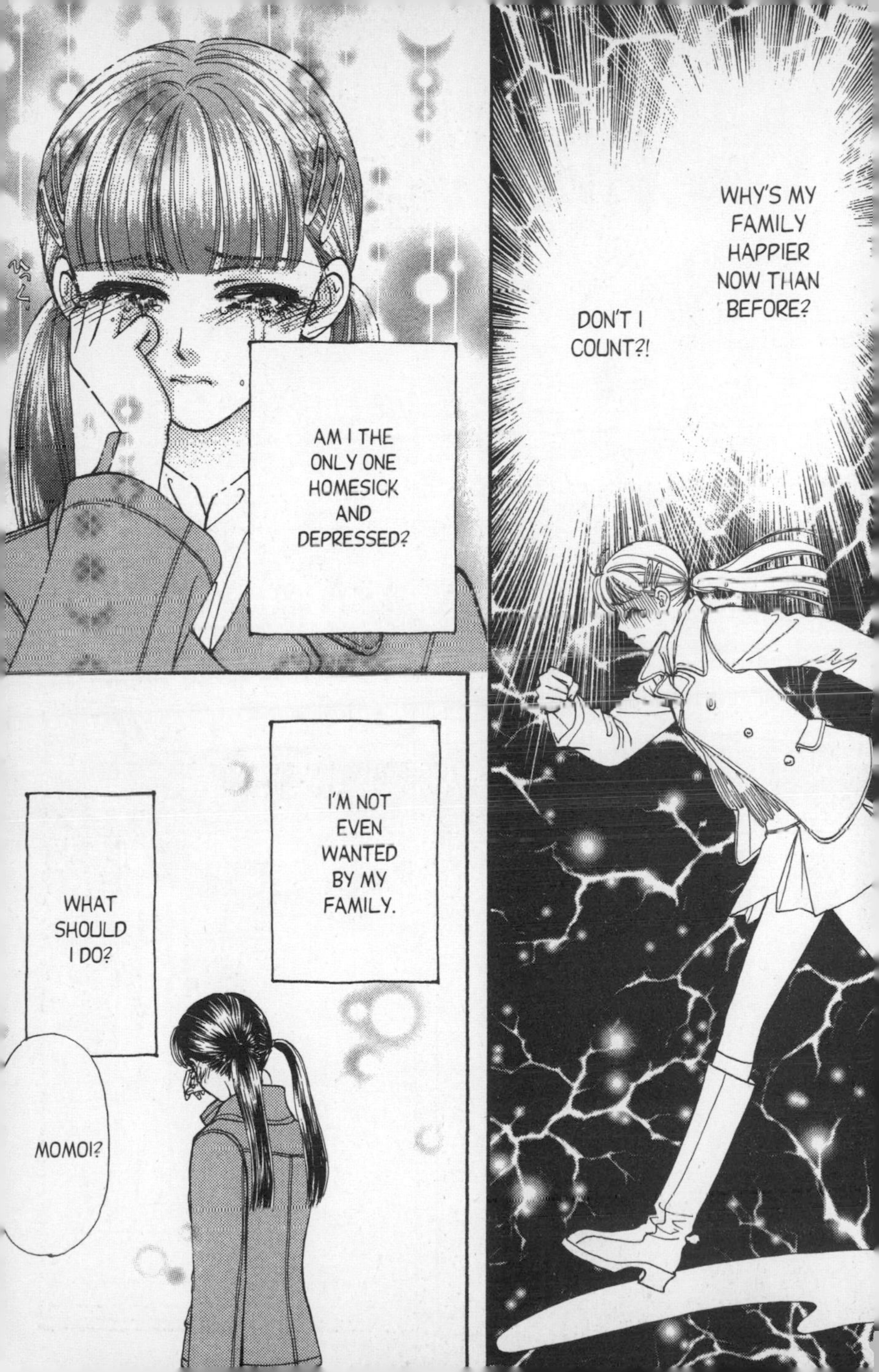

WHY'S MY FAMILY HAPPIER NOW THAN BEFORE?
DON'T I COUNT?!
AM I THE ONLY ONE HOMESICK AND DEPRESSED?
I'M NOT EVEN WANTED BY MY FAMILY.
WHAT SHOULD I DO?
MOMOI?

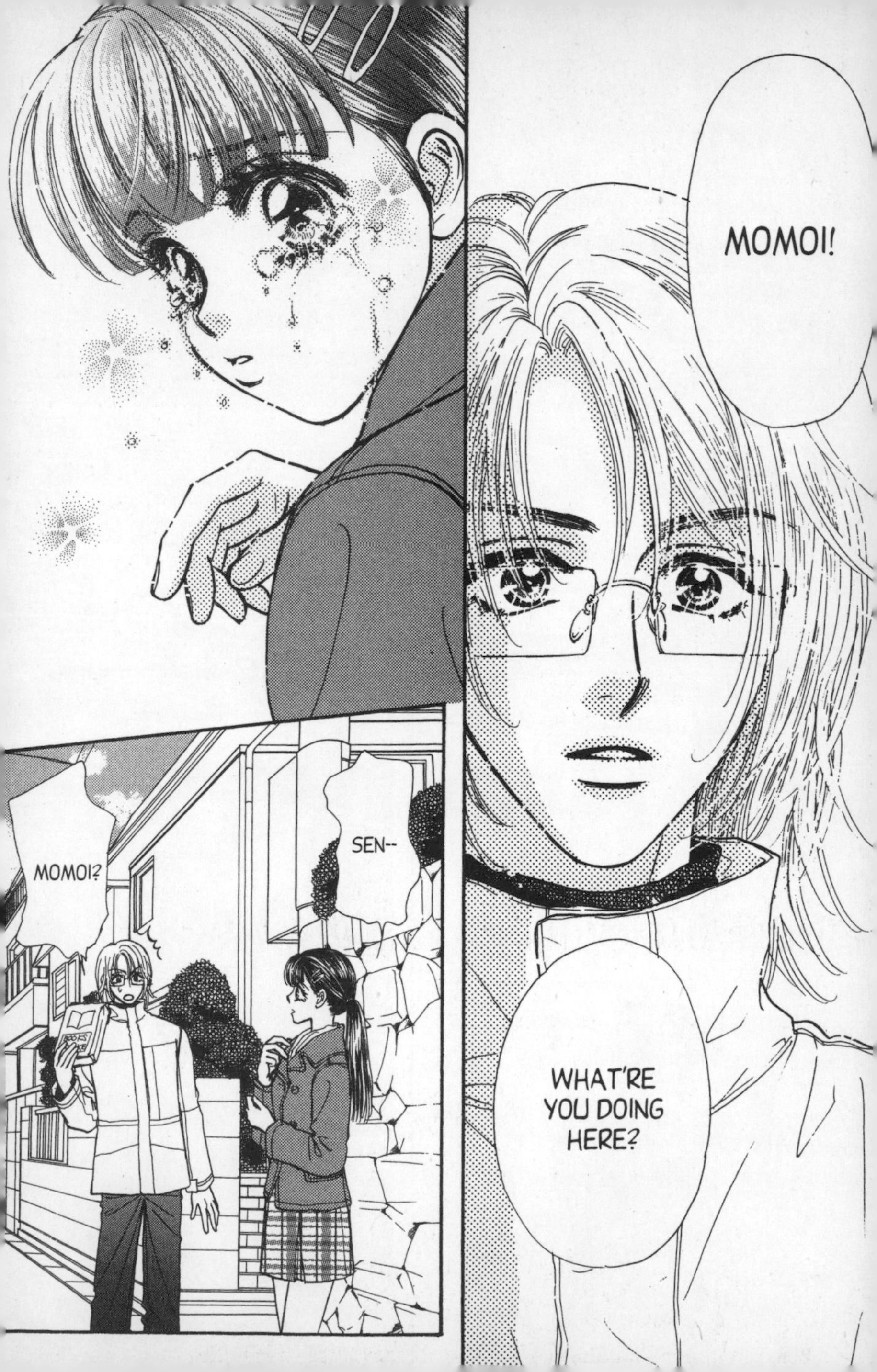
MOMOI!
WHAT'RE YOU DOING HERE?
SEN--
MOMOI?

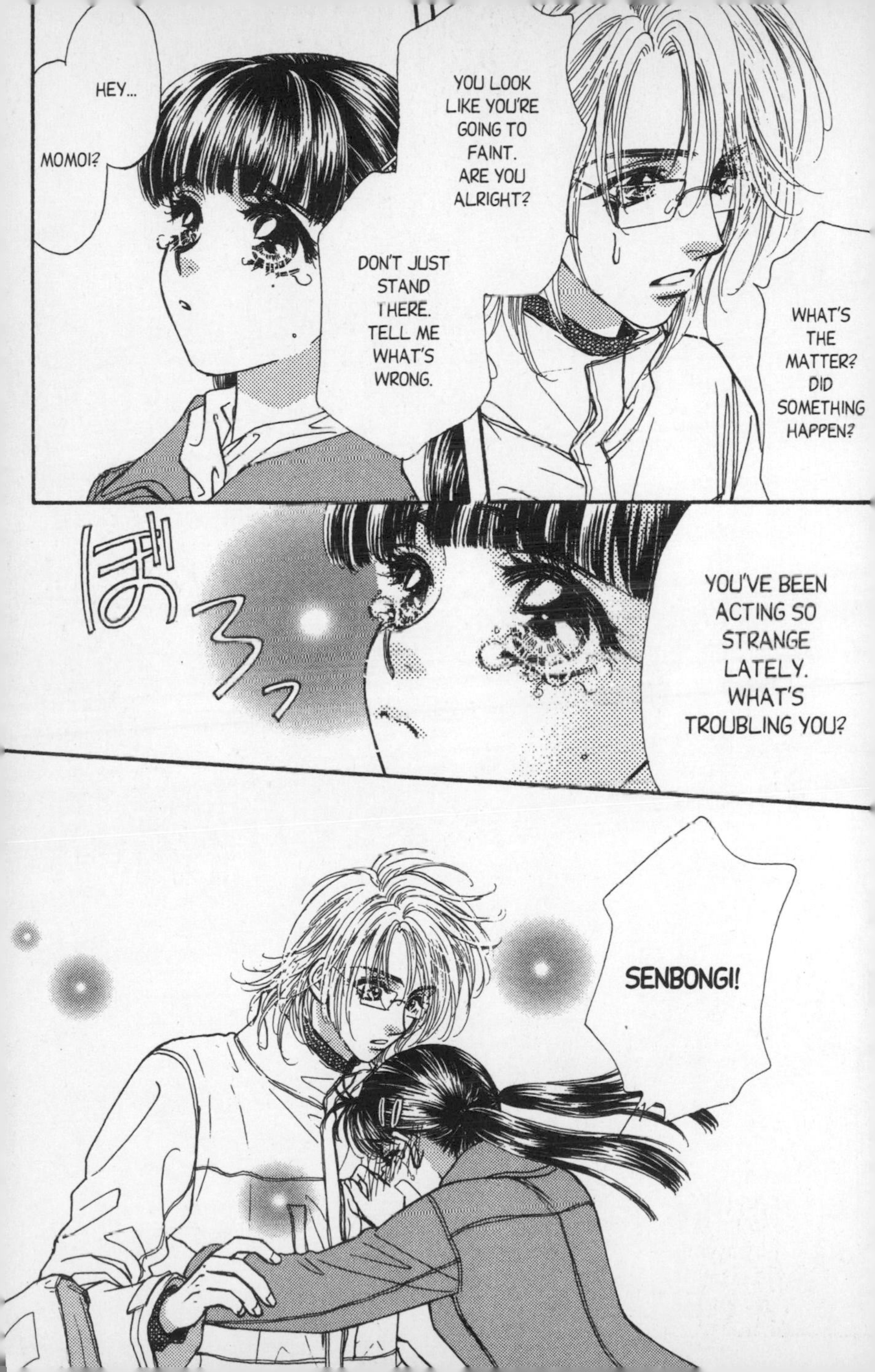
WHAT'S THE MATTER? DID SOMETHING HAPPEN?
YOU LOOK LIKE YOU'RE GOING TO FAINT. ARE YOU ALRIGHT?
DON'T JUST STAND THERE. TELL ME WHAT'S WRONG.
HEY...
MOMOI?
YOU'VE BEEN ACTING SO STRANGE LATELY. WHAT'S TROUBLING YOU?
ぽろっ
SENBONGI!

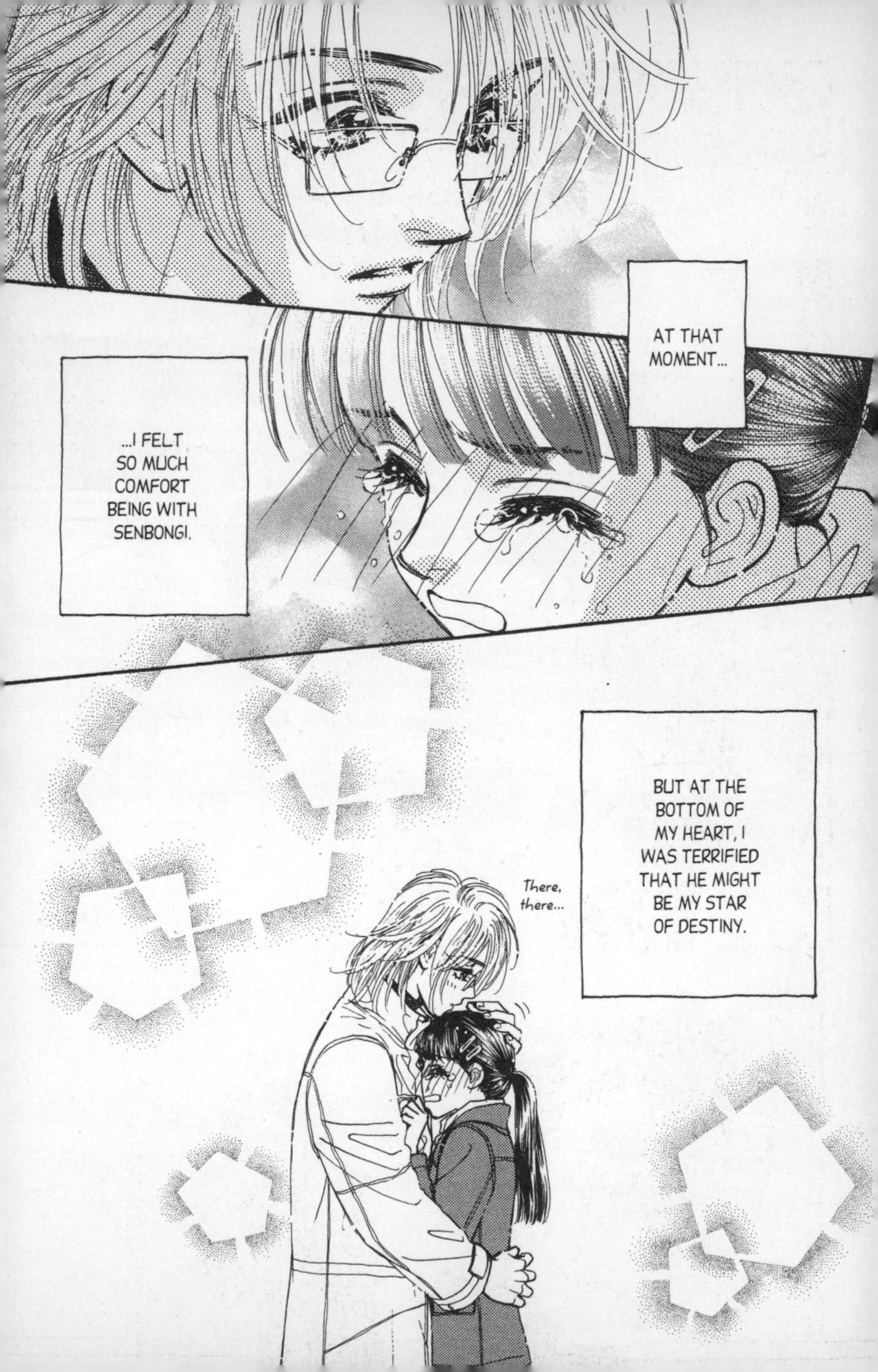
AT THAT MOMENT...
...I FELT SO MUCH COMFORT BEING WITH SENBONGI.
BUT AT THE BOTTOM OF MY HEART, I WAS TERRIFIED THAT HE MIGHT BE MY STAR OF DESTINY.
There, there...

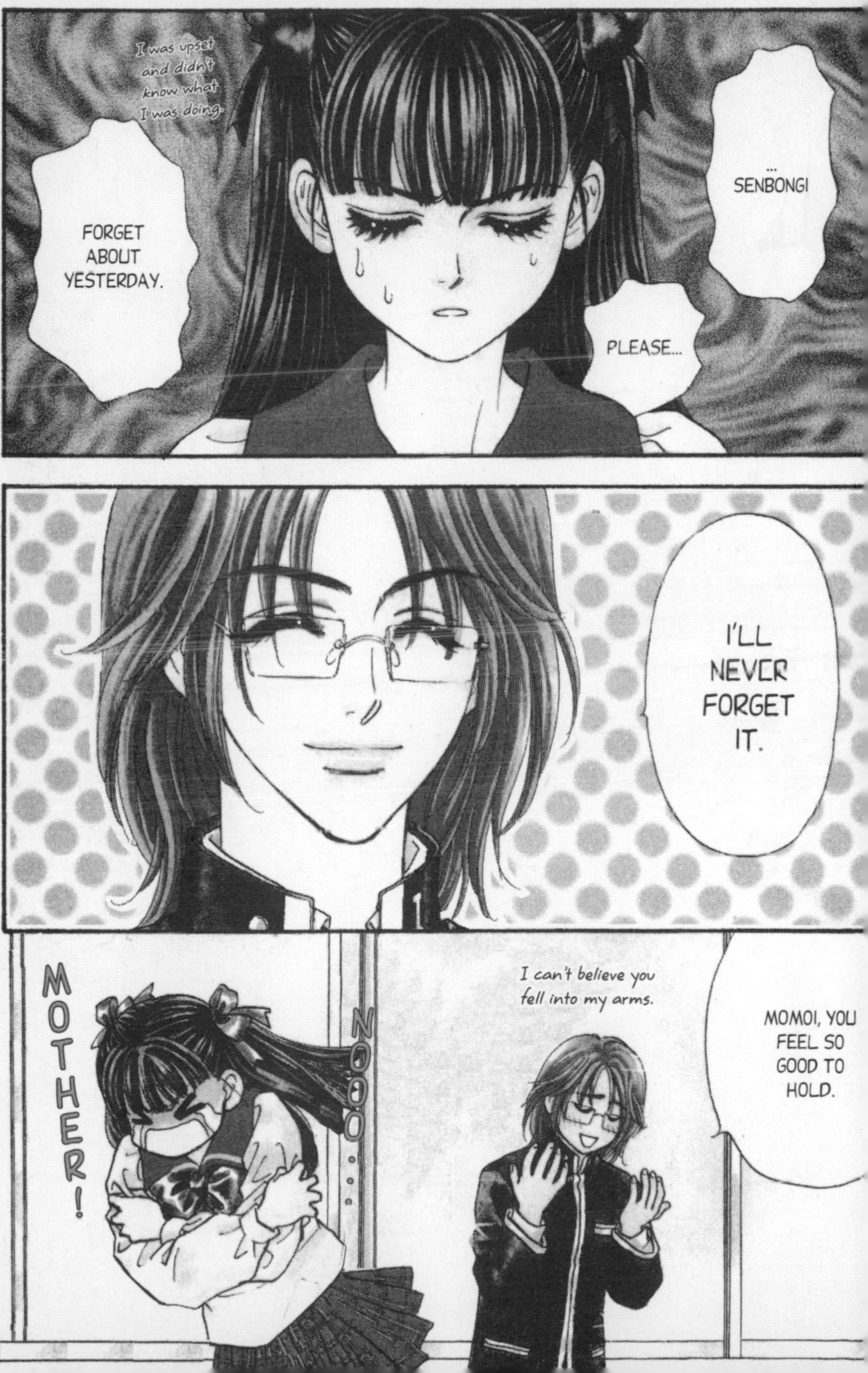
...SENBONGI
PLEASE...
I was upset and didn't know what I was doing.
FORGET ABOUT YESTERDAY.
I'LL NEVER FORGET IT.
MOMOI, YOU FEEL SO GOOD TO HOLD.
I can't believe you fell into my arms.
NOOO...
MOTHER!

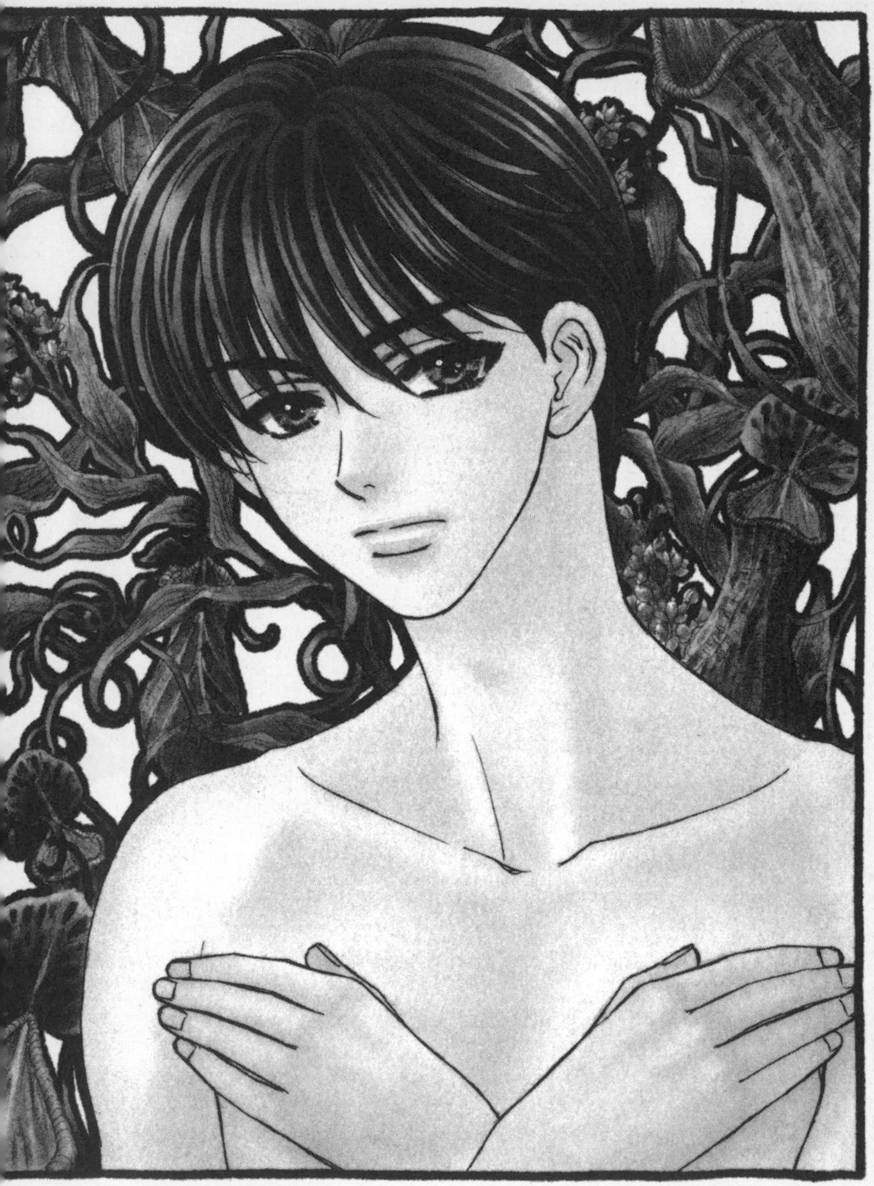

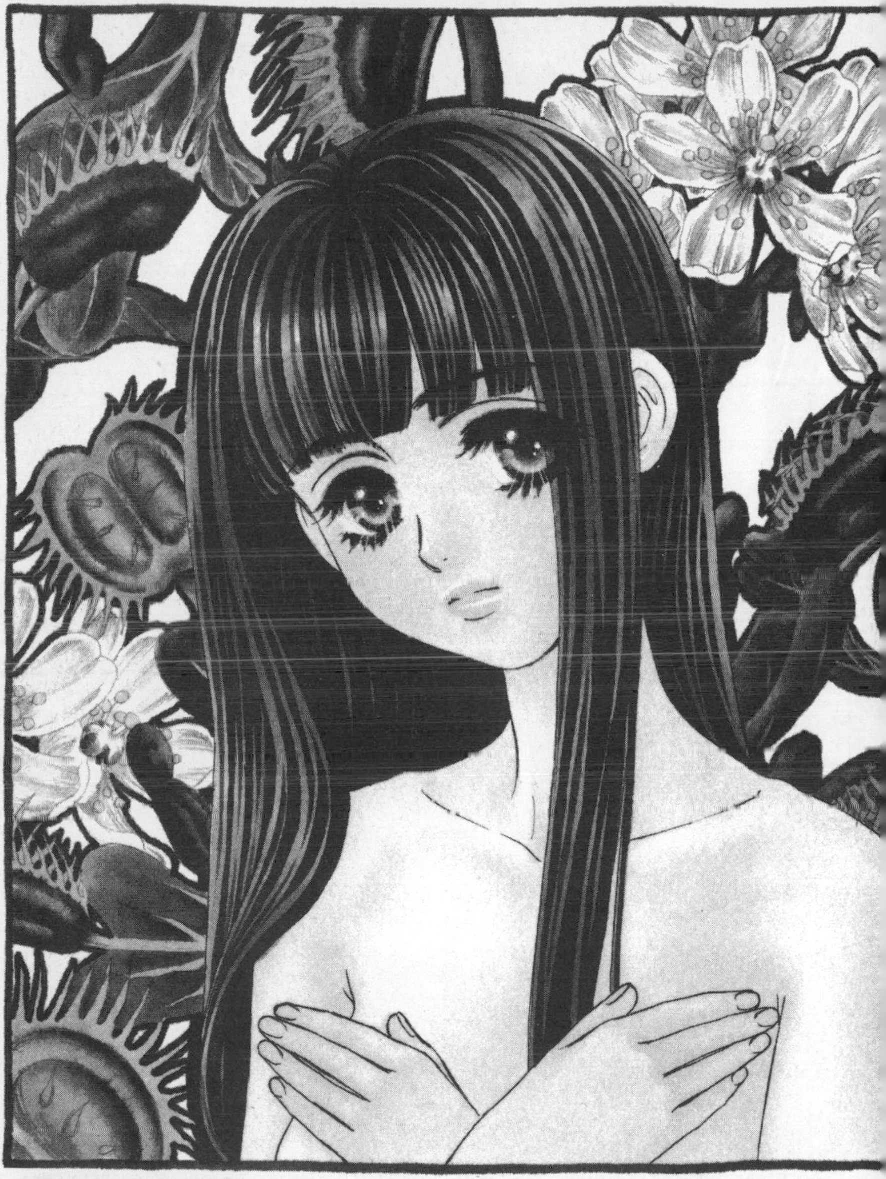

Episode 8
Exam Study

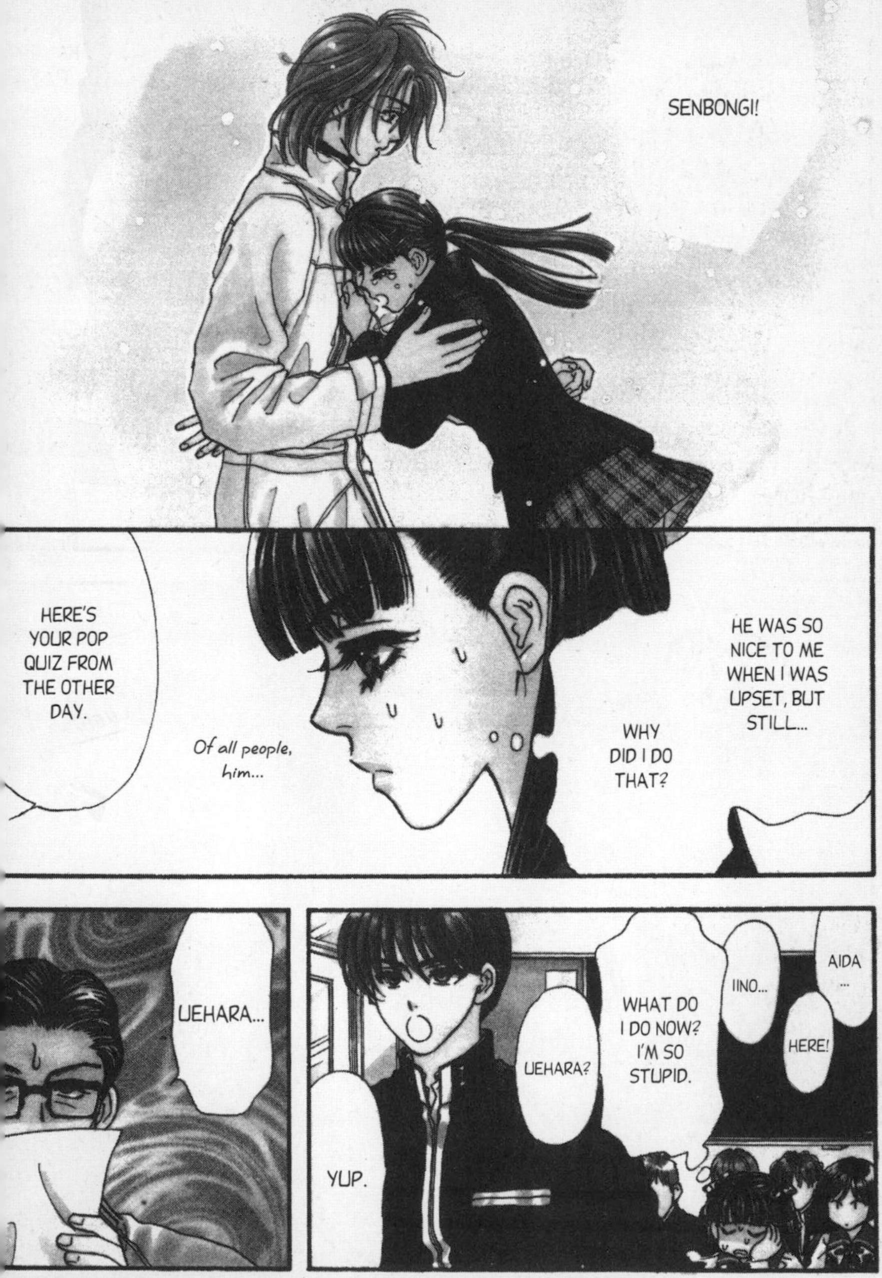
SENBONGI!
HE WAS SO NICE TO ME WHEN I WAS UPSET, BUT STILL...
WHY DID I DO THAT?
Of all people, him...
HERE'S YOUR POP QUIZ FROM THE OTHER DAY.
AIDA ...
IINO...
HERE!
WHAT DO I DO NOW? I'M SO STUPID.
UEHARA?
YUP.
UEHARA...

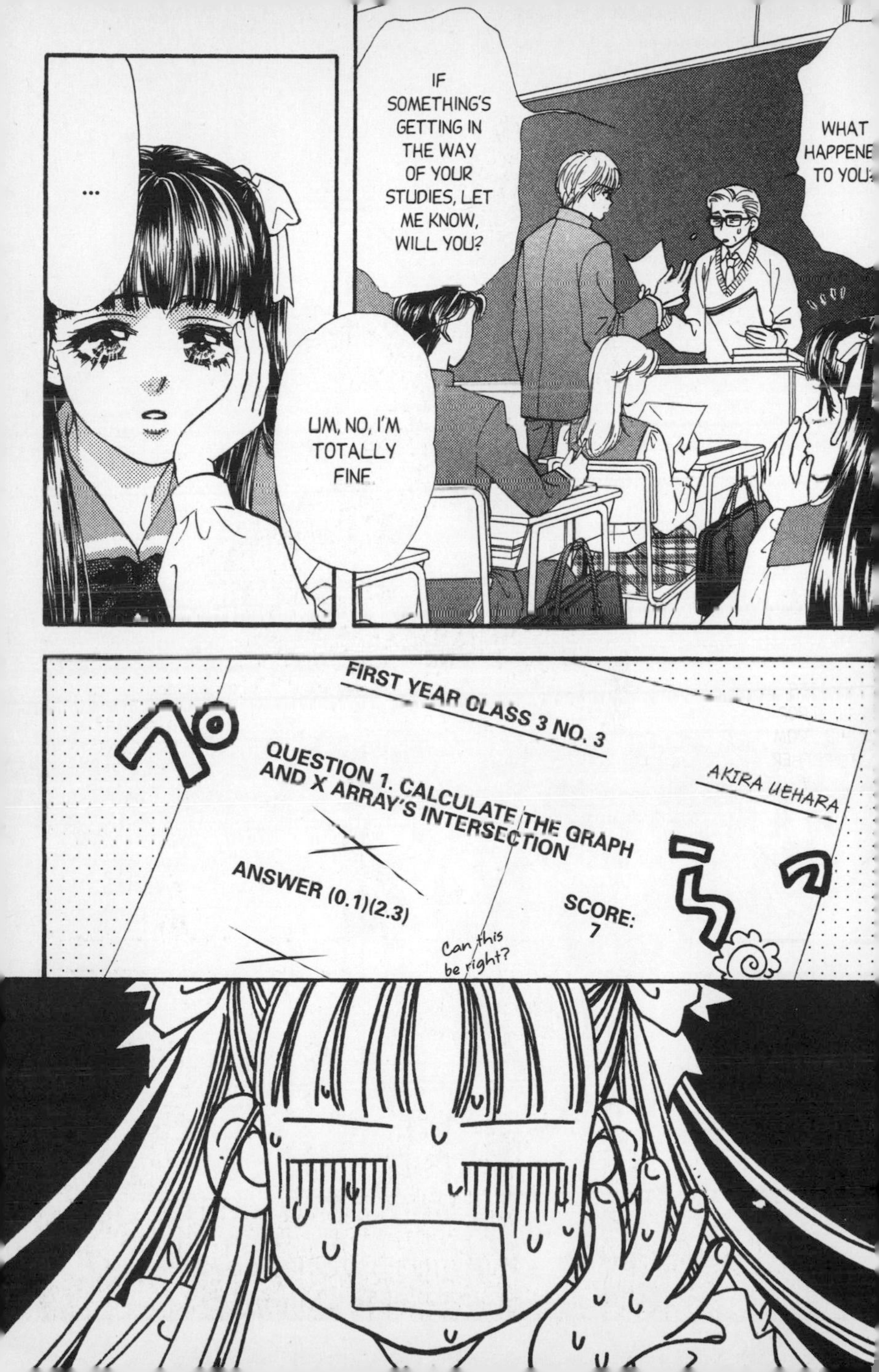
WHAT HAPPENE TO YOU
IF SOMETHING'S GETTING IN THE WAY OF YOUR STUDIES, LET ME KNOW, WILL YOU?
UM, NO, I'M TOTALLY FINE.
...
FIRST YEAR CLASS 3 NO. 3
AKIRA UEHARA
QUESTION 1. CALCULATE THE GRAPH AND X ARRAY'S INTERSECTION
ANSWER (0.1)(2.3)
SCORE: 7
Can this be right?

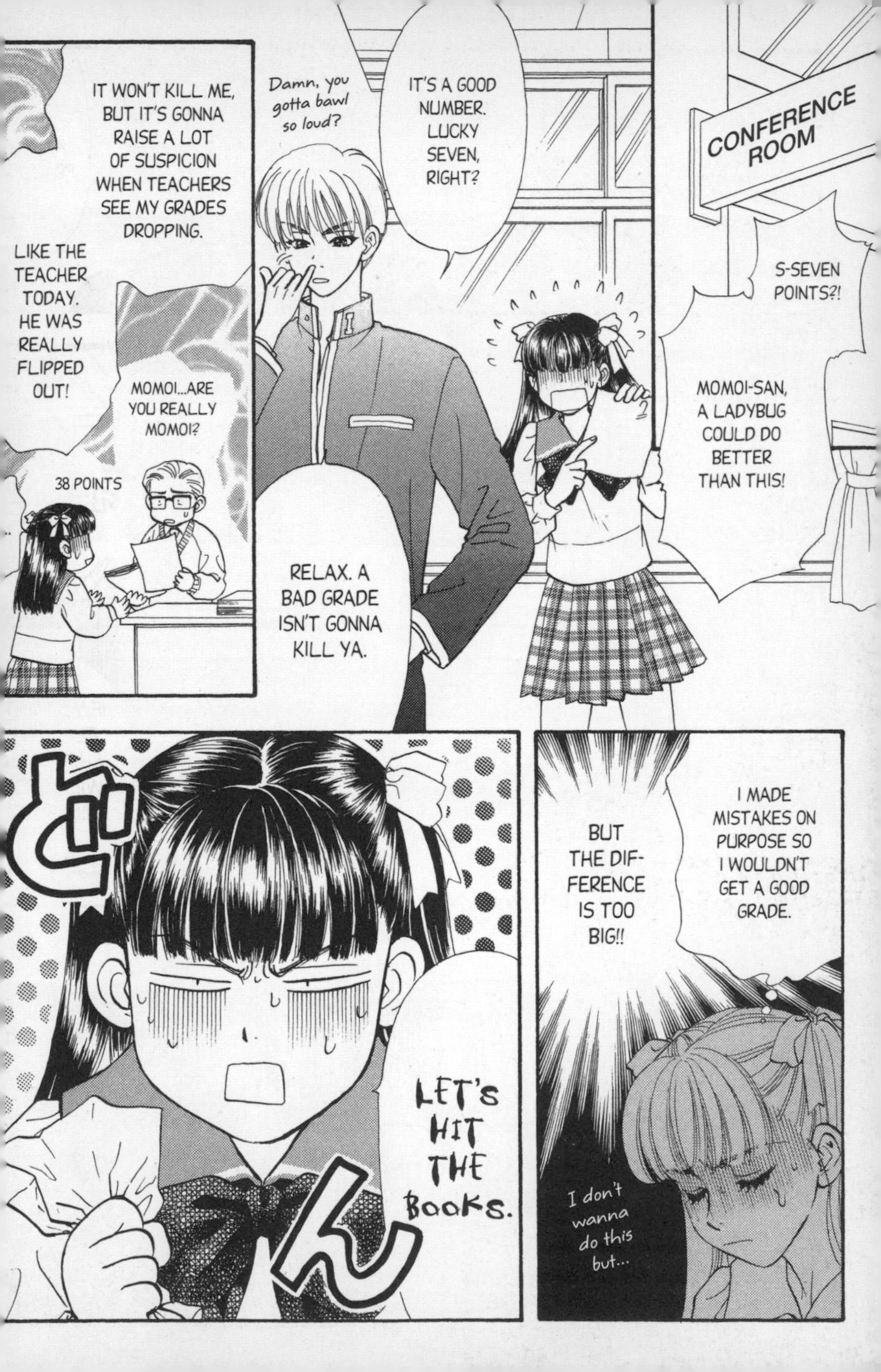
CONFERENCE ROOM
S-SEVEN POINTS?!
MOMOI-SAN, A LADYBUG COULD DO BETTER THAN THIS!
IT'S A GOOD NUMBER. LUCKY SEVEN, RIGHT?
Damn, you gotta bawl so loud?
RELAX. A BAD GRADE ISN'T GONNA KILL YA.
IT WON'T KILL ME, BUT IT'S GONNA RAISE A LOT OF SUSPICION WHEN TEACHERS SEE MY GRADES DROPPING.
LIKE THE TEACHER TODAY. HE WAS REALLY FLIPPED OUT!
MOMOI...ARE YOU REALLY MOMOI?
38 POINTS
I MADE MISTAKES ON PURPOSE SO I WOULDN'T GET A GOOD GRADE.
BUT THE DIF-FERENCE IS TOO BIG!!
I don't wanna do this but...
どん
LET's HIT THE Books.

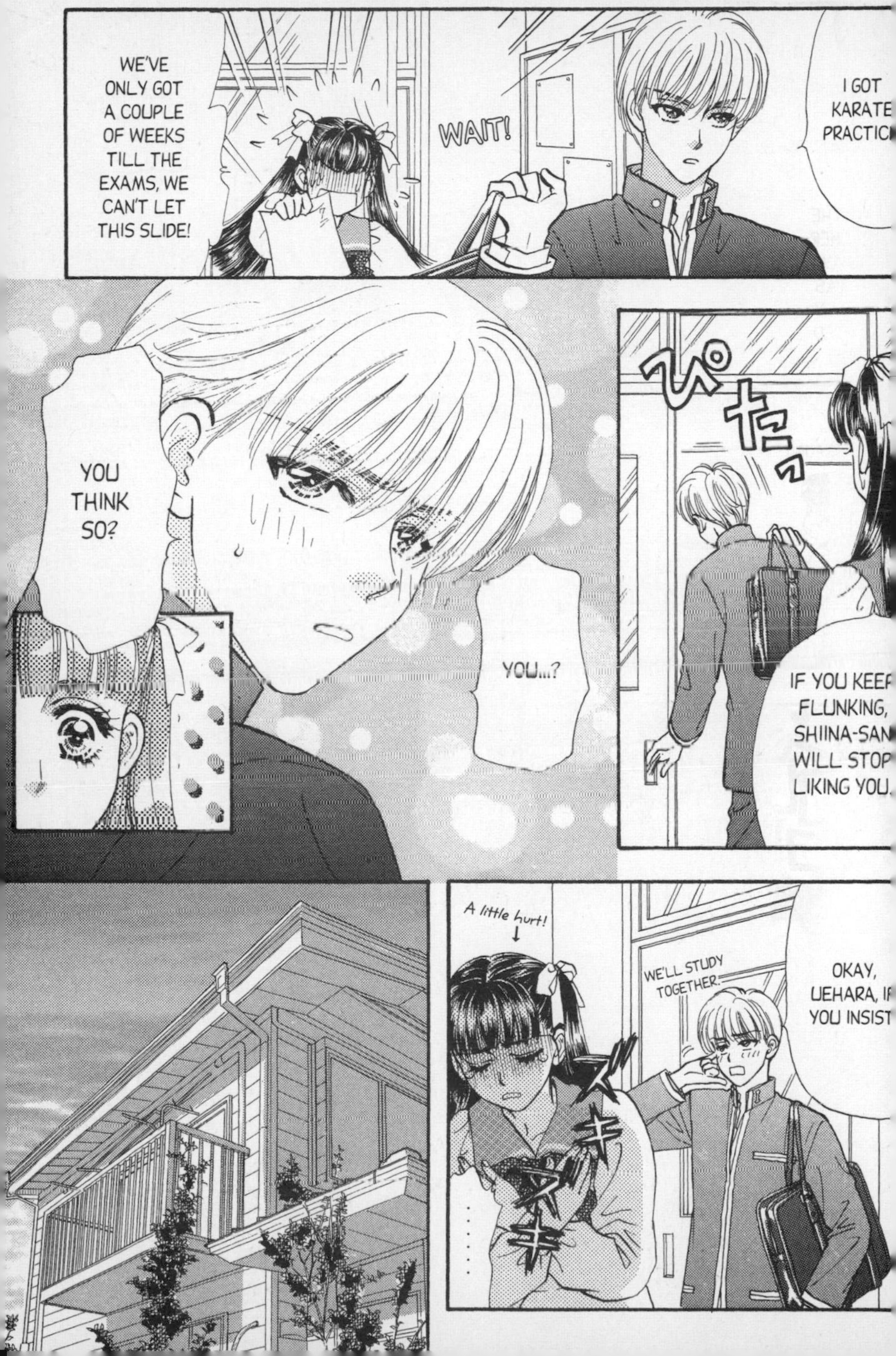
I GOT KARATE PRACTIC
WAIT!
WE'VE ONLY GOT A COUPLE OF WEEKS TILL THE EXAMS, WE CAN'T LET THIS SLIDE!
ぴたっ
IF YOU KEEP FLUNKING, SHIINA-SAN WILL STOP LIKING YOU.
YOU...?
YOU THINK SO?
OKAY, UEHARA, IF YOU INSIST
WE'LL STUDY TOGETHER.
A little hurt!
ズキズキ

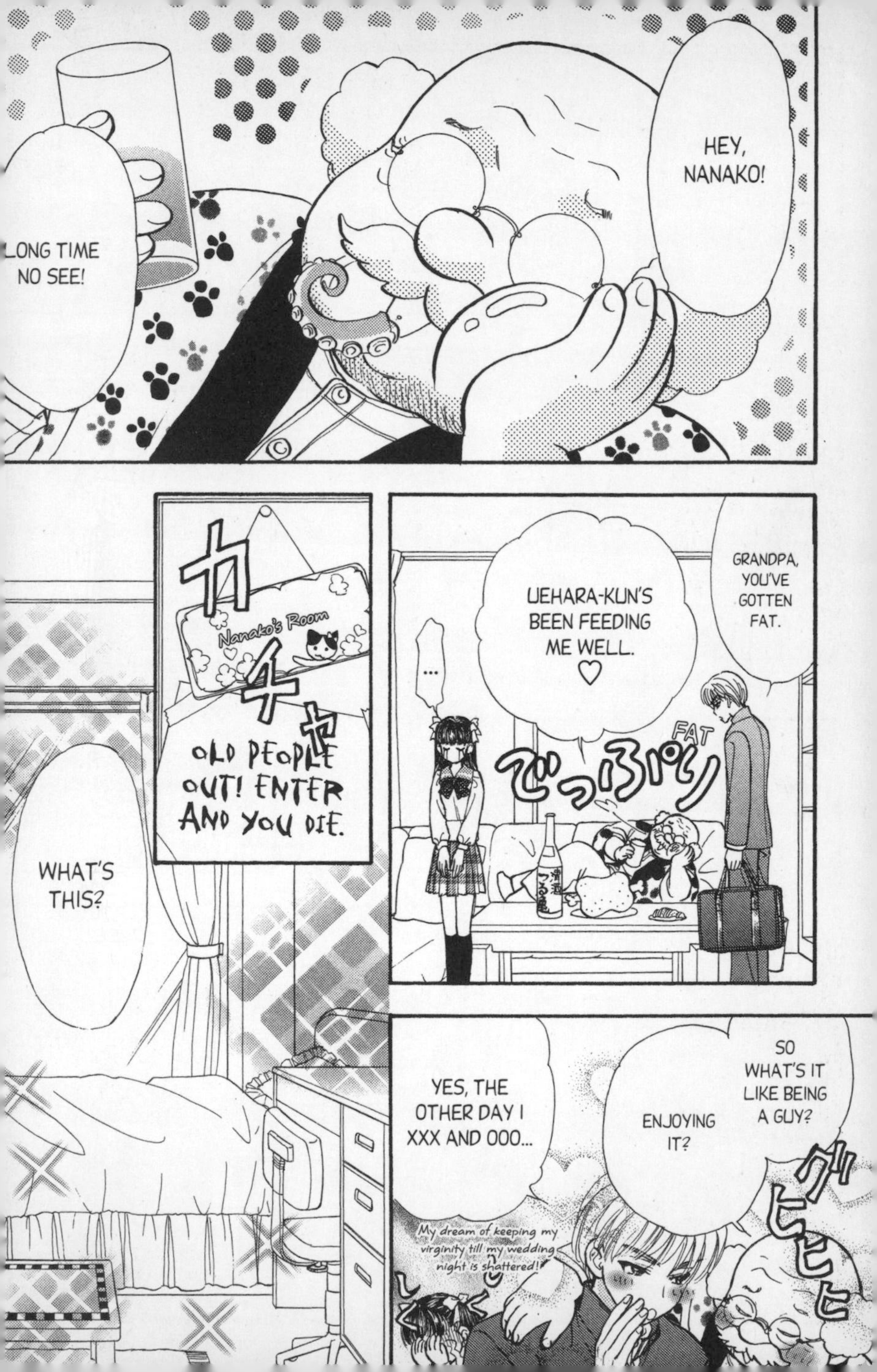
HEY, NANAKO!
LONG TIME NO SEE!
GRANDPA, YOU'VE GOTTEN FAT.
UEHARA-KUN'S BEEN FEEDING ME WELL. ♡
FAT
...
SO WHAT'S IT LIKE BEING A GUY?
ENJOYING IT?
YES, THE OTHER DAY I XXX AND OOO...
My dream of keeping my virginity till my wedding night is shattered!
Nanako's Room
OLD PEOPLE OUT! ENTER AND YOU DIE.
WHAT'S THIS?

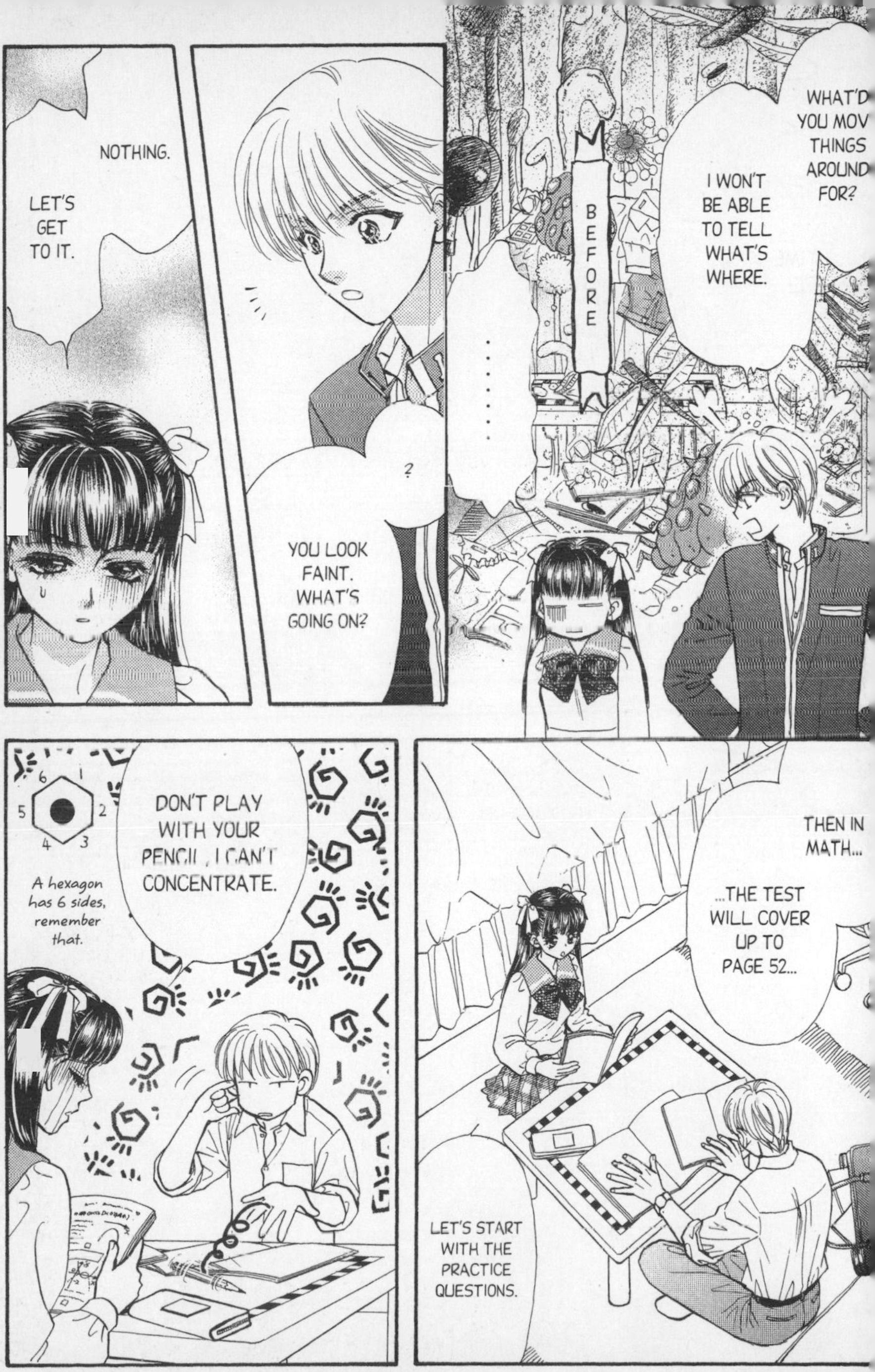
WHAT'D YOU MOV THINGS AROUND FOR?
I WON'T BE ABLE TO TELL WHAT'S WHERE.
BEFORE
......
?
YOU LOOK FAINT. WHAT'S GOING ON?
NOTHING.
LET'S GET TO IT.
THEN IN MATH...
...THE TEST WILL COVER UP TO PAGE 52...
LET'S START WITH THE PRACTICE QUESTIONS.
DON'T PLAY WITH YOUR PENCIL, I CAN'T CONCENTRATE.
A hexagon has 6 sides, remember that.

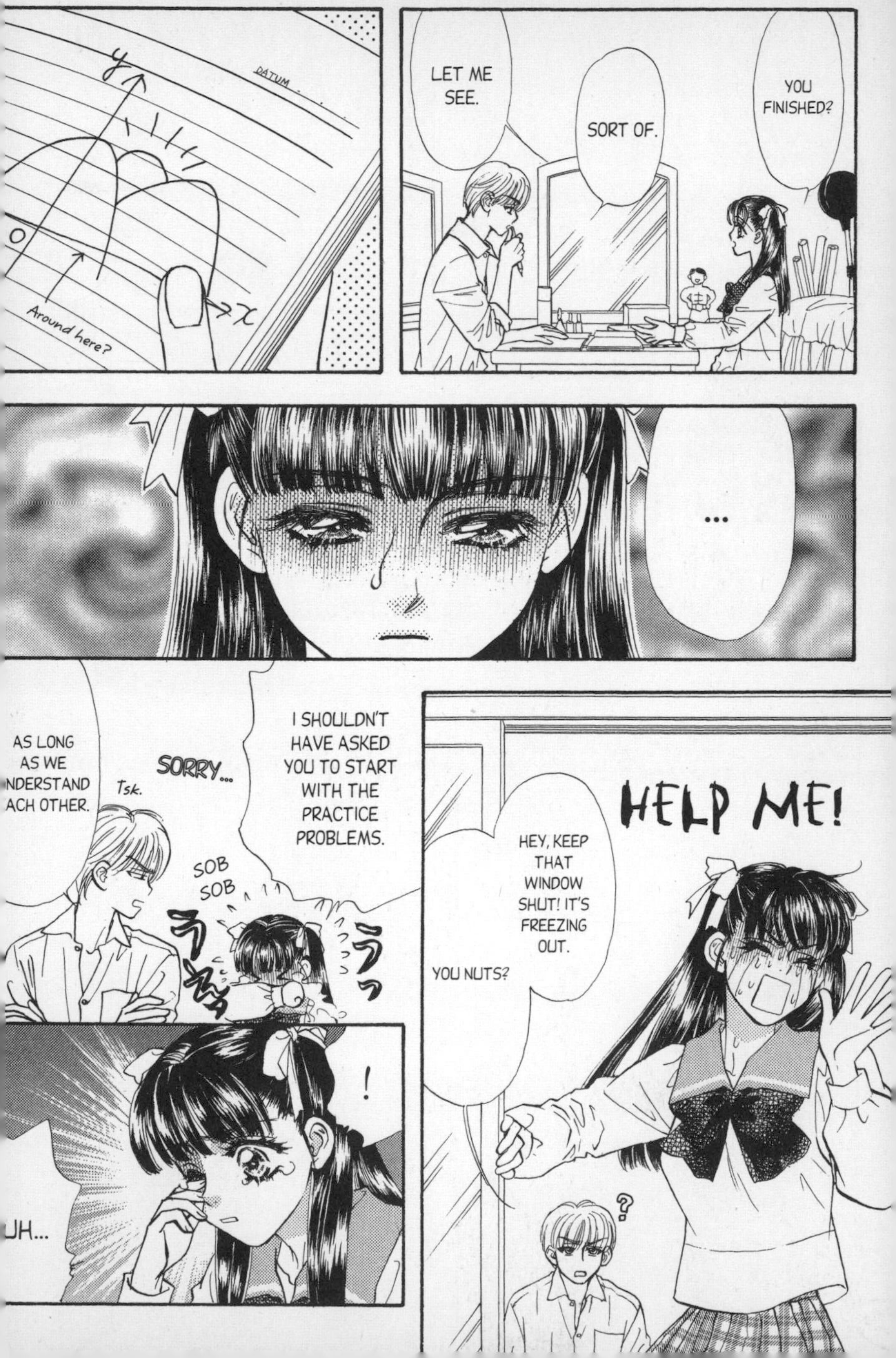
YOU FINISHED?
SORT OF.
LET ME SEE.
DATUM
Around here?
...
HELP ME!
HEY, KEEP THAT WINDOW SHUT! IT'S FREEZING OUT.
YOU NUTS?
I SHOULDN'T HAVE ASKED YOU TO START WITH THE PRACTICE PROBLEMS.
SORRY...
Tsk.
AS LONG AS WE NDERSTAND ACH OTHER.
SOB SOB
!
JH...

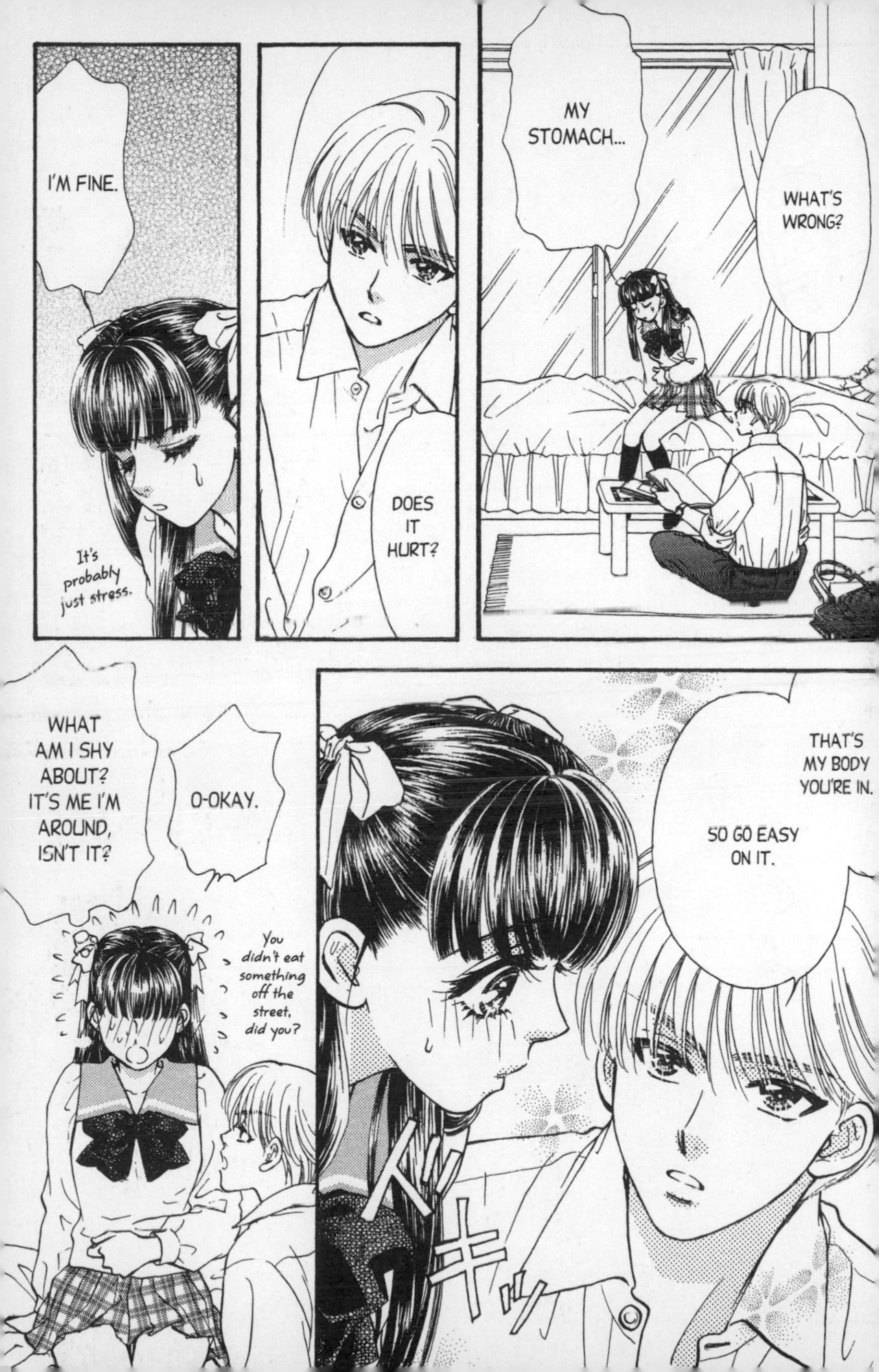
WHAT'S WRONG?
MY STOMACH...
DOES IT HURT?
I'M FINE.
It's probably just stress.
THAT'S MY BODY YOU'RE IN.
SO GO EASY ON IT.
ドキッ
O-OKAY.
WHAT AM I SHY ABOUT? IT'S ME I'M AROUND, ISN'T IT?
You didn't eat something off the street, did you?

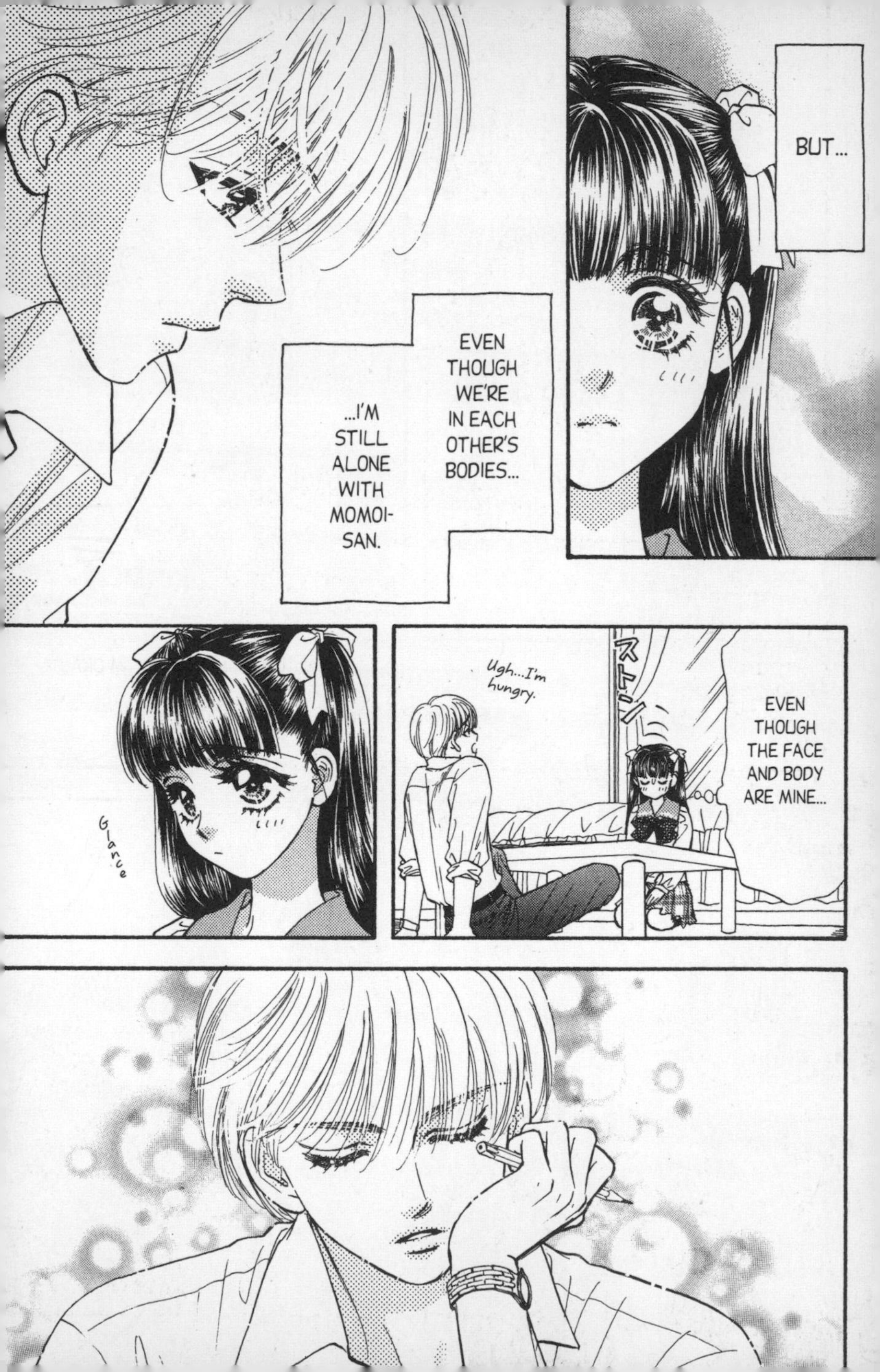
BUT...
EVEN THOUGH WE'RE IN EACH OTHER'S BODIES...
...I'M STILL ALONE WITH MOMOI-SAN.
ストン
EVEN THOUGH THE FACE AND BODY ARE MINE...
Ugh...I'm hungry.
Glance

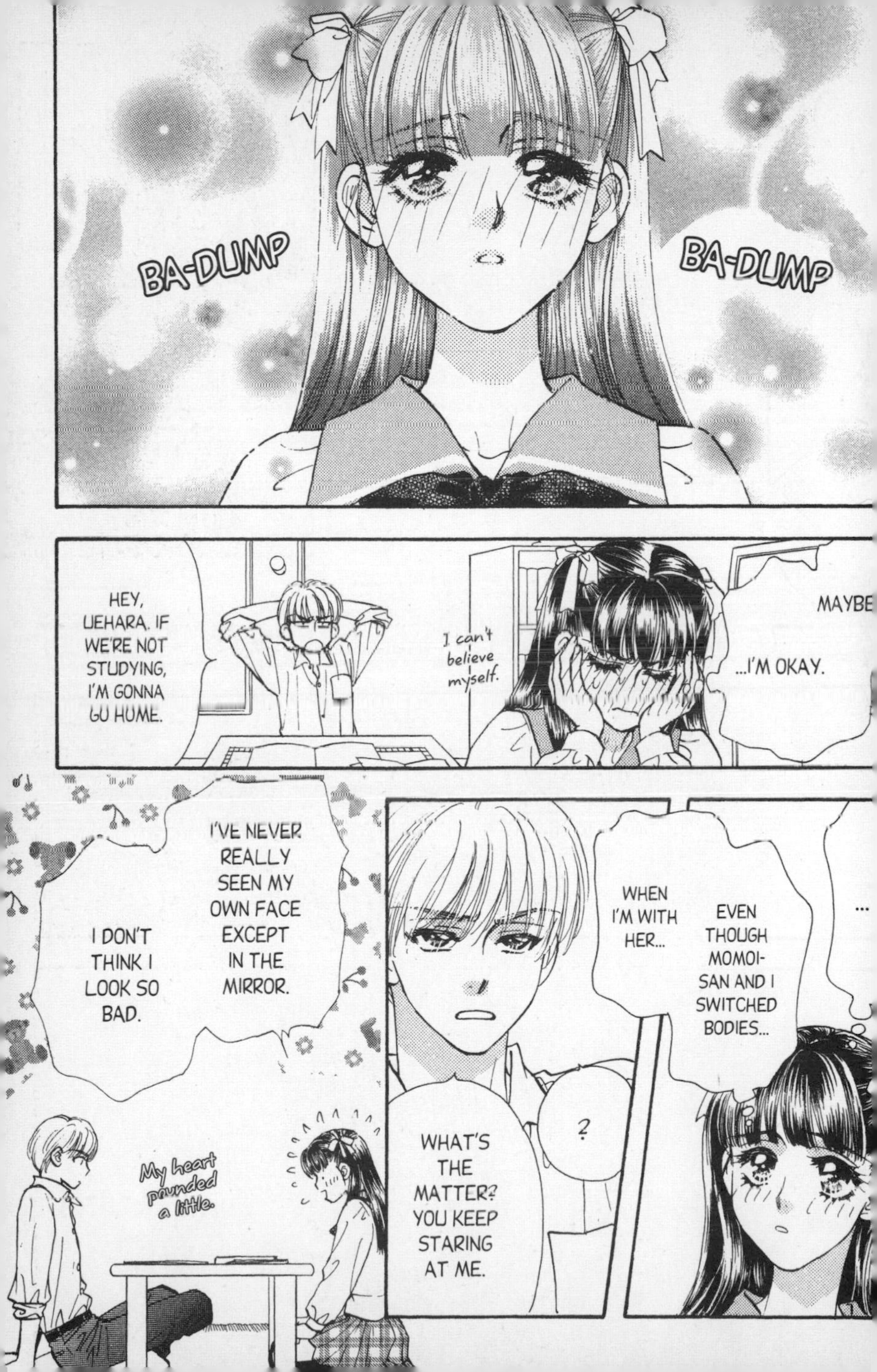
BA-DUMP
BA-DUMP
MAYBE ...I'M OKAY.
I can't believe myself.
HEY, UEHARA. IF WE'RE NOT STUDYING, I'M GONNA GO HOME.
...
EVEN THOUGH MOMOI-SAN AND I SWITCHED BODIES...
WHEN I'M WITH HER...
?
WHAT'S THE MATTER? YOU KEEP STARING AT ME.
I'VE NEVER REALLY SEEN MY OWN FACE EXCEPT IN THE MIRROR.
I DON'T THINK I LOOK SO BAD.
My heart pounded a little.

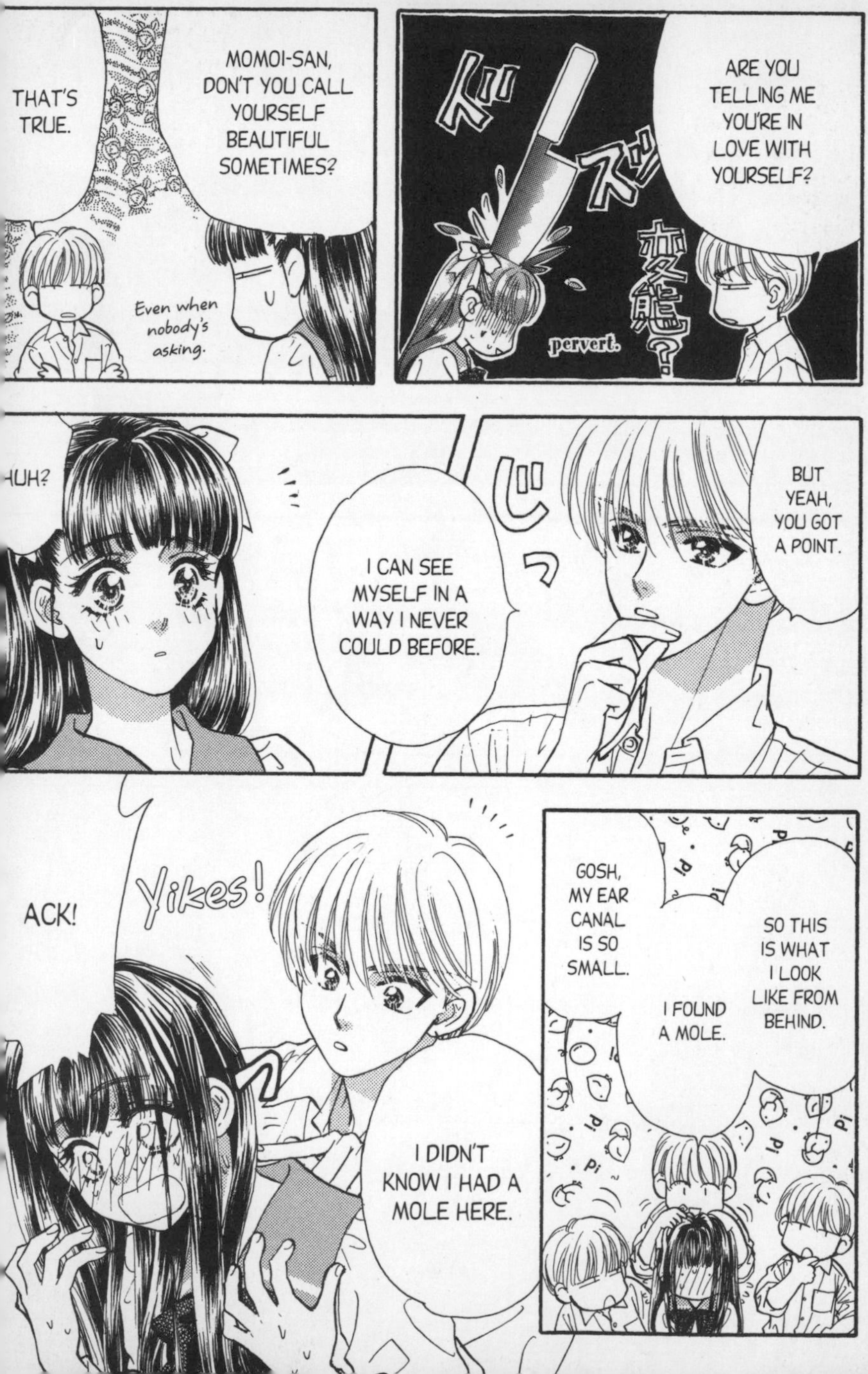
ARE YOU TELLING ME YOU'RE IN LOVE WITH YOURSELF?
変態?
pervert.
MOMOI-SAN, DON'T YOU CALL YOURSELF BEAUTIFUL SOMETIMES?
THAT'S TRUE.
Even when nobody's asking.
BUT YEAH, YOU GOT A POINT.
じっ
I CAN SEE MYSELF IN A WAY I NEVER COULD BEFORE.
HUH?
GOSH, MY EAR CANAL IS SO SMALL.
SO THIS IS WHAT I LOOK LIKE FROM BEHIND.
I FOUND A MOLE.
Pi
I DIDN'T KNOW I HAD A MOLE HERE.
Yikes!
ACK!

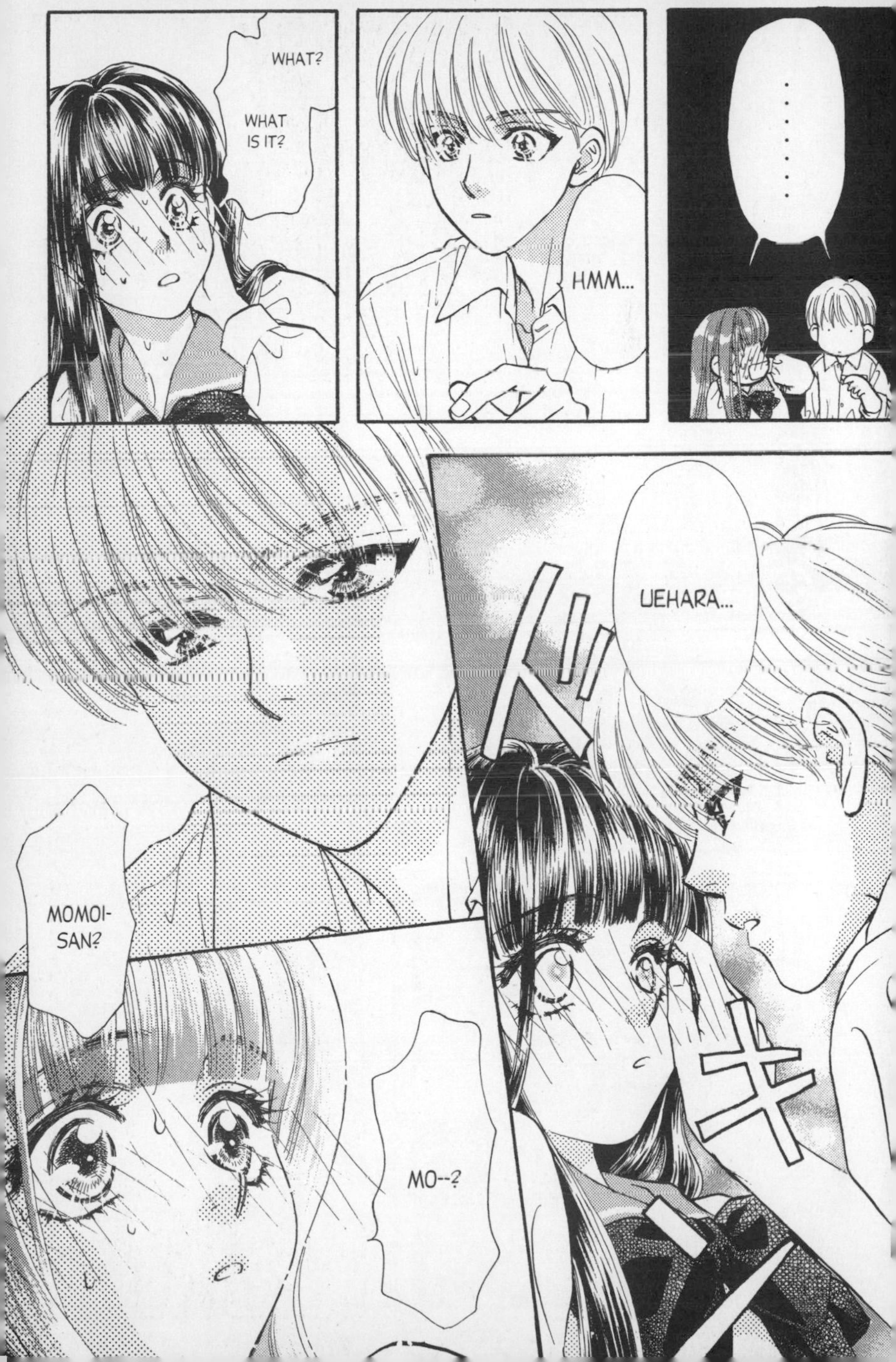
......
HMM...
WHAT?
WHAT IS IT?
UEHARA...
MOMOI-SAN?
MO--?

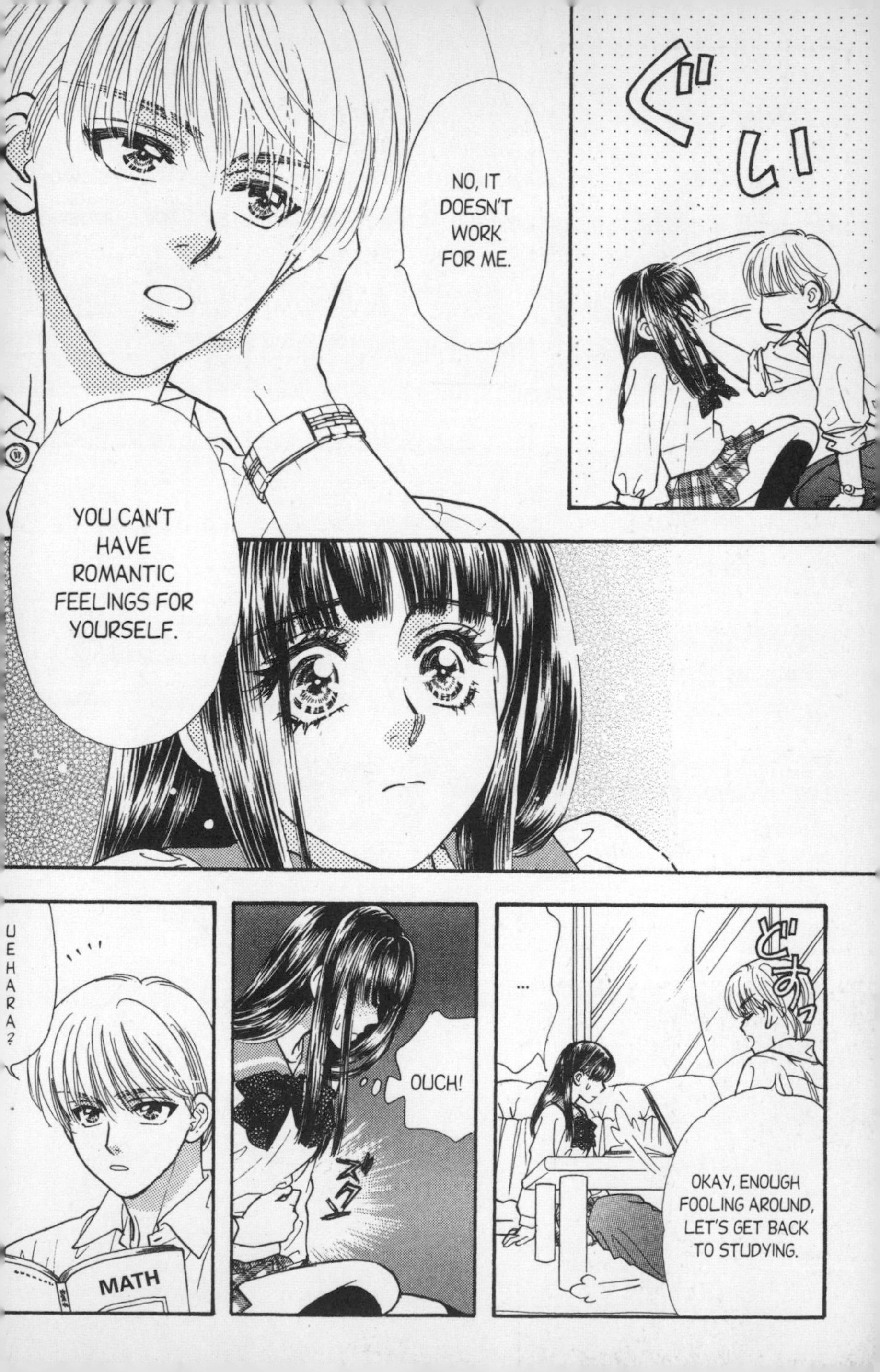
ぐい
NO, IT DOESN'T WORK FOR ME.
YOU CAN'T HAVE ROMANTIC FEELINGS FOR YOURSELF.
OKAY, ENOUGH FOOLING AROUND, LET'S GET BACK TO STUDYING.
...
OUCH!
UEHARA?
MATH

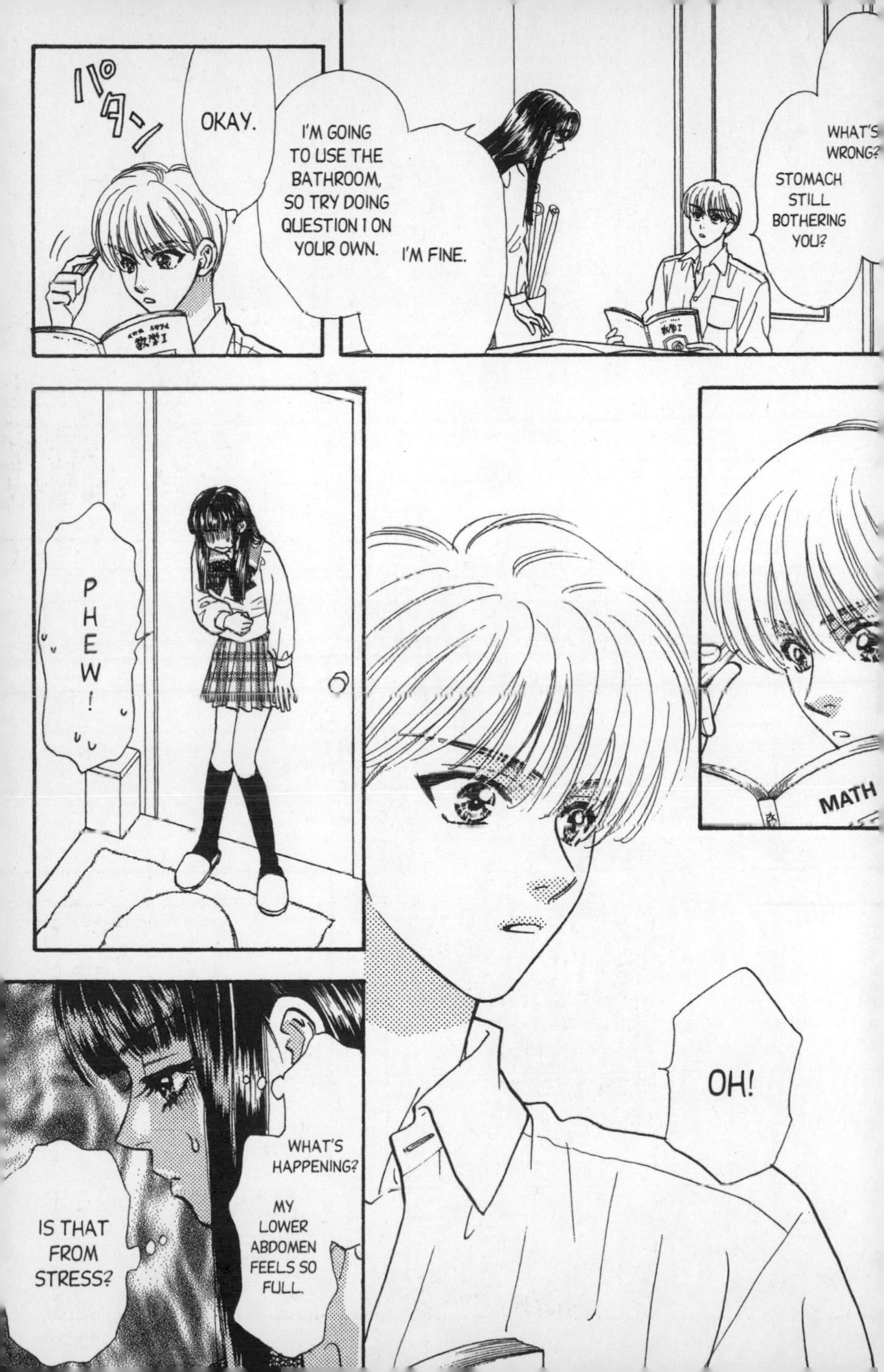
WHAT'S WRONG?
STOMACH STILL BOTHERING YOU?
I'M FINE.
I'M GOING TO USE THE BATHROOM, SO TRY DOING QUESTION 1 ON YOUR OWN.
OKAY.
パターン
MATH
OH!
PHEW!
WHAT'S HAPPENING?
MY LOWER ABDOMEN FEELS SO FULL.
IS THAT FROM STRESS?

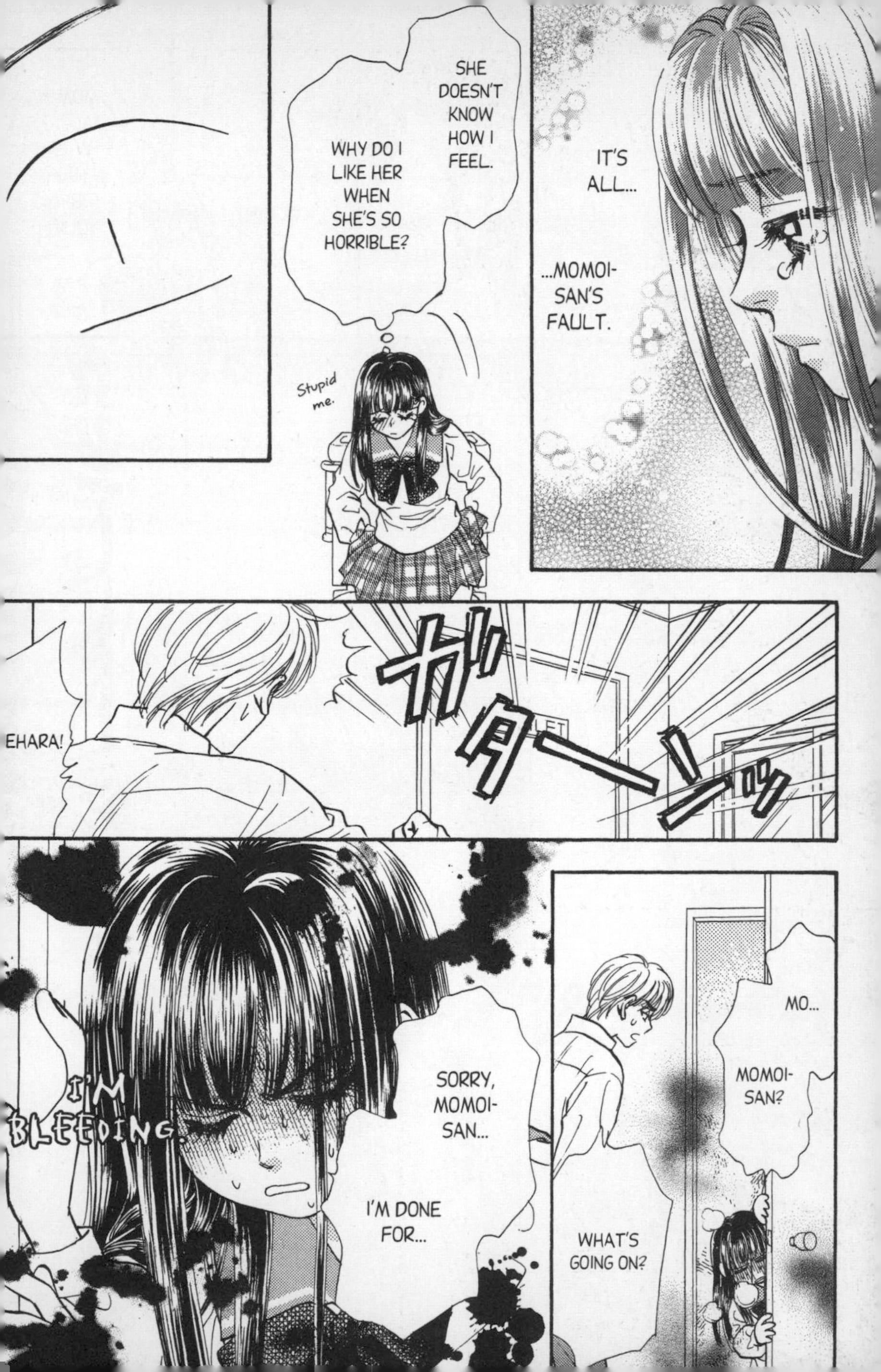
IT'S ALL...
...MOMOI-SAN'S FAULT.
SHE DOESN'T KNOW HOW I FEEL.
WHY DO I LIKE HER WHEN SHE'S SO HORRIBLE?
Stupid me.
ガターンッ
EHARA!
MO...
MOMOI-SAN?
WHAT'S GOING ON?
SORRY, MOMOI-SAN...
I'M DONE FOR...
I'M BLEEDING.

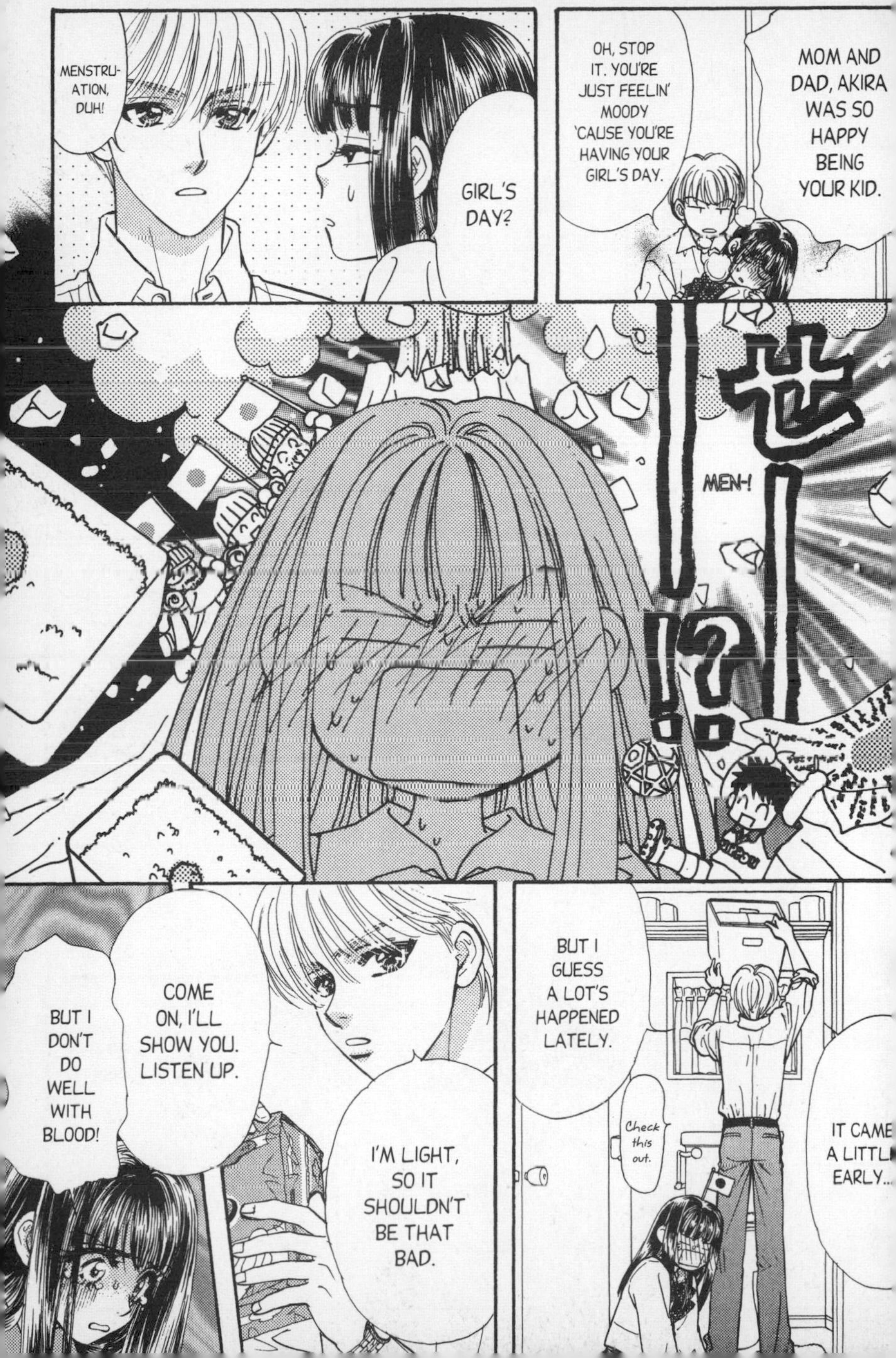
MOM AND DAD, AKIRA WAS SO HAPPY BEING YOUR KID.
OH, STOP IT. YOU'RE JUST FEELIN' MOODY 'CAUSE YOU'RE HAVING YOUR GIRL'S DAY.
GIRL'S DAY?
MENSTRU-ATION, DUH!
MEN-!
IT CAME A LITTL EARLY...
BUT I GUESS A LOT'S HAPPENED LATELY.
Check this out.
I'M LIGHT, SO IT SHOULDN'T BE THAT BAD.
COME ON, I'LL SHOW YOU. LISTEN UP.
BUT I DON'T DO WELL WITH BLOOD!

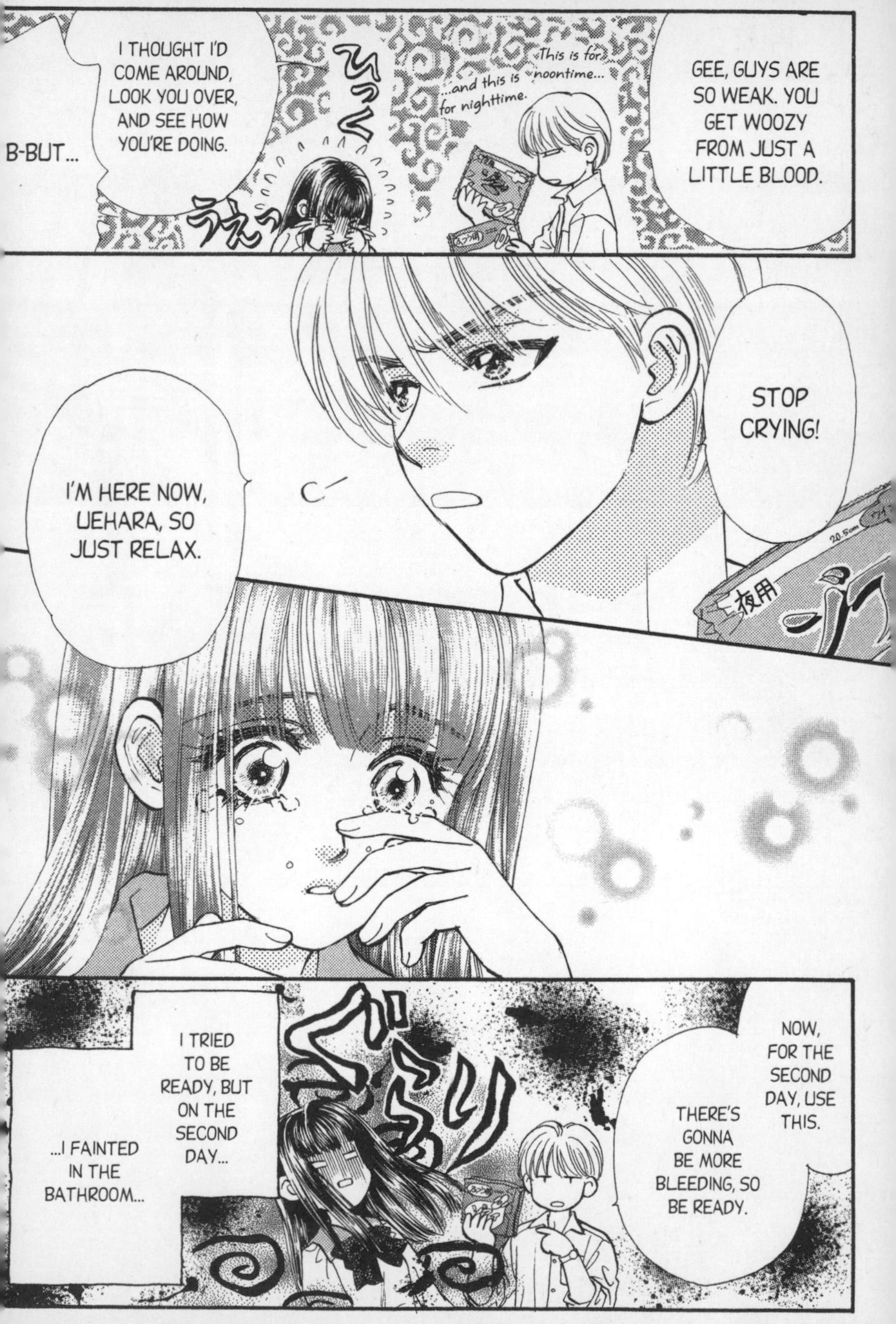

GEE, GUYS ARE SO WEAK. YOU GET WOOZY FROM JUST A LITTLE BLOOD.
This is for noontime...
...and this is for nighttime.
ひっく
うえっ
I THOUGHT I'D COME AROUND, LOOK YOU OVER, AND SEE HOW YOU'RE DOING.
B-BUT...
STOP CRYING!
I'M HERE NOW, UEHARA, SO JUST RELAX.
夜用
NOW, FOR THE SECOND DAY, USE THIS.
THERE'S GONNA BE MORE BLEEDING, SO BE READY.
I TRIED TO BE READY, BUT ON THE SECOND DAY...
...I FAINTED IN THE BATHROOM...

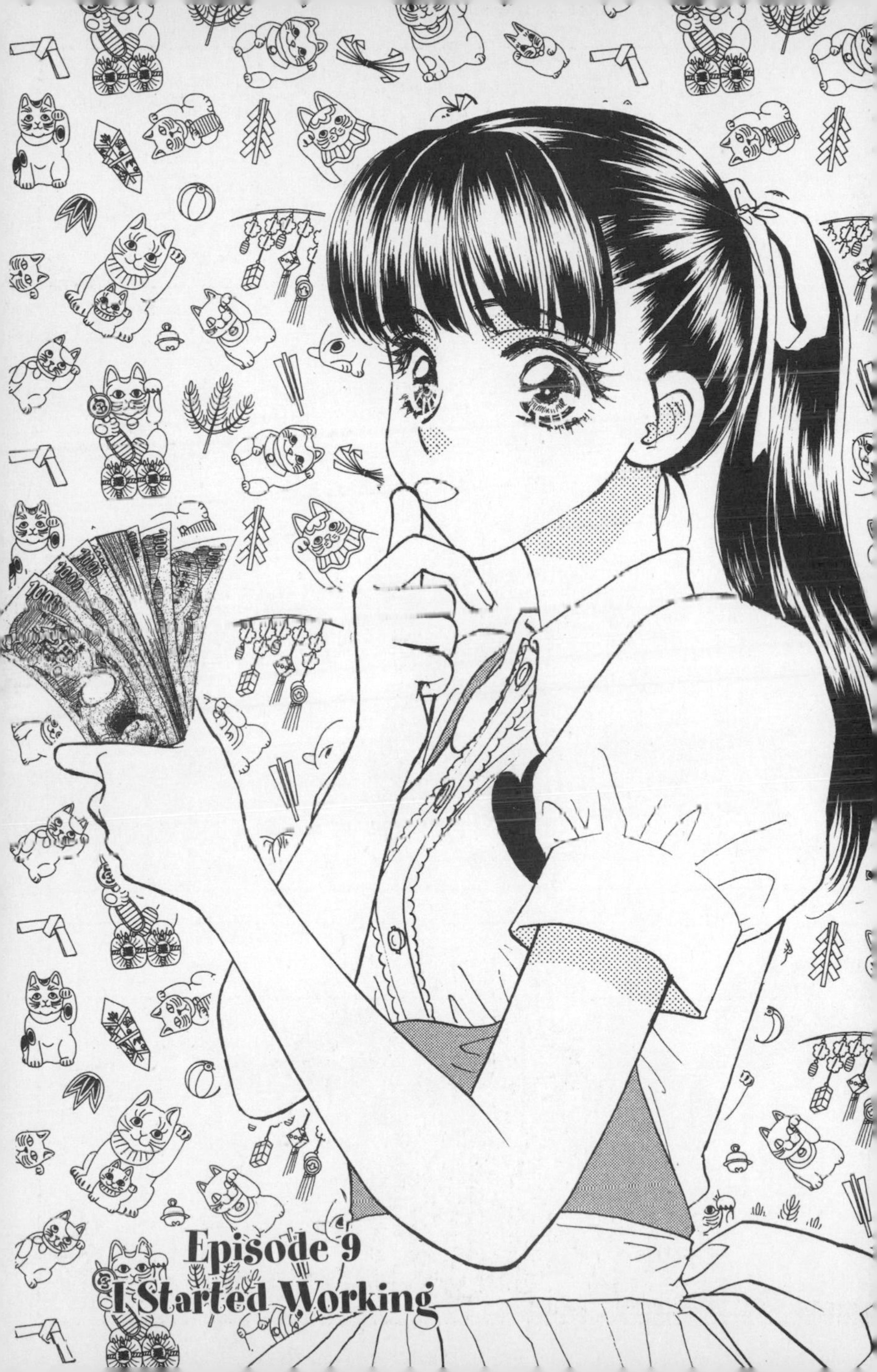
Episode 9
I Started Working

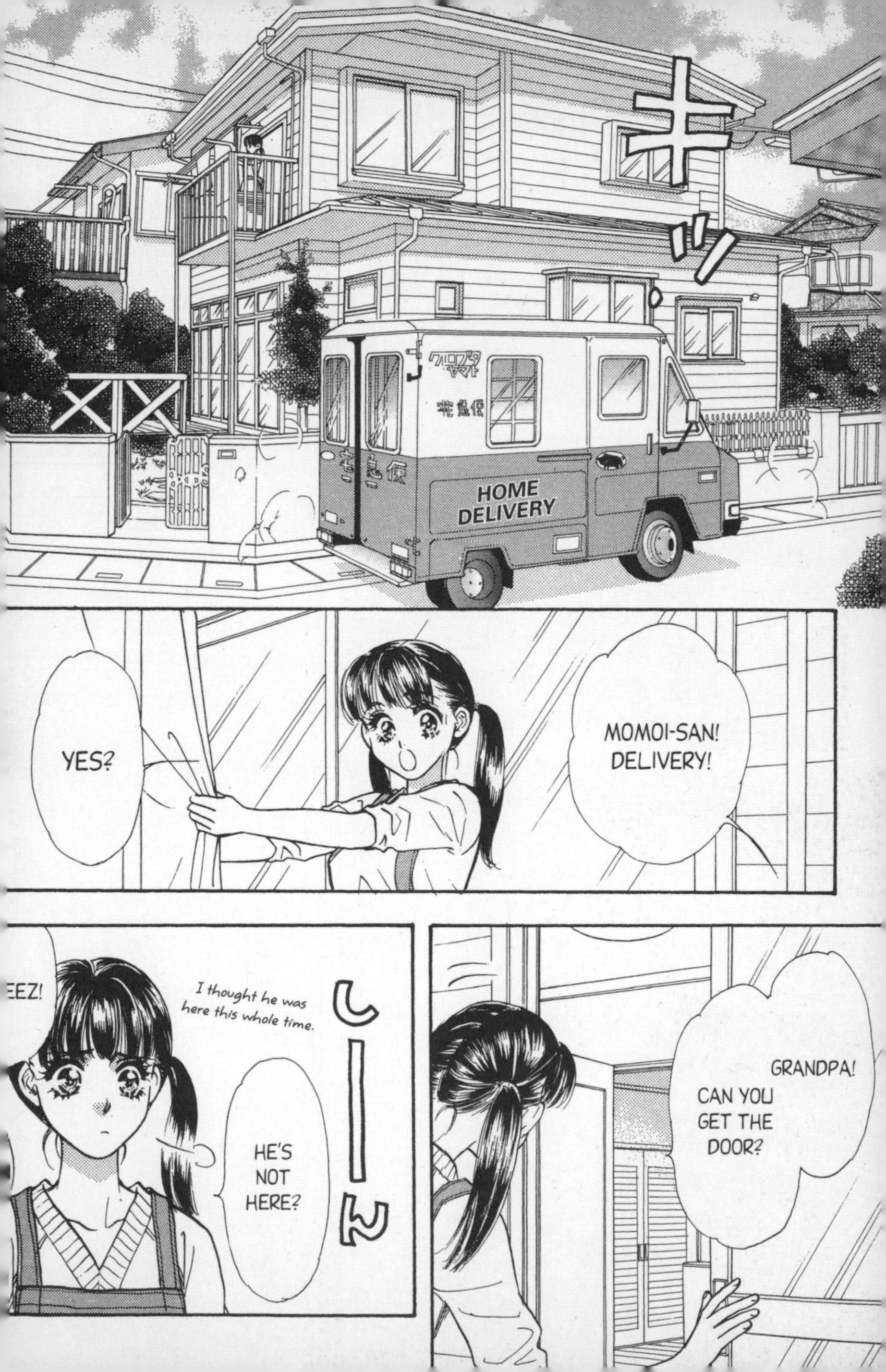
キッ
HOME DELIVERY
MOMOI-SAN! DELIVERY!
YES?
GRANDPA! CAN YOU GET THE DOOR?
しーーん
I thought he was here this whole time.
HE'S NOT HERE?
EEZ!

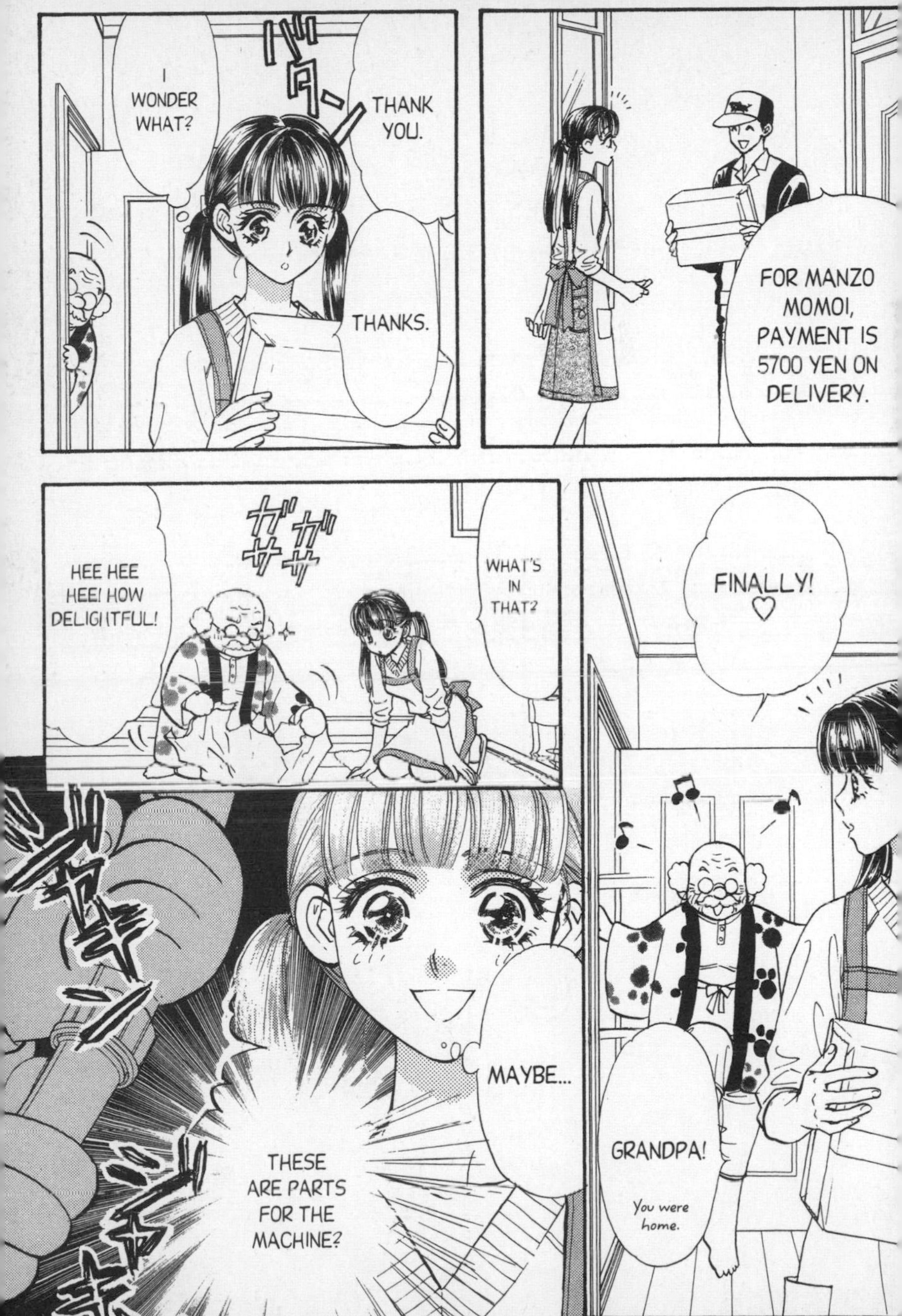
FOR MANZO MOMOI, PAYMENT IS 5700 YEN ON DELIVERY.
THANK YOU.
I WONDER WHAT?
THANKS.
FINALLY! ♡
GRANDPA!
You were home.
WHAT'S IN THAT?
HEE HEE HEE! HOW DELIGHTFUL!
MAYBE...
THESE ARE PARTS FOR THE MACHINE?

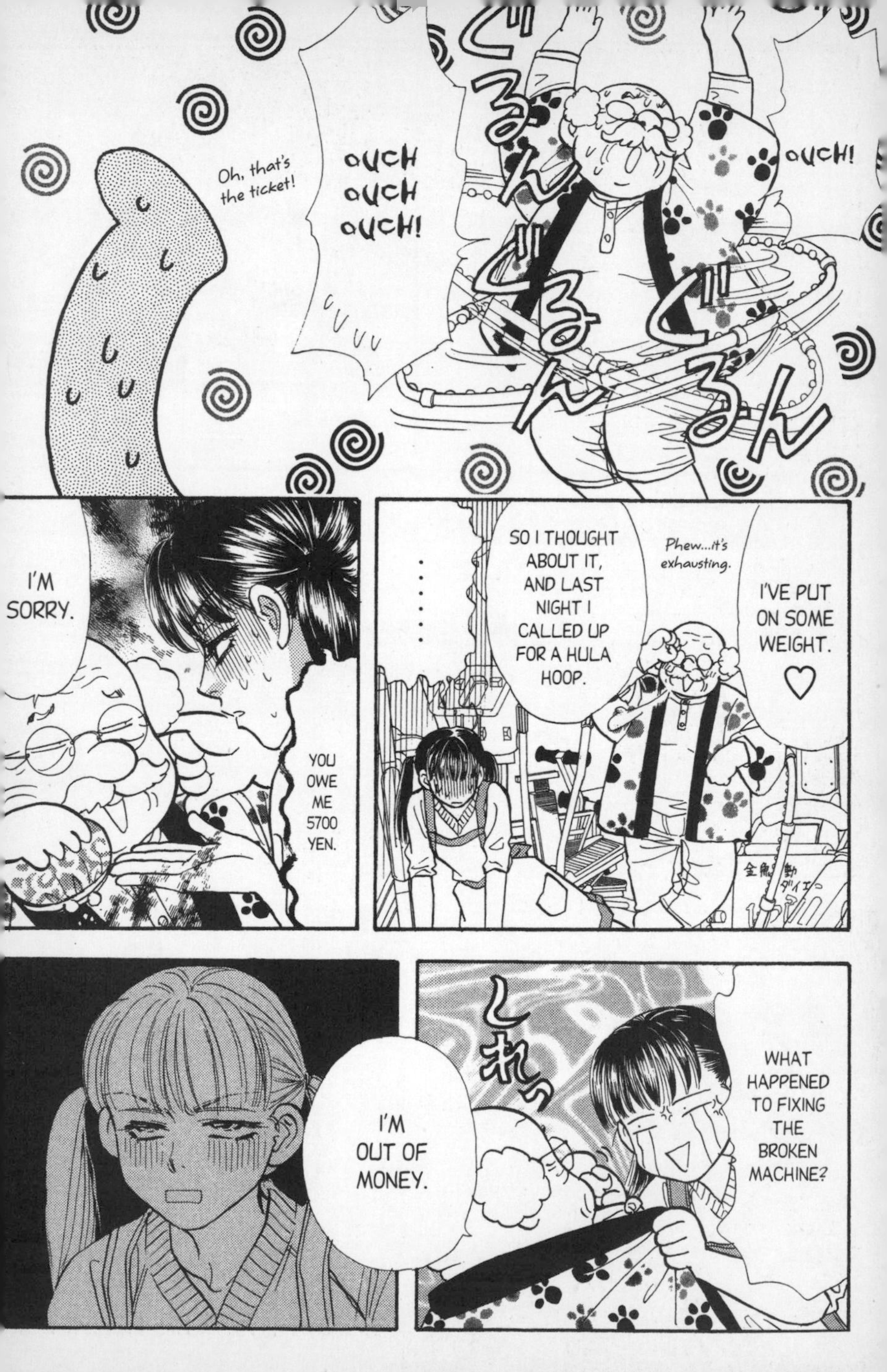
OUCH!
ぐるんぐるん
OUCH
OUCH
OUCH!
Oh, that's the ticket!
I'VE PUT ON SOME WEIGHT. ♡
Phew...it's exhausting.
SO I THOUGHT ABOUT IT, AND LAST NIGHT I CALLED UP FOR A HULA HOOP.
......
YOU OWE ME 5700 YEN.
I'M SORRY.
WHAT HAPPENED TO FIXING THE BROKEN MACHINE?
しれっ
I'M OUT OF MONEY.

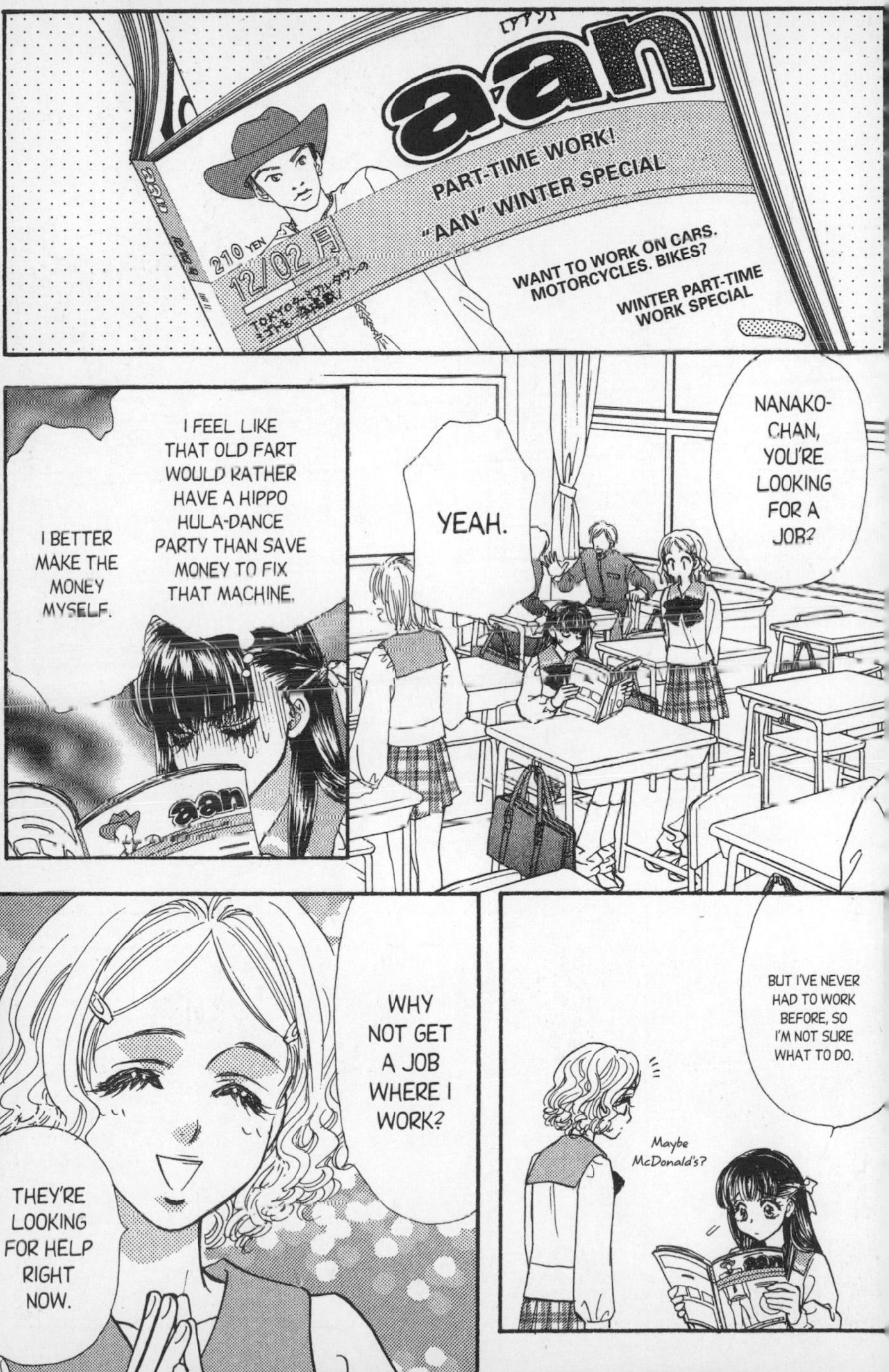
aan
PART-TIME WORK!
"AAN" WINTER SPECIAL
210 YEN
12/02 月
WANT TO WORK ON CARS. MOTORCYCLES. BIKES?
WINTER PART-TIME WORK SPECIAL
NANAKO-CHAN, YOU'RE LOOKING FOR A JOB?
YEAH.
I FEEL LIKE THAT OLD FART WOULD RATHER HAVE A HIPPO HULA-DANCE PARTY THAN SAVE MONEY TO FIX THAT MACHINE.
I BETTER MAKE THE MONEY MYSELF.
aan
BUT I'VE NEVER HAD TO WORK BEFORE, SO I'M NOT SURE WHAT TO DO.
Maybe McDonald's?
WHY NOT GET A JOB WHERE I WORK?
THEY'RE LOOKING FOR HELP RIGHT NOW.

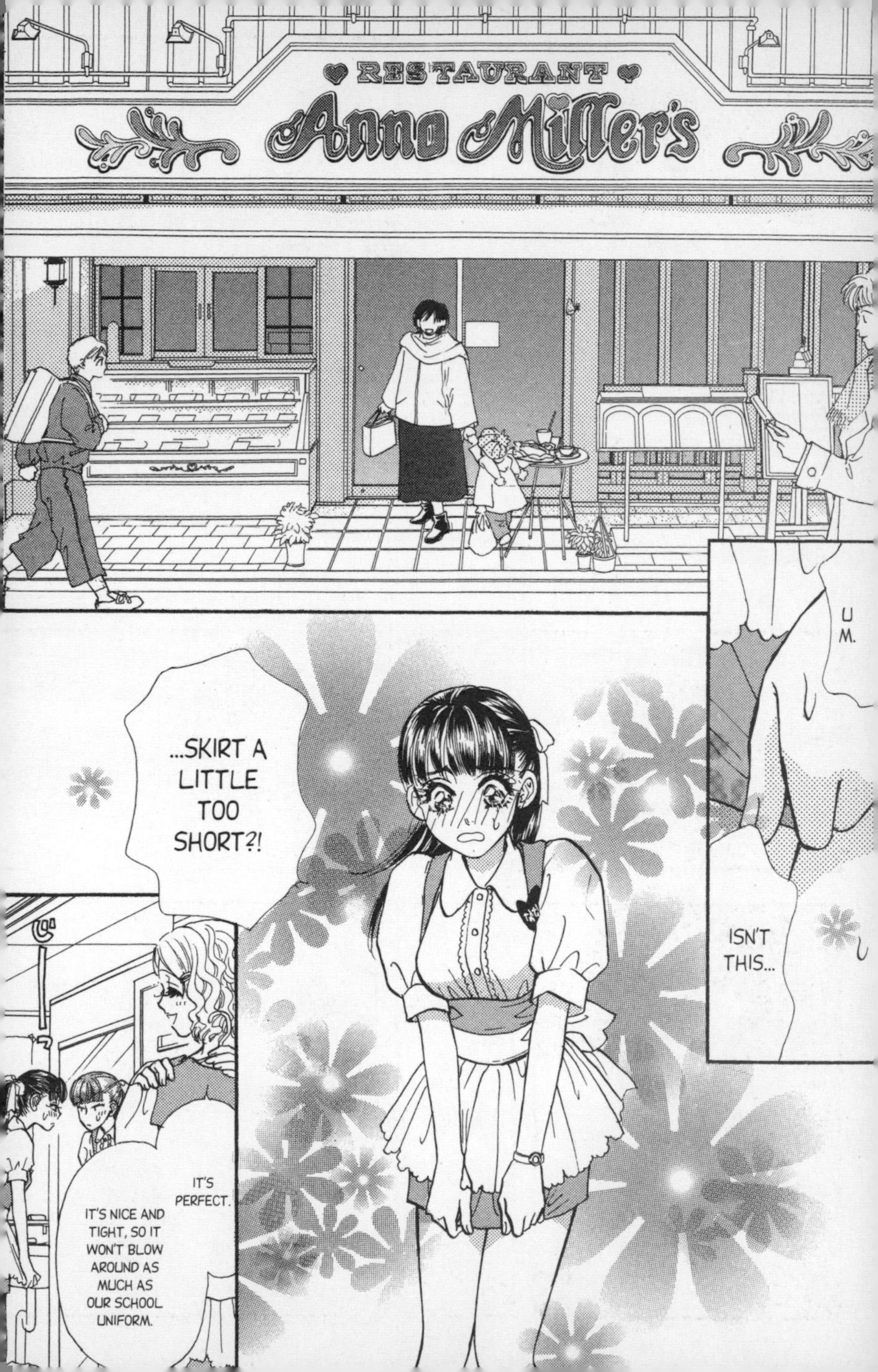
RESTAURANT
Anno Miller's
UM.
ISN'T THIS...
...SKIRT A LITTLE TOO SHORT?!
IT'S PERFECT.
IT'S NICE AND TIGHT, SO IT WON'T BLOW AROUND AS MUCH AS OUR SCHOOL UNIFORM.

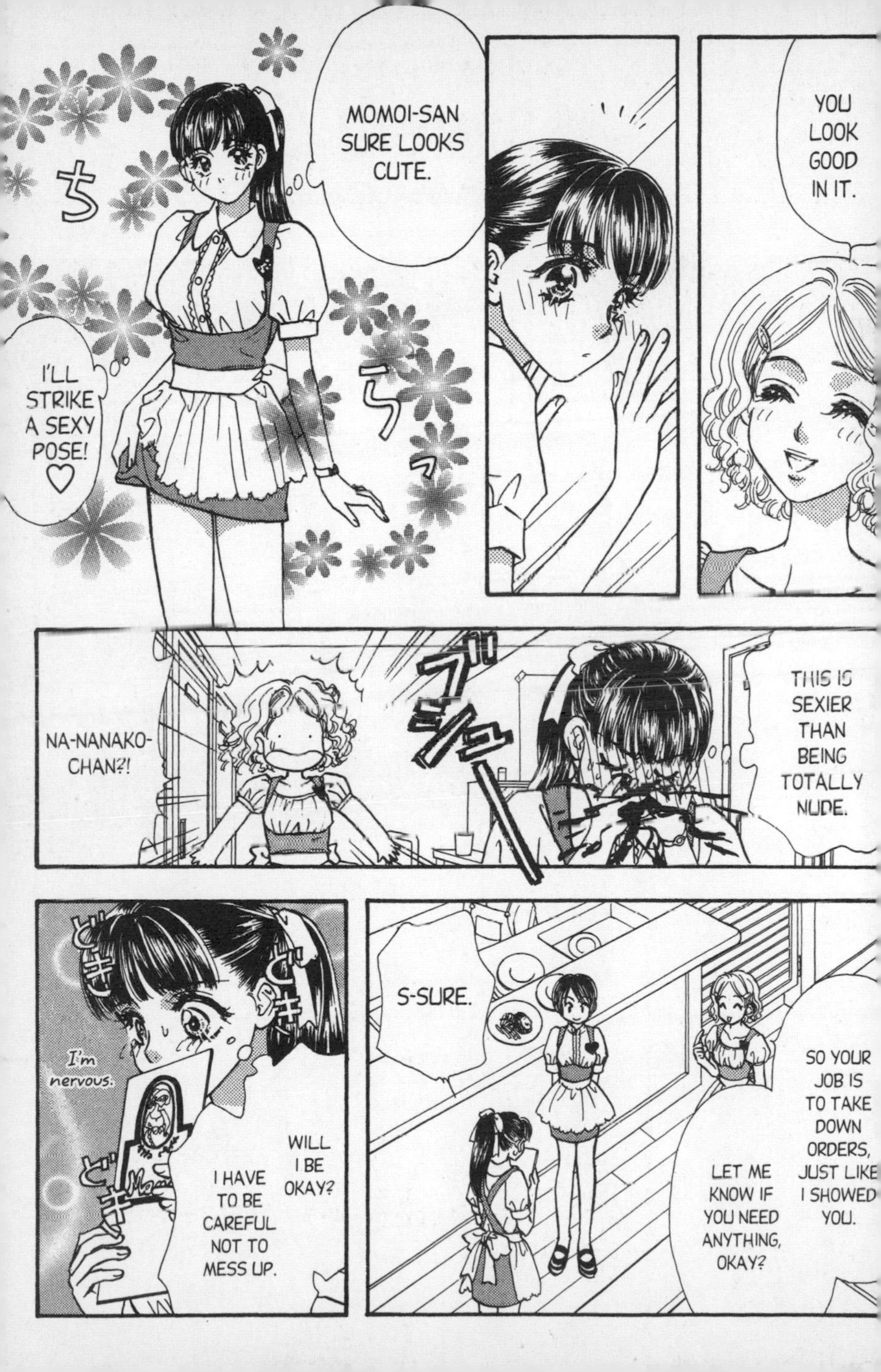
YOU LOOK GOOD IN IT.
MOMOI-SAN SURE LOOKS CUTE.
I'LL STRIKE A SEXY POSE! ♡
THIS IS SEXIER THAN BEING TOTALLY NUDE.
NA-NANAKO-CHAN?!
SO YOUR JOB IS TO TAKE DOWN ORDERS, JUST LIKE I SHOWED YOU.
LET ME KNOW IF YOU NEED ANYTHING, OKAY?
S-SURE.
WILL I BE OKAY?
I HAVE TO BE CAREFUL NOT TO MESS UP.
I'm nervous.

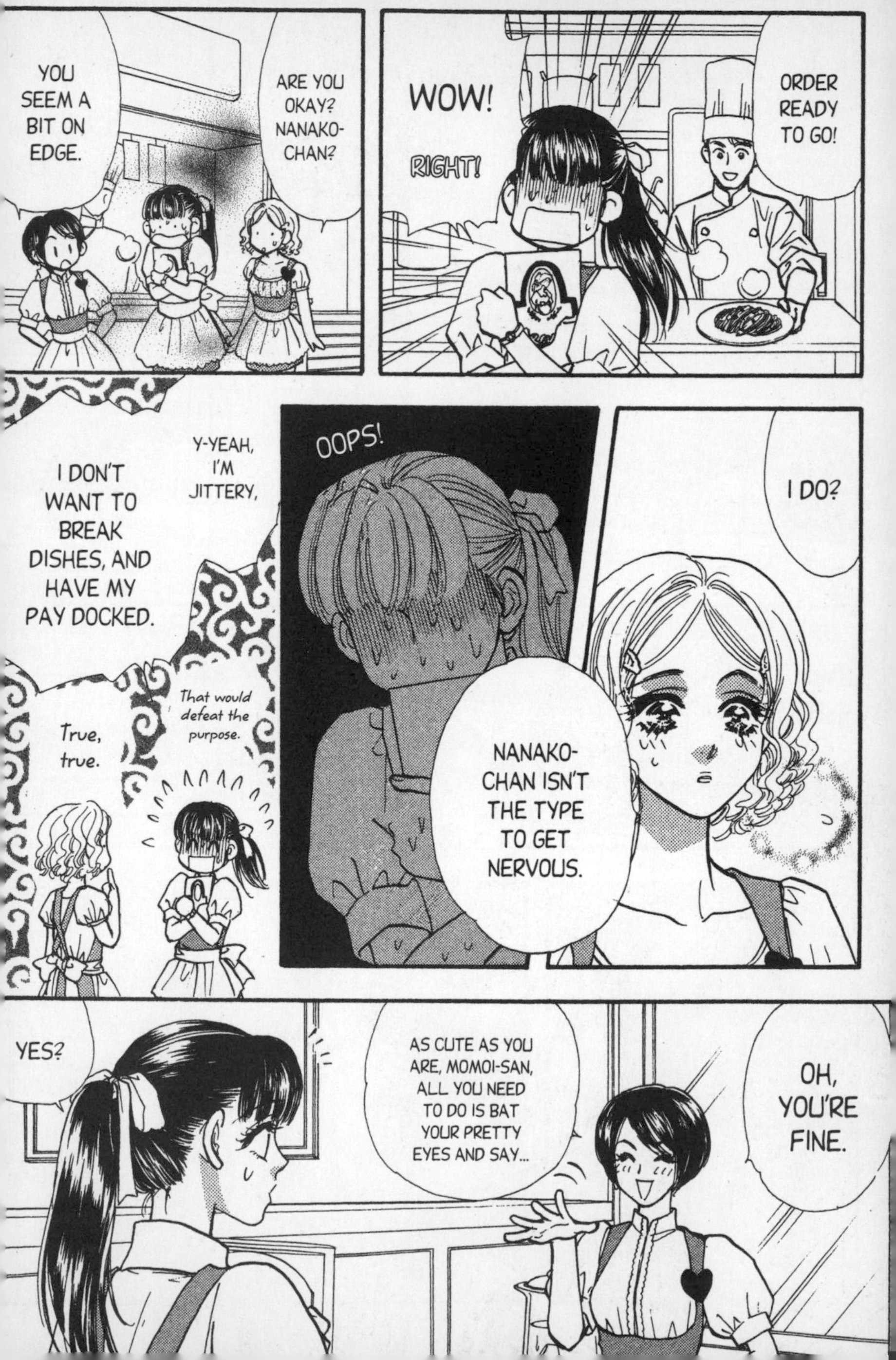
ORDER READY TO GO!
WOW!
RIGHT!
ARE YOU OKAY? NANAKO-CHAN?
YOU SEEM A BIT ON EDGE.
I DO?
NANAKO-CHAN ISN'T THE TYPE TO GET NERVOUS.
OOPS!
Y-YEAH, I'M JITTERY,
I DON'T WANT TO BREAK DISHES, AND HAVE MY PAY DOCKED.
That would defeat the purpose.
True, true.
OH, YOU'RE FINE.
AS CUTE AS YOU ARE, MOMOI-SAN, ALL YOU NEED TO DO IS BAT YOUR PRETTY EYES AND SAY...
YES?

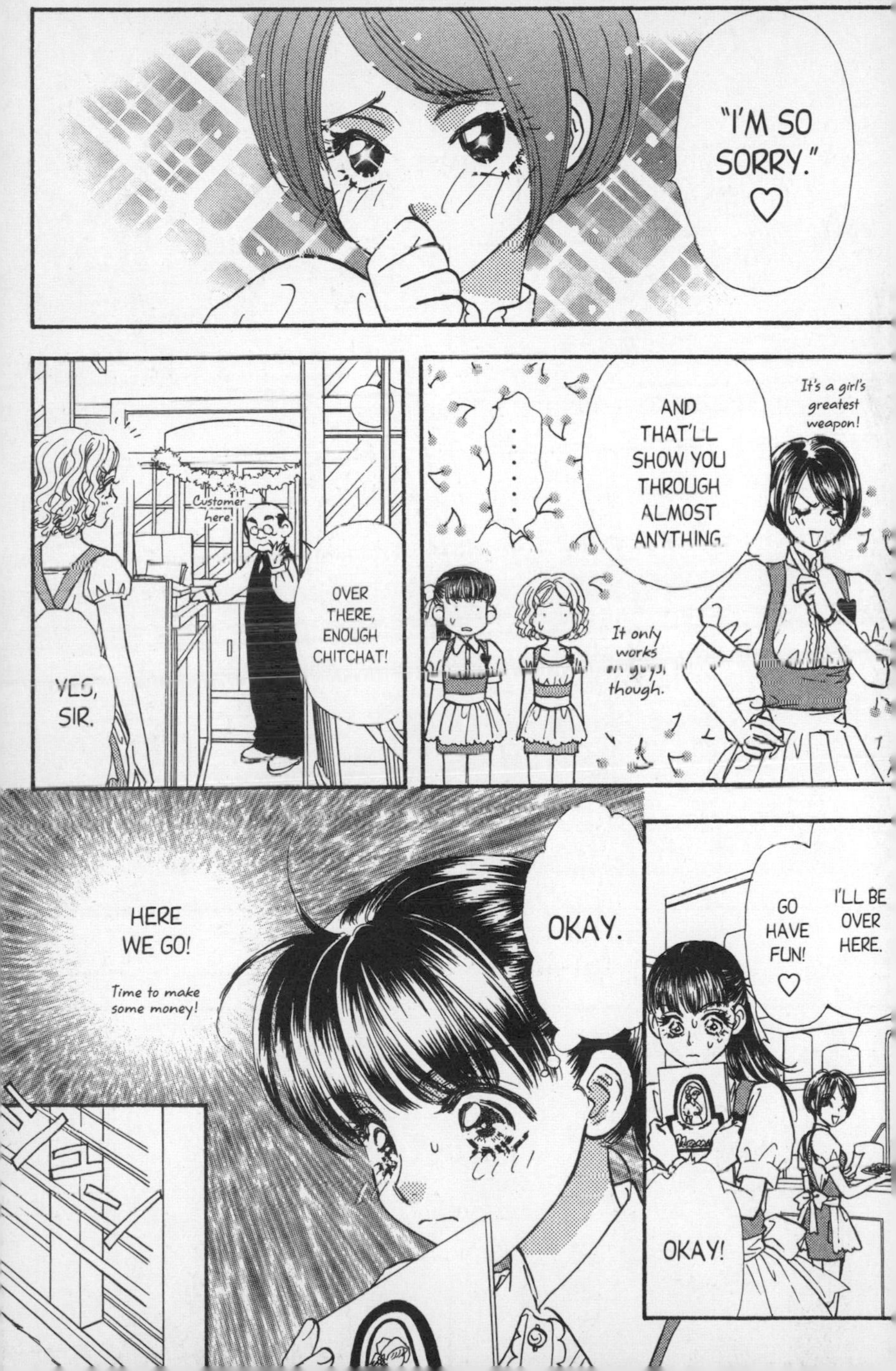
"I'M SO SORRY." ♡
It's a girl's greatest weapon!
AND THAT'LL SHOW YOU THROUGH ALMOST ANYTHING.
......
It only works on guys, though.
Customer here.
OVER THERE, ENOUGH CHITCHAT!
YES, SIR.
I'LL BE OVER HERE.
GO HAVE FUN! ♡
OKAY!
OKAY.
HERE WE GO!
Time to make some money!

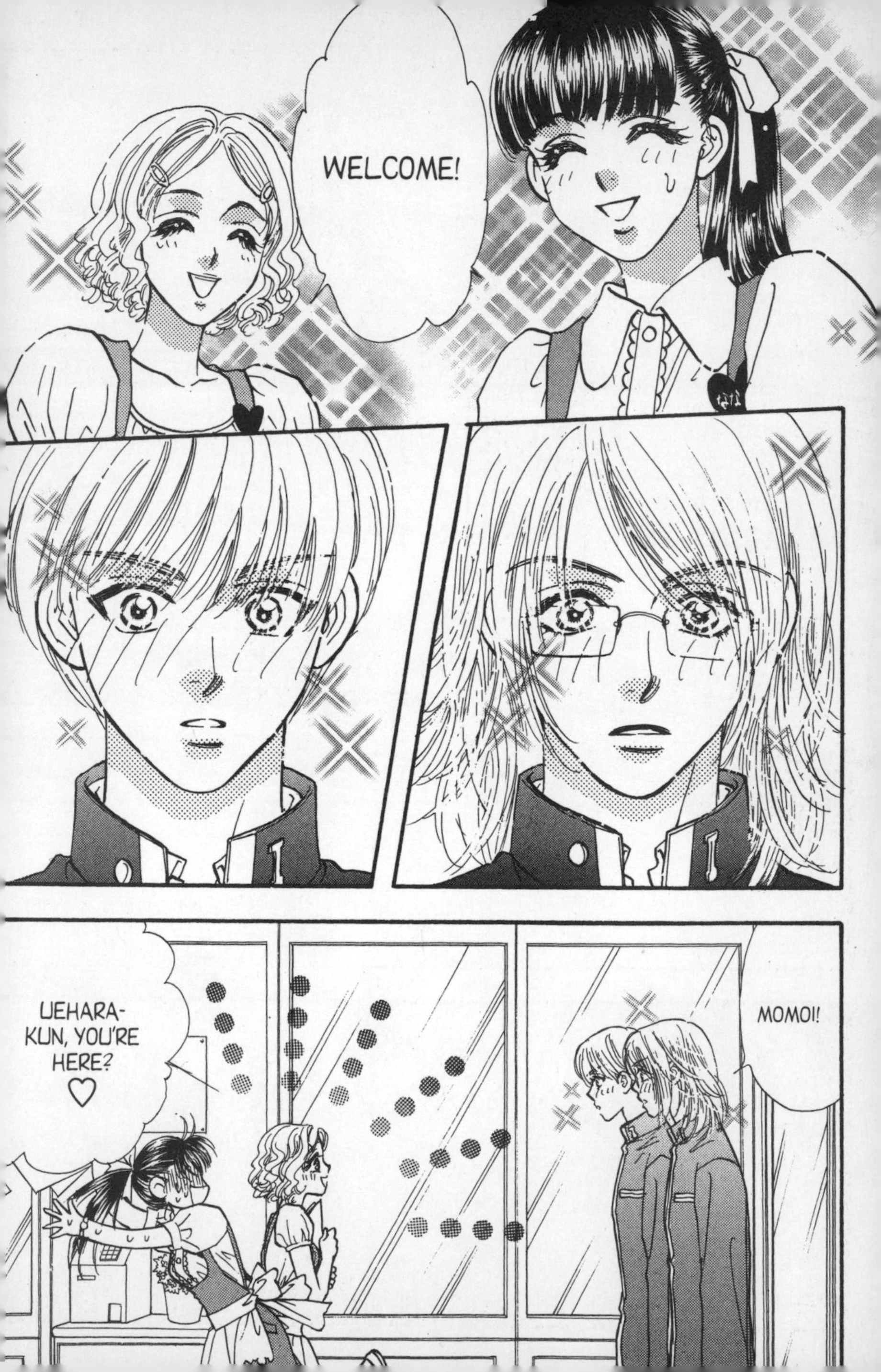
WELCOME!
MOMOI!
UEHARA-KUN, YOU'RE HERE? ♡

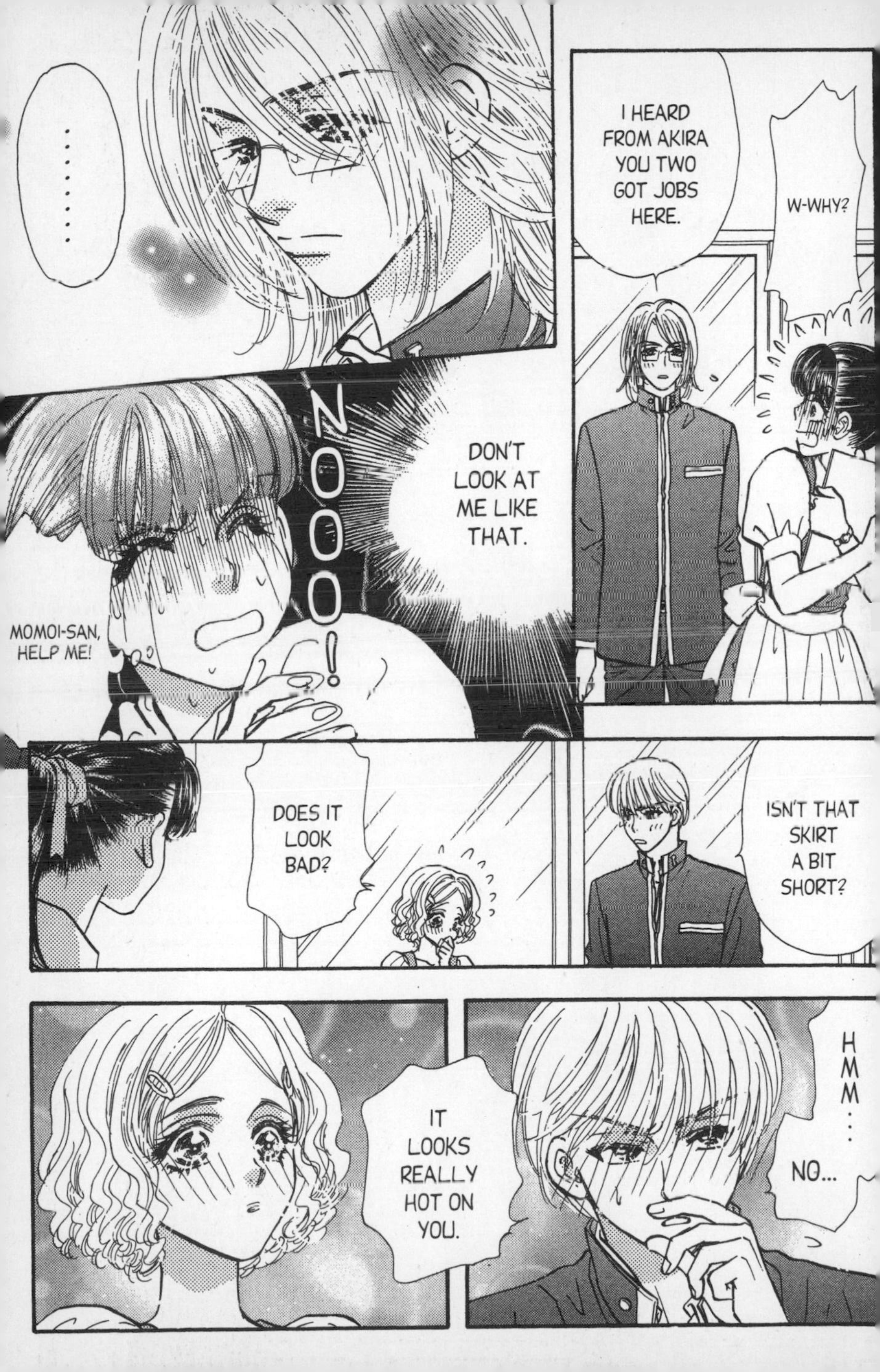
W-WHY?
I HEARD FROM AKIRA YOU TWO GOT JOBS HERE.
......
NOOO!
DON'T LOOK AT ME LIKE THAT.
MOMOI-SAN, HELP ME!
ISN'T THAT SKIRT A BIT SHORT?
DOES IT LOOK BAD?
HMM...
NO...
IT LOOKS REALLY HOT ON YOU.

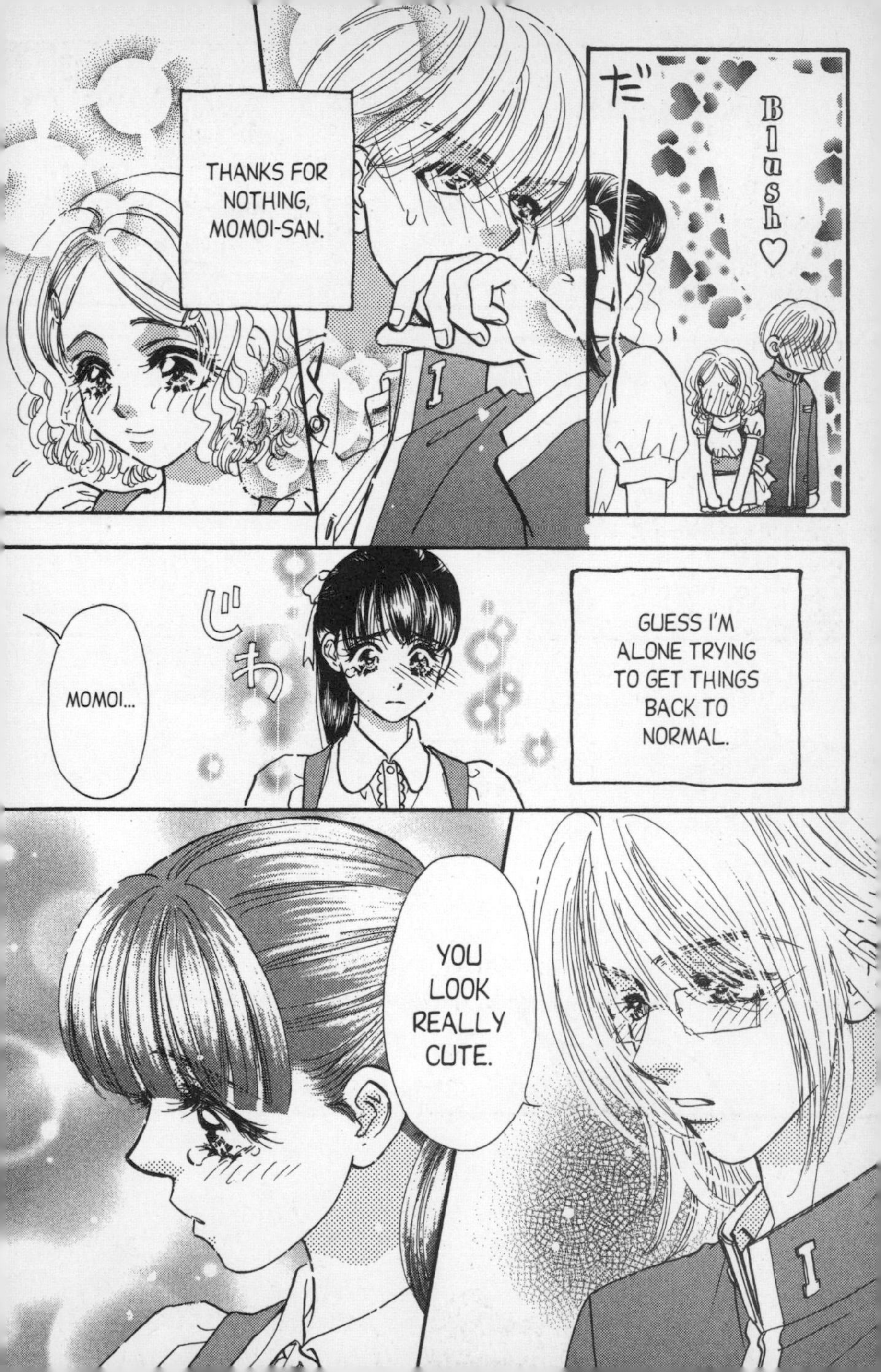
だ
Blush♥
THANKS FOR NOTHING, MOMOI-SAN.
GUESS I'M ALONE TRYING TO GET THINGS BACK TO NORMAL.
じわ
MOMOI...
YOU LOOK REALLY CUTE.

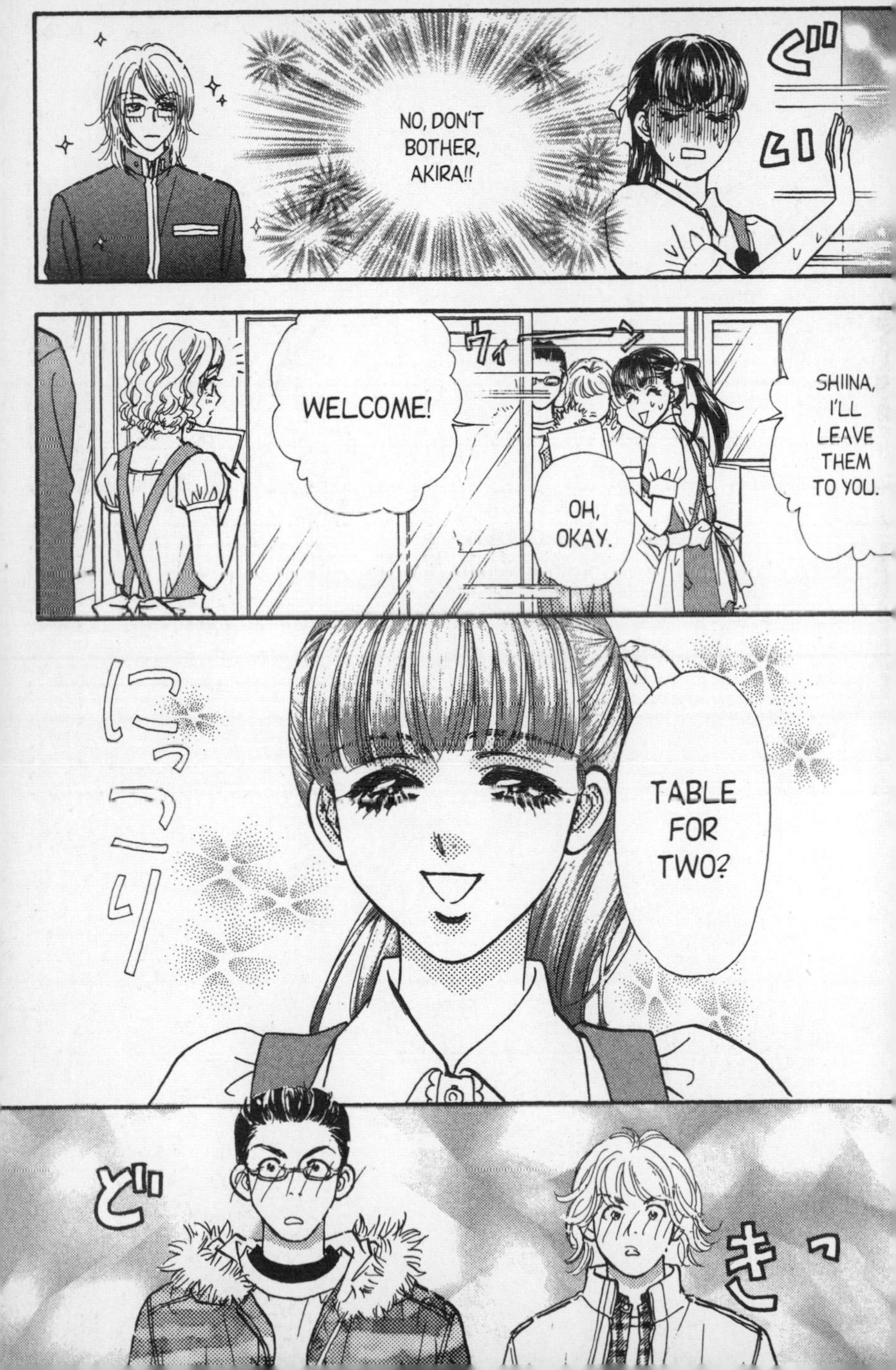
NO, DON'T BOTHER, AKIRA!!
SHIINA, I'LL LEAVE THEM TO YOU.
OH, OKAY.
WELCOME!
TABLE FOR TWO?
にっこーり

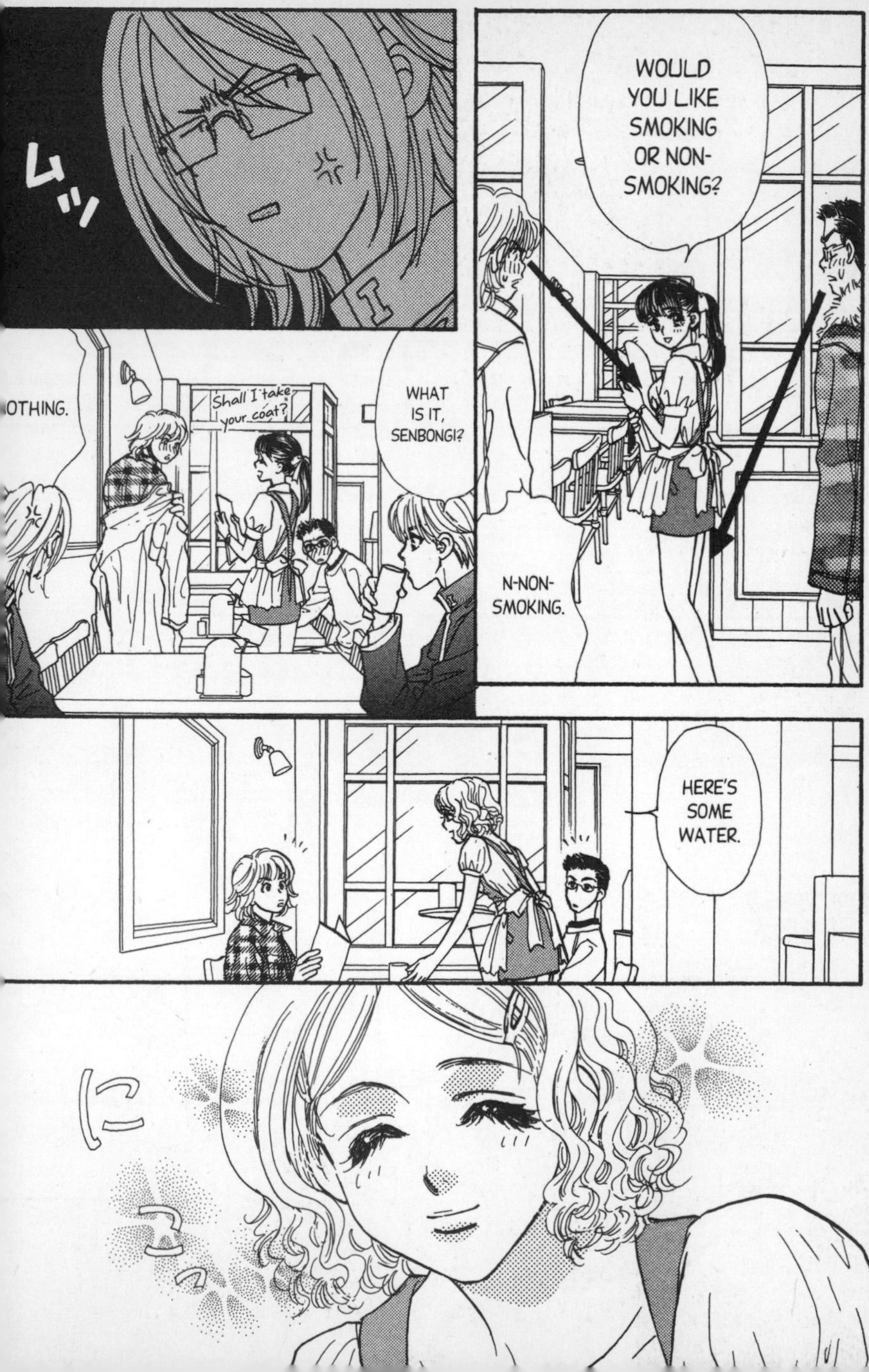
WOULD YOU LIKE SMOKING OR NON-SMOKING?
N-NON-SMOKING.
ムッ
WHAT IS IT, SENBONGI?
Shall I take your coat?
OTHING.
HERE'S SOME WATER.
にこっ

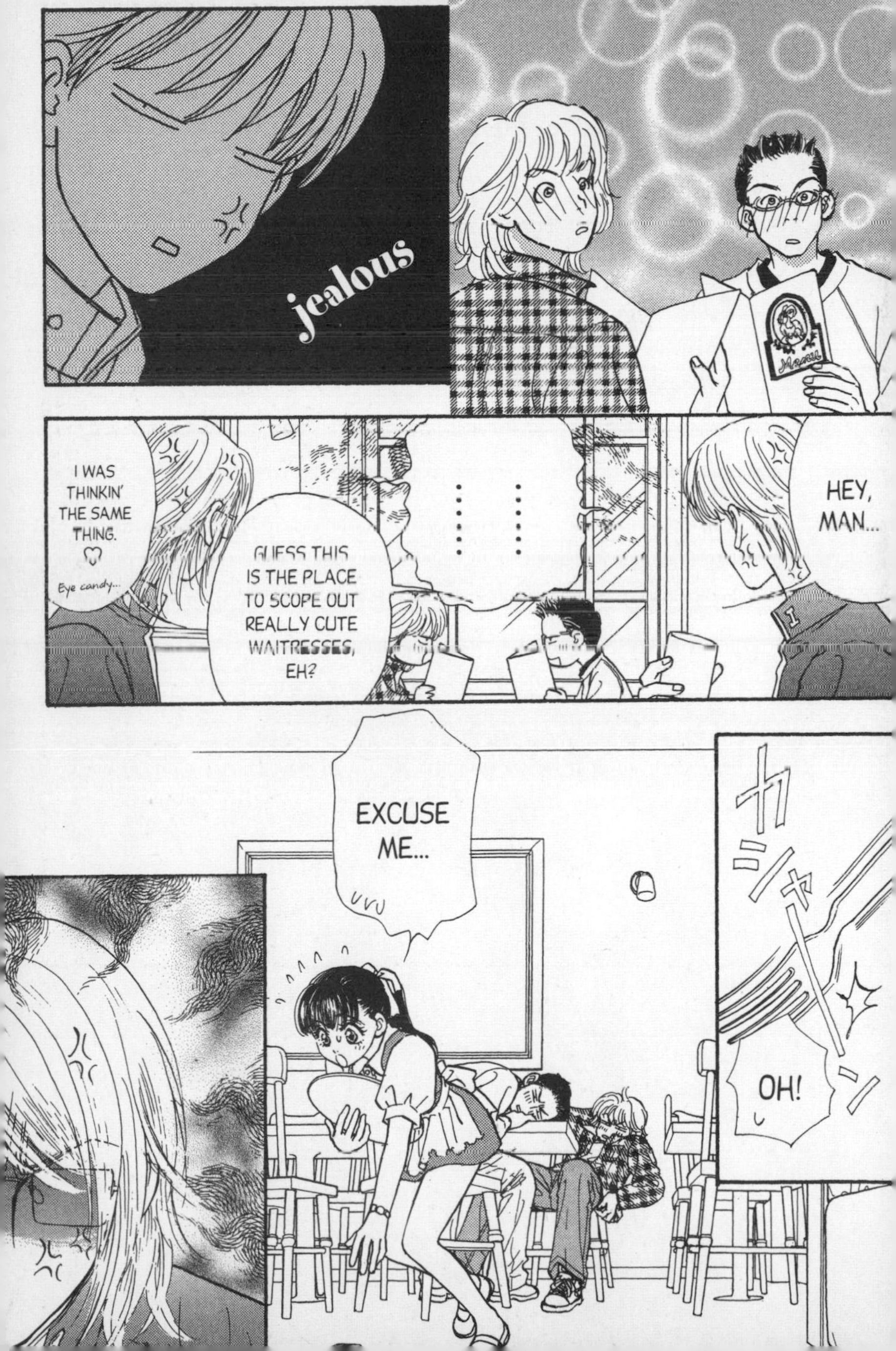
jealous
HEY, MAN...
....
GUESS THIS IS THE PLACE TO SCOPE OUT REALLY CUTE WAITRESSES, EH?
I WAS THINKIN' THE SAME THING. ♡
Eye candy...
カシャーン
OH!
EXCUSE ME...

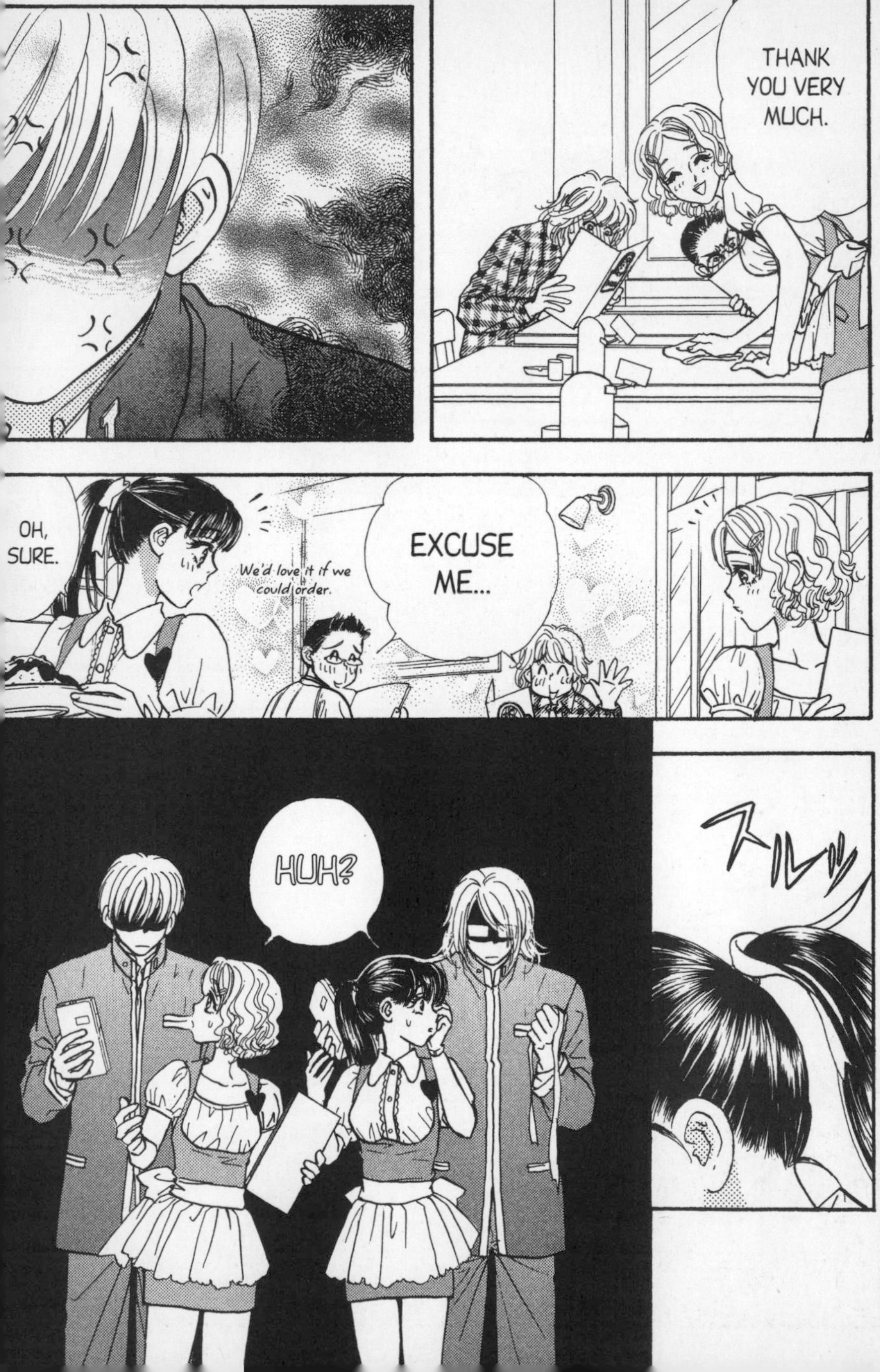
THANK YOU VERY MUCH.
EXCUSE ME...
We'd love it if we could order.
OH, SURE.
スルッ
HUH?

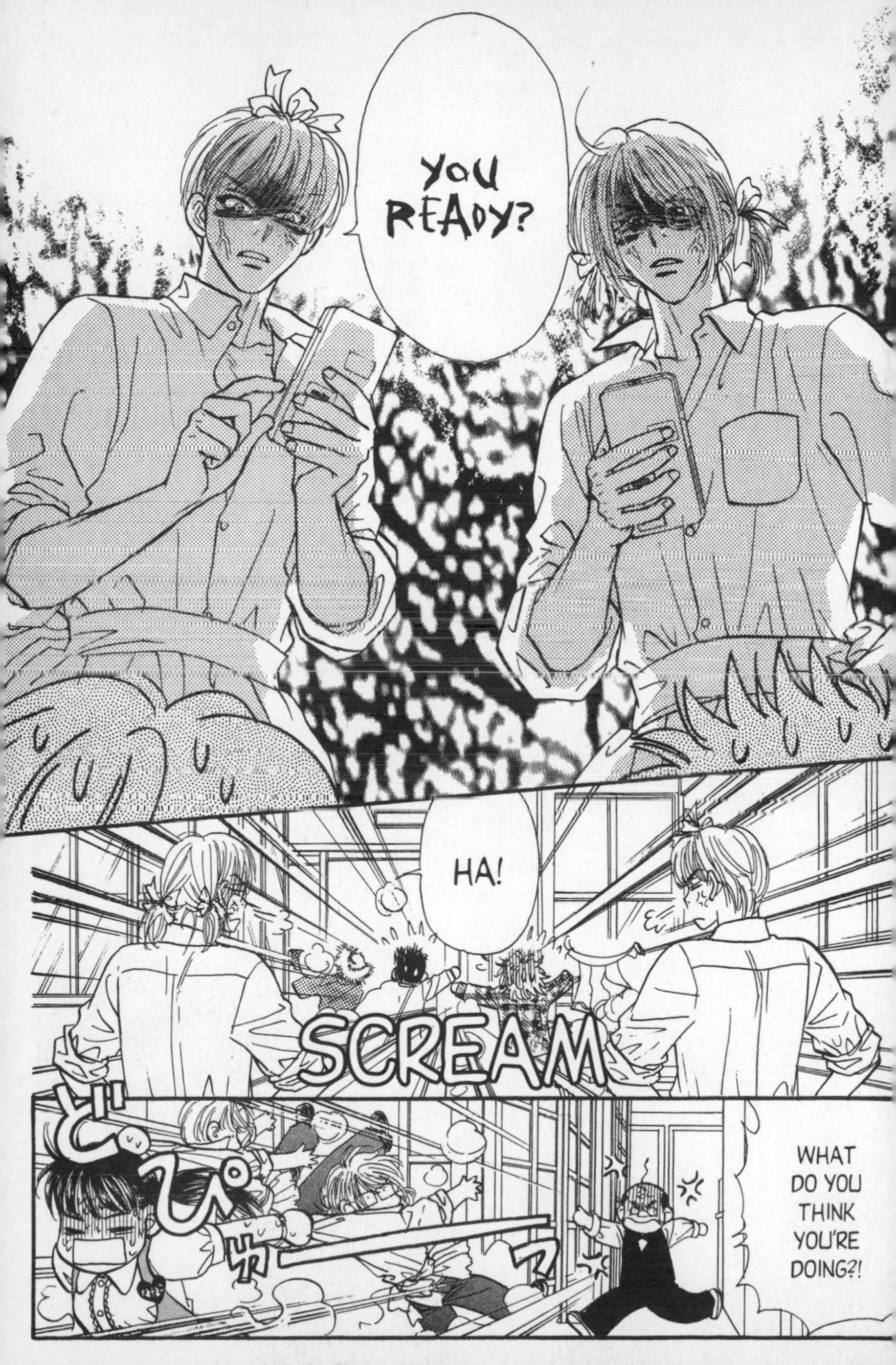
YOU READY?
HA!
SCREAM
WHAT DO YOU THINK YOU'RE DOING?!
どぴゅっ

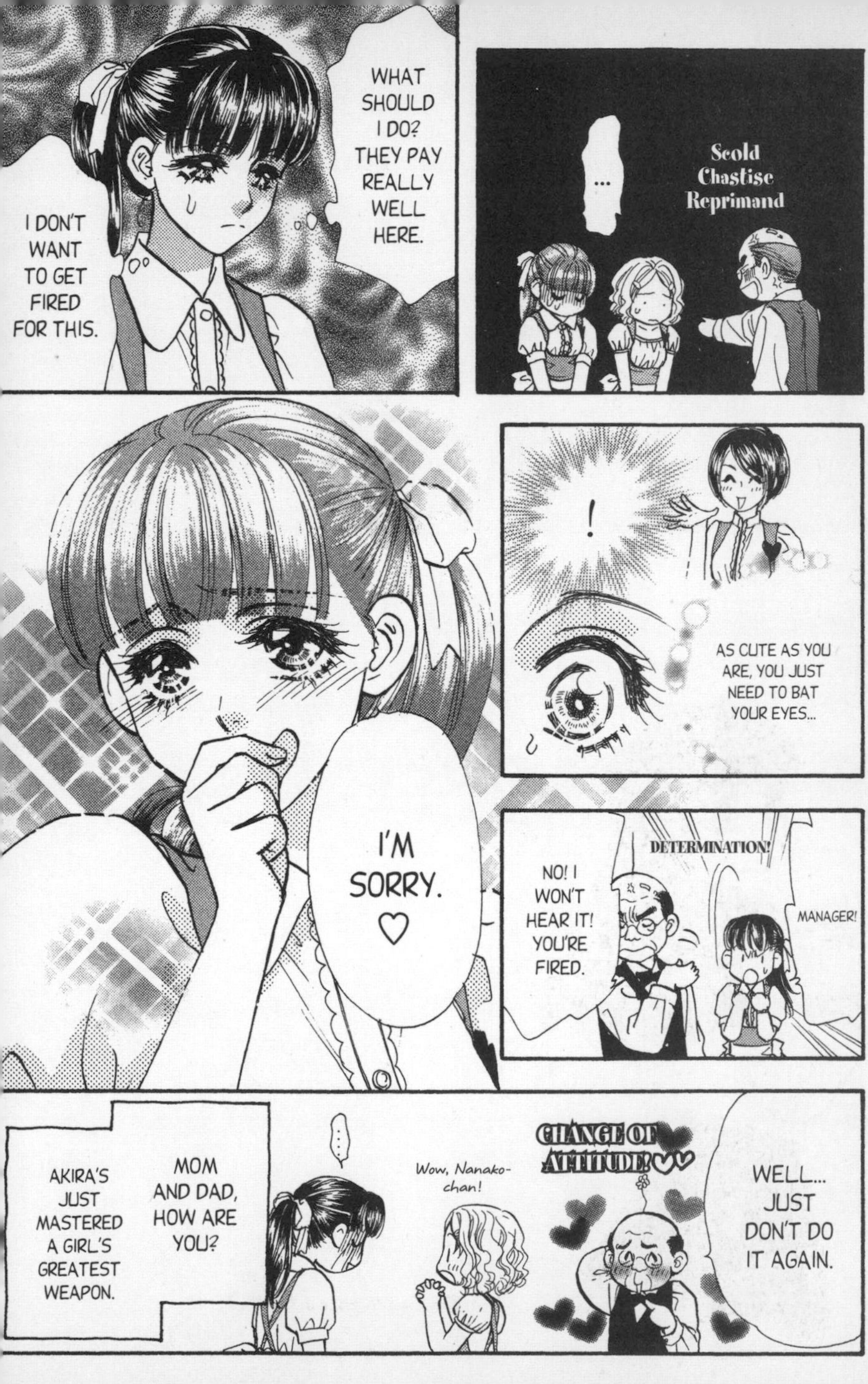
...
Scold
Chastise
Reprimand
WHAT SHOULD I DO? THEY PAY REALLY WELL HERE.
I DON'T WANT TO GET FIRED FOR THIS.
!
AS CUTE AS YOU ARE, YOU JUST NEED TO BAT YOUR EYES...
DETERMINATION!
MANAGER!
NO! I WON'T HEAR IT! YOU'RE FIRED.
I'M SORRY. ♡
WELL... JUST DON'T DO IT AGAIN.
CHANGE OF ATTITUDE!
Wow, Nanako-chan!
...
MOM AND DAD, HOW ARE YOU?
AKIRA'S JUST MASTERED A GIRL'S GREATEST WEAPON.

To Be Continued in Vol. 2!

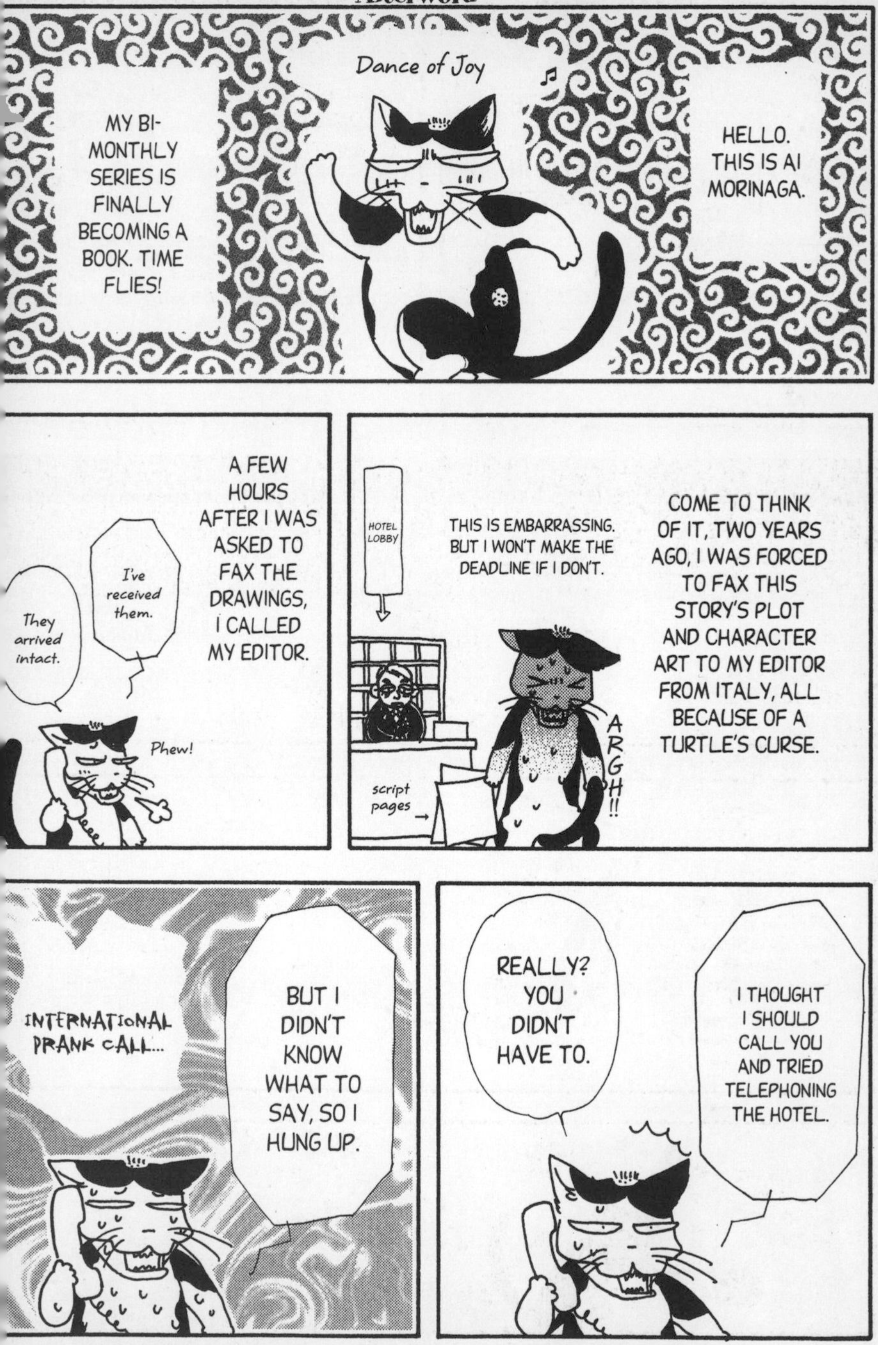
HELLO. THIS IS AI MORINAGA.
Dance of Joy
MY BI-MONTHLY SERIES IS FINALLY BECOMING A BOOK. TIME FLIES!
COME TO THINK OF IT, TWO YEARS AGO, I WAS FORCED TO FAX THIS STORY'S PLOT AND CHARACTER ART TO MY EDITOR FROM ITALY, ALL BECAUSE OF A TURTLE'S CURSE.
THIS IS EMBARRASSING. BUT I WON'T MAKE THE DEADLINE IF I DON'T.
HOTEL LOBBY
ARGH!!
script pages
A FEW HOURS AFTER I WAS ASKED TO FAX THE DRAWINGS, I CALLED MY EDITOR.
I've received them.
They arrived intact.
Phew!
I THOUGHT I SHOULD CALL YOU AND TRIED TELEPHONING THE HOTEL.
REALLY? YOU DIDN'T HAVE TO.
BUT I DIDN'T KNOW WHAT TO SAY, SO I HUNG UP.
INTERNATIONAL PRANK CALL...

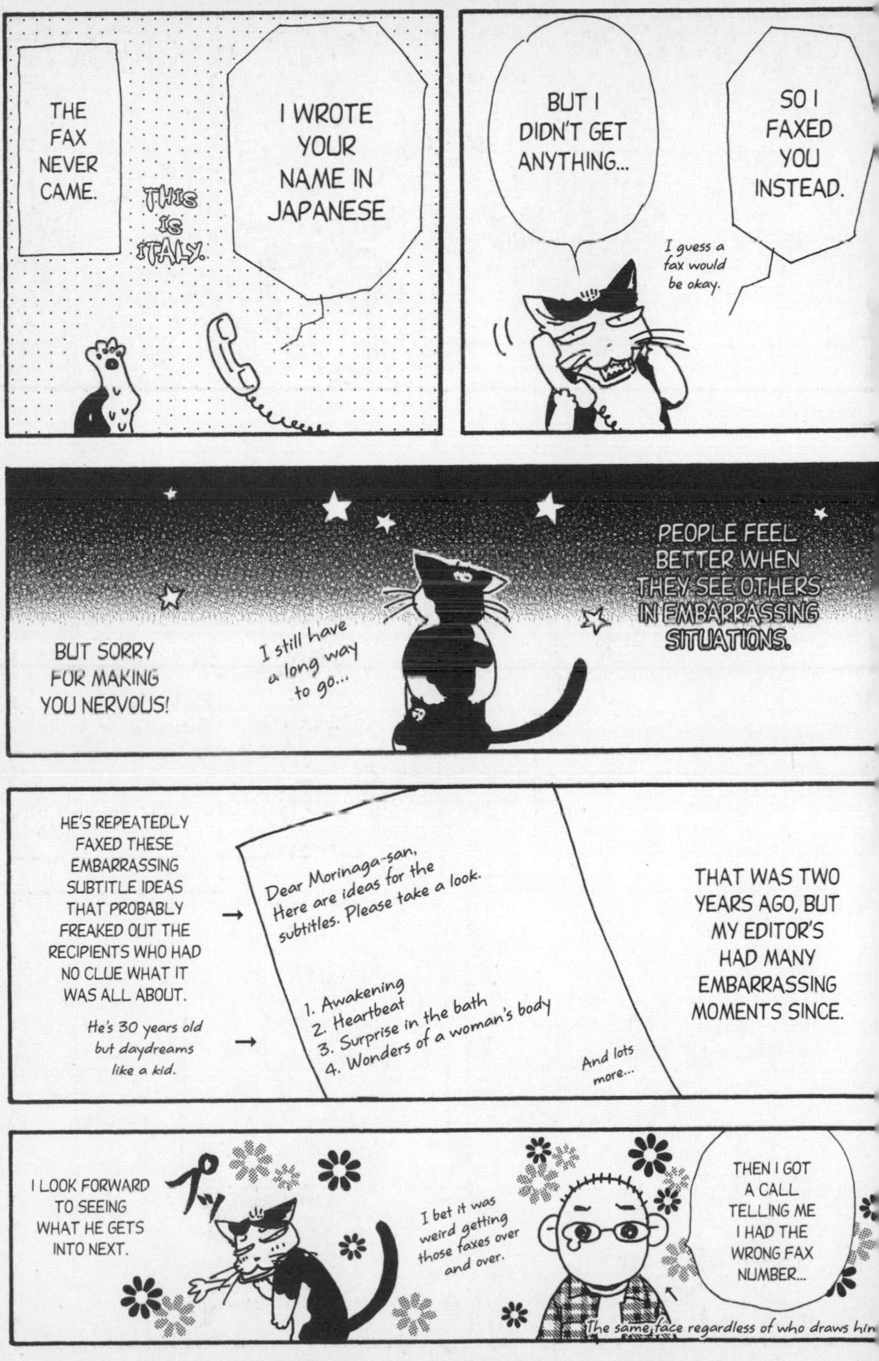
SO I FAXED YOU INSTEAD.
BUT I DIDN'T GET ANYTHING...
I guess a fax would be okay.
I WROTE YOUR NAME IN JAPANESE
THIS IS ITALY.
THE FAX NEVER CAME.
PEOPLE FEEL BETTER WHEN THEY SEE OTHERS IN EMBARRASSING SITUATIONS.
I still have a long way to go...
BUT SORRY FOR MAKING YOU NERVOUS!
THAT WAS TWO YEARS AGO, BUT MY EDITOR'S HAD MANY EMBARRASSING MOMENTS SINCE.
Dear Morinaga-san, Here are ideas for the subtitles. Please take a look.
1. Awakening
2. Heartbeat
3. Surprise in the bath
4. Wonders of a woman's body
And lots more...
HE'S REPEATEDLY FAXED THESE EMBARRASSING SUBTITLE IDEAS THAT PROBABLY FREAKED OUT THE RECIPIENTS WHO HAD NO CLUE WHAT IT WAS ALL ABOUT.
He's 30 years old but daydreams like a kid.
THEN I GOT A CALL TELLING ME I HAD THE WRONG FAX NUMBER...
The same face regardless of who draws him
I bet it was weird getting those faxes over and over.
I LOOK FORWARD TO SEEING WHAT HE GETS INTO NEXT.

In the Next Volume of...

Your & My Secret

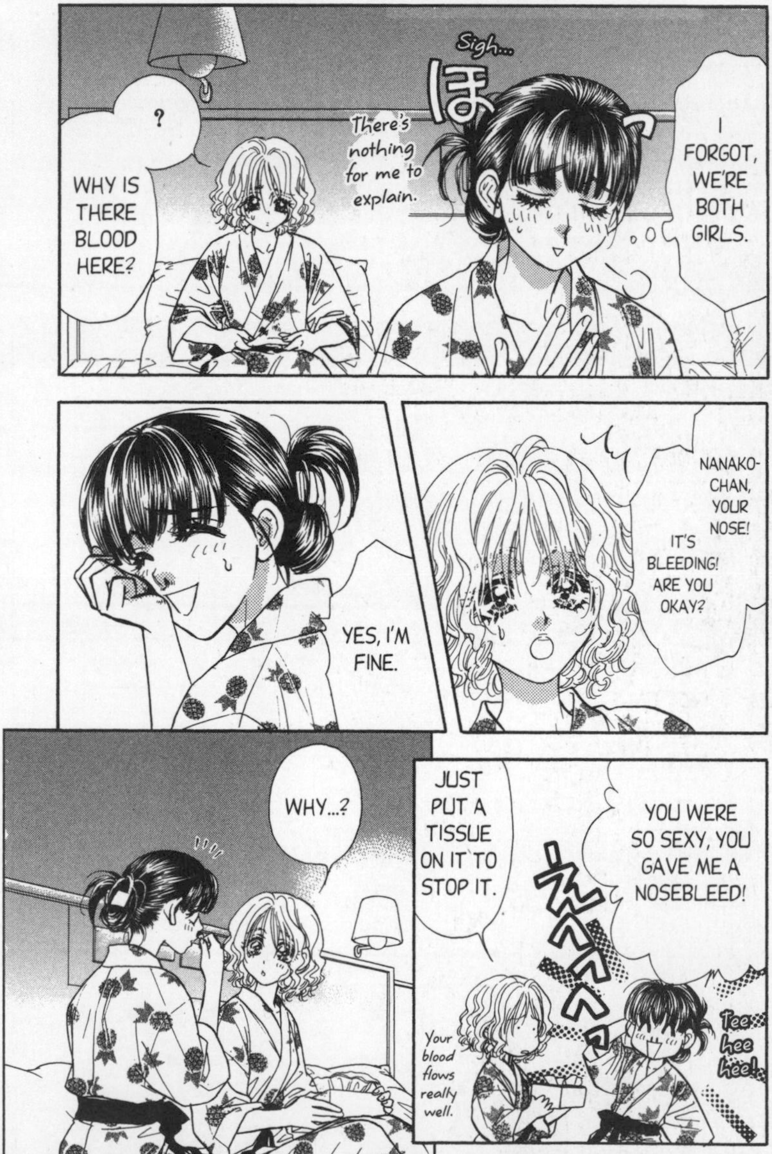
I FORGOT, WE'RE BOTH GIRLS.
Sigh...
ほっ
There's nothing for me to explain.
?
WHY IS THERE BLOOD HERE?
NANAKO-CHAN, YOUR NOSE!
IT'S BLEEDING! ARE YOU OKAY?
YES, I'M FINE.
YOU WERE SO SEXY, YOU GAVE ME A NOSEBLEED!
Tee hee hee!
えへへへっ
JUST PUT A TISSUE ON IT TO STOP IT.
Your blood flows really well.
WHY...?

Available July 2008!

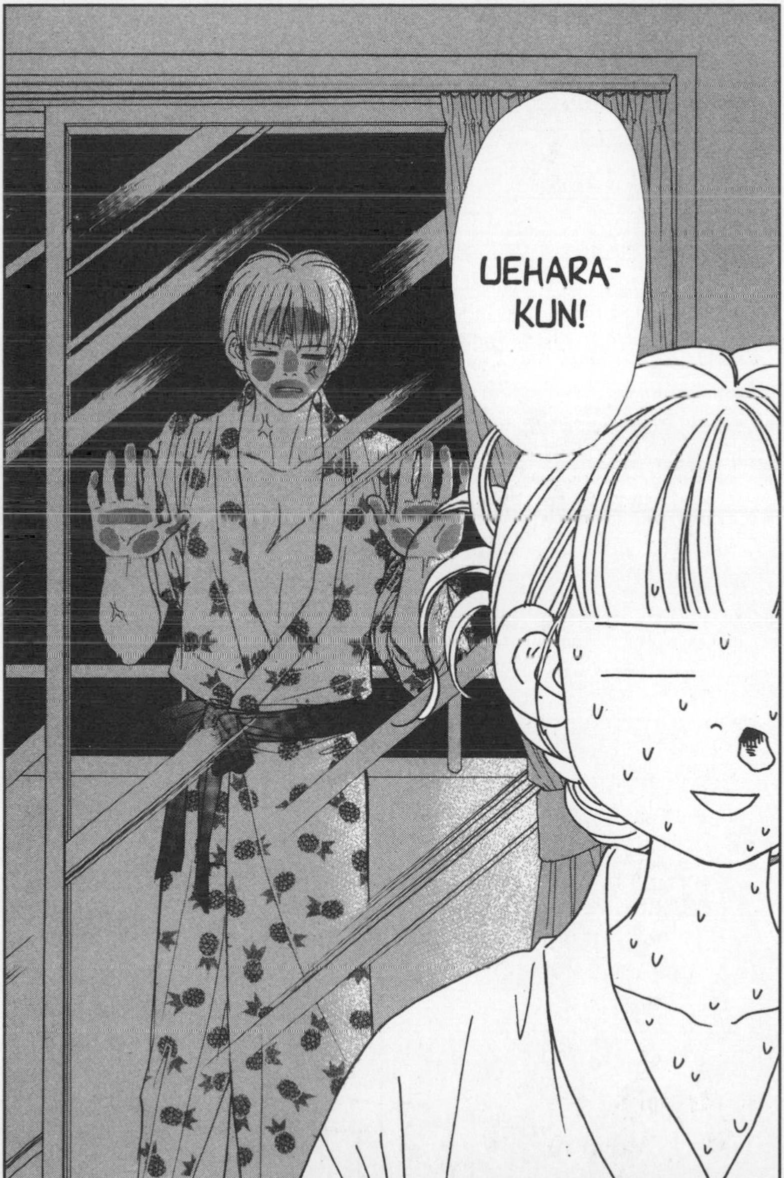
UEHARA-KUN!

STOP!

This is the back of the book.
You wouldn't want to spoil a great ending!

This book is printed "manga-style," in the authentic Japanese right-to-left format. Since none of the artwork has been flipped or altered, readers get to experience the story just as the creator intended. You've been asking for it, so TOKYOPOP® delivered: authentic, hot-off-the-press, and far more fun!

DIRECTIONS

If this is your first time reading manga-style, here's a quick guide to help you understand how it works.

It's easy... just start in the top right panel and follow the numbers. Have fun, and look for more 100% authentic manga from TOKYOPOP®!

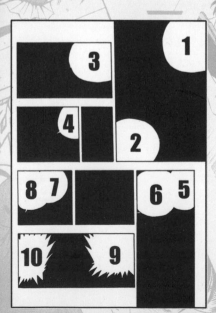